THE CRIME TIME FILMBOOK

Having just staggered, dazed and confused, into his thirties, John Ashbrook set himself three tasks for 1996: Get a job; buy a car, and make that long hoped-for trip to the States. He got the job, but was fired; which conveniently gave him enough free time to write and edit this book. He bought the car, which is still running well, but seems to need a new battery.
As for America, that'll still be there next year!

1997
No Exit Press,
18 Coleswood Road
Harpenden, Herts, AL5 IEQ

Published in association with **Crime Time** magazine

A CIP catalogue record for this book is available from the British Library.

ISBN 1 - 874061 - 84 - X

9 8 7 6 5 4 3 2 1

Book Design By Crow Design

Cover Illustration from the Electric Pictures release *Fallen Angels*, used by kind permission.

THE CRIME TIME FILMBOOK

JOHN ASHBROOK

AND

RICHARD ARMSTRONG
GRAHAM BARNFIELD
STEVEN CHRISTIAN
JOHN COSTELLO
PAUL DUNCAN
JOHN FOSTER
JOHN GORE
CHRIS HOLDING
STEVE HOLLAND
GERALD HOUGHTON
RICHARD LUCK

NO EXIT PRESS

CONTENTS

QUENTIN'S REVENGE

PROFILING

HARD CASES

THE YEAR IN REVIEW

THE THIRD DEGREE

ACKNOWLEDGEMENTS

Paul pushed, Peter pulled, Ion suffered in silence. Andi couldn't wait.
Ian and Merlin lost their computer, Steve lost the use of one ear.
Maureen and Andy, my marvellous mum and dad, never had a moment's doubt.

RAMBLE WITHOUT A CLUE

OR: HOW TO WRITE A BOOK FOR (CONSIDERABLY) LESS THAN $7,000

JULY 4:

IT NEVER HAPPENS this way. Never. The proud and valiant publisher of *Crime Time* magazine sidled up to me during an editorial meeting, and quietly asked if I felt like writing a book about crime films. *When for?* I asked. *Christmas!* He answered casually, as if such things happened every year.

Which never happens. Ask anyone who has any knowledge of publishing and they'll tell you that it generally takes between one and three years to get a book out. I had five months. It was a ridiculous proposition; it couldn't possibly happen; there aren't enough hours in the day. Obviously, I didn't hesitate in treating his query with the contempt it deserved: I said *Yes!!*

JULY 12:

One of the great sadnesses of the crime genre - at least to my mind - is that it is not taken more seriously by the media in general. It's a 'genre', you see, and therefore of less significance than the 'mainstream' movies critics adore and audiences stay away from. Genres evolve when film after film use similar motifs and tropes to a similar end. You can call on an infinite variety of characters, but the style of the piece, the techniques employed, or the nature of the tale being told, will carry resonances of the other films in the genre. In this way, as Graham Barnfield points out in 'Hard Boiled Cities', modern films as varied as *Devil in a Blue Dress* and *Seven* can both owe an obvious debt to forties *noir* films like *Double Indemnity* and *The Big Sleep*. They all concern the dark side of the human personality, but they represent and evaluate this in radically different ways.

Personally, I have always considered 'mainstream' to be just another genre; its stock in trade being its lack of easily-identified motifs and tropes, its lack of, if you will, plot.

JULY 13:

Paul Duncan (erstwhile editor of *Crime Time*, and recipient of his own 'write a book by Christmas' offer) and I sat down for a bit of a brain-stormer. His book, *The 3rd Degree*, would be made up entirely of interviews with crime writers; mine, on the other hand, would take a more variable form;

JOHN ASHBROOK

interviews, sure, but also essays and reviews.

JULY 14:

This structure would afford me an opportunity to compensate for one of the great frustrations of magazine publishing - lack of space. Alongside the new material I could present uncut or updated versions of interviews which had already seen print, in a much truncated form, in *Crime Time*. Smashing.

JULY 15 - 25:

Essays and reviews. This book presents me with a golden opportunity to use 1995/6's glut of astounding crime films, to make some detailed and serious points about the Significance of crime films. Better not call it that, though; claims to Significance are the battle-cry of The Pretentious!

Therefore, make some interesting and sincere points, but keep it entertaining.

One thing that never ceases to amaze me, is how The Classics never lose their power. Modern film-makers are still tipping their celluloid hats to the likes of Hitchcock and Billy Wilder; so it is worth pointing out why.

But, by the same token, it's important to keep an eye on what's new, and left of centre. Analysing inspiration is good, but it can become very insular if it isn't coupled with an awareness of the work being done away from the limelight. The Hong Kong film industry, for example, is a perfect representation of a force which almost no-one noticed until it was too late. The influence film-makers like John Woo have had on film-makers like Quentin Tarantino is tangible and electrifying. And, let's face it, five years ago, who the hell had heard of Quentin?

This gives me a great excuse to include pieces which explore and explain the phenomena which are burning a path through Hollywood at the moment, whilst the background material will anchor this into a continuum ... a genre.

SEPTEMBER 1:

Well, enough of thinking about how good this book is going to be. Mayhap 'tis time I actually put finger to keyboard ...

SEPTEMBER 4:

Of course, the problem is, much as I'd like to believe what they tell me (in my dreams), I'm not really the fount of all knowledge. There are people whose knowledge and opinions are far more interesting than mine. Although I have as much ego as the next guy, I'm not going to jealously hold this book to my chest and insist that every word has to hewn from rock by my own fair hands. After all, opinions are like ass-holes, we've all got 'em, and everyone thinks everyone else's stinks!

The key to good writing is the ability to communicate your opinion in a witty, concise and literate way. The key to a good book (and, I suppose, to good editing) is to assemble the best writing, whoever it is by, whatever opinion it espouses. Basically, any piece I wish I had written, will go in the book.

SEPTEMBER 9:

It looks like my plan to assemble a review section of 'The Top 100 Crime Films' isn't going to run. Partly because it would consume the book and turn it into another Movie Guide, which I don't want. Also, to be blunt, I'm gonna find myself reviewing a lot of crap just to make up the numbers. Pages that could be spent on an intelligent consideration of *Fargo*, will be wasted on trashing *Barb Wire*, or *Four Rooms*. Do I really want the book to be that negative? No.

So, instead, I'll pick out a selection of the good and the bad . The point being to give pages to ALL the good stuff, then find interesting things to say about the bad stuff with the proviso that, if there's nothing useful to say, say nothing.

SEPTEMBER 20 - 27:

I've started to receive the pieces I commissioned from other authors. This is a completely new experience for me, to see other writer's work in its raw, uncut form. It not only confirms my initial feeling that other voices in this book will add weight and credence to it, it is actually quite humbling to see just how talented these writers are.

Every piece, however long, from whatever source, has been a revelation to me. This delightful process is comparable to one of those animated pub conversations you have with other people who share your fascinations and passion, but not your opinions. The difference is, the arm-waving and yelling has been replaced with considered and tightly-crafted writing.

OCTOBER 1 - 5:

Unfortunately, great as the writing I have received is, I'm running out of space and am having to edit. I've just cut out some 25 pages of my own mildewed meanderings to make room for a couple of late arrivals, but I still find myself in the unenviable position of having to trim some of their magnificent work. I hope they'll forgive me.

OCTOBER 10 - 25:

The review section is coming along. A few 'avoid for your own safety' type reviews (included purely as a public service) but the rest are a genuine evaluation of the incredibly broad spectrum of crime films released this year. I'm finding that, as even more are unleashed, I'm having to drop a few sub-genres. The terrorist/action-movies have had to go, so no *Goldeneye*, and no *Escape From LA*, however enjoyable they were. I've left *Batman Forever* and *Judge Dredd* in because they are, at heart, good old-fashioned pulp fiction crime-busters.

Films released on video in '96, but at the movies in '95 (like the two above examples), have been included were relevant, because, arguably, video is where they will receive their largest and keenest audience.

Rather than ranking them into a chart, I've listed them alphabetically, but included their American box-office take. I've used this rather than the English figures, simply because the American information is more reliable. Also, as a general rule of thumb, what a movie makes in America is about half of what it will make world-wide. So, for global take, multiply the American figure by two.

There are exceptions to this rule, of course: *Trainspotting* and *Things To Do In Denver When You're Dead* spring to mind from the crop included here, which only serves to make their success in Britain all the more exciting.

NOVEMBER 1:

Well, it's as good as done, just a few tees to dot and eyes to cross; and what's more, I'm only two weeks past my deadline.

It's been a curiously exhilarating experience. There have been moments, though, when I needed climbing gear to get up my Learning Curve. Firstly I didn't know I could write so much so quickly. Secondly, I didn't know that *Crime Time* magazine had earned such a reputation that damn good writers were prepared to trust me with their work without ever having met me. Thirdly, there is no thirdly.

NOVEMBER 5:

Bugger. Better think of an introduction ... quick!

The best I can hope for this book is that it contains a representative sample of the crime-films available in the mid-nineties, a period which is an undoubted renaissance for this much-maligned genre. If *The Crime Time Filmbook* tells you, the reader, things you didn't know, points you in new directions, inspires you to give such-and-such a movie a second chance, or fills you so full of wrath that you have to put pen to paper and write a riposte, then it will have succeeded.

I am not setting myself, or any writers here represented, up as the absolute arbiters of taste, but rather presenting discussion documents and personality interviews which will, hopefully, inform and improve your enjoyment of the crime films which are playing across our big and small screens with unheard-of frequency.

Now, more than ever, is the time for crime.

JOHN ASHBROOK

Coventry, November (what *is* the date, anyway?) 1996

QUENTIN'S REVENGE

"So, on the 563rd day, God made lead and chrome plating and these he fashioned into a gun. And he gave the gun to Adam and said *"Kill the filthy motherfucker"*"

Genesis 2:16

LOS HOOLIGAN

by John Ashbrook

ON THE TRAIN *coming down to London for a press-screening, I had finished reading a book called* Rebel Without A Crew. *It is a film diary, telling of the year in the life of a 23-year-old Texan, who made a home movie called* El Mariachi *for $7,000 then sold it to Columbia Tri-Star for a quarter of a million. It is a startlingly honest and inspirational book which leaves the reader with the unshakeable belief that any shmoe with a little money, a lot of gullible friends and a determined streak a mile wide can make a movie. In years to come a lot of film-school rejects will see their names in lights because of this book.*

I arrived at Columbia Tri-Star's preview theatre, in London's West End, sporting my favourite baseball cap (well, it's always a good idea to dress up for these formal occasions). It bore the legend Hard Boiled *in bolshy gold letters. The choice of this hat was a strategic move on my part as I was about to interview Robert Rodriguez, the fore-mentioned Texan; one-man film crew, post-Tarantino phenomenon and, not coincidentally, lover of John Woo films.*

This'll get his attention! I thought. Little did I know ...

First they screened Desperado, *the sort-of sequel to* El Mariachi, *then, as the lights rose, in wandered the director, dressed in jeans and a lumberjack shirt with the sleeves rolled up. Oh good, I thought, at least I'm not the only scruffy bugger here! After our brief introduction I switched on my microphone and set about checking levels on my tape machine, the first words it recorded were:*

"Cool hat! Wow, where do I get one of those? Damn."

"Ehm ... who distributed the film? ...Metro Tartan; I think. I got it off them!"

"That's great!"

[Trying hard to act surprised] *"Thank you. Ehm ... So, has your reputation for making films cheaply helped or hindered you in Hollywood?"*

"Oh, completely helped! I'll work forever off *Desperado* alone, because Hollywood just doesn't know how to make movies that look big, that can be sold like a big movie, but that cost under ten million. It's really funny, 'cos they just can't see how to do it, and I dunno why.

"*Desperado* cost seven million, which is, y'know, a lot for me but it's nothing for a big action film. Action movies start at thirty and, if it's a summer movie, which this one was in the States, they start at fifty. In fact, there was an article

A (C)HAT WITH ROBERT RODRIGUEZ

in one of the industry magazines and it showed all the hits and all the disasters - the big bombs that cost a lot and made nothing - and there were only seven films on the list that made it. *Desperado* was one of 'em, simply by the ratio of what it cost to what it made."

"So, are the days of monsters like Waterworld *over?"*

"No, they'll still do them. They'll salivate over the idea of a *Jurassic Park* forever and spend maybe sixty or seventy million dollars, but make back over a billion after merchandising and video sales etc. They roll the big dice. It's risky making small movies because you don't know if they'll even make profit, they almost certainly won't do the *Pulp Fiction* business, that's a rare thing! So it's hard for them to know how to run their business,

"No one in Hollywood really knows what they're doing, they're all dependent on somebody else. The studio guys don't know how to make movies, they're all accountants who're totally dependent on guys like me, who can tell 'em anything. They don't know. They haven't learned what you need. They should, then they wouldn't get shafted so much! On the other side, creative guys aren't usually very technical so they're dependent on technicians and on the crew, who tell 'em it'll take so long and cost so much to do, so there's another waste.

"Something I learned from my first job in high school was that the last thing a creative person does is learn to be technical, they're just too lazy to do that. But, if you're creative and you become technical, then you're unstoppable. That's what I did, I learned how to make a movie from the ground up, I learned all the camera stuff, I learned how to cut it, all so I wouldn't be dependent on anybody."

"And you'll continue doing it this way?"

"Yeah, 'cos once I'd set the precedent with *El Mariachi* (and then they made the mistake of letting me do it again with *Desperado*) that really locked it in. I was able to persuade them to let me direct and shoot and edit *Desperado* like that because I was doing it for so little money. They had nothing to lose, so they let me do it. Now it's standard operating procedure. From now on, when a producer hires me, he knows already that I'm gonna shoot it and edit it and arrange the music myself, he won't even question it.

"It used to be that you either made big movies which everybody had to go see so were really watered down, and had no one person in control; or you had to make really small independent movies where you had a lot of freedom, but no one would go see 'em. But movies like *Pulp Fiction, Desperado*, and *From Dusk Till Dawn* satisfy everybody because we make 'em cheap enough that the investors'll get back their money back plus a little profit."

"I can imagine that you won't make yourself too popular in Hollywood saying things like that!"

"But they love what I'm saying. They want me to make movies that make money and don't cost anything. True, when they see how cheap I can work, they sweat a little; it makes it harder for them to justify such great expense. At the premier of *Desperado* I was sitting next to, I dunno, they musta been two agents or something, and they just kept looking at each other and whispering *"Seven million dollars! This didn't cost seven million dollars!?" "Yeah, seven million dollars!"* and they were sweating 'cos they were making one for forty million and if it blows they're gonna lose their jobs; so they're scared out of their pants."

"So the rumblings have already started in Hollywood?"

"Yeah, but that's good; the whole industry has gotten too big, it's time it was shaken up a little bit. That's what young people are supposed to do, shake things up. Then I'll be there in a coupla years and some new guys'll breeze into town and tell me what an idiot I am. I guess what goes around comes around! I'm just making the most of it while I can."

"But a lot of film-makers get on the ladder by calling in favours, getting someone high up to give them a break, and they do on condition that later on you do them favours back ..."

"That's one way to get in, but I tried not to do that. There are people who borrow money from their parents to make their first movie, but I tell people *"Go sell your body to science for a few months, then you can do it with your own dime. Put yourself on the line, don't drag someone else into it."* That's what I did, and if it's your own risk you're actually more careful with the money.

"Then you don't owe any favours and you own your own picture. That's what happened with *Mariachi*, I put myself on the line and then, when it was a success, I didn't have to pay anybody back, it was all my own thing."

"Does working so cheaply make the job easier?"

"Well it's never easy with any budget, but with a bigger budget you've just got other kinds of problems. You're always gonna have problems, it's just that you solve 'em differently when you don't have a lot of money. It wasn't like 'Hey, now I've got seven million dollars, I can relax', 'cos I was making something that, by Hollywood standards, would cost much more. So it was still a struggle, but when you don't have very much money you end up solving your problems creatively. What a movie is, is a whole series of creative problems that you have to solve, that's why big movies get into trouble, 'cos when they get a problem they don't stop and think about how to fix it creatively and make the movie better, they just wash the problem away with the money hose. That's easy and it doesn't really solve your problem."

"So how does seven million dollars get spent?"

"I shot the whole movie, put everything in the can, for $3.1 million. The rest went on wages for the actors, producers, post-production, the SDDS eight-track sound mix, the release prints, all the post stuff which we didn't think we needed to spend so much on, but the studio thought we did. I'll be controlling more of that from now on! But to actually make the movie, all the sets, all the explosions and all the stunts came in at 3.1. That's nothing."

"Does more money mean bigger names?"

"On *Desperado*, Antonio Banderas cost a little bit, not much. He was on the way up. The same is true of George Clooney in *Dusk*. You can either pay twenty million dollars for these big actors, or you can find new guys and make them into twenty million dollar actors. We got George Clooney for a song 'cos no one was offering him movie rôles when I hired him, now he's been offered *Batman and Robin* which is great. I'd rather make someone a star and then not be able to afford 'em, so have to go find someone else and make them a star instead! That keeps the budgets down and sparks your creativity."

"Do you resent the way that you and Tarantino are grouped together in people's minds?"

"I think film makers have always worked together, Spielberg and Lucas worked together for years, and that happens all the time, because Hollywood is a small community where you find that people you relate to are few and far between. Quentin and I worked together three times in a row [*Desperado, Four Rooms* and *From Dusk Till Dawn*]... but on *Desperado*, he was only there for one day. Actually I hardly ever see him these days, he's always leaving the country, I dunno where he is half the time."

"Did he write his own lines for Desperado?"

"Ehm ... it was an old joke he told. I told him to make it his own, so he added stuff and made a six minute version of a three minute joke, which I cut down to two minutes. He knew he was only gonna be there for a day, so he knew it wasn't gonna be pretty. I think he had a bad feeling from the moment he walked on the set and saw I had a smile on my face. He knew he was gonna get it!"

"He has a much more substantial rôle in From Dusk Till Dawn, *so I guess you must rate him as an actor!"*

"Well he always wanted to be an actor, he studied acting, and he took it very seriously on *Dusk*. After I saw him in *Desperado*, he seemed like a real natural. It's true that he needs a strong director while he's still learning, especially when he comes up against a guy like George Clooney who's been in awful stuff for years, but got away with it because no one even paid enough attention to dismiss him. The critics wouldn't say *"George Clooney was terrible in this movie"* because they didn't even care who George Clooney was. He had years to get the seasoning that Quentin has to get very quickly; and, as you see in *Dusk*, he got there very fast.

"Are you a strong director with him, then?"

"I didn't really have to do that much, he actually studied and worked hard on just the acting and didn't take anything else on. He really worked on the character, and therefore he's not playing another loudmouthed guy, he's playing someone very subdued and backwards and very different. I think he's extremely entertaining and completely twisted, and the audience just starts laughing whenever he does anything wrong, which is really great.

"How do you respond when your films are compared to John Woo's?"

"That's great, 'cos that was our major inspiration. American action movies were getting really stale because, I found out, action is usually shot by second unit, a stunt guy who takes the camera and a whole other crew and shoots the action stuff. They usually move so slow on a big movie that the director will spend all his time directing the main sequences with the main actors while the difficult stuff is passed on to second and third crews. We did everything first unit on *Desperado*, I wanted to shoot everything. I was horrified when I found out that I was supposed to hand all the fun stuff to somebody else, that's what I was waiting for the most, I didn't wanna do the dialogue scenes, I wanted to blow things up.

"It was the John Woo movies that made me realise that the difference between our films and films from other countries is the way they would commit to the action. I hadn't been excited about an action movie like *The Killer* or *Hard Boiled* since I was a kid watching James Bond movies, and I thought it was just 'cos I was getting older, but I realise now that it's just that our movies are getting stale. Those Hong Kong movies made that catharsis come back again, they made you wanna be Chinese and do all that neat stuff."

"I noticed a lot of rather playful imagery around sex and guns ..."

"Yeah, well, I think that whole obsession with pistols and guns, it's just guy fantasies and it's really funny, so I just played it up. In fact, that one phallic symbol gun that Salma Hayek pulls out of the mariachi's guitar-case was used later in the movie, but I had to cut it out 'cos it was too funny. However, it shows up in *Dusk*. A character named Sex Machine has it and it's like a mini cannon that rises up out of the crotch area. It's for when you've got your hands up and you wanna shoot someone ... well, it's got a big long barrel and two revolvers for the testicles ... it's really gross. But it gets a huge laugh 'cos it's in a leather cod-piece, and it just takes the whole idea of a guy with his pistol ... cocked ... and, I dunno, I was just playing with that whole mentality."

"Do you think there's a bias against Hispanic actors in Hollywood?"

"I guess you could call it that. They certainly don't jump at the chance to hire 'em unless they need a token character for a demographic - maybe they'll make a little extra money in the Latin market if they put a few in - but they won't give 'em anything cool to do; he'll be the first one to get shot or the first to run chicken, nothing like what we do with 'em in this movie. Even the bad guys are cool in my movie! They'll jump off a building shooting all the way down. They're tenacious and exciting.

"You'll see the same faces show up in *From Dusk Till Dawn* playing different parts, and this creates an audience for them. You're able to say "But these guys are stars, they've been in two and a half movies now, people know who they are!" Normally they'd say that there aren't any Latin stars so you must use this guy and paint him brown, or whatever. You've gotta make stars from the ground up, so I've been bringing them along and putting 'em in as many secondary rôles as possible. Even the guy who throws knives in *Desperado*, it's a small bit part but I give him a lot to do so that he stands out; then, when he showed up again in *Dusk Till Dawn* I heard people cheer 'cos they remembered him. That's cool, that's how to create your own stars, and partly why I did *Desperado* and *Dusk Till Dawn* back to back, to heighten people's awareness and make these guys stars."

"Where do you find your actors?"

"All over the place. People sometimes have very little acting experience because they don't get the chances, so I start them sometimes from nowhere. I saw Salma Hayek on Spanish television saying how she couldn't get work in the States 'cos of her accent, even though she is a big soap star in Mexico. In *Desperado*, for instance, since we were shooting in this little town, we couldn't afford to fly a lot of actors out of Los Angeles, so a lot of the actors, even in bigger parts, are my crew people. I deliberately hired a Mexican crew, so my first assistant director's in the movie, my director of photography, my grip, my gaffer, my make-up artist, they're all in there.

"You know that bit where Antonio slides across the bar and the other guy slides up to him and they run out of bullets and they're shooting empty guns at each other *[a sequence ripped whole and bleeding from John Woo's* A Better Tomorrow *it must be noted!]*, well that's my second assistant director. As soon as we killed him he went back to work. I just looked at my crew and said *"Man, you guys look like movie stars"*, so I put 'em all in. That was fun, every day a different crew guy got to be in the movie, which kept the morale up!"

"Did you get much co-operation from the small town you filmed in?"

"Tons. We'd shot *Mariachi* there, but they didn't notice us when we were there first time because there was no crew, just me with a camera running around shooting one take and then off to the next location, really fast. That's how we made it look expensive by filming on the real streets, with real cars rolling by. Normally you have to pay the city to clear the streets, hire people to rent cars, bring in guys to drive 'em - it's all that backwards kind of thinking, the old way is just to let real cars go by and film your actors running between 'em. This time we wanted to go back because we wanted to pay back the town. Everyone got to work on the movie in some capacity, 'cos it's only a small place."

"At one point, when the bad guy is after Banderas' blood, he says "Just go into town and, if you see someone you don't know, you shoot 'em! How hard can that be?" *Is this your philosophy for making films?"*

"Exactly. Bucho *[the bad guy]* says all of my lines: *"Do I gotta do everything myself?*", that's my favourite line, I say that all the time on the set. In all honesty that film was just an excuse to kill people in crazy and exciting ways. It was supposed to be a really over the top, blown out, fun action movie with this ridiculous story idea about a guy with a guitar-case full of guns. I was surprised when the first movie got out the way it did, but I thought it would be great to make a bigger, more extreme second one."

"Will there be a third Mariachi *movie?"*

"We'll see. Maybe I'll call it *Once Upon A Time In Mexico. [Don't worry folks, he's joking. Honest.]* I heard about this small town in Mexico where all they do is make guitars, so I thought, maybe that's where he'll be holed up, building guitars."

"Obviously you've got a reputation for action movies, but in Rebel Without A Crew *you talk about starting out with animations -"*

" - And family comedies, yeah, that's mainly what I do. I'm the blood and guts guy now, but what I've always been is Mr Family Comedy. I wrote a comic strip for a few years called *Los Hooligans* which was based on my family, and that's what's coming next. I mean, *From Dusk Till Dawn* is by far the capper on all this, I can't go any further than that, it's like completely an exploitation, drive-in, horror, action, splatter thriller with Tarantino and me together at our most extreme. You can't go beyond that. So it's time to go the other way, I'll probably do a family comedy and after that maybe a biopic on Stevie Ray Vaughan."

"Does your drawing lead you to storyboard everything?"

"Not so much these days, 'cos there's so many shots; if I had to draw 'em all ... If I didn't operate the camera myself I'd probably do that, but since I'm framing the shot anyway and I'm choosing the lens, I just tell people to move fast and follow me. You just use a storyboard to tell your crew what you want. That's what directing is in Hollywood, it's more of a power position where you tell people what to do; I don't like to do that. I don't wanna be the boss, I wanna be making the film, so rather than telling the crew what to do, I'll work with them and lead by example, that's how we can move so quickly and make the movie so cheaply, not because I'm cracking the whip but because I'm leading the way, and I'm moving very, very fast.

"I see 'em already cut in my head, which comes from. over the years, just making so many movies and seeing 'em through the editing. Like, if I was making a movie about us two guys talking, I'd think about it for a minute and know not only how to shoot it but how it would look cut on the screen, so I could just get those little pieces that I need."

"You're not good at deputising then?"

"No, I don't deputise. I can't imagine who even thought of that. Editing is the best part of making a movie. Who thought to give that to someone else? In fact, they don't just give someone else the chance to have all the fun, they pay them to have all the fun, that's ridiculous. To call yourself a cook when all you do is buy the groceries doesn't make any sense, y'know. Too much of this and not enough of that can screw up the whole thing, so editing's very, very important, the most important part of the job."

"Rebel Without a Crew *almost reads like a manifesto of how you think people should make films ...*"

"I've had several people tell me that, does it really sound like that? When people quote me they say *"You said 'You should do this'."* But I never said *"You should do -"* anything, 'cos I hate it when people tell me that. All I said was what I did, and I wrote it to show you that it is all completely against everything you've ever heard, but it worked for me. It should make you realise that all that stuff you thought you needed to know, all those people you thought you needed to be in with, you don't need that at all.

"I just wanted to demystify it, make it seem less frightening, because that's what held me back for so long - just not knowing the nature of the beast I was confronting. It turns out to be a little rabbit. So, I thought I'd better tell some people, 'cos no one else wants to let people know or there'll be too much competition, but I don't care. I know what I can do, it's the other filmmakers who are scared; they didn't want anyone to know how easy it all is, which makes me mad, so I decided I'm not gonna keep the secret, I'm gonna blurt it out."

And with that, his next appointment arrived. However, so won over was I by the man's disarming honesty, by his refusal to be precious about his 'art', I felt foolish getting him to autograph my copy of Rebel. *Instead of just acting like a fan-boy, I offered him a trade. Consequently he went to his next interview happy, and I walked to the tube clutching my treasured book, while the wind whipped around my bare head.*

Rebel Without A Crew *is published by Faber and Faber. My hat appeared in* The Observer *newspaper that weekend, sported by its new owner. To this day I don't have a* Desperado *hat!*

Reservoir Dogs

by Chris Holding.

THE ATTEMPT IN THIS ESSAY *is to present a critical analysis and overview of* Reservoir Dogs. *It is of particular interest because, unlike much of what has seen print on the subject of Tarantino, it was written in 1993, before the release of* Pulp Fiction, *and therefore before his work had entered the popular consciousness. Granted, he was a source of much excitement amongst gatherings of film-critics and students, but he hadn't begun to be lauded, parodied or worshipped as he became after the success of* Pulp Fiction. *Very little had, at the time of writing, been published on* Reservoir Dogs, *but what there was concentrated on the violence of the movie. This was a trend which was, of course, to continue.*

"Let's Go To Work ..." has not been published before, and it therefore has interest not only as an historical document, but also because it assesses Tarantino's work (and the early responses to that work) in a balanced and objective way which would be quite impossible now. Chris makes some amazingly portentous comments, especially given the developments of Pulp Fiction, *and in the light of the effect Tarantino has had on American independent film-making since 1993.*

CRITICS ARGUE that films like *Reservoir Dogs*, *Bad Lieutenant* and *Man Bites Dog* represent a 'new aesthetic' of cinema violence. The two main juxtaposed views then represent a critique of the films as a) simply art-house violence, filmed as pop video, or b) as a legitimate emergence of a 'new' style and scope of movie within independent cinema. Whether the view adopted is the former or the latter, *Reservoir Dogs* is a problematic film in many senses, some of which this essay will attempt to uncover. In so doing, I will provide a discussion of the text, drawing on contemporary writings, analyses, and the subsequent theory which arises from them.

One of the most noticeable features of the film is its position as a strongly post-modern movie. Of course, post-modernism has any number of guises within cinema, for instance, the jazzy nostalgia of Woody Allen films, combined with their intimation at a hope for the future. In contrast, the more extreme post-modernism of David Lynch, especially in *Blue Velvet*, which conflates the worlds of small-town fifties America with an underclass dominion of sexual perversion and violence. *Reservoir Dogs* sits uncomfortably among these

LET'S GO TO WORK

particular definitions, whilst sharing a mixture of their characteristics.

As an understanding of the post-modernism within *Reservoir Dogs*, refer to David Harvey; in his book *The Condition of Post-modernity*, he, in turn, refers to the idea of Deconstructionism as instigated by Derrida in the '60s:

" ... *[Deconstructionism is] less a philosophical position than a way of thinking about and reading texts ... Writers who create texts or use words, do so on the basis of all the other texts and words they have encountered, while readers deal with them in the same way. This intertextual weaving has a life of its own. Whatever we write conveys meaning we do not or could not possibly intend, and our words cannot say what we do mean."* Harvey continues: *"It is vain to try and master a text, because the perpetual interweaving of texts and meanings is beyond our control."*

The effect is to 'deconstruct' the power of the producer so that the understanding of the text passes towards , firstly, the meaning of the text in relation to its origins (author, director, influences, etc.) and secondly, the meaning of the text with regards to our own incorporation of it as a new whole, created or interpreted from the 'fragments' of its origin.

With this Desconstructionist concept in mind, it is perhaps clearer to see the territory within which *Reservoir Dogs* operates. As an authored piece, it must be read in relation to how it was penned, and by whom; but, moreover, how the spectator perceives this. As a fragmentary and referential piece, *Reservoir Dogs* relies not only on its in-built themes and references, but also on the individual's own decoding of these elements which, unlike Harvey's statement, may not allow us to 'try and master the text' but simply provide a reading of it.

The film mixes various genres, such as Gangster, Black comedy/Parody, Horror and B-movie; along with acting styles, such as the '50s Method of Harvey Keitel, the late '60s speediness of Steve Buscemi, the understated '70s heroism of Tim Roth and the '90s retro-cool of Michael Madsen, locations are restricted to '90s downtown LA (where mobile phones abound), yet the *mise-en-scène*, dialogue and music locate it between the mythical '50s and '70s, largely thanks to *K-Billy's Super Sounds Of The Seventies*.

The film also cross-references Group/Posse movies like *The Magnificent Seven* and *The Wild Bunch*, the dress sense of *The Blues Brothers*, and the cult appeal of directors like Scorsese (Italian mobsters), John Woo and Ringo Lam (designer violence) and the Westerns of *Reservoir Dogs*' executive producer Monty Hellman.

Indeed, many describe *Reservoir Dogs* as a filmic film. Devin McKinney in *Violence: The Strong and the Weak*, portrays it as:

" ... *a jaunty, hyperbolic comedy of horrors that aspires to no particular realism or social import. It occurs in a comic existential dead zone, and is as non-referential to a reality outside itself as a (theoretically) mimetic work can be."*

So it is non-referential to 'real life', but is very referential to a whole host of filmic realities. *Reservoir Dogs*' multiplicity of meanings and juxtapositions are located within a reference to, respect for, and send-up of Film School values, which makes the movie's 'real' meaning or dominant discourse difficult (if not impossible) to decipher. The text is layered thickly enough to ensure that the individual's subjectivity may decode or perceive the film in any number of ways: straight-cut Gangster Movie, Comedy of Horrors, Empowerment of Gun-Culture, or critique of White, Male Masculinity and The Underclass ... and so on.

To this effect, Amy Taubin, in *The Men's Room*, reflects that the film is: " ... *self conscious, a black comedy of manners that both brags on and derides its genre and characters* ..." Moreover, it is a " ... *film about film, about fiction*."

In this light, *Reservoir Dogs* represents a truly post-modern encoding of a cultural text, a concentration of The Signifier over The Signified, fragmentary by nature but cohesive as a whole, referential but not reverent to a particular style. It is on this level that much of the criticism around the movie has centred.

The film's overt referencing of both the traditions and the tribulations of Hollywood has led some critics to decry it as 'hip' and 'self-consciously smug'. By replaying or imitating so many Hollywood story-lines and genres, the call is that the film purports not to be 'real' (whatever that may be) or original. In much the same way that dance music mixes together and reprocesses samples from recordings by other artists, located in a new context, *Reservoir Dogs* replays its story in a new but strangely familiar vein.

Under the ethos of this argument, the criticism is aimed not at the film itself , but at the strongly post-modern directive it supports through its storyline - the themes are standard film stock, " ... *loyalty and betrayal, cops and robbers, the humanist versus the psycho*" as B. Ruby Rich observes in *Art House Killers*.

The criticism then lies in what the film is saying because of how it is saying it. 'Proper' films, it may be argued, represent art and representations of reality in the format of post-modern parody, or as an entertainment or celebration. This has unsurprisingly ruffled the feathers of more tradition film theory/ cinema (note: Frederic Jameson discusses this 'Paraliterature' in *Post-modernism and Cultural Society*). Certainly, laughing at tough physical violence (which is the crux of the issue for many, with regard to *Reservoir Dogs*) is problematic. For most critics, the issue appears to be whether *Reservoir Dogs*' metalanguage is perceived as an exploitatively violent movie hiding behind the ethos of post-modern reference and art-house cool, or if its message has a critique of its own other than just reference or entertainment.

This is perhaps an oversimplification, after all, post-modern movies abound within Hollywood without any real discussion of ethics. What makes *Reservoir Dogs* different is its unashamed use of fiction combined with the seriousness of the subject of violence. To many, it seems taboo to place harsh violence so closely to comedy and 'the fiction of film', and in this sense *Reservoir Dogs* merges all three elements in a bold manner. The arguments proliferate, whilst Tarantino has simply stated *"I love violence in the movies!"* B. Ruby Rich claims that *"Nobody is likely to confuse movies with real life after seeing [Reservoir Dogs] despite a publicity campaign that seems to want to sell us on authenticity."*

Paradoxically, Tim Roth, who plays Mr Orange, states: *"Quentin shows you that violence has consequences ... people have been lulled into advertising violence, nicely shot, beautifully lit ... this guy dies and you've forgotten about the person who's been killed because he never was real."* The quotes highlighted here articulate the diversity of views on offer and the rhetorical nature of the questions asked: Is the violence the shock value, gimmick, or intrinsic element and underpin of the story?

Linked with these concepts of violence is the pleasure which the movie delivers to the audience. With *Reservoir Dogs*, this comes in a variety of references, firstly to the whole cinematic tradition, but also, to pop culture in general, i.e.: the discussion of *Like A Virgin*, the inane babbling about Pam Griers and the omni-present *K-Billys*.

In conjunction with this is a referential form of type-casting, wherein the pleasure in the movie is linked with the baggage each actor brings to the text. For example, Harvey Keitel's rôle as Mr White places him in familiar Scorsese territory. Equally, Michael Madsen's ultra-cool *"I'll bet you're a Lee Marvin fan"* Mr Blonde posturing is a direct cross-over from previous rôles in *Thelma and Louise* and *Kill Me Again*. In his *Sight and Sound* review, Kim Newman states that Lawrence Tierney (Joe. Cabot) " ... *carries a freightload of genre history which goes back to* Dillinger." In other words, the pleasure is in placing familiar forms in a new combination and familiar actors into rôles we, the audience, would like to see. In *Reservoir Dogs*, the added twist comes from the change in chemistry, i.e.: Tim Roth as an Englishman playing an American undercover cop, or Eddie Bunker as a real-life ex-con bringing added authenticity to Mr Blue.

Once again, the pleasure derived is related to our knowledge (or lack of it) with regards to the text's references. In this way *Reservoir Dogs* represents a melting pot of the known (Keitel, Madsen, pop references, genre tropes) and the unknown (Tarantino himself, Roth, the slap/kiss titillation of the story). As a result, the mixture is simultaneously aesthetic/nostalgic and yet volatile.

Continuing on this theme, Roland Barthes, in his article *The Pleasure of the Text*, rhetorically asks: *"Is not the most erotic portion of a body where the garment gapes?"* Consequently, if we view the text from this angle, the pleasure is also wrapped up in the gaps and in the difficulties which the film provides; the mystery or mythology which the text creates. As an illustration, the paradox of difference and unity is carried in the story itself as the band of robbers are compelled to become both a professional unit or team, whilst at the same time remaining detached and anonymous, hiding behind colour-coded names.

Moving on, the second main area of pleasure on offer is tied up with the idea of a new aesthetic of violence. In simple terms, a shift in the focus of cinema from portrayal of sex or romance as entertainment, to the voyeurism of watching violence. B. Ruby Rich claims that it is:

" ... too angry and uptight for the old sexual fix. How much better to sign on to violence and see that rage explode on screen, but comfortingly restrained within the cosy familiarity of genre."

Under this label, the charge aimed at *Reservoir Dogs* and films like it, is that, through its lack of traditional pleasures (women, love interest, sex) the voyeuristic nature of the cinema audience is subverted from the 'perversional pleasure' of viewing sex on screen, to the ghoulish voyeurism of watching violence. In effect, the psychological thrill is the same although the subject has changed.

In much the same way, Amy Taubin in *The Men's Room* asserts:

" ... the problem with Reservoir Dogs *is that its critique of masculinity is tied-up in its money shots; they're the one and the same. Mr Blonde carving up the cop, and the final bad joke shoot-out are guarantees of box-office success."*

The fear, then, is that the same cinematic mythologising of sex (no need for condoms, no unwanted pregnancies, no AIDS, no homosexuals) as the traditional selling point of many movies, will be transferred to violence.

In answering this reprimand, *Reservoir Dogs* provides both fuel for the criticism and counterpoints to the charges. Arguably, excessive violence is utilised, but the text also highlights the consequences of this violence. For example, the film places Tim Roth bleeding to death before our eyes as its central time-frame. Equally 'good' overcomes 'evil', but at a cost. Similarly, comedy is used as a tool to funnel the nervous release for the horrors the spectator witnesses (perhaps not always to good effect).

But the study of violence is not always weakened through humour. Two particular instances are when Roth must shoot the woman whose car he must steal, in order to maintain his cover, and the final scene when he confesses his betrayal to Keitel, who executes him. Certainly, such moments disrupt the fictive storyline and cause the spectator to think more deeply of the film's 'true intent'.

In contrast to this, there appears to be transgressive areas within the text, where the affection for the characters and the humour appears to cross over, where the story goes beyond parody in its depiction of a shared cultural acceptance of homophobia, racism and anti-feminism. In some senses, the line drawn is a very thin one, whilst many would consider those elements intrinsic to the critique of masculinity in '70s culture. The argument is also whether such dubious and arguably 'discarded' fragments of culture require such impassioned play-acting. B. Ruby Rich neatly summarises the struggle when he discusses the Neo-violence movie 'trick' of switching the audience from horror to laughter: " ... *some of us never started to laugh. Some of them never stopped*".

If *Reservoir Dogs* appears regressive in its portrayal (or rather, lack of portrayal) of women and race, its subject matter (white gangsters) and referential style (post-modern) give it the credibility to carry such regression off. However, it might also be argued that a nostalgic nod towards racism is uncalled-for.

As it is, we are unsure whether we are watching a truthful or cynical moment, a reference or a reality. One moment the text discusses 'black bitches' with a grudging respect, then, at another point, the genuine concern for a young black-girl shot by Mr Blonde, is illustrated. In the same way, Mr Orange represents the juxtaposition of the characterisations: As an undercover cop, he stands as the collective consciousness of 'right', and of the audience (once his identity is revealed), yet, to maintain his cover, he must act and speak as the epitome of 'wrong'. Whilst he both abhors the gang's actions, and will betray them, he shares a masochistic respect for, and bond to, their code, into which we, the spectator, are also drawn.

It is perhaps this love/hate relationship which provides the basic premise of the movie, incorporating both a nostalgic love of the regressive characterisations, with an abhorrence of the values for which they stand. As a celebration of disgust, the film escapes reality through fiction, whilst also striving for authenticity. In this way, *Reservoir Dogs* appears schizophrenic by nature, constantly seeking to balance its fragmentary elements in a fictive auditorium of its own creation.

The ultimate position of the movie is unstable, or debatable. Tarantino mixes not only genre, acting styles, time-lines and story-lines, but also emotions. The spectator is placed in a variety of positions; the story being picked up after the heist, allows an entanglement of contradictory views as the plot is relayed through anecdote and flashback.

The camera places the spectator initially as objective observer, but swaps throughout from Mr White to Mr Orange; Mr Pink, to Nash, the tortured cop. One moment the audience sees Mr White's charitable and humane side as he fosters a bond with the rookie Orange, the next he 'professionally' disposes of two cops in a squad car, and once again alienates the audience. As Amy Taubin observes:

"Tarantino lays bare the sado-masochistic dynamic between the film and the spectator. The masochistic (feminised) position of the audience is inscribed in Mr Orange's bleeding body."

But, also in Mr White's attempts to save Mr Orange, and through the audience's location as concurrently the tortured cop and the torturer Blonde. Indeed, emotionally, the film takes the spectator on a roller-coaster ride of perspectives and empathies, from comedy, affection, nostalgia and mythology to horror and disgust.

It would seem that the best way to view *Reservoir Dogs* is as an entirety, in an historical context. Whilst many may consider much of the material when taken out of context, or even in context, as overtly violent, racist, homophobic and anti-female, as a whole, the film provides (or attempts to provide) critiques of these elements. Of course, how well the film addresses the issues, or answers the charges about portraying its characters the way it does, is largely down to the spectator's subjectivity.

In the final analysis, Tarantino seems more than keen to promote a multiplicity of meanings. In his article, *A Rare Sorrow*, he states *"As can be seen from the film I made, I like what I call Kitchen Sink Movies, which means* 'there's everything in it but...'" Perhaps, ultimately, the question with such problematic movies should not be 'what did you think of the film?' so much as 'was the journey worth it?' I think it was.

QUOTES AND REFERENCES ARE TAKEN FROM:

The Condition of Post-modernity
by David Harvey. Basil Blackwell, 1989.
The Men's Room, *by Amy Taubin.*
Sight and Sound, *December 1992, Vol 2/8.*
Art House Killers, *by B. Ruby Rich.*
Sight and Sound, *December 1992, Vol 2/8. Violence:*
The Strong and the Weak, *by Devin McKinney.*
Film Quarterly, *Vol 46/4, Summer 1993.*
Harvey Keitel - Staying Power *by David Thompson.*
Sight and Sound, *January 1993, Vol 2/9.*
Reservoir Dogs *(review) by Kim Newman.*
Sight and Sound, *January 1993, Vol 3/1.*
A Rare Sorrow *by Quentin Tarantino.*
Sight and Sound, *February 1993, Vol 3/2*
The Pleasure of the Text *by Roland Barthes, 1973.*

PULP FICTION

Richard Luck on Tarantino, Travolta and learning to love Bruce Willis

"Every once in a while, you encounter a work of art that permanently affects the way you see the world." For editor Paul Seydor (*White Men Can't Jump*, *Cobb*) that film was Sam Peckinpah's *The Wild Bunch*. For this writer, the decision is not so clear cut. *Chinatown*, *Gregory's Girl*, *A Matter of Life and Death*, *Bring Me the Head of Alfredo Garcia*; all manner of different movies have had a life-shaping impact upon me. If we're talking contemporary movies, as I think Seydor is, there really is only one contender. I first saw Quentin Tarantino's *Pulp Fiction* at the 1994 *Birmingham Film Festival*, and I've been carrying it around ever since.

It's been said, and Tarantino said it better than anybody else, that there is "*nothing more exciting than a hip, contemporary director*". For Tarantino, that director was Brian DePalma. Personally, I have never been able to tap into the attraction of DePalma. Tarantino, on the other hand, I latched onto instantly. As someone who grew up in the '70s, on a steady diet of breakfast cereals, *Spiderman*, Baccara and *The Brady Bunch*, it took me less than ten minutes of watching *Reservoir Dogs* to realise that, for the first time ever, I was watching a movie that was made by someone a bit like me. A frightening thought, yes, but a comforting one, too.

Not that nostalgia is my main reason for liking Tarantino. If I wanted to get back to the '70s, I'd just go out and buy a packet of Black Jacks. It's not the humour, either (although it is a pleasure to watch films that have been made by clever, witty people. To write a wonderful indictment of all those balls 'n' glory 'Nam movies, and then get Christopher *The Deer Hunter* Walken to perform it, was a stroke of genius). No, the real source of my infatuation is that one word that has become attached to Quentin's work ever since it first appeared on the big screen. Yep, you guessed it: 'morals'.

"The problem with Pulp Fiction", Ben Elton commented in issue four of *Crime Time*, *"Is that there is no sense of heroism."* This statement is complete balls. So, too, are all the arguments concerning Tarantino's masterpiece and its portrayal of violence. Not only does *Pulp Fiction* contain more heroic actions than your average Seagal or Van Damme movie, its body count is minuscule (six compared to over a hundred in the second *Die Hard*). More to the point, *Pulp Fiction* has

DID YOU GET THE PANCAKES?

a moral structure way beyond the grasp your average American movie. So complex are the arguments Tarantino is trying to get to grips with, they might even look out of place in European film. No wonder the good people of Pig's Knuckle, Alabama, found the film so disturbing. It's not everyday you find movies that address biblical morality at your local multiplex.

"The path of the righteous man is beset on all sides by the iniquities of the selfish and the tyranny of evil men."- Jules Winnfield

Anyone who wants to argue about the immorality of *Pulp Fiction*, really ought to focus on the riff Samuel L. Jackson delivers before offing the floundering Brad. Within the context of the movie, there is much to be made of the way in which Jules ponders its meaning while pointing 'Mr Nine-Millimetre' at Pumpkin. Outside of the film, the inclusion of the quote saw Quentin Tarantino achieve something that Cliff Richard, Simon Mayo and Alvin Stardust had spent decades trying to do; he got young people to pick up *The Bible*. Whether fans kept reading after their futile attempts to find *Ezekial 25:17* (it doesn't exist) is besides the point. Tarantino pulled off a coup of Church of England-pleasing proportions. The moral aspect of *Pulp Fiction* extends well beyond a reference to the good book. In detailing the story of Jules Winnfields's redemption, the writer/director sets up a moral conundrum of Peckinpahesque proportions.

I have long been a fan of Sam Peckinpah's Westerns. Its not just the guns and blood, you understand. What struck me as instinctively right about Peckinpah's world-view was the idea that received concepts of morality, such as obeying the letter of the law, sometimes breached more important binds such as family and friendship. In *Pulp Fiction*, Tarantino sets up a moral quandary that Bloody Sam would have been proud of. During their bacon breakfast debate, Jules tells Vincent (John Travolta) that, having felt the touch of God, he is going to quit the gangster game. It is a noble decision, and one that surely saves the lives of Pumpkin and Honeybunny. In the long run, however, it will also lead to the death of his colleague and best friend. Without his partner to cover his back, Vincent Vega is left holding the loo rôle when he encounters the gun-totin' Butch. The moral complexities of Jules's change of heart are so deep they make the 'are guns a good thing?' debate look like a subject that could be resolved by classroom discussion.

And the moral dilemmas don't end there. With his boss's wife dying from an overdose, Vincent Vega has to decide whether to skip town or save her life. In the end, he does the right thing. So, in fact, do most of the characters in *Pulp Fiction*. Not only does Jules spare the life of Pumpkin, he also has grave concerns about being seen to disrespect his friend Jimmy, the man with the 'dead nigger storage' problem. As it tries to deal with the big moral questions, *Pulp Fiction* also manages to address everyday dilemmas in a manner more realistic that most modern movies (not that dead niggers form a part of everyday life, but you get the picture).

Tenderness, redemption, friendship; there are so many incredible things going on in *Pulp Fiction*, you really want to grab hold of the pro-censorship lobby and say *"Hey! Look at this! You're missing the point!"* I wouldn't mind having a pop at these talentless sods who are lining up to have a go at Tarantino. In lieu of this, I would just like to say to all of these people, one thing: before Quentin Tarantino came along, movies were crap. The '80s was, without doubt, the worst decade for film since the 1880s, when moving pictures didn't even exist. Bimbo comedies, sequel procreators, thirty-something angst; you really couldn't move for the all the highly-polished shit that was about. Whatever else you might say about Tarantino, he has actually bullied people into caring about film. The smug laziness of recent times has been replaced by urgency and enthusiasm. University courses, rock videos, adverts; the old gateways to Hollywood have been rendered redundant by a generation of people who have just got off their arses and made movies. Thanks to Tarantino, there are now thousands of office clerks, factory workers, butchers, bakers and tallow handlers who are secretly writing scripts in their spare-time. It's a legacy which Our Quentin should be very proud of.

But back to *Pulp Fiction*, and after a work of such unrivalled genius, where does Tarantino go now? Will he make his guys-on-a-mission movie? Will he adapt Elmore Leonard's *Kill Shot* for the big screen? After *Four Rooms*, there are even some unkind souls who are suggesting that Quentin might already have shot his bolt. Personally, I would much rather see Tarantino blow some of his kudos on a small, portmanteau movie than a big-time epic. More to the point, all the great directors have made the occasional dog. John Huston spent the best part of thirty years making crap; it doesn't make *The Maltese Falcon*, *Fat City* and *Wise Blood* any the less good. And even if Tarantino doesn't have anything else up his sleeve, he has left us with one of the great moments in modern cinema. Battered and bloody, Butch (Willis, superb throughout) prepares to leave his pawn shop prison. Reaching the door and the daylight, he listens to the screams of a man, who, had things worked out differently, would have gladly killed him. In a moment of almost biblical self-sacrifice, he turns away from the daylight, arms himself and literally walks back into Hell. It is a moment of truly awesome power, spoilt only by Willis' choice of weapons. If it'd been me, I'd have picked the chain-saw. That would have really pissed James Ferman off.

PULP FICTION

...by the immensely brave (or foolish) Gerald Houghton

PULP FICTION is to '90s what Coppola's *Godfather* pictures were to the '70s, or Scorsese's *Raging Bull* was to the '80s. It is an icon, a touchstone for a whole generation of movie-heads. That poster of a manifestly un-PC Uma Thurman (low-cut, hot pistol, smouldering cigarette) is now as *de rigueur* student issue as *Betty Blue* was in my day. It made the almost unthinkable vault from Cannes success to the *Golden Globes, BAFTAs,* even *Oscars,* and still raked in over a $100 million at the US box office. You cannot argue with Tarantino's über-progeny. So why are we?

Get it straight - *Pulp Fiction* is a film that contains much to be admired. Tarantino is there to be praised for bringing back some balls to contemporary, *popular* cinema. Since *Reservoir Dogs* (1992) people have been writing better dialogue, and, even if we cannot prove it, we only really have one usual suspect to round-up for questioning. That is manifestly not the point.

Nor indeed are we here to debate the man's talent behind the camera: Quentin Tarantino can direct. His style is distinct and undoubtedly owes much to his legendary time in the video store watching whatever they put in front of him. For all he's a new young Turk, Tarantino is very much the classicist. Check the number of extraordinarily long takes in this film (Bruce Willis' introduction; Travolta and Samuel Jackson's arrival at the apartment building; the backyard walk to Willis' apartment), and its director's frugal use of close-up. The very non-TV use of widescreen and medium shots make this very much a cinema film. For this, for now, we applaud him.

Similarly, author Will Self might have found the screenplay hackneyed and crass and walked out after ten minutes, but as a writer, Tarantino is at least unsparing of his audience's TV-bred narrative mentality. We have here a film that starts and ends in the middle and proceeds to spin itself out from there. It is clever and proves that there is a mass audience in cinemas and, perhaps more significantly, on video for films that refuse the ordinary. But then again didn't Stanley Kubrick do something similar way back in 1956 with *The Killing*? *Dogs* owes Kubrick more of a debt (royalties, even), but two pictures in and Tarantino's structural borrowings could so easily become affectation. For now we'll forgive him, if only because that is arguably the least of *Pulp Fiction*'s troubles.

This film is a bloated mess.

GETTIN' MEDIEVAL ON YO' ASS

The clue as to why is hidden in the title. Not even so much hidden. This is *pulp* fiction. We think pulp, we think *film noir*, we think cheap paperbacks, sleazy, lurid, garish. You only have to look to the opening and its American Heritage Dictionary definitions: Tarantino tempts providence when he allows us to know that it can also mean *"a soft, moist, shapeless mass of matter"*.

New *noir* cinema (Neo-*noir*, if you must) tries so hard at emulating its forebears, but just cannot shake-off the weight of contemporary film. The results are too often either wax museums to past glories or, worse, parody. Think of Greenwald's *The Kill-Off* or Dahl's *Kill Me Again*, both from 1989, or the following year's *The Hot Spot*. That latter is the perfect example - Dennis Hopper is aiming for the same sweaty, over-sensitised passions that inform, say, *The Postman Always Rings Twice* (Tay Garnett's 1946 original - not Rafelson's soggy, redundant remake) or *Double Indemnity* (1944), or best of all, Joseph H. Lewis' marvellous *Gun Crazy* (1949). But *The Hot Spot* misses on most bases: it's too explicit, too ponderous (*noir* was never that), and, worst of all, at 148 minutes, much, much too long.

That last is the iceberg that does for almost every Neo-*noir* (and most contemporary film-making into the bargain). Which brings us back to the film under discussion. *Pulp Fiction* is, at most, an hour-forty masquerading as a two and half hour epic. Where *Dogs* is 99 beautifully sustained, tightly written and edited minutes, *Pulp* is suffused with longueurs. In his first film Tarantino the writer was in league with Tarantino the director to integrate and streamline the little riffs (the torture sequence; Roth's cover story). Here they sit over the action like an ill-fitting wig. Like a dance routine in a musical, they bring everything to a shuddering halt for three or four minutes; for every monologue like Christopher Walken's Captain Koons (one of Tarantino's single best pieces of writing, quite brilliantly delivered) there are two or three burger routines to be endured.

Evidence: immediately post the (excellent) title sequence we are gifted the whole celebrated *"Royale wi' Cheese"* schtick. What we learn is no more than is repeated a few minutes later in the apartment, to more immediately comic effect. What it tells us is that the screenwriter learned something vaguely amusing on his travels around Europe. That Vincent Vega recently toured Europe is established again - and better - during the drug buy. Excise the car-ride and the film is immediately lighter almost two minutes. Which brings us, you will be relieved to know, to the point of all this.

Let us establish some ground-rules. All times mentioned from hereon are not cast in stone, and everything is cited under the proviso that some tidying of dialogue and, occasionally, motivation may be necessary. That settled, the following is based around recutting the letterboxed UK video release of *Pulp Fiction* released by *Touchstone Home Video*, complete with its one slight trim by the blessed BBFC, and recognises the disparity in PAL running times. So, with the admonition that video copying is illegal and under absolutely NO circumstances should be indulged, pull up a blank VHS and, forgive me, let's go to work.

CUT 1: As established, the entire first dialogue between Vincent Vega (John Travolta) and Jules Winfield (Samuel L. Jackson). Post-titles the film opens far more effectively on the trunk-lid being lifted: welcome to our movie.

APPROX 2 MINUTES

CUT 2: The dialogue between Jody (Rosanna Arquette) and Vega about piercing. Like the burgers, Tarantino is crow-barring in something cool he's learned. This time from the women-folk who've so recently entered his life! Aside from the time recovered, it renders more effective and enigmatic Vega's reference in the subsequent scene, particularly as we cannot see clearly when she appears around the door, and removes the irrelevant Bronagh Gallagher altogether.

APPROX 1 MINUTE

CUT 3: The most dramatic (and to some, undoubtedly perplexing) edit. The film now leaps from one of the its best sequences (the whole drug fetishisation) to Lance's (Eric Stoltz) house almost a half-hour later. What's missing? In a nutshell, Uma Thurman.

Quentin Tarantino cannot write women.

In *Dogs*, of course, it was never an issue. But with *Pulp* he cannot avoid bringing the girls out to play in his boy-world, and finds himself wanting. They puppet around this picture like expensive props. When Thurman is not riffing about pop culture (all that 'Fox Force Five' nonsense) she has zip. Thus, Tarantino takes her to *Jack Rabbit Slim's* but has nothing to do with her and Vega once they get there. (Likewise, the restaurant itself is simply a Tarantino wank-fantasy, its celeb-waiters are crude, its movie-poster chic tiresome, its architecture lifted bodily from an Elvis movie, and worse yet, it wastes the excellent Steve Buscemi.) The whole rôle is patently predicated on Tarantino's idea of the perfect date. The only woman in the entire picture to have any measure of credibility is surely Honeybunny (Amanda Plummer), and only then because he gives her a gun and lets her play at being a boy in a skirt.

Plus, Thurman is supernaturally bad. Sticking on a black wig and walking barefoot does not a performance make. Admittedly, even a half-decent actress (say, Jennifer Jason Leigh) would have her work cut-out with such underwriting, but Uma just compounds the horror. To work, the whole sequence demands a sexual chemistry between Vega and Mia that Travolta and Thurman cannot supply. To quote Keitel's Wolf later in the film: *"Just because you are a character doesn't mean you have character."*

And again, there is a structural justification for her expulsion: in place of the inane will-they-won't-they bull we do get, we substitute an ambiguity that will never be explained, strengthening any scene that follows involving Vega with his boss. We leap from Vega's post-hit euphoria to the slam-injection on Lance's floor. The Mia we first see is almost dead. Naturally her subsequent joke is also axed. The only other time we see Mrs. Wallace is after the fight, the exchange now far more pregnant with menace and subterfuge. We also get to lose a stack of frankly irrelevant and misused songs (Dusty Springfield? Urge Overkill?), and the single biggest misjudgement in the entire picture - drawing that bloody square on the screen.

APPROX 28 MINUTES

CUT 4: Tarantino shows the same remarkable economy he displayed on the robbery in *Dogs* in *not* showing Butch's (Bruce Willis') fatal fight, only to spoil it when the film runs slap-bang into another of his awful women. And all taxi driver, Angela Jones, wants to know is: *"What does eet feel like? Keelling a man?"* It's an outbreak of the exotic-accent disease that will strike again only minutes later, and offers us a gratingly dull cab ride for our trouble. Keeping Butch's phone-call, everything else is out the door.

APPROX 3 MINUTES

CUT 5: A second dose of cute foreign accents, in the Björkish shape of Maria de Medeiros. Her childish wide-eyes and bafflingly dim talk of pot bellies and Madonna is, if anything, *Pulp Fiction* at its most irksome. Arguably the worst character ever to flow from his pen, it's shocking to consider that Tarantino reputedly penned the rôle originally for the astonishing Swiss actress Irene Jacob after seeing her in Kieslowski's masterly *The Double Life of Veronique* (1992). She would have carried it better, but even she would not have been safe from career-flattening embarrassment. (Ironic then that *Pulp Fiction* should beat Kieslowski's far superior *Three Colours: Red* - starring Jacob - to the *Palme d'Or.*) The Fabienne rôle is necessary, thus various trims to reduce her scenes to the barest minimum.

APPROX 3 MINUTES

CUT 6: The most problematic sequence in the entire film. There is no obvious explanation for the extended rape in this movie. It could be a tribute of sorts to Boorman's *Deliverance* (1972), or maybe just the director's particular fetish, but there is no question that it is anything other than dim-witted, ill-advised and homophobic. Over ten minutes of Tarantino at his most ugly, it is never funny, only repulsive and ignorant; the most otiose scene he has yet committed to film. Things can only be improved by its loss. And again, structurally it leaves open the conflict between Marcellus (Ving Rhames) and Butch. As it stands the film cheats badly - given what Butch has done and what he's just witnessed, no way would he be allowed to walk.

APPROX 11 MINUTES

CUT 7: Given the debt he owes to Keitel, Tarantino serves the actor very badly in this film. The Wolf is joke. It's a rôle Keitel had already essayed as The Cleaner in Badham's grisly *The Assassin* (1993), where, at least, he got to keep a measure of self-respect. Instead, here he gets to recite pedantic dialogue directed exclusively towards a couple of ropey punchlines, that awful on-screen gag about how fast he drives, and suffers the indignity of a scene opposite Tarantino, who should frankly be ashamed of himself for continually sticking his no-talent mug in front of the camera. Trims here, and, finally, axing the feeble-minded washing scene.

APPROX 4 MINUTES

What we have here, crudely speaking, are something like 52 minutes of cuts. The resulting picture runs around 96 minutes, of which 6 are titles and credits. There are other individual lines that could stand removal, and it is arguable that, without the rape, Butch's car crash is no longer strictly necessary. (And just what is Marcellus Wallace doing on that street corner anyway?)

Net result of all this? Principally the women's rôles are reduced to absolute essentials only. For us as viewers - and for Tarantino's future - this is no bad thing. *Dogs* was essentially theatrical, a boys town. Women served no purpose other than as cannon fodder. It's no wonder he should use that as his calling card picture. This time out he could not avoid the consequences of the other half of the population and all we get are a parade of idealised dates who obviously watch too much TV (Thurman), and strange and alluring foreign cuties (everyone else). *Pulp Fiction* does little to further the cause of feminism.

Christopher Walken's rôle (play to your strengths) becomes more significant, and better yet, Jackson is now effectively the star of the film, for which, to all intents and purposes, we had him pegged anyway.

There is still a slight question remaining over what some (in particular) cited at the time as the film's racism. This is debatable. Certainly the epithet 'nigger' is universal, albeit the bulk from the lips of either Jackson or Rhames. If there is a problem, it's not a conscious one. Tarantino is using it for seasoning, even though after a while it does seem more like affectation than character. Certainly, Spike Lee is reported to have suggested Tarantino (who appeared in the former's *Girl 6*) hold it down in future. Tarantino can be held accountable, but largely acquitted on grounds of laziness.

Of course, this is sacrificing a sacred cow (or at the very least applying some major plastic surgery). The film made a mint, collected awards like fallen apples, and has now been reissued on video with two EXTRA scenes tacked on, BOTH expanding the women's rôles. Some people never learn.

Even this drastic surgery could be seen as merely papering over the cracks while the house crumbles about our ears. The great Paul Schrader is down on record as being unsure what Tarantino's success tells us about the future. He contrasts these nihilist wits with the existential anti-heroes of the '70s and finds them wanting. For all it thrills us, for all it makes us laugh, for all it looks great, *Pulp Fiction* is really a film about nothing except maybe itself, and as we toast the end of cinema's first century, that has to be just the tiniest bit depressing. But then that, as they say, is another story.

PULP FICTION Dir: Quentin Tarantino Dist: Touchstone Home Video. Cert: 18. Dur: 148 mins (but subject to negotiation!) Released: 14/10/94 US Box-office: $107.75 million.

CRUISIN' FOR QUENTIN

...with Steve Holland...

HOW MANY WORDS must be written before people realise that Quentin Tarantino is not God. Quite a few more than the gigabytes of discussion, argument, chat and banter that passes for *alt.fan.tarantino*, the Internet newsgroup dedicated to QT. OK, so amongst the requests for Quentin's e-mail address, votes for best quotes and solutions to the enigma of what's in the briefcase, which forms a pretty regular thread, there's the odd dissenting (if badly spelt) voice: *"the worst film he(and r.rodr.) ever made - DUSK TILL DAWN"* claims one participant (and since QT only briefly acted in *Desperado* and *Four Rooms* was a quartet of solo stories with linking material, *From Dusk Till Dawn* is actually the *only* film they've made together, so you could argue it's also the best film they've done). Without getting too deeply into this, when someone claiming to be Travis Bickle starts asking about The Gimp, it's time to heed your mother and stop talking to strangers.

So there I am, cruisin' for Quentin on the Internet, thinking that The Man has only made a couple of full-length features, so it should be pretty easy to see quite a bit of what's been written. Wrong. Big time. I can't quite access *The Church of Tarantino* (http://www.aston.ac.uk/~smallmj), but a search via Yahoo throws up 35 sites alone - and a check at *The Ultimate Quentin Tarantino Links* (http://www.idb.hist.no/~kennetha/tarlink.html) will send you to the four corners of the planet. Some of them I couldn't access, some have vanished (like the *Pulp Fiction World Wide Website*), and others just take too damn long or are too graphics heavy or require certain software to view (*Quentin Tarantino Central*, for instance); but that still leaves the likes of *Tarantinomania*, *Tarantino World*, *The Shrine* and *The Not Quite Definitive Quentin Tarantino Page* to cruise.

There are some serious fans out there. Their addiction is total. There are pages and pages dedicated to the question of 'Who shot Nice Guy Eddie?' and, you know, they've got it all wrong. Here's the *Quentin Tarantino FAQ* (Frequently Asked Questions) version:

'What is the order of gunfire in the triangular shoot-out?'

"Joe shoots Mr Orange, Mr White shoots Joe, Nice Guy Eddie shoots Mr White, Nice Guy Eddie shoots Mr White again and Mr White shoots Nice Guy Eddie as he falls from his wounds."

But, as Mr Nice Guy himself (Chris Penn) revealed recently when visiting this country on a promotional tour, it ain't necessarily so: In fact, nobody shot Nice Guy Eddie. The squib (the small explosive charge and blood-bag, designed to simulate a bullet hit) went off by accident, even though nobody actually shot at him. Will this from-the-horse's-mouth information stem the speculation? Of course not, the fan-boys always know better!

Something you see a lot of on the Internet is parodying, and who better to parody than Tarantino? The man has made a living from paying homage (to put it politely) to his favourite films, directors, songs and stars, so it's not surprising that other people are going to pay homage to him by repositioning his characters, re-using his dialogue in unusual ways, and generally having a good time. So, for you lucky folks without the Internet (and, therefore, without my last quarterly phone bill), here are a few highlights from the alternatives to Tarantino. Let us start with something simple: how about *The X-Files*, Tarantino style? Remember folks, it only makes sense if you've seen *Pulp Fiction*...

We pick up the story some time into the dialogue. Basically Scully and Mulder have replaced Vincent and Jules, and...well, read on:

MAN: Everybody be cool! This is a robbery!

WOMAN: Any one of you fuckin' pricks move and I'll execute every motherfuckin' last one of you!

(*Mulder and Scully leap from behind their table, drawing their Glocks, still looking incredibly cool.*)

MULDER: Drop the fucking guns! We're with the FBI!

SCULLY (*Copping an attitude*): Yeah!

WOMAN: We're not dropping the fuckin' guns! You drop them!

MULDER: No, you drop them - we're better dressed.

SCULLY: Yeah!

You get the drift. Now, I don't know about you, but simply replacing two characters with two other characters doesn't quite add up to biting satire as far as I'm concerned. If it's to work, Scully and Mulder should be acting in character for starters; they are, after all, still supposed to be Scully and Mulder. So, sadly, this one from *alt.tv.xfiles* gets the thumbs down. Rather than put you through the torture of all the hundreds of parodies, I'm going to stick my neck out and offer you my own top three favourites. I make no apology for quoting these at length.

Excerpts from *The Holy Bible Quentin Tarantino Version:*

"GENESIS 2:16

But of the fruit of the tree which is in the midst of the garden, God hath said, Ye shall not eat of it, neither shall ye touch it. Eat instead Royale wi' Cheese or Le Big Mac.

And the Lord God called unto Adam and said unto him, Where art thou?

And He said, Hast thou eaten of the tree whereof I commanded thee that thou shouldst not eat?

And the Lord God said unto the woman, What the FUCK is this that thou hast done? And the woman said, The serpent beguiled me and I did eat.

And the Lord God said unto the serpent Because thou hast done this, thou art cursed above every beast.

So on the 563rd day, God made lead and chrome plating and these he fashioned into a gun. And he gave the gun unto Adam and said Kill the filthy motherfucker!"

"GENESIS 4:8

And Cain talked with Abel, his brother; and it came to pass when they were in the field, that Cain rose up against Abel, his brother and duct taped him to a chair, cut his ear off, poured gasoline on him and blew him away."

"LEVITICUS 11:7

And the swine though he divide the hoof and be clovenfooted, yet he cheweth not the cud; he hath no respect for his own faeces. Pigs sleep and root in shit; they are filthy animals.

And Moses said unto the Lord, I beseech thee, bacon tastes good.

And Aaron spake unto the Lord, Pork chops taste good.

And the Lord spake, No. Of their flesh shall ye not eat and their carcass shall ye not touch; they are unclean to you. As for dogs, dogs are filthy animals, but they got personality and personality goes a long way."

- Matt McCarney

Republic Dogs:

Narrator: Thrasymachus. Alcibiades. Aristotle. Socrates — are Quentin Tarantino's Republic Dogs.

[Enter Alcibiades and Aristotle]

Aristotle: So you're saying you'd give Helen of Troy a foot massage?

Alcibiades: Fuck yeah, in a minute.

Aristotle: You'd touch her feet? She might be the most beautiful bitch since fucking Aphrodite, but trust me, her feet stink. And her armpits stink too. Just cuz she's beautiful don't mean she don't smell like the rest of us. And don't you go telling no deodorant story, either, cuz you know and I know it wasn't invented during the Trojan war.

Alcibiades: What, you wouldn't do her?

Aristotle: I didn't say I wouldn't do her. I said I wouldn't give her a foot massage. I don't dig on feet.

Alcibiades: Well, what if before you did her you'd have to give her a foot massage to get her in the mood?

Aristotle: Allow me to inquire, Alcibiades. What if you had to massage her armpits to get her in the mood?

Alcibiades: Fuck you, Aristotle.

Socrates: You guys have got it all wrong.

Alcibiades: What, you don't like foot massages either?

Socrates: No, motherfucker, *The Iliad*, you've got *The Iliad* all wrong. Do you wanna know what *The Iliad* is about? Well, I'll tell you what I is about. It ain't about no bitches, that's for fucking sure.

Alcibiades: Sure it is. You're saying Helen of Troy ain't one hot bitch?

Socrates: I'm not saying Helen of Troy ain't a hot bitch, I'm saying *The Iliad* ain't about her. She ain't even in it. *The Odyssey* is about bitches, I'll grant you that. But I'll tell you what *The Iliad* is about. It's about big boats. Didn't you ever read the second Canto? Boats boats boats boats boats boats boats. Hence, The Trojan War.

Aristotle: You're full of shit.

Alcibiades: Fuck yeah you are; *The Iliad* is about Achilles' struggle with his own homosexuality.

Socrates: Maybe I should frame my theory a bit more emphatically. [Drawing his gun.] Didn't you ever hear of the face that launched a thousand...boats?

Alcibiades: Uh...

Socrates: WELL?

Alcibiades: Yeah.

Socrates: Well, how'd you like me to launch your face?

Alcibiades: Uh...

Socrates: Ahh, I guess that example cleared up all your objections then. [Points weapon at Aristotle] You don't have any problems with that, do you?

Aristotle: Hey, man, it's cool. Cool. Boats are cool by me. I was just on a boat recently.

Socrates: [Putting away his gun.] Well good for fucking you. This makes you special?

Aristotle: From Mycinea.

Alcibiades: What's it like? I hear they do some crazy-ass shit there.

Aristotle: Man, that place is like Mount-fucking-Olympus. Every night, they gather round the fire in certain legally designated areas, where government-licensed civil servants throw the roots of a domestically cultivated plant in the fire.

Socrates: So fucking what?

Aristotle: So the smoke makes them giddy and lighthearted as if they had drunk on wine, only they don't have a headache in the morning, that's fucking what.

Socrates: That's it, I'm fucking going. It's the perfect fucking city.

Aristotle: It ain't the perfect fucking city.

Socrates: You know a better city?

Aristotle: No, I don't know a better city, motherfucker, but that don't mean fucking Mycinea is fucking perfect. 'Perfect' doesn't mean that there ain't nothing better, it means perfect.

Socrates: Can you explain that lofty idea in terms a base, wandering street philosopher like myself might be able to understand?

Aristotle: Well, allow me to demonstrate. Let's say there was an imaginary city, and all the people were divided into three groups. Let's say I represent the Gold group, I'd be Mr. Gold, you, Socrates would be Mr. Silver, and, you, Alcibiades, Mr. Bronze.

Alcibiades: Why do I have to be Mr. Bronze?

Aristotle: Because it's only a demonstration. So me, Gold, I'd be the philosopher king.

Alcibiades: But why can't I be the philosopher king? Look, Socrates, I'll trade with you.

Aristotle: [Draws a gun, fires a shot into the air, and points it at Alcibiades] Interrupt me again, motherfucker. Interrupt me again. Nobody's trading with anybody. This is my allegory.

[Alcibiades gestures submission.]

Aristotle: [Putting away gun.] So as the philosopher king, it would be my duty to keep seditious literature out of the city—

Socrates: I got it. I understand.

Aristotle: Shut up, motherfucker, how can you understand my perfect city when I haven't explained it yet?

Socrates: No, dickhead, not that, I understand what you were saying before, about perfection. It's all about forms.

Aristotle: Forms?

Socrates: Yeah, motherfucker, forms. Like, something don't have to physically exist for it to be perfect; it exists as the perfect ideal, the perfect form, beyond mortal comprehension.

Alcibiades: Socrates, you're supposed to pour your libations on the ground, not drink them till you're talking like a crazy Bacchae bitch.

Socrates: Normally, I'd be pouring libations with your spinal fluid right now, but since I'm feeling at peace with the universe I'll try to enlighten your sorry ass instead. Imagine there's this dark, underground cave.

Alcibiades: Yeah?

Socrates: And there's this rapist-motherfucker, and he's got this gimp, right, tied up in the cave. See that?

Aristotle: Okay.

Socrates: And this rapist, he's a sick motherfucker, so let's say one day he sends down a coupla pipe-hittin' negroes to cut the gimp's ear right off.

Alcibiades: Cut his ear off?

Socrates: Yeah, and gouge out his fucking eyes. Now wouldn't you say that the ear and eye are the proper receptacles of the senses of sight and hearing, respectively?

Alcibiades: Clearly so.

Socrates: So, moreover, would you not agree that this gimp's senses are imperfect?

Aristotle: Why, yes, Socrates, I suppose they would be a trifle damaged.

Socrates: And what do things look like to someone with imperfect senses?

Alcibiades: Dark?

Socrates: No, motherfucker, nine letters, begins with 'I.'

Aristotle: Imperfect.

Socrates: Bingo. So you'd say this gimp, you'd say this gimp motherfucker would be unable to perceive true perfection - but that don't mean it don't exist. Now if you brought him out of the cave, into the light, things would be less dark, and his eyes might heal a little, he might begin to see a glimmer of light, thereby gaining the idea of true perfection.

Aristotle: What kind of argument is that? Your theory of the forms rests on an arbitrary and vicious act of violence.

Socrates: [Draws his gun.] Aristotle, you're Plato's student, I respect you, but I will put fucking bullets through your heart if you don't take back what you said about me being violent now!

Aristotle: [Also drawing gun] You shoot, you'll be dining with Lord Hades tonight. I repeat. You kill me, your ass is eating pomegranate fucking casserole for the rest of eternity.

Alcibiades: Shit, man, you're acting like a bunch of fuckin' Spartans. Am I the only philosopher around here?

Socrates and Aristotle: [To Alcibiades] Shut up!

- Nathaniel Daw.

I have to admit that *Republic Dogs* is by far my favourite sustained QT parody, and it goes on for quite a bit longer. But I thought I'd leave enough space for this little item, my favourite bit of Tarantino-inspired writing to date (for inspired is just what it is): What if Dr Seuss had written *Pulp Fiction*?

I would not eat Royale wi' Cheese,
So do not even ask me, please.
I won't eat fries and mayonnaise,
I would not touch them anyways.
I would not drink five-dollar shake,
'Cause it gives me a tummy-ache.
If I snort some uncut smack,
Blood and mucous I will yak.
"Why don't you eat pork?" you whine,
It's just 'cause I don't dig on swine.
Would you could you with a shrimp?
Would you could you with the Gimp?
I would not do so, but instead,
I think I'll blow off Marvin's head.

- Chris Pierson

The above extracts are culled from the innumerable items you can find on the Internet, these particular examples can be found at the following URL addresses:

Holy Bible: http://rmd-www.mr.ic.ac.uk/~dan/tarantino/bible.html

Republic Dogs: http://rmd-www.mr.ic.ac.uk/~dan/tarantino/republic_dogs.html

Dr. Seuss: alt.cult.movies

Alternatively, most are available indirectly as links from the better Tarantino websites like:

The Tarantinoverse: http://rmd-www.mr.ic.ac.uk/~dan/tarantino.html

Church of Tarantino: http://www.aston.ac.uk/~smallmj

Tarantino World: http://www.tarantino.com/top.shtml

Newsgroup: alt.fan.tarantino

Some people just have too much time on their hands ... me included.

TALKING HEADS

by John Ashbrook

The closing event of the 1996 *Shots In The Dark* festival (held, as usual, in Nottingham) was also the world premiere of *Curdled*, the first full-length feature film from writing-producing-directing partnership Reb Braddock and John Maass. Come with us for a brief but bizarre journey into the heat and the steam of downtown Miami where vibrant music and bright colour-schemes hide the hunting grounds of the notorious Blue-Blood Headsman ...

We meet Gabriella (Angela Jones), a young, sultry and seemingly quite normal Colombian immigrant who has a hobby; she collects news cuttings about murders. She has been following with interest the exploits of Miami's latest serial killer, who woos rich, lonely women, gets them to take him home, then beheads them with a sword.

When Gabriella sees an advert for the company P.F.C.S. - Post Forensic Cleaning Service, an organisation which cleans up murder-sites after the police have finished with them - she cannot resist the temptation to get more involved with her favourite subject.

Like star-crossed lovers, Gabriella and the Blue-Blood Headsman (played enthusiastically by a fresh-faced William Baldwin) are fated to meet and get to know each other ... intimately.

Curdled is a film which demonstrates a fresh and wittily skewed view on life, and which will not suffer conspicuously for having been executive produced by one-man new-wave Quentin Tarantino.

After seeing the film at its world premiere, our intrepid reporter tracked down the writer/producer/director partnership of Maass and Braddock, along with the film's star Angela Jones. They spoke at great length and with much enthusiasm (it being their first big interview of what, undoubtedly, developed into hundreds) about *Curdled's* evolution and execution.

Although the dialogue is accurate, the scene was nothing like what follows, but, had it occurred in a film, rather than in what passes for the real world, it would *undoubtedly* have gone *exactly* like this. Needless to add (but I'll add it anyway): Only the facts have been changed to protect the innocent ...

EXT. AN ENGLISH INNER-CITY STREET DURING RUSH HOUR, DUSK.

This is Nottingham, England, consequently it is raining. Men in long coats hurry past, tipping their hats to the girls in mini-skirts who are huddling out of the rain. A big red London bus rumbles past, splashing everyone's legs, including a bobby, who pulls out his pocketbook and notes down the driver's number.

A subtitle gives us the setting:

NOTTINGHAM, ENGLAND. PRESENT DAY.

INT. Q.T.'s CAFE.

This is a typical English caff, with a picture window that looks out on the delightful spectacle above described. Rain pounds against the window, blurring and smearing the street-scene beyond. The pink and blue 'Q.T.' neon sign reflects back into the cafe, giving the otherwise grey decor a splash of cheap, hazy colour.

A row of chipped grey cubicles are lined up against the window, awaiting customers. We dolly past these slowly, taking in the ambience of a damp English caff. A wrinkled menu sits in a pool of coagulated tea. A copy of The Sun sits folded up, the cross-word half-finished. Off screen we can hear typical English conversations being carried out - discussions about football teams, etc, all conducted in classic Hollywood English accents: the "Cor lummy guvnor, sure as eggs is eggs I'm a cheerful Cockney sparrah from ol' Edinburgh town, an' no mistyke" type of thing!

In the corner cubicle, four people sit, three Americans and a rather shabby looking English reporter. The Americans are taller, smarter and much better lit than anyone else. Their tans nicely contrast their gleaming teeth. The shabby English reporter is drinking stewed tea from a cracked cup. The Americans all have cappuccinos.

In the aisle seat sits producer and writer JOHN MAASS, in an Armani suit. He usually has to interrupt his conversations like this by chatting enthusiastically on his portable phone: "Arnold, loved 'Eraser'!", "Clint, let's do lunch." That sort of thing. Of course, this reckons without the incomparable telecommunications network we have in Britain!

Next to him sits director REB BRADDOCK, slightly shorter and stockier, with designer stubble, wearing a genuine fifties motorcycle jacket with an Indian logo on the back. He has a zoom lens on a cord around his neck, and occasionally uses it to frame some incident outside - such as when two black London cabs smash into each other and their drivers start fighting. Cabbies are much the same the world over!

Opposite him sits star ANGELA JONES, wearing a simple off-the-shoulder black dress. Despite the gloom of an English summer, she is loath to surrender her designer shades. She has masses of brushed black hair, dark lipstick, and generally gives the impression that she wishes she were being filmed in black and white. As a concession, all of her close-ups are shot in soft-focus!

She is crammed into one side of her seat, trying to get as far away as the window will allow from THE SHABBY REPORTER, who sits next to her in an ill-fitting old suit with worn elbows. His shirt gapes between the buttons as it stretches over his beer gut, and he absently scratches the exposed flesh from time to time. He has his stained hat pushed back to reveal a lot of shiny forehead. As he chats with his 'guests' he makes, when he can be bothered, the occasional note in a ring-bound note pad. He writes with a stubby blue biro stolen from a bookies.

ANGELA JONES pushes her glasses up so she can see, and is scrutinising the menu.

JONES: Do they do key lime pie?

SHABBY REPORTER The only pie they do here comes with mash.

JONES doesn't quite understand, but she smiles anyway.

SHABBY: (*to JOHN MAASS*) Let's get this road on the show. So, this is your first film!?

BRADDOCK and JONES smirk to each other, since MAASS was lucky enough to be picked first.

MAASS: It is, it's our first feature. We've worked on other features before, in different capacities, Reb has worked as cinematographer and I've line-produced; but this is the first one we've done on our own.

SHABBY: When we mere mortals see the credits of movies, you see *executive producers* and *line producers* and just plain *producers*, what do these various people actually do?

MAASS: The degree of involvement of those titles vary in a given film, depending on who the individuals are. In our case, Quentin was the executive producer, which meant that he arranged for financing by taking the film to Miramax, he also basically convinced Billy Baldwin to appear in the film. After that he helped us with certain specific goals, if Miramax needed persuading about something. Basically, he had more influence and more impact than us and was essential to our film getting made, and made the way we wanted.

SHABBY: How did 'Quentin' become involved?

MAASS: In the first place because he saw the half-hour short version of *Curdled*, starring Angela. We sent it around to various festivals, hoping that someone would pick it up and help us develop it into a feature.

Speaking of help, MAASS looks encouragingly over at BRADDOCK, who pulls himself up from the slumped position he had slid into, and starts paying attention.

SHABBY: So you were always intending to expand it!

BRADDOCK: We really liked the whole concept of the short *Curdled*, so, while we were making it, we decided that, if we made a good job of it, we could write the feature length version and use the short as our calling card. Hopefully some studio would see it and like the way that it and Angela worked, and agree to help us make it into a feature. That was the plan, anyway, and by sheer luck it happened exactly that way.

MAASS: Quentin saw the short at a festival in Italy. It was 1992 and he was there with *Reservoir Dogs*. At first his involvement was informal, just lending us advice and making a few calls for us, but ultimately, once we had finished the screenplay for the feature version, he agreed to come aboard formally.

CUT TO BLACK AND WHITE & SILENT SHOT:

EXT. SUNNY AMERICAN STREET. DAY. SUNNY.

A tall, thin man, looking not dissimilar to Quentin Tarantino, garbed in black suit, white shirt, black tie and shades, is knocking on a metal door flush against a brick wall. He has a can of film tucked under his arm. The sign on the door says 'COLOSSAL PICTURES'. The door opens and a fat man in a vest, with a half-chewed cigar in his mouth, looks out. Quentin Nobody shows him the film-can and talks to him about it. The door silently slams and Quentin Nobody slinks away, head hanging in despair.

SHABBY (*as voice-over*): So, presumably, if he was taking *Res Dogs* around the festivals, he was still Quentin Nobody!?

CUT BACK TO THE CAFE:

INT. Q.T's, THE SAME TABLE.

MAASS: Well he was already developing something of a name because the film had shown at *The Sundance Festival* in January and Cannes.

CUT TO ANOTHER BLACK AND WHITE & SILENT SCENE:

EXT. ANOTHER AMERICAN STREET, DAY. SUNNY.

The same Quentin Nobody, carrying the same can of film, is now being held aloft on the shoulders of a silently cheering crowd, they are waving their arms, and the air is full of confetti and ticker-tape.

MAASS (*in voice over*): Having said that, *I* didn't know who he was.

The black and white cutaway ends abruptly.

CUT BACK TO THE CAFE:

INT. Q.T's, THE SAME TABLE.

MAASS: In fact I only saw *Reservoir Dogs* for the first time the night before I met him. That was my first contact with him, and I loved the film, so I was flattered that he was interested in us. Of course, none of realised just how far he was likely to go in such a short time. Excuse me.

MAASS picks up his mobile and stabs out a long series of numbers on it, then sits with it pressed to his ear, deliberately avoiding catching SHABBY's eyes. BRADDOCK is starting to warm to this whole interviewing thing, so begins to volunteer information.

BRADDOCK: We were on the outside of his rise to success. People already had a sense of the success the film would be, as he was nearing the end of the festival circuit. Of course, it didn't really happen for him until *Pulp Fiction*;. He was still writing that when we met him. That's when he said that he really liked Angela's performance in *Curdled*, so ended up writing a part for her in *Pulp Fiction.*

SHABBY suddenly sits up and looks in surprise at JONES, who blushes slightly.

SHABBY: Really?

BRADDOCK: Oh sure. I dunno if you remember the scene with Bruce Willis and the cab driver ... well that's Angela. Same character as in the short, wearing the same dress ... he just changed her name. He was determined to cast her in that rôle, so kinda helped her get started professionally.

JONES, being the thespian of the bunch, suddenly launches into character - and frightens the life out of SHABBY. She leans over to him and, glowering over her shades, purrs:

JONES: What's eet like, beating a man to death weeth your bare 'ands?

SHABBY: Ehm ... well, I wouldn't ... ehm ...

DISSOLVE TO CLIP FROM PULP FICTION:

INT. A MOVING TAXI CAB (WHICH IS REALLY ON ROCKERS IN FRONT OF A SCREEN). NIGHT.

It's another rainy night, in a different city, on a different continent. JONES is Esmarelda, the sassy taxi-driver, in an exotic floral dress. Behind her, progressively divesting himself of boxing gloves and tape, is BRUCE WILLIS as Butch Coolidge. Out of the cab's rear window we can see a deliberately shaky back-projection of rain-washed city streets rolling past.

ESMARELDA: It's a soobject I have mooch eenterest een. You are the forrst porrson I ever met 'oo 'as keeled somebody!

As their conversation continues, ESMARELDA's eyes (which never deviate from the road ahead) shine with excitement. As you watch this scene, familiar from a dozen previous viewings, you realise that, for the first time, you're ignoring WILLIS and concentrating on the foreground action.

INT: Q.T's CAFE

BRADDOCK, MAASS, JONES and SHABBY are still sitting together. Having regained his composure (thanks to a fortifying swig of lukewarm tea) SHABBY gets ready to continue with the cross examination, but first he needs a fag. He lights one casually, then notices the others glaring daggers at him. Failing to find an ashtray, he grinds the cigarette out on his heel and resumes questions, hanging on to as much nonchalance as his exposed belly allows. Meanwhile, MAASS has taken to tapping suspiciously at his phone, then listening to it, to no avail.

SHABBY: So, Angela, what's your background in acting?

JONES: Well I started out studying music as I was growing up, and I was going to go to school for that ... classical flute and piano. Then I did some theatre work at grade school and just changed my mind. I majored in Drama in college, then got my graduate degree in Theatre. Through graduate school at Florida State U., I got to work in the Film Programme, and that's how I met Reb and John.

SHABBY: Did you do a lot of student films?

JONES: Oh sure, the film students needed warm bodies in their films, and we needed the acting experience.

SHABBY licks his lips as he writes down 'warm body'.

JONES: Reb and John weren't like any other students I'd worked with, they ran a completely professional set. Of course, we had no idea that the film would be seen at festivals and turn out as well as it did.

SHABBY: And now you're living in la-la land!

JONES: That's right, I've moved to Los Angeles and I'm working there now.

SHABBY: How's that going?

JONES: *Pulp Fiction* was my first film there ...

SHABBY: Not a bad way to start!

JONES: True. It certainly helped a lot. After that I was able to establish an agent and a manager, and concentrated on getting *Curdled* together, which took nearly three years. Since then I did the episode of *ER* that Quentin directed, the Denis Leary film *Underworld*, then another film called *Morella*, and another called *Skinheads*... and now I'm waiting for all of them to open!

SHABBY: So you're trapped in the Twilight Zone, you've been

busy but no one's yet heard of you!

JONES: Exactly!

MAASS stands up, muttering about The Twilight Zone, and heads towards the counter to ask about a pay phone. The saggy old man who runs the cafe and drops cigarette ash in the eggs, points outside to the balmy, rain-soaked summer evening.

SHABBY (*continuing to JONES*): It must be so frustrating!

JONES: Oh, it is; but I know I can do the work, I know that I have done the work. That was something Quentin always said:

CUT TO BLACK AND WHITE SHOT :

EXT. AN ALLEYWAY BEHIND A BOXING RING.

Someone looking suspiciously like QUENTIN TARANTINO, dressed in black suit and shades, is standing next to the stationary cab, the same one as in the Pulp Fiction *clip. QUENTIN is leaning on the cab, arms folded, a pair of director's headphones dangling around his neck. JONES, in her* Pulp Fiction *costume, is sitting in the driver's seat, leaning on the sill of the driver's window, she is looking disconsolate. In the background someone looking not unlike BRUCE WILLIS is sitting in the make-up chair, having his head waxed.*

QUENTIN: Look, Anj, don't worry about it, man; you're gonna work, it's just a matter of time. Ah-right!?

CUT BACK TO THE CAFE:

INT. Q.T's, THE SAME TABLE.

JONES (Continuing): Some actors believe that you've got to pay your dues, so to speak, but that's kinda crazy. If you think less of yourself when you're not acting, so take anything, then that's the kind of work you're always gonna be doing. You've gotta be patient, stay above it all and have a sense of humour about it. That's the only thing that keeps me going!

MAASS returns to the table and, using a coin, begins to unscrew the back of his mobile. BRADDOCK has his lens to his eye and is watching MAASS's hands in macro close-up.

SHABBY: So what was Quentin like to work with?

JONES: He's a lot of fun. When I first moved over to LA he looked me up and we got to hang out together.

SHABBY writes down 'she hung out with Quentin!!!!' JONES tries to read over his shoulder, but fails because he tilts the book away from her.

JONES (*Carrying on, unperturbed*): The *Pulp Fiction* set was like a big party. Everyone was just having a good time, which is great, 'cos a lot of times it can get a bit tense. But, technically, that scene was tough to do, because of all the back projection, and because I couldn't see what Bruce was doing behind me. But we got it all done in, like, three days.

SHABBY: I suppose, thinking on it, Quentin must have been pretty nervous himself, working with all these big stars on only his second film. Looking at it now, everyone can say they knew it was gonna be a big hit ...

JONES: But at the time we had no idea. I think Columbia Tri-Star were originally gonna make it, and they dropped it, so we didn't even know if it would get made until Miramax picked it up. Nobody had any idea it was gonna be as huge as it was, we thought we were making an art-house film.

MAASS has the phone in pieces on the table now, he is poking at them with his coffee spoon. Before he starts measuring things with it, SHABBY starts addressing his questions to him.

SHABBY (*To MAASS*): So Gabriella was specially written with Angela in mind!?.

MAASS: For the feature film, yes. When we were in pre-production on the short version at Florida State, Angela showed up for audition and was absolutely the best actress for the rôle, although, at that stage, we hadn't literally written it for her. We actually auditioned some other actresses for it, but she turned out to be the best. With the feature though, there was never any question. Do you know anything about mobile phones?

SHABBY: I know I can't afford one. How involved did you let Angela get with the full-length adaptation?

MAASS: Well, we've known and been working with her for ... five years. She was involved throughout the evolution, in terms of our talking to her about new ideas for scenes. She'd keep us informed on how she was preparing for the rôle, what kind of research she was doing so, even though she was in Los Angeles and Reb and I were still in Miami, we were in contact throughout.

SHABBY (*Quietly*): Though not by mobile phone.

MAASS (*Ignoring this*): One of the great things about this is that all of us have been in this together for a long time. It's kind of a rare thing for an actor to be that in-tune with a script. I think it really paid off, because she had been thinking about the rôle for years even before we had finished the script. Consequently she was in a great place, regarding the rôle, when it came time to get the film rolling.

SHABBY (*Turning back to Jones*): How did you cope with the years of waiting?

JONES: It was just a matter of keeping the character alive. At times it was frustrating, but when we did get to shoot I was completely ready for it and just glad to get the character out of my system.

CUT TO CLOSE-UP FLASH-FRAMES OF HACKING AND BLOOD SPRAYING.

JONES (*Continuing as voice-over*): I'd been reading a lot of serial killer books and watching videos of pretty harsh stuff, executions and things like that.

CUT BACK TO THE CAFE:

SHABBY is looking distinctly queasy.

JONES (*Not noticing, continues*): I was researching too much and it got really depressing after a while, so I pulled away from it. But even now, when I go to a book store, I still gravitate towards the crime section, I just have to keep telling myself, I cannot buy one more book on this stuff! It does wear on you, you know!

SHABBY (*Looking very green*): You're not talking about films of real executions?

CUT TO FLASH-FRAMES OF FACES AND BLOOD

JONES (*In voice over*): Yeah. There's a series of films called *The Faces Of Death.*

CUT BACK TO THE CAFE:

SHABBY is hanging over the back of his seat, throwing up, but Jones, the bit firmly between her teeth, so to speak, is undaunted ...

JONES (*Very serious*): Well, I found some really intense underground stuff, which you can't even buy over there, and I got to see some of that. It was ... harsh. But I wanted to get over that fear and, you know, see what that was like.

SHABBY (*Wiping his mouth with his sleeve*): Yes ... yes, of course. And after spending so many years inside this weirdo's head, how much of you would you say there is in her character?

JONES: Well, I try not to think of her as weird, but her curiosity certainly takes her to places most people don't go. And, I suppose, she's taken me to some of those places. But, for her, the fascination isn't with blood and guts but with what getting beyond that will lead her to understand.

As for my influence on her ... Well, the script was all John and Reb's work. Choosing the direction to go in, getting the balance right, making her innocent and inquisitive, that was all Reb and John. At times I thought I was playing her too young and too much like a little girl ...

CUT TO SEPIA TONE SHOT:

Angela, as Gabriella, in a gingham Shirley Temple dress, with pigtails and a lollipop.

JONES (*continuing in voice-over*): ... and Reb said 'yeah, you have to grow up a little bit'!

The image morphs into the Gabriella as seen in the film.

CUT BACK TO THE CAFE TABLE:

JONES (*nodding emphatically*): The creative decisions were always theirs!

MAASS: Angela isn't obsessed with finding out if decapitated heads talk, if that's what you mean. No, although, obviously, we pictured her as Gabriella as we were writing, but I wouldn't say that her actual personality made its way into the character.

(*Scratching his chin and looking quizzically at JONES*)

MAASS (*Continuing*): Although, maybe subliminally I suppose, it's not the sort of thing you can put your finger on ... maybe it'll dawn on us in a couple of years' time.. Given how well we know Angela, something may have rubbed off.

SHABBY: It must have put a lot of pressure on you to take on a leading rôle like that ... you're in every scene almost, and usually by yourself ...

JONES: Oh, it was a gruelling schedule; eighteen-hour days sometimes. But, when I was working, I was happiest, it's only in the small amount of time that you get to yourself that you get tired. But, I'd been working on the character for so long, I was about as prepared as anyone can be, and I was completely confident. I wasn't worrying about how I was going to carry the film, or anything like that. I kinda blindly just got on and did it.

SHABBY: You know, with the lightning reflexes of the trained professional, I've just noticed you're speaking with a distinct lack of South American accent!

JONES: No, that was a dialect I had just for the film.

SHABBY: I suppose, with an adopted accent, you need a lot of rehearsal.

JONES: Yeah, that was important for me. Reb seemed pretty happy with what I was doing, but I wanted it to be precise. I wanted to be as true to her heritage as possible, and I didn't want people to doubt me as an actor, 'cos I know I can be a bit touchy!

All the while MAASS has been tinkering with his pile of phone pieces, trying to fit them together again. Finally, deciding that dignity is the better part of telephone maintenance, he brushes the pieces into his hand and shoves them ignominiously into his jacket pocket, when no one is looking

BRADDOCK (*gazing out of the window through his viewfinder*): Does it always rain in England?

SHABBY: Only when Americans are visiting. But why did you choose Nottingham in England for the world premiere ... it's hardly the most obvious place!?

BRADDOCK: Primarily it was because of *Shots in the Dark* founder Adrian Wooton. He was there in Italy with Quentin when they saw our short, and so is possibly one of the reasons we ever got to make the feature at all. I also met him when the short showed at the London Film Festival, and he was very encouraging, and he's always checked in on us. Plus, the Nottingham festival came along just after we finished the movie, so the timing was perfect.

It's kinda cool when you do a movie of any substantial budget and backed by a big Hollywood studio, to still be able to keep something in the family, as it were. So many times the company takes it away from you and make decisions about marketing and money. Well, in this case, we were able to repay the debt to the people who helped us make the movie.

Their coffees finished, MAASS' phone finished, the group depart.

EXT. NOTTINGHAM'S STREETS. NIGHT.

The same menagerie of cheerful cockney sparrahs step gingerly around the group (tipping their hats respectfully at JONES as they do so) as they walk through the now slackening rain. When the quartet pass the open doorway of a pub, they can hear a piano playing and a group of drunken revellers singing 'Roll Out The Barrel'. On the other side of the road, a man is patiently working his way down the street, igniting all the gas-lights.

JONES has BRADDOCK's leather jacket round her shoulders. MAASS is blowing smoke rings with his breath, amazed at how English people can survive such summers, and wondering what on earth the winters must be like.

SHABBY (*flicking back through his notebook, trying to find a page that isn't covered in doodles*): So, the script is written, Quentin's interested ... then what?

MAASS: By the time the screenplay was finished, which would be around the May of '93, Quentin was close to going into pre-production on *Pulp Fiction*, at which point he would become immersed and unreachable, so he couldn't become too involved in getting *Curdled* set up. But by December of '93, he had wrapped *Pulp Fiction* and so we went to LA and met with him and he agreed to be executive producer. After that, it still took a while to get the funding in place, and getting Billy Baldwin involved took a long time ... so we didn't finally get the cameras rolling until May of '95.

SHABBY: So, you've explained how Tarantino helped get Baldwin, but you haven't said why you *wanted* Baldwin particularly?

MAASS: Well, Reb and I see the character of Guell - the serial killer - as a very charming and alluring figure, but with an earthy quality to him too - he's not as sophisticated as he would like to appear. Even though he's charming and handsome, underneath there's just a conventional guy, and that's a big part of what Guell was about. We'd seen Billy Baldwin in various rôles where he demonstrated that type of character, so we thought he was very fitting.

Even though he hadn't done any independent films before, we showed him the script and he showed enthusiasm for the rôle, and we were really comfortable with the idea of him playing it. So that's how it worked out - you start off with understanding that he is the right type and is a good actor, and then from there you meet with him and get the sense that he has a real understanding of where the character's coming from.

SHABBY: He's coming from LA, presumably.

BRADDOCK: Well, actually, he was in Miami at the time, and our agent knew someone who knew him, and showed him the short version.

CUT TO STILL SHOTS OF BALDWIN FROM 'CURDLED'

BRADDOCK (*In voice over*): He was an interesting choice for that character, 'cos he really is this good looking guy who has a real sense of the way he looks. You watch him in movies and you'll see that he's very aware of himself, which I thought worked well for Guell.

He's completely obsessed with appearing aristocratic, and that's kinda what it's all about, he's trying to get the women to let him be part of the upper, upper class (this is all subtext, it's not something we dwell on in the movie). But there's also a real vulnerability to him, which is important to his relationship with Gabriella.

CUT BACK TO THE STREET:

BRADDOCK (*Continuing*): As vicious a criminal as he is, he really just wants these women to respect him, and when he meets Gabriella, here's a woman who can actually understand him and even respect him for a moment. Billy had a really good understanding of the character, and really liked the script.

SHABBY: It must have been a leap for him to go from the big-budget excesses of *Fair Game* to a low-budget first-film. Weren't you intimidated working with a big star on your first film?

BRADDOCK: At first it was strange 'cos I didn't know how he would react, this being a very small movie. But he was very accessible and he really wanted to do this, because it was something different. Taking a risk like that was a pretty major thing for him ...

SHABBY: I can imagine the conversations he must have had with his agent.

CUT TO:

INT. BILLY BALDWIN'S FANTASY AGENT'S OFFICE

It's a cluttered room, over-flowing with files and videos and piles of photographs. It's lit and shot to look like something from a Terry Gilliam movie - with a wide angle lens. Behind a huge desk sits a very, very small man - several sizes too small for the padded leather chair and desk around him. He is bald, incredibly tense, and his worried eyes are magnified tenfold by thick glasses. He holds an old black, dial phone to his ear.

AGENT *(Screaming into the phone in rage and horror)*: How much??????

CUT TO:

EXT: THE RAINY STREET:

BRADDOCK: Oh yeah, we had many, many long conversations with his agent. Getting Billy aboard was a long and painful process, but finally he took the risk, and I had a lot of respect for him for that, which made working with him much easier.

He really wanted to do something different and cool, so I didn't ever really feel intimidated by him. I kinda let him and Angela evolve, to get them into the set and let them rehearse and find their own space, which worked for them really well. It ended up being a lot of fun.

SHABBY: And the last third of the movie is just the two of them and the camera ...

BRADDOCK: Yep, just them and what they do. When you watch that, it's cut, but we shot it in actual time - five minute blocks. I had the camera on a steadicam rig and we just followed them around until the film ran out. That way they were allowed to do each scene almost in it's entirety, which gives it a great organic feel.

SHABBY: Was there much improvising?

BRADDOCK: Not a lot. In rehearsal there was a certain amount of that, but when we went to the set we went back to the script, that made it easier to cut the different takes together. We had to work those scenes out carefully in advance, because it's difficult to maintain interest in such a small space as a kitchen. We had a great space to shoot in, so logistically it was much easier than I would normally have expected on a location. Even though it was a real house, it shot like a custom-built stage.

The main difficulty, of course, is always time. We shot the film in twenty-six days, which isn't long at all. There were many days when I was finishing off ten pages of script, and it's hard to do any sort of interesting work at that pace. So, knowing that there's only a certain amount of time, and you've got to spend so much of it in this one room - normally you'd throw in a lot of things to keep it moving, different angles and stuff, but we didn't have that luxury, so we had to be very careful and very specific and do it mostly through the actors.

SHABBY: Which again demonstrates the benefit of having a strong script.

BRADDOCK: Yeah, and two really good actors who are perfectly in synch. Angela's an amazing, phenomenal actress, and I think she helped bring out some of the best work Billy's ever done. They really got into it.

JONES is looking at her feet, embarrassed by the barrage of compliments. Because she's not looking where she's going, she walks straight into a bus stop. Everyone stops to pick her up, then notice that the bus stop hoarding bears an illuminated poster for the Shots In The Dark *festival, with her face emblazoned across it.*

As the group carry on their way, the people who are queuing at the bus-stop, take a good look at the poster, then look at JONES, then double-take. One starts nodding his head. Another starts shaking his. As the Curdled *crowd disappear around the next corner, a fist-fight breaks out at the bus-stop.*

SHABBY (*TO JONES*): I don't know if it's just the way they lit you, but you have a very striking 1940s look in the film, and especially in the poster. It's a lot like Jane Russell in Howard Hughes' *The Outlaw*.

CUT TO THAT *(IN)FAMOUS POSTER, ROSTRUM CAMERA ZOOMS IN ON JANE RUSSELL IN THE STRAW:*

JONES (*Voice over*): It's a look I like. I guess I've never felt very modern.

CUT BACK TO:

EXT: THE STREET, NIGHT:

SHABBY: So you must long for the days when women ruled the roost ...

JONES(*handkerchief pressed to her nose to stop it bleeding*): And had all the interesting characters; sure. We don't have those powerful rôles so much any more, now we're the girlfriend and the damsel in distress.

MAASS: I suppose Gabriella also has something of that *femme fatale*, the female-is-deadlier-than-the-male aspect to her.

SHABBY: I was thinking that she's playing almost a man's rôle, in that it's not a romance, it's a dark film about dark things and she's a rather sullen loner of a character, the type that masculine cinema is dotted with.

MAASS: That's probably true, although there's no equivalent antagonist, for her, there's no *homme fatale*, because what drives her is pretty internal, she's not lured into danger by anyone else, it comes strictly from her own psyche. So she's maybe her own *fatale*. But it is true that's its pretty unusual for a film like this to be about a woman.

SHABBY: And the film is filled to bursting with that Latin music ...

BRADDOCK: I wanted to build the whole world as if it were her world, so there's a lot of warm, saturated colours, which is very Latin, and the music is the kind of music that she would listen to. We tried to find something that was really unique, and the basis for what we used is a Colombian folk-music called *Cumbia*, which isn't *Salsa*, it's kinda like very early rock. It's very up-beat, but always has a dark tone to it. If you could classify music as black comedy, that's Cumbia!

One of the songs is about a guy who goes to a city to get his sick wife medicine, and while he's in that city he finds himself in the middle of a street-party. He stays there all-night then, when he gets home, his wife is dead. And this is a very happy, uplifting piece of music, with these grim, fateful lyrics. So, you see, it was perfect for *Curdled*.

SHABBY (*TO JONES*): I've gotta ask, what was it like for you, first time out of the gate, working with Mr. Sex-on-legs.

JONES: He was very sweet. We got to meet before going down there to film. I wouldn't say I got to know him real well, like I did with some of the other cast members, but not knowing him too well worked for the character, anyway!

CUT TO SCENE FROM CURDLED.

BALDWIN and JONES are waltzing around the kitchen, as she asks question after question. The sound is mixed down so the voice-over takes precedent.

JONES (*Voice-over*): We choreographed the dance together ... you know, when we're dancing and I'm asking him all those questions. But that was concentrated mostly in those last two weeks because, after we rehearsed, he had to leave town, then came back for the filming. He was in the process of getting married at the time, so he had a few other things to worry about! He trusted me though, he didn't let my lack of experience get in the way, which was nice.

CUT TO:

EXT: THE STREET, NIGHT:

SHABBY: So you weren't star-struck at all.

JONES: Well, no. When you're working with someone, you can't look at them that way. Although I was very, very nervous of meeting Bruce Willis on *Pulp Fiction*, but he was very cool. We got to hang out during rehearsal and he put me completely at ease.

SHABBY jots down 'letting it all hang out with Willis too!!!'

JONES (*Trying to see what he's written, and failing*): I think it's more how the people who work for them act, than how they really are. On the set with Billy, the more people treated him like a star, the more he acted like a star. It was fascinating to see the obvious difference.

SHABBY: Looking back at that period when Quentin came aboard back in the early nineties, there must have been something in the water in LA, cos you get Harvey Keitel signing on for *Reservoir Dogs* for an unknown director, for his second film he gets Bruce Willis, Uma Thurman and Eric Stoltz and brings back John Travolta, and they all turned up for minimum pay. Same story for *The Usual Suspects* and now *you've* got Baldwin ...

MAASS: Well, what they're doing is looking for work that is interesting and compelling, and they're not too proud to look everywhere. Also, actors who are smart see it as potentially enhancing their careers. If you do a film that's off-beat or unconventional, and draws a lot of attention for that reason, then people in the business are going to see you in a different light and consider you for rôles that maybe they previously wouldn't. If you're established as a romantic lead, the studios aren't going to risk a lot of money on allowing you to play a homicidal maniac.

SHABBY: *Curdled* not only has this indefinable period feel, it has the feel of a European movie, too!

BRADDOCK: Yeah. Letting the story evolve in a single shot rather than having a lot of cutting, relying on the actors to move around and create the atmosphere, that's very South American *and* European. And it is very enclosed, so the spaces are important, and how they act in them. I'd say there was a definite European influence.

SHABBY: And when the film is released there, I think the audiences will recognise that.

BRADDOCK: Sure, it's just too bad that the U.S. is so commercially driven, to the exclusion of everything else. It's hard for large, widespread audiences to see films like this.

SHABBY: But, surely Tarantino has broken that hold ...

BRADDOCK: To an extent. But Quentin's films are a little bit easier to access because of the crime element. He also happens to be an amazing writer, his dialogue is incredible, and his characterisations are fascinating, which has forced other writers to produce better work. Dialogue has been seriously neglected, it was believed that it there were more than three sentences of dialogue on a script page, it was too long, but you look at Quentin's scripts and there's a monologue on every page.

The group arrive at the taxi-rank. SHABBY hails a taxi (because, being local, he knows the appropriate threats and insults to use) and they begin to clamber into the back of a big black cab. MAASS tells the driver to head for the local Odeon. This being a journey of some forty yards (they hadn't noticed the cinema facade behind them) the driver smiles and sets off in completely the wrong direction, looking forward to a long and leisurely circuit of the city.

CUT TO:

INT. A TAXI, TRAVELLING THROUGH THE STREETS OF NOTTINGHAM. NIGHT.

This taxi bears no similarity to the one JONES drove in Pulp Fiction. *The three Americans sit wedged on the back seat whilst Shabby is sandwiched into the drop-down seat, his back to the driver. Because his seat is higher than theirs, his head is tilted to one side by the roof. In no small state of discomfort, he chooses this moment to hit them with his big theory about their film:*

SHABBY: You know how pretentious film-crits always have to have their own little theory about other-people's films ...

BRADDOCK (*over-compensating, in case what follows really is preposterous*): I understand that completely, It's true that a film, once it's done, takes on a life of its own!

SHABBY: So, my pet theory about your film is that there seems to be a very basic Freudian structure to the piece. Gabriella is the *Id*, curious and demanding on the subject of death; Guell is the *Ego*, going out and satisfying his curiosity about death, and then you have Helena who's very pragmatic and practical about coping with death, and very involved in stopping people from doing these compulsive things ...

MAASS: ... right, right, the *Superego*.

BRADDOCK: That's interesting, I wouldn't say that I ever thought of Freud when I was doing it. But, essentially, those *are* the characterisations of those people in the film.

We approached it more from the perspective of how people deal with violence, Gabriella and Helena and the men in Gabriella's life, all have their own particular approaches. Eduardo has the approach that most everyone has, he's curious but he'll only investigate so far, he'll slow down at the car accident, but no more. Guell, of course, is the extreme, he *is* the violence. He's the person who takes it too far, but there isn't any thought behind it, no curiosity, it's just pure violence.

Then there's Lodger, just trying to run his clean-up business. He has a very pragmatic way of dealing with it: he says that this is a reality, you don't go too far with it, you just accept and deal with it. Gabriella, of course, is convinced it's better to see it and experience it to understand it in order to control it and live happily. That was our approach. Which isn't quite Freudian.

SHABBY (*Unwilling to let go just yet*): Well, to explain where I got my idea from: the thing that made me notice all that is the mirroring between Guell and Helena.

CUT TO APPROPRIATE SHOTS OF GUELL AND HELENA, ARRANGED SIDE-BY-SIDE LIKE MUG-SHOTS.

SHABBY (*Voice-over*): She has a scar on one side of her face, he has a scar on the other. How do you see the connection between Guell and Helena?

CUT BACK TO:

INT: THE TAXI:

MAASS (*Scratching his chin, thinking*): Even though Paul is exploring something, he's not exploring it in order to make him grow as a person, obviously. He's psychotic and what drives him is a misguided impulse. Helena has placed a lot of boundaries around her behaviour and has created a world that she thinks will keep her safe. So, they have both limited where they can grow as people, but I never really thought of them as being that closely connected. Maybe Reb will give you a different answer on that.

SHABBY: I couldn't remember if Mel Gorham - who I last saw as Harvey Keitel's girlfriend in *Smoke* and *Blue in the Face* - actually has a scar. But then, why would Baldwin have one added too, cos I know he hasn't. So there's that connection, and the fact that they both smoke like chimneys ...

BRADDOCK: Yeah, Billy suggested that he should have a scar, a recent wound from one of his victims, something that marred this veneer, this perfect look that he was trying to obtain. Mel, on the other hand, suggested that it would be good for Helena to have a scar, to show that she was very hard and weather-beaten, in a way that is opposite to Gabriella. And I thought that this was gonna cause trouble, 'cos I'd got two actors who wanna have scars, it'll look really strange.

So, I decided, if we put them on different sides of the face, but in roughly the same place, it'll make people think there's a connection, and make them read into that, now what the significance of that may be, I wasn't sure, but, I thought, as they both stand on either side of Gabriella, that might spark off some curiosity and some questioning. It's great that you've figured out a connection.

SHABBY feigns bashful modesty.

MAASS: Part of that was just that Helena was constantly warning against exploring this dark world, and exploring fear and what it is that frightens us, which, for most people, really isn't the best way to deal with what's out there. I guess she is meant to be the healthy one, in terms of what she is keeping Gabriella away from, and yet she is the smoker, which indicates that she might be actually being destructive in the way that Paul Guell is being destructive. We're not trying to say that she was evil, it was nothing more than an ironic and possible amusing comparison.

The motion of the car has put JONES to sleep by this point. She will be glad to know that she doesn't snore. Out of the back window, the Dome of Saint Paul's Cathedral can be clearly seen.

CUT TO A SILENT SCENE FROM CURDLED.

Gabriella and Helena are sitting, in overalls, in front of an old black wall-oven. Gabriella is chatting until Helena gets up and walks away.

SHABBY (*Voice over*): I also though it was interesting, when Gabriella starts talking about Hansel and Gretel, that Helena just walks away, she doesn't want to know about fairy tales or fantasies.

CUT BACK TO:

INT: THE CAB, STILL NIGHT:

MAASS: Well fairy-tales tie-in very closely with Gabriella, although, if you don't pick this up from the film, that's fine, it doesn't really matter all that much. One of the things people theorise about fairy tales, particularly the disturbing or horrific ones, is that they allowed people in less sophisticated societies to categorise the nebulous, frightening things out there, whether it be noises in the woods or highwaymen or wolves or whatever. If you create a story which sets ground rules for these horrific things, they're easier to deal with, for a child or for a parent.

For us, the idea was that the more you understand frightening things, the easier it is to cope with them, and the less disturbing they become. This doesn't work with everyone, for some people it's *more* disturbing to read a Stephen King novel or watch a Hitchcock movie, and ultimately it doesn't help them. But with a whole lot of people, maybe the majority, that kind of vicarious exposure to horrific things makes it easier to cope with life.

That's exactly what's happened with Gabriella, the more she understands violent crime and what makes someone commit a heinous act, the more she understands what goes on when somebody is attacked and facing death, the more comfortable she feels. It's not something that she studies formally, it's just a feel that she gets as she reads about this process, she feels better. For her, the job allows her to learn more about that than she would ever be able to otherwise.

SHABBY: So you're saying that horror films serve a similar purpose?

MAASS: Yeah, except that there's a point when they become purely visceral and less intellectual. There's a wide range in horror films from slasher films to something like *Alien*, and there's really a different impact with all of 'em. But horror films can have that effect.

SHABBY looks out his side window and sees the Eiffel Tower in the distance. He frowns and looks over his shoulder at the driver, who glares back at him in the rear-view. Deciding that it's really none of his business, he carries on questioning ...

SHABBY: And so, obviously you know where I'm going to go with this next ... into the whole debate about censorship. *Natural Born Killers* still isn't available on video in this country, *Reservoir Dogs* only came out after several years' wait. There seems to be a real paranoia about images of violence in the home. Consequently, films that get cinema releases, don't automatically make it to video. How do you react to the whole censorship and media effects debate?

BRADDOCK: So do they have a separate rating system for videos?

SHABBY: Oh yes.

BRADDOCK: So what's permitted in theatres, isn't necessarily permitted on video. How interesting. Well, obviously, I hope *Curdled* will get seen, I wouldn't like them to ban it ... but it's hard to tell these days ... It's just strange how two countries can be so different.

SHABBY: I think the main problem you will encounter will be when the film transfers to that video market, because the concern is generally around images of violence seen in the home.

BRADDOCK: I can't see how watching acts of violence in films can make a person want to go out and commit acts of violence themselves. I think watching it is a particularly safe way of vicariously living through feelings like that. Everybody has violent thoughts and deals with them every day, and it is absolutely absurd to repress it.

I really do believe that repressed feelings of violence will backlash into greater acts of violence, if you don't let off steam some other way. To express it, try to do something creative with it and deal with it has got to be much better. That's really Gabriella's message to Helena, she's saying you can't hide from these emotions, you have to explore them to see and understand them. Of course, Gabriella goes a little further than I would recommend ...

The Red Square minarets sweep by the window, which is rapidly frosting over. Everyone is ignoring this now, because it's too silly!

MAASS: There are probably some cases where people who are already well on the way of committing some kind of violent or anti-social act may see a movie, or read a book, and somehow relate to the person therein, but I definitely question the idea that films can be responsible for people getting that way in the first place.

BRADDOCK: I think that people are offended by certain things because they have certain worries and repressions and things they are afraid of. They react to those things by saying 'stop it, ban it' rather than dealing with *why* it bothers them. If they thought about it maybe they'd realise 'okay, now I've addressed it, so I've realised it's not dangerous to me any more, and therefore, what I see on the screen isn't dangerous to me either'.

Steven Spielberg said something interesting in an interview I saw with him ...

DISSOLVE TO GRAINY BLACK AND WHITE, SILENT FILM (GIVING THE IMPRESSION OF OLD 8MM):

INT. A CLUTTERED PLAYROOM IN THE EARLY SIXTIES.

A young boy, looking not unlike how an eight-year-old Steven Spielberg might have looked, with military haircut and shorts with razor-sharp creases down them, is playing with a train-set. It's a table-top job, quite elaborate, obviously not cheap, with all the foliage and signal-boxes that go to make a really impressive model railway.

We see a montage of train crashes as he smashes his electric trains into each other, over and over again, laughing and clapping at the carnage each time.

BRADDOCK (*In voice over*): He was talking about when he was younger he had a train-set, and used to set it up so trains would crash into each other all the time. Over and over and over and over, and his dad got really angry with him because he was destroying his train-set.

Generic middle-American dad stands over the diminutive boy, waggling a finger accusingly and yelling at him. Lap dissolve: Now the boy has a little camera on a tripod, and is filming trains travelling down the tracks. We cut to the camera's view-point, two trains inter-cutting in progressive close-ups, building up speed, building up tension, then smashing into each other in marvellous slow-motion.

BRADDOCK (*Voice over*): Later, when he got his first super-8 camera, he filmed each train coming from different directions then filmed them colliding and made a little movie.

A darkened room, lit only by a cone of light being thrown out by a little movie projector. The boy sits, hugging his knees, watching open mouthed as his film is projected on the wall. Lap dissolve to another boy, clearly the same boy only several years older, watching the same movie.

BRADDOCK (*Voice over*): And he said, after he'd watched that movie, immortalising the crash, he never made his trains crash into each other again. After he's filmed it, it wasn't an interesting thing for him to do anymore, he preferred watching the film.

DISSOLVE BACK TO BRADDOCK IN FULL COLOUR IN THE TAXI:

INT. TAXI. NIGHT.

The surface of the Moon can now be seen out of the rear window.

BRADDOCK (*Continuing*): If you take that statement to a point of violence, you'll see that there can be a sort of cathartic effect in watching it on the screen. It maybe takes the desire out of you.

MAASS: Reb and I have talked about it and we don't think there's anything that goes beyond the pale in our film, unless someone thinks that having an appealing character who's fascinated by violence is somehow dangerous. I hope that it makes people think about why they're fascinated with violence, and explore that side of themselves, though not by going out and doing what Gabriella does. It's a very weird phenomenon that people who are generally gentle, kind-hearted, considerate people, would like to watch a movie where these horrific things are taking place.

I think it's really interesting to look at ourselves and wonder why we find these things interesting. Why do people love Hitchcock; why were Agatha Christie novels so popular for so long? Hopefully our film will be interesting to these same kind of people in the same way. So I think that it's a perfectly healthy subject matter to treat, maybe we go a bit farther than most people do in films.

BRADDOCK: I'm getting the feeling that we might encounter censor problem over here. But then, I actually thought that we'd have trouble in the US because the MPAA tends to frown upon women committing acts of violence. They're perfectly okay with men stabbing people, but if a woman does it, they get freaked out. But we passed them without any trouble at all, with an R rating, which is 17 years-old and up. I was surprised. But, I've heard people talk more and more about these things over here, and I'm starting to wonder.

SHABBY: Some people may try to stir up some dirt just because you've got the name Tarantino in the titles.

MAASS: Exactly.

SHABBY: In a way, the kinds of people who get off on violence will probably be bored by your film because it's more contemplative than active.

MAASS: Well there is action in it, but it's not *Reservoir Dogs* .... although *Reservoir Dogs* didn't have that much action in it. Let's say it's not *Desperado*! It doesn't have that kind of body count. There are some very dynamic scenes but that's not what we're into, the movie's more about a woman's transformation.

With that, JONES wakes and the taxi pulls up outside the Odeon. Everyone piles out and MAASS attempts to pay the cabby with American Express. After this is less than enthusiastically received, MAASS retrieves the two pieces of his card from the gutter, and the four have a quick whip-round, pay the fare in a wide variety of currencies, and join the end of the queue outside the cinema.

EXT. CINEMA QUEUE. NIGHT.

It's raining again, so the cheerful cockney sparrahs have pulled-up their collars and are hugging the mini-skirted 'birds' to keep them warm. A few sanguine souls thought to bring umbrellas. Some less far-sighted queuers try to buy the umbrellas off them, when their offers are refused, a fist fight breaks out.

MAASS (*watching the pummelling with distaste*): Does this go on a lot in England?

SHABBY (*Headfirst in his notebook*): Only when you mix male egos with alcohol. Now, I know you credit The Coen Brothers with being an influence, and I can see why, their films are slow paced, with gradual revelation of details and ...

MAASS: Deliberately paced!

SHABBY: Ah, sorry ... deliberately paced - but it's not a comparison you mind?

MAASS: No, nonono, compare us to the Coens all you like and we'll be thrilled. I think influence is a pretty harmless phenomenon. When you see other films and are aware of other film-makers, your opinion of their films will be influenced by your knowledge of their other work. You may not sit down and say 'oh, I'm going to write this scene like that one in *Miller's Crossing*' but, at the same time, all of that knowledge is floating around in your brain, so similarities can make their way into the work. I don't think that there's anything overt in *Curdled*, it's more tonal.

SHABBY: Given the break-neck pace you filmed at, this 'deliberate' pace the film proceeds at is quite remarkable.

CUT TO SCENE FROM CURDLED.

Its an almost static shot, of Guell standing behind a bar, motionless. Waiting.

SHABBY (*Voice over*): There's one moment when you just show Guell motionless at work, just watching, waiting, thinking, and that shot seemed to go on for ... well, ages. It's a very Kubrick moment!

BRADDOCK: Yeah. That's something that I and the Director of Photography designed, based on *The Shining*, it's meant to be that way, to have that formalism. There was some stuff where we tried to create a formal feeling, because there's some really interesting tension that comes out of a formal shot like that.

CUT BACK TO THE QUEUE:

SHABBY: But when you're pushed for time, isn't there just a temptation to rush things along to get on to he next set-up?

BRADDOCK: Yeah, definitely. But the Director of Photography and I sat down before we commenced filming and drew up a shot-list for the entire movie, we just sat in my office and talked the whole thing out. We decided there on the motifs, on what was important - overhead shots, certain kinds of push-ins, a certain kind of formalism, fluidity; and those things we hung on to. We knew they were essential, so we would shoot them first, or sacrifice other things in order to get them done. We took the time before-hand to establish the style that we were trying to create so, at the very worst, when we had to start losing shots, these key shots would remain.

SHABBY: Cunning.

BRADDOCK: That comes from me having shot films before, as a Director of Photography, and I know only too painfully well what has to get sacrificed when you have to shoot in only four weeks.

SHABBY (*Glaring at his biro, which seems to have run inconveniently out of ink*): Last question: PFCS - Post Forensic Cleaning Service, this is far too good an idea to be untrue.

BRADDOCK: In the States, the police really have no involvement with a crime-scene once the body has gone and they've dusted for prints, that's it, they're outta there. Now, seemingly co-incidental to our film, there's been a mini-boom of these cleaning businesses. There's two or three now, it's quite remarkable! There's one called

1-800 Autopsy. They do autopsies and what they call 'decomp clean-up', which is decompositional removal.

MAASS: When we wrote the original short film script, I wasn't aware of any company that did it exclusively, And I called around several general cleaning services and asked them if they'd ever done a crime-scene clean-up, and some of them had, so I gathered some knowledge of what that was like through them.

JONES is refreshing her lipstick, SHABBY eyes the lipstick thoughtfully, then asks if he can borrow it. Surprised and amused, she surrenders it to him.

MAASS (*Oblivious to this*): A-guy-in-LA we talked to, is probably more colourful a personality than Lodger. It's one of those jobs where you have to have a certain constitution to decide you wanna do it. I couldn't even begin to do it.

The-guy-in-LA invited us to go on one of the crime-scene clean-ups, but first he said we had to go to a second opinion autopsy with him. I couldn't handle that, but Reb and Angela went; he took 'em to an autopsy, working on the theory that, if you can handle that then maybe you could handle a crime-scene clean-up, which is supposed to be worse. So they went to the autopsy, then we got into pre-production so they never made it to the crime-scene.

SHABBY (*Already feeling another attack of nausea coming on, he never-the-less turns to JONES*): How was that? I suppose after watching all those snuff videos it wasn't so bad.

JONES: It was weird ... it was really weird. Kinda icky, but interesting though.

He writes 'icky but interesting' down in his book, in thick, smeary red letters.

SHABBY: But not gruesome?

JONES: Ehm ... I kept trying to personalise the guy.

CUT TO SILENT BLACK AND WHITE

Hand-held camera shots, deliberately shaky, looking over the doctor's shoulder as he is slices up a cadaver. The tag on the toe says JOE NOBODY. JONES and BRADDOCK, in smocks and masks are standing next to him, watching. JONES is paying particular attention, craning to see what's going on. She looks down at the body and the face changes, morphing slowly from JOE NOBODY to a different JOE NOBODY to BRADDOCK to BALDWIN and finally to JONES , all laying pale and still on the metal slab.

JONES (*In voice-over*): Who was this cold, grey man lying there on the table? I wanted to know, to feel sorry for him. But, I also wanted to pass that test. I wanted to go to the crime-scene too, I was really disappointed that we didn't.

CUT BACK TO:

EXT: THE QUEUE:

It has stopped raining now.

SHABBY: Lodger actually tells Gabriella that the biggest thing people are surprised by is the smell. I suppose that's something that you can only imagine if you've been that close to a corpse.

JONES: Right. The guy-in-LA helped us with the sensory information - what it looks like, what it smells like, 'cos I had no idea, I don't suppose many people do. I asked him 'is it that bad' and he said, from his point of view, it was. That kind of prepared me for the first time you walk in the room and see the blood which is rotting. I never really though that blood could curdle, but it does.

BRADDOCK: Lodger is actually a good deal more compassionate than some of the people we met, but essentially he's exactly the same, fussing over missed skull-fragments, they would talk about this stuff totally routinely, and throw a little dark joke in there once in a while. But they take their business very seriously.

CUT TO SILENT FILM WITHIN THE FILM:

INT: A LARGE LIVING ROOM, LIT THROUGH THE FRENCH WINDOW. DAY

Shot at bizarre MTV angles, in saturated colours, two cleaning ladies in over-alls straighten-up, holding their aching backs. They have a trolley full of cleaning fluids, cloths and buckets - like the ones maids push down hotel corridors every morning. Sillhouetted in the doorway, their boss is pulling on a white cotton glove. He is a large, ex-football-player type. He walks around the room, running a finger over the surfaces, checking under the corner of the rug and behind a couple of picture-frames. This is edited together in that irritating, spastic manner so beloved of pop-videos, and is run through at 18 frames per second to make it look slightly foolish.

BRADDOCK (*Voice over*); One guy charges per room, a flat fee, no matter how bad it is. He told us about a clean-up job he had done at one particular house where someone had shot himself. He cleaned up the room and left, satisfied at another job well done ...

CUT TO;

INT. THE EX-FOOTBALL-PLAYER'S OFFICE. DAY.

Feet on desk, he takes a phone-call.

CUT TO:

EXT. THE LAWN OUTSIDE THE LIVING ROOM.

Various members of the deceased's family cluster in the French windows looking in horror at the woman kneeling on the grass in the foreground. Wearing a pink marigold, she picks up a lump of grey and pink flesh, holding it by the dark hairs which are sprouting from one side of it. She is holding it at arms length, so the camera gets it in glorious close-up. Another wide-angle lens extends her arm and enlarges the lump of brain.

BRADDOCK (*Continuing the voice-over*): But he got a call the next day from the relatives and they said 'we were out in the yard and found some brain matter out there' 'cos, apparently the guy had shot himself with his back to a window, or something. Anyway, the cleaner said 'I'll come right over and get it'.

INT. THE LIVING ROOM. DAY.

The same woman has the lump of brain in a clear plastic evidence bag - still held in a Marigolden hand, at arms length. With her other hand she holds an ornamental phone, she is talking to The Cleaner. Her lips synch with BRADDOCK's voice-over. She is still shot in caricaturish wide-angle, and is still slightly speeded up.:

BRADDOCK (*Still in voice-over*): 'No,' They said, 'It's already been dealt with, but we want our money back!!!'.

INT. CLEANER'S OFFICE

His heels slip off the desk and he falls forward in shock. Then he gets stroppy, telling her what's what - with his lips synching to BRADDOCK's words - then slams the phone down triumphantly.

BRADDOCK (*Finishing the voice-over*): So he said 'Hey, I billed you for the *room*, it's not my fault if there was something out on the lawn!' and hung up.

CUT BACK TO:

EXT: THE QUEUE AND THE RAIN:

We also return to normal colour and normal speed.

BRADDOCK: In the end they took him to court, and they haggled over the money, and he won. Lodger would never do that, he would say 'Think about the customer'.

SHABBY: That's one of those stories which you have to fictionalise, 'cos if you presented it as truth no one would believe it!

BRADDOCK: Exactly. In fact we toned down a lot of the details, some of the stories are quite horrific.

MAASS: What is so amazing about it - which we kinda played down - was how physically unsettling it is to go into one of those places. Supposedly the smell, even if it's just blood that's been decomposing for a few hours, will make anyone retch, it's so horrible, and the rooms are generally filled with insects.

JONES is nodding knowledgably at this.

MAASS (*Continuing*): Physically and psychologically it's just a nightmare scene, but we didn't want to dwell too much on how horrible the reality is. Never the less, for me, it's amazing that anybody can actually do that, go into a room and clean up bits of people.

SHABBY: In a way, you'd have to be like Helena and be a deeply unimaginative person to deal with it.

MAASS: Or like Gabriella. You must remember that she's not interested in the gore, that's not what draws her in, she's not into running her fingers through puddles of blood, she's motivated to go there because it allows her to better understand the psychological goings-on of the assailant and the victim, because she sees the dynamics of the scene, it's much easier to picture and get a sense of it. She's not wallowing in blood and getting off on that. And, of course, this is where the film gets its title from.

CUT TO SCENE FROM CURDLED.

Lodger is handing out the day's work-duties to his girls. Gabriella plumps for the Blue-Blood Headsman job, much to Helena's irritation.

SHABBY (*In voice-over*): I'll tell you, seeing Lodger standing on his little balcony, despatching his PFCS cleaning-ladies to the crime-scenes of Miami, it all reminded me of nothing so much as *Charlie's Angels*!

CUT BACK TO: EXT: THE QUEUE:

BRADDOCK: Really? That's funny, 'cos on the set, we called 'em *Lodger's Angels*!

SHABBY: I think there's a TV series waiting to happen here: *The Further Adventures of PFCS.*

CUT TO TACKY TITLE SQUENCE:

Deliberately reminiscent of 'Charlie's Angels' the sequence shows sillhouettes of young women equipped with cleaning implements, intercut with shots of Gabriella ringing out a bloody wash-cloth, picking an eye-ball out of a fish-tank, using her nail-file to dig a bullet out of a wall, then looking at it through a magnifying glass she just happens to have in her pocket. The sequence ends with a freeze-frame of four girls, all in blood-stained overalls, walking down a pavement, grinning, their hair flowing behind them. Over this is stencilled the logo 'PFCS'.

BRADDOCK (*Voice over*): Well, I'll tell ya, John and I wrote a proposal for a TV series, and we've been having a hard time getting anybody to read it, but it is completely based on the maid service! We were planning to turn it into a mystery/thriller series though, 'cos Gabriella's able to figure out how the various crimes were committed before the detectives are.

CUT TO:

An obviously posed shot of ANGELA LANSBURY trying to look natural and spontaneous. This is subtitled: 'Tonight's Guest Star: Angela

Lansbury'

SHABBY (*Voice over*): All you need then is Angela Lansbury to sign on in a cameo ...

BRADDOCK (*Voice over*): ... As Mrs Lodger!!

CUT BACK TO THE QUEUE:

The foursome have nearly made it to the head of the queue now, where a doorman is tearing tickets and tipping his hat at the mini-skirted girls.

SHABBY: Humour is a great way of dealing with serious subjects, you do get some big laughs out of the audience, especially with those oh-so-innocent facial expressions Angela has.

MAASS (*Who has been digging around in his jacket's breast pocket, instead of paying attention*): Which Angela? Jones or Lansbury?

SHABBY (*Ignoring him*): They're funny without needing to fall-back on jokes or one-liners. (*To Jones:*) How do you go about performing without dialogue?

JONES: I think one of the most important things I learned in school was that acting is often re-acting. You have to keep an inner monologue in your head, instead of just acting when you're speaking, and those are some of my favourite moments, to take in information, process it and put it out, without speaking. I think that that's much more important than just speaking a line.

This was especially important with the last shot of the film. I didn't want her to come across as evil, but simply curious. She's gotta find out the big questions about death, so she doesn't think about it too much before acting on her impulse.

BRADDOCK: It's not often you encounter an actor who you can put the camera on and they just sit there and you know what they're thinking. That's pretty remarkable. I hope, after this film, she gets other opportunities to show off her talent and create other good work.

MAASS has produced three cinema tickets from his pocket and is divvying them out to BRADDOCK and JONES. There is pointedly no ticket for SHABBY.

SHABBY: So, are you planning on continuing in this vein?

BRADDOCK: I think we're gonna do a little exploring into crime, actually. We have an idea to look at the criminal mind, the outlaw, of sorts. I think people are always fascinated with outlaws, you know, people who live outside The System, looking at what makes a criminal a criminal. That's kinda the idea that we'll be dealing with, but we'll look at in our own way and it'll probably be set in Miami. And it'll be odd!

SHABBY: To feature Angela?

BRADDOCK: No doubt we'll feature Angela in there somewhere! I think she is such a great actor. I mean, you've only seen her play a Colombian girl. I've seen her do a really wide range of things and as you've noticed, she's got great comedic timing, and so I'll be using her in ... just about everything I ever do!

JONES: I love comedy far more than drama. I feel more comfortable in that, but I don't think a lot of people see me as the comedy type. It would be nice to do something in my own voice, at last.

SHABBY (*Eyeing up the cinema-tickets suspiciously, but carrying gamely on, regardless*): Are you ready for fame?

JONES: I guess ... I don't actually know what it means. I'm very curious about it. Hopefully it'll mean that more people see my work, and I get more opportunity to work! But fame ... I don't quite know what to expect from that. I guess there's no way to plan it.

JONES: Well you'll just have to hire someone to sort through your fan-mail, and you won't have to queue at cinemas.

JONES: Ooh, that would be nice!

SHABBY (*Brightening, and addressing MAASS*): So, what film are we going to see, anyway?

MAASS (*Handing his ticket to the doorman*): *We* are going to see *Trainspotting*!

BRADDOCK: (*Handing his ticket to the doorman*): It's not been released in the States, yet, you see!

JONES (Handing her ticket to the doorman, who tips his hat to her): Apparently we won't understand a word of the dialogue, so we'll just listen to the music!

DOORMAN: That'll do nicely, ma'am.

He then unhooks a cord from the wall and drapes it across the doorway. It carries a plaque bearing the legend 'sold out'.

MAAS (*Emptying bits of broken phone from his pocket into the ashtray by the door*): Well, it's been fun. What's the traditional English saying? Oh yes: Cheers!

MUSIC: Iggy Pop's 'Lust For Life' strikes up and continues through the credits.

The threesome give SHABBY an enthusiastic thumbs-up, then disappear into the gloom inside the cinema. SHABBY stands on the pavement, JONES' lipstick still in his hand, flicking through his bookfull of semi-coherent notes.

It begins to rain again.

FADE OUT.

ROLL CREDITS.

PROFILING

"I can't tell the difference between a good script and a bad script, it all looks horrible on paper, but hopefully it'll be a wonderful experience on film. For me the key has always been the experience and the process, and that means the people."

Christopher Doyle

DANNY BOYLE AND ANDREW MACDONALD

by Richard Luck, John Ashbrook and John Gore

IN THE TIME BEFORE *Trainspotting*, the Scottish New Wave unleashed their first surprise attack on the British cinema industry, *Shallow Grave*. Director Danny Boyle and producer Andrew MacDonald made a whistle-stop tour of the country, personally introducing the film (which they co-created with writer John Hodge) to audiences. One such event was held at *The Warwick Arts Centre* and was hosted by that hallowed establishment's Film Programmer, John Gore. John recorded the event for posterity and, late one night, surreptitiously passed the tapes over to John Ashbrook in a deserted bus station. The tapes were transcribed under conditions of the greatest secrecy ...

Before their highly sensitive contents can be revealed, it would be a good idea to get late-comers up to speed. And when it comes to speed - Richard Luck's y'man ...

With the availability of video, the added intimacy of a home-based media allows you to understand exactly what it is about *Shallow Grave* that makes it work so well. A major reason for the film's success is the simplicity of its story line: the new flat-mate dies leaving a suitcase full of dosh, they decide to bury the body, keep the loot and all hell breaks loose. No tricks, no red herrings, this is story-telling at its straight-forward best.

The performances are uniformly excellent: As Alex, Ewan McGregor shows exactly why is he is the current golden boy of British cinema. New Zealander Kerry Fox, meanwhile, makes a fine stab at an Edinburgh accent. Christopher Eccleston is also impressive in a, typically, unsympathetic rôle. There are also fine cameos from Ken Stott, as a lugubrious DI, and Keith Allen as Hugo.

Of course, *Shallow Grave* has its feathers. It changes gear learner-driver style and the violent set-pieces are a bit too Wily E. Coyote-ish for their own good. There is, however, a sense of something really special going on here. You only need to look at the absence of guns to see that this isn't a rip-off of a successful American formula. What's more, Boyle's direction and Hodge's script are so assured, so sincere in their belief in the story, one really couldn't give a shit that the whole thing doesn't make sense. *Shallow Grave* suspends disbelief. So what? Isn't that what good movies are supposed to do?

DIGGING SHALLOW GRAVE

Like all films about money, greed and madness, *Shallow Grave* exists in the shadow of John Huston's *The Treasure of Sierra Madre*. Indeed, it is possible to draw parallels between the characters here and those played by Humphrey Bogart, Walter Huston and Tim Holt in the latter. However, while it might share thematic concerns with Huston, *Shallow Grave* isn't a homage to an esteemed classic. This is an angry nineties film that, somehow, still retains a fierce pride in its British roots. This is a picture that dares to be daring, and for that we should all be grateful.

... As the *Shallow Grave* credits ended and the lights rose, John Gore bounded on to the stage to introduce the makers:

JOHN GORE; "Good evening ladies and gentlemen, thank you all very much for coming. Good film, innit! I'd now like very much to introduce you to Andrew MacDonald and Danny Boyle, who are respectively producer and director of this evening's film.

[Pause for Applause]

"Nice house Andrew, where'd you find it?"

ANDREW MACDONALD: "We built the flat in a warehouse in Glasgow. A lot of people think it was real, I wish it was, I'd be living in it now! However, it is based upon real flats in Edinburgh, in New Town, where they have these tiny, dingy little staircases, but once you get the door open, they're just massive inside.

"Of course, we decided to build it even bigger! The living-room is literally the size of this 300-seater cinema, it was just massive, by far the biggest set that has ever been built in Scotland. We shot the film in six weeks, thirty days to be exact, and we shot on that set for twenty-two days; and so that's where we spent our money ... every penny of it. We almost went broke several times."

JOHN GORE: "Danny, you take your name actor, and you kill him off in the first twenty minutes! Was this intentional?"

DANNY BOYLE: "For that part, we wanted someone who, when the door swung open and you get your first look at him, everyone thinks 'Crumpet!' Boys and girls were meant to look at him and think 'Oh, he's gorgeous'. So we tried Daniel Day-Lewis, Jean-Marc Barr ... Keanu Reeves ... all The Crumpet really; and we ended up with Keith Allen.

"But, yeah, that was one of things that was brilliant about the script, each time you got hooked into something, and you started predicting where it was going, it always suddenly jumped away from you. For example: late on in the film, the thugs arrive and you think that they're gonna take over and all the violence you've heard about is gonna take place. Through the last thirty minutes they're just gonna be torturing the inhabitants of the flat, and you're thinking that, in a way, they deserve it ... but then the thugs get killed off.

"That was one of our principles when we set the film up, we wanted to try and make an intelligent film that just kept ahead of the audience, make it a bit of a roller-coaster, but try to stay one jump ahead. A big influence on the film was

Blood Simple which, although it's not as deliberately funny as this, is a tremendous thriller. When I went to audition for the film, that was the first film I mentioned and, thank goodness, it was the right one to mention, so I got the job."

JOHN GORE: "So how do you go about getting the money for something like this, these days?"

ANDREW MACDONALD: "The funding was relatively easy, Channel Four were the principle funders, putting up about 85% of the £1 million, and the Glasgow Film Fund topped it up once we'd got Channel Four on board. It can be so difficult, because it's your first film, it's the first one I had produced, the first that John Hodge had written (by the way, he apologises for not being here, but we've got him locked up writing our, with any luck, next film).

"We'd worked together on the script for about eighteen months, before we met the Head of Drama at Channel Four at a script-writing conference in Inverness of all places. I was working in Glasgow making documentaries, and John was working in the hospital there, and we met through having similar interests, as people do, But the whole reason the film got made was because of the script, and Danny told the script as a storyteller, as a director, with the actors, and improved it. But basically it was all there, you could see it on the page, and everyone saw the same film, which made it very easy to finance.

"Channel Four make television drama, but they also invest partially in a film like *Four Weddings* or *The Crying Game*, and *Shallow Grave* was made for the same department, 'Film On Four', who always intend that their films are to be shown, if possible, at the cinema. The reason they can get away with such a diverse slate, is because it is all guaranteed to end up on television, and they own it forever, and they can show it as many times as they like. The BBC's *Middlemarch* cost £1 million an hour, we spent that on a whole feature film, which they've already sold all through the world and therefore have made a profit on before it opens anywhere. But this film worked out, a lot don't, so they do take a lot of risks. It's something the BBC should pay more attention to, in my opinion. You could make a nice little industry out of twenty films a year."

JOHN GORE; "It seems brave, to me, that you've made the bunch in this film the kind of people you'd rather not have living next door to you."

DANNY BOYLE: "We could have made them sympathetic very easily by making them poor. Keep all the gags but make them poor, and immediately you look through that to excuse what happens, because they really need the money. So it was very important to set it up that they had comfortable lives, as secure employment as you can get nowadays, and they seem to have everything that they could ever want. That was crucial.

"It was an aesthetic decision that, as all great films do, you use your imagination much more than actually seeing things. It's weird the way that people ... I know that I do ... see a film and think they've seen things; you're absolutely sure you've seen things, but, when you look very closely, you realise that the film is so well made, you haven't actually needed to see it. You've created it. There's no way that we can get anyway near what you are imaginatively capable of, and this was absolutely true, right up until the very last moments of the film, we held it back until then.

"We also took a very important decision very early on that we would have no guns in the film, and it's worked out very well for us. It was one of those decisions which you look back on and realise was a really good step. Unfortunately, that's not true of all decisions. But we shied away from guns because we realised how little a part guns play in our lives, as Britons, thankfully. You can spend your whole life without ever seeing a *real* gun, unless you've been in Northern Ireland. We realised how easy it is to ape American culture. It's a thriller, there's drugs, there's drugs money, we've gotta have guns. There's violence, we've gotta blow people away. No you don't.

"So. that decision led us on to thinking 'Well, what are we gonna have then?' We decide to have pain that people really understand, which is why the thugs smack them across the shins. Everybody has banged their shins on a coffee table at some point, we all know what agony that can be. Good decisions like that feed upon each other and they grow, they become strong factors that work in your favour."

AUDIENCE MEMBER: "But most of the weapons used are domestic."

ANDREW MACDONALD: 'Exactly. The idea is, if you have a gun, it's a machine, it's very easy to use, that's why eight-year-old kids can shoot somebody. But a kid of eight would find it very difficult to batter somebody to death with a crow-bar. To do that, to actually hit somebody, is much more difficult."

SAME AUDIENCE MEMBER: "It will be interesting to see if that point is made even more forcefully when watching the film on video or TV, because you'll be watching it at home."

DANNY BOYLE: "Yes, don't try any of these things at home, kids."

AUDIENCE MEMBER: "The violence, especially at the end, seemed to be a reference to seventies and early eighties domestic horror movies, stalk and slash movies, or something like *Driller Killer*."

DANNY BOYLE: "The temptation with a question like that is always to just say 'yes'. There's lots of influences on you when you're working, and I'm sure *Driller Killer* was an influence on John, there's a little homage to it in there. The flesh piecing at the end was because we wanted to climax the film with a release of the tension we'd built up, you can't just let it float away, you've got to bring people to a climax ... so to speak ... which is why we saved that moment to the end. We wanted it to be very small, so that you don't see it at first, there's a beat before they see it, and hopefully you're on a trip with the film in some kind of way, and moments like that which you experience collectively, are great.

"That's been one of the exciting things for me, having worked in television but before that in theatre, you lose the sense of how important it is to experience things collectively. Whether it be a thriller like this, or *Four Weddings*, which I saw in a packed cinema, and people were there to enjoy a ride together, it was absolutely a communal experience, which is a very important function of cinema."

JOHN GORE: "What a nice man, you can come again."

AUDIENCE MEMBER: "How irritated are you at being called The Scottish Tarantino?"

DANNY BOYLE: "I really take offence at that, 'cos I'm from Manchester.

"But it's very flattering. If we can make a second film that's as big a move forward as *Pulp Fiction* was from *Reservoir Dogs*, that will be tremendous. He has mobilised a wonderful energy in the cinema, which is fantastic, and he's done it through his work, but also through his personal energy, and it's great for some of that to rub off. You've gotta be careful, because, for instance, people are disappointed with *Killing Zoë*, just because of how that's been marketed.

"For us, although there's lots of American influences, there's lots of influences from elsewhere too. We wanted to make very much a British film, we wanted it to work at home, more than anywhere else, that was our aim. Andrew's grandfather's films, the Powell/Pressburger films (his grandfather is Emeric Pressburger), are just as much an influence. If someone cares to compare us to Powell/Pressburger, that would be really ... really ... intimidating."

AUDIENCE MEMBER: "When films like *True Lies* take up to two hundred days to shoot, how can you turn out a film in six weeks?"

ANDREW MACDONALD: "Right from the beginning, John, being a doctor and therefore a more practical writer than some, conceived the idea of a film that would take place in a confined space, with a dramatic event that a small number of characters had to encounter. He designed it as a film which it would be possible for he and I to make for a few hundred thousand pounds, although God knew where even that amount would come from, at weekends, in real flats, with our friends. Kind of in the way that *Leon The Pig Farmer* was made. It was only when we got decent finance that we were able to widen things out, actually build the ideal flat, and go for the best young actors in the country."

AUDIENCE MEMBER: "You say that you wanted to make this film British, but will you be tempted to follow Neil Jordan and all the rest and head for America?"

DANNY BOYLE: "To be honest, we've had quite a job to establish that this is very much the work of three film-makers, and Hollywood doesn't see things that way. They tend to treat writers appallingly, and I don't quite know what they think about producers, but they certainly want to head-hunt directors. You see that again and again and again.

"I've been offered a Sharon Stone film and all sorts of things like that, which is just silly really. I think you have to make films that you know about. Lots of people want to make films about things they don't know about ... I don't know much about Sharon Stone.

"It seems stupid to abandon the actual process which made *Shallow Grave* good, y'know, it's like, if you're a pop group and you have a good album, you don't kick people out, you try and stick together ... unless you're *Suede*. The next film is gonna be on an even smaller budget, but will show a very different side of life in Edinburgh, based on Irvine Welsh's book *Trainspotting*. which, if you've read it, you'll relish the thought of it being made into a film. And if you haven't read it, you should, it's a tremendous read."

AUDIENCE MEMBER: "How can a cheap film like this compete in an open market with the big Hollywood blockbusters and their massive marketing budgets?"

ANDREW MACDONALD: "Don't know, but we've just earned two million in our opening weekend. To an extent, Tarantino's success has helped us, by laying the groundwork for thrillers and smaller films ... even set in one room. *Four Weddings* has helped us especially. We're not exactly similar, except we are British.

"Previously, anything that had 'Channel Four' or 'British Film' attached to it would turn people off because they hadn't, on the whole, enjoyed those films. You don't really want to see 'A Great British Film' on the poster, you just want it to be taken as a film. The audience always knows better than anybody else. Opening in London and Scotland in the same cinemas as *Pulp Fiction* last year, we've beaten its records. That must be because *Four Weddings* has taught people that it can be good if it's British, in fact, you might even enjoy it more, because its British."

DANNY BOYLE: "Also, ideas are free, and they come from you lot out there. Hollywood thinks it can buy ideas, it buys, buys, buys, but hopefully there's an energy amongst this audience that wants to go and see something a little bit different, that's actually prepared to take a few risks. At the kind of budget levels British films are made, you can afford to take risks. This becomes impossible when there's forty million dollars invested in a film. It becomes predictable and safe."

AUDIENCE MEMBER: "You make the point in the film about friends and friendship ... it seemed to me that Kerry Fox's character was the most faithless in that regard."

ANDREW MACDONALD: "She was always the outsider, that's partly why we cast Kerry, because she's a New Zealander. The idea with her was that she controlled these two boys, and they, of course, thought they controlled her, like every shared flat in those circumstances. She was meant to be in complete control both of the two, and the situation, and she gives such a great performance that that manages to come across. In a way, she has a little bit of the *femme fatale* type figure, a kind of Kim Novak. Whether she was any better or worse a human being than the other two, I'll leave up to you."

SAME AUDIENCE MEMBER: "But the male still wins out in the end, because she doesn't get the cash."

ANDREW MACDONALD: "But she gets away, that's not bad!"

DANNY BOYLE: "It's quite interesting that the body count is male, and she survives. She doesn't get the money, but she survives, leaving men nailed to the

AUDIENCE MEMBER: "I very much enjoyed the opening race around the streets, was that scripted or an editorial decision?"

DANNY BOYLE: "We worked very hard on that. It wasn't absolutely specific in the script, but you did get the sense that John wanted to announce the film with an enormous energy. In all those films you see ... usually British ... they pan slowly across a city at the beginning, and you think 'Oh God, 'ere we go'. So we talked and talked and talked and actually that opening sequence particularly developed out of an enormous number of people who worked on the film, contributing ideas. We worked very hard to make it gel, both in how it was shot and in the post-production, and in choosing the Leftfield music, so that the film really grabs you. Like David Lean says, *"You grab that audience early on, you announce what you wanna do, early on.""*

AUDIENCE MEMBER: "Did Channel Four try to exert any editorial control over the film or just let you get on with it?"

ANDREW MACDONALD: "They let us get on with it; but the bottom line is: they're putting up the bulk of a million quid, if they want to do anything to your film, they can. But they're so used to working with first-timers that they put up with the mistakes you make ... like spending all the money in the first week on building a bloody great set, things like that. They're well used to it, and I don't think they even execute final cut.

"With something like *Naked*, they made suggestions, but if Mike Leigh said he wanted it like that, they're not gonna change it, that's not really what they're about. That's partly why they've become so successful, because they trust film makers.

"Ultimately, what they do is support you, so when you do spend all the money in the first week, they help you get out of the shit rather than sacking you. If we'd been working for someone like Miramax, that would have been it. So I think they're great, any one who is lucky enough to make their first film with them knows that there's no one else like them in the country, basically because they're used to working with independents."

AUDIENCE MEMBER: "How difficult was it to cast."

ANDREW MACDONALD: "Keith Allen was very difficult."

DANNY BOYLE: "Yeah, but he wasn't at all concerned about the nudity. When you're casting a part that requires nudity, you have to tell 'em before-hand, so that they won't come up with the idea of a towel on the morning of the shoot. But he was delighted at the opportunity to take his clothes off, he couldn't wait. Although, I have to say, we showed the film at The London Film Festival, and did a Q&A like this afterwards, without realising he was in the audience. And he stood up and shouted 'That wasn't my willy!' There's probably somebody here who can comment on that, but we won't ask you to stand up."

AUDIENCE MEMBER: "Did you encounter any censorship problems?"

ANDREW MACDONALD: "None. We were a little concerned at one stage, more about its eventual television screening than cinema. If it hadn't been successful and got a cinema release, and taken lots of money, won a few awards, and been legitimised as a work of art of some kind, then it could have been different. But now they're gonna show *Reservoir Dogs* on Channel Four, they show Martin Scorsese films, and because they're perceived by the media and critics as 'art' they're accepted. Based on that precedent, we won't have any problem now."

AUDIENCE MEMBER: "Do you see it as a moral story?"

DANNY BOYLE: "One of the things I learned from making this film, was to make A Story. We decided that the god of the film would be the narrative, and all our other private agendas, little obsessions that you can't help developing, had to be abandoned. They would get cut if we shot them. And everybody on the film knew that.

"It's funny, but when you do that, rather than set off with a different agenda, for instance, to make a really moral film, or to try and teach or express highly individual ideas to people, it's curious how a film can find its own place in a society. We didn't have The Lottery in mind, the North London football managers who were taking huge bungs hadn't been exposed yet, but when the film comes out, those kinds of things come into focus with it. Its a great lesson, to trust the narrative, really, and if you make a good narrative, like so many great films, they'll come in and out of focus at different times, like Hitchcock and Billy Wilder films. The principle idea is just to tell a great story.

"One of the brilliant things about the story is that that body's already dead. Their first step over the line, in to blood, is actually not a crime, it's in that shady area. It's very clever, particularly as one of them was a doctor, who deals with corpses every day. What John's implying is that, we're all capable of things that we think, at least publicly, that we're not.

"The film has its own cinematic life, they could take the sensible honourable option and not do it, but they take the other path. In cinematic terms its a much more pure act, to cut the body up."

AUDIENCE MEMBER: "Is that a reflection of society in the 1990s or is it more universal than that, bringing in Thatcherism, for example?"

ANDREW MACDONALD: "I think it comes out of that, because John and I grew up in the eighties. Danny's a little older. However, in no way did we set out with that intent. There was always the simple truth: What's it about ? It's about how greed messes you up! Everybody knows that and I don't think that's ever changed. The only other place it has opened is Australia, and its doing very well there, and I haven't a clue what they had in the eighties. It seems to play at festivals, and through that they've sold it to Korea, South America, and therefore I think it works just on the thriller level if nothing else. Half the time, when they translate a film, there's no way they can translate the jokes, so that can't be the appeal."

DANNY BOYLE: "I think it has some serious implications about doctors. The next time a junior doctor hovers over you ... think about it. In fact, John told us that doctors have abbreviations that they use, so they can talk about a patient without them realising what they're talking about. And one of his favourites is 'T.F. Bundy', which stands for 'Totally Fucked, But Not Dead Yet'."

ANDREW MACDONALD: "Someone at the Q&A we did in Manchester said, that's the same for the British film industry!"

AUDIENCE MEMBER: "It's tempting with an intelligent film like this, to play hunt the image; could you talk us through some of the images you used, such as flesh and water and what have you. Was that deliberate?"

DANNY BOYLE: "Again, the honest answer is that it's very easy to be bewitched by what you did, especially if it achieves any success. But we set out, plainly and simply, to make a thriller with jokes."

ANDREW MACDONALD: "One of the things was the drum kit. John and I got really excited about this, 'Great', we thought, 'homage to *Gregory's Girl*', our favourite film. We want to make the most successful Scottish film next to that. Of course, it never dawned on Danny or the art director, and they had Ewan smashing the drums around like Gregory. There are lots of those touches, some of John's, for example, the opening and ending is *Sunset Boulevard* ..."

DANNY BOYLE: "But one thing we did do, is have a huge collection of photographs and images that we all contributed to, and showed to each other, 'cos language, which is the normal method you use to communicate ideas before you film, is very imprecise. If you give a person a photograph of something red, they don't turn up fourteen weeks later having made you a blue one.

"This is wonderful, because it allows people to have a sense of the film while they're working on it, because you forget that people who are not working in such elevated jobs as us two, often feel completely remote from the film. That often happens in filming. Whereas, if you include everyone, you can nick all sorts of ideas of those people you would otherwise ignore.

"You steal from everywhere, all the time. People don't usually own up to it, which is one of the great things about Tarantino, he will own up to that fact that basically we're all really magpies. Whether the ingredients you steal are any good depends on how you cook 'em."

AUDIENCE MEMBER: "With that attention to detail, how did you go about accessorising that big a flat?"

ANDREW MACDONALD: "A lot of it's from my dad's place! A lot of the kitchen stuff seemed to come from there. The big dark painting that Kerry and that man Keith Allen stand in front of, that's by a Scottish artist called Steven Conroy, who became a real influence. Danny came in and said 'Have you see this guy's work', I grew up with the man, he's a friend of mine, so we went along and borrowed some of his paintings, and now he's a bit of a mega-star and only opens in New York. Those paintings are worth like fifty grand each, and he lent 'em to us."

AUDIENCE MEMBER: "I don't know if it's gaps in my perception, but I couldn't follow how the dealers found them, and how the police got suspicious? Are there deliberate holes in the narrative?"

ANDREW MACDONALD (*To Danny*): "Are you gonna tell the truth?"

DANNY BOYLE: "One of the wonderful things that I loved about the script was that it didn't try to explain everything, it didn't try to moralise. One of the things that's wrong with British films is that we often carry around too much luggage, we feel we have to explain ourselves all the time, both in terms of story and in terms of what we want to imply. The problem with that is, you don't trust the audience. You know that feeling when you're watching a film and you're ahead of it the whole time, thinking, 'I know this, I've seen this, I don't need it explaining'. John took some deliberate jumps. When you're working, you talk about holes in the script, and we decided that we would plough on and forget that. It's how things happen."

ANDREW MACDONALD: "You just know, from the tradition of the thriller and the *noir*, which way the action will proceed. There are holes in the plot, such as when the police fail to notice the holes in the ceiling, and those are our fault. But the two you pointed out were there right from the beginning.

"The audience has to know just enough so it doesn't feel cheated, which is why we show the newspapers, before making it clear exactly what they are. When did he swap the money for the newspapers? But everybody is half expecting a final twist. And that was something that Danny very much wanted to do, and, as ever, we were running out of time, so we had to cut this and change that to make time, but Danny insisted on doing that. It works because it gives the audience more information to explain the ending, so it doesn't come completely out of the blue. It's a matter of balance."

AUDIENCE MEMBER: "If you found a dead body with a suitcase full of money, what would you do?"

DANNY BOYLE: "In films, Hollywood is the dead body with huge sums of money in its suitcase. When you get sight of that, before long, there's little whispers about 'Oh, it wasn't that well written, after all, was it!?' Best friends start conspiring against each other. So we like to think that we're very loyal to each other. But who knows. When I actually get to meet Sharon, it might all change!"

JOHN GORE: "And with that thought, I'm afraid we're gonna have to wind up, we've got another showing to get in tonight. Thank you very much to Andrew and Danny for coming along this evening, and thank you all for showing up."

ANDREW MACDONALD: "And if you did like the film, don't forget to tell your friends!"

JOEL AND ETHAN COEN

by John Foster

THE WELCOME RE-RELEASE of *Blood Simple*, the quite exceptional Neo-*noir* and impactive debut from the Coen brothers, offers opportunity to re-evaluate this powerful and complex thriller. Although the movie established the Coen brothers as a new force in popular American cinema, some critical reaction to this poetic melodrama, upon its initial release in 1983, relegated the film to a cheapjack exploitation picture which dealt in buckets of blood and mindless violence. The film was almost too successful in concealing its thematics, in laterally deploying meaning under its dark, seedy surface.

Some critical response to *Blood Simple* was not dissimilar to that which greeted Michael Reeve's English historical thriller *Witchfinder General*, upon its release in 1968. *Witchfinder General*, a masterpiece of British cinema, was re-released by *Tartan Video* in 1996, a label fast establishing itself as the prime publisher of 'lost' seminal movies. The re-release followed the restoration of certain sequences cut by the producers from the original print in a movie which also identified a director able to embrace melodrama, satisfy the needs of an audience, yet utilise genre in an expression of deeply personal and impassioned themes, and in so doing, usurp the conventions of the form and the expectations of the audience.

Both *Blood Simple* and *Witchfinder General* can be defined as horror flicks, especially given the plentiful helpings of gruesome mayhem offered by each movie. Yet the films, more interested in the elements of *Psycho*-drama interlacing character relationships, also primarily function as *Psycho*logical thrillers, eliciting the fall from grace of their characters, who systematically prosecute their own destruction.

Reeves' narrative, like Michael Mann's *Manhunter* (1986) and Don Siegel's *Dirty Harry* (1971), is structured upon the döppleganger principle, where the lead-character's adversary becomes a mirror-image of himself, and his descent into violence first evokes him as a romantic hero, then as a revenge hero, and finally as an antihero. The Coens present us with the paranoid world of *noir* in all its treacle-black sleaze, depicting the ruthless if neurotic pragmatics of survival, leading the deceit, betrayal and brutal murder in a murky underbelly of lowlife Texas, where only the picture's femme fatale finally comes through the mean season the film depicts.

DREADFUL SUMMIT

The Coens were luckier than Reeves who, although half-American, functioned in the moribund context of sixties British cinema and fell victim to English cultural snobbery and its obstinate, self-regarding illiteracy concerning genre and popular art. *Blood Simple* hit the movie-houses at the right time, following the rise of the auteur theory and the explosion in film culture studies, which involved fundamental re-evaluation of popular cinema. Suddenly movie melodrama could be entertaining and meaningful at the same time, serious fun, and directors who could achieve this elusive combination became the high-priests of popular art. *Blood Simple* therefore benefited from having amongst its audience a new generation of the media literate.

Their first movie established Joel and Ethan Coen as popularist, mainstream film-makers with box-office potential, embraced hungrily by Hollywood as new-born Spielberg wunderkinds. However, their movie was too uncomfortable to become a big hit and they disabusingly insisted upon developing their own deeply personal, highly individualistic, idiosyncratic cinema. It wasn't until after the Coens flatly refused to go to LA that their own brand of oddball unpredictability was established in their subsequent films and, developing into a cult, they became impossible to pigeon-hole.

The ingredients to be later part of a richer brew were already to be in evidence in *Blood Simple*. An air of farce and some diabolical black humour, especially accompanying scenes of grisly violence, co-existed convincingly with the formal elements of realism: an intensely visual eye, a strong sense of place and atmosphere, a keen ear for dialogue. Their laconic, implicitly jaundiced view of America seemed to be the result of a European influence, being reminiscent of the sprightly irreverence of French New-Wave trace-kickers like Godard and Truffaut. Their joint sensibility, especially in its refusal to sell-out to Hollywood and their rejection of West Coast glitz and megabuck film-making, appeared closer to the tradition of experimental, innovative art-house, East Coast cinema, à la Cassavetes, Scorsese and early De Palma. Their raw, edgy cinema was not smoothed-out, diluted and plasticised; and epitomised the erstwhile tension between East Coast creativity and West Coast avarice.

There is a sense in which the Coens understood with absolute clarity that the pulp story does not get published in the slick magazine, no way does it belong there, and any attempt to streamline it would be dishonest and self-destructive; as Raymond Chandler found with self-disgust when he wrote his story *I'll Be Waiting* not for the hard-boiled pulp, *Black Mask*, but for the soft-boiled slick, *The Saturday Evening Post*. For the Coens' the power of solar-plexus film-making could only exist outside contemporary Hollywood, which had its eye on the crowd, not on the ball.

B-picture melodrama stemmed from the economic demands of studio conveyor-belt production, and its denizens worked quietly away, unheralded and unsung until the French began to discover them decades later. These seeming journeyman directors produced personal films within formulaic structures with an enviable lack of self-consciousness. That kind of freedom is not available today in the deal-driven, high-budget, A-picture Hollywood, encapsulated somewhat smugly by Robert Altman's *The Player* (1992). So artifice and compromise were banished by the Coens in favour of uniqueness of voice.

Yet the Coens also sustained the paradox that whilst exhibiting a love for the mainstream genre in their cinema - *noir*, thriller, screwball comedy, gangsters - they also appeared suspiciously satirical of it. Their laughter in the dark revealed an unease with the conventions of popular form and the reluctant tendency to ridicule it, as if wishing to distance the inevitable compromise acceptance of genre implies. And *Miller's Crossing* (1990), itself the superior film, predicted *Reservoir Dogs* (1992) with its deliberately enclosed, claustrophobic, theatrically dialogue-led ethos. In an American cinema dominated by *mise en scène*, the Coens were, perhaps perversely, prepared to go against the grain and the theology of visual gymnastics to make a movie which was stubbornly dense with dialogue and audaciously anti-imagistic.

Written by both Joel and Ethan and directed by Joel - formerly assistant editor on 1982's *The Evil Dead* - and produced by them both, *Blood Simple* occupies a deeply cynical and sanguine world. No character is unambiguous, no action pure, and certainly no one behaves with what could remotely be described as altruism. As a calling-card movie, its success was to be smartly aware of its genre and to make passing-nod references to it without appearing to pleased with itself, yet most particularly to present a genuinely minted *film noir*, pulsating with energy and tension. Some movies, such as Stephen Frears' lacklustre version of Jim Thompson's *The Grifters*(1990), and John Dahl's formidably underwhelming *Kill Me Again* (1989), borrow the clothes of *film noir* simply to look cute. They are performing poodles of movies, acutely aware of their own virtuosity, yet sunk by a lack of vitality, a failure derived of an inability to generate narrative not wholly dependent upon a film form very much of its own time, a film movement which was responsive to a particular era of contemporary America.

Roman Polanski's Neo-*noir Chinatown* (1974) refreshed the form whilst forging its own dynamic by reversing the signifying codes of *noir* and presenting us with a sunlit environment where rain, fog and darkness where omitted. Jack Nicholson can be perceived almost as an antihero and Chinatown itself becomes a country of the mind, that locale from your past which brought you low and will do so again. But the Coens went one better. Whereas Polanski's film sustains a period setting, lovingly realised, *Blood Simple* is the Texas of the eighties, bled through with all the recognisable atmospherics of film *noir*, yet with newly coined content. The movie does not simply borrow, but emulates whilst being insistent upon its own originality. The movie refuses merely to copycat. It is authored.

The surface of the film resembles the vulgar illustration from the cover of a pulp magazine, an animated *Black Mask* or *Dime Detective Weekly*. It provides echoes of the past in faithful reprise of those gaudy melodramas of the dark side. In utilising the clichés of film *noir*, the movie also reinvents them with sensuous power. The opening title sequence, compulsively gripping, classically denotes the icons of *noir*, yet with a sturdy storytelling élan, whilst even referencing a sister genre, the adrenaline-rush, young-couple-on-the-run film *noir* road movie, derived from the true story of Bonnie and Clyde, created by Fritz Lang's 1937 movie, *You Only Live Once*.

The titles of *Blood Simple* hammer B-picture style upon a car's rain-swept windscreen, also doubling as the movie-screen, in affectionate tribute to Robert Aldrich's *noir* masterpiece, *Kiss Me Deadly* (1955), which sustains a similar opening title sequence. We are given the smogged night, the steaming rain, the lone car travelling into danger, the windscreen wipers swishing, the young couple in flight from imagined threat as well as from themselves. There is no music. The music is the sound of the rain, the car engine, the windscreen wipers' regular heartbeat rhythm. There is a low key, throttled, Chandleresque exchange between the nervous duo, night people, scared of being followed, driving to a doomed love affair. It is a totally electric opening, brimming with menace and veracity.

It is quite difficult to relate to the main characters in *Blood Simple*, the Coens do not make it easy for us, and this perhaps accounts for the film's mixed reception amongst audiences: there is no hero figure to root for. The protagonists are not especially glamorous and the film is conceived with the eye of a documentarian, which again extends it beyond its genre status. The raw reality and its abrasive way of seeing the world invests the film with a harsh perception. The story is also entirely unpredictable, so that it delivers none of the reassuring outcomes associated with the formulaic. It continually arrests and startles. A dour cloud hovers over the characters and their environs, which are mood-laden and effectively evoke trapped, dead-end lives. Lonely highways, cheap motel rooms, tacky office interiors, down-at-heel bars. This could be a Jim Thompson novel.

The protagonists are confused and inconsistent, itinerants in this alienating urban landscape. They seem directionless, pulled by the whim of ship-that-pass passion, as selfish as they are impersonal. Accurate and well-realised creations, empathy with them and their tawdry ambitions is consistently undercut by the capricious verve of real, unpredictable people, populating a real world. Yet they occupy the dead-man's shoes of noir stereotypes without ever becoming stereotypical, without their individuality ever being effaced or undermined.

Frances McDormand's slyly predacious femme fatale, the lone survivor of the debacle, has earned accusations of misogyny. She is an updated femme, conforming to the image of streetwise allure, yet emboldened and modishly self-sufficient. The men die around her, yet she is equally vulnerable to fear and violence, and overcomes through intelligence, nous and good fortune. She seduces with lithe but unceremonious animalism, down-to-earth, non-rococo and without coyness in her ministrations, and a million miles from Dietrich. Her violence is sudden and vehement, sourced in her independence and feisty desire for self-determination. She is a feminist femme.

John Getz, her lover, is the hapless, limp-wristed victim-hero from countless film noirs, perhaps most famously realised in the character of Walter Neff in Billy Wilder's *Double Indemnity* (1944), and, fifty years subsequently by the afore-mentioned John Dahl with his well-crafted but spineless post-modern noir, *The Last Seduction* (1994). The noir victim-hero is the masochistic protagonist who is compromised and used with cool ruthlessness by his De Sadean mistress; she presents an image of strong independence in a patriarchal society and offers sexual imperialism which feminism has responded ambiguously towards, but who clearly is a product of male infantile sexual insecurity. Yet the Coens' victim -hero is more lifelike because of characterisation again subjected to rehabilitating realism. He becomes drawn into a situation which will end in his death through stupidity and lack of resilience rather than any proactive stitching-up of the femme he lamely falls for.

He is his own fallguy. Non A-list actors without the egos which come with superstar status greatly contribute to the authentic intensity and brooding naturalism this has on offer, and Getz's appropriately self-effacing performance serves the unsensational ethos of the movie well. His Hickville wimp becomes a killer by default rather than through any femmed spider-web, and thus, in rejecting this over-familiar plot-line, the film quietly comments upon the unlikelihood of any such preconceived feline gambit, the stuff of formulaic fiction: the events in the film result not from womanly wiles but from star-crossed love, they ferment in the dark oasis of mistrust and paranoia, the bizarre chaos of the narrative echoing the neurosis of the characters. In adapting the noir scenario of James M Cain's steamy lovers' triangle, the Coens modernise it and imbue it with credibility.

The *Psycho*drama-oriented plot-lines of thrillers such as *Double Indemnity* and *The Postman Always Rings Twice* (made in 1946 & 1981) concern the unfaithful deadly nightshade who pressurises her lover to murder the cuckolded husband, usually for money. In *Blood Simple*, only passion counts. The Coens turn this traditional victim-hero storyline on its head, for it is the husband (Dan Hedaya) who hires M. Emmett Walsh's balefully corrupt private eye. And, by imposing his own crazed agenda, the eye vents havoc, with an ensuing rollercoaster of violence, including a premature burial which is grotesque in humour as well as horror.

M. Emmett Walsh, combining threat with absurdity, brutality with facetiousness, provides a delicious performance of Wellesian stature, reminiscent in fact, of Welles' own corrupt lawman in *Touch Of Evil* (1958), yet benefiting here from greater restraint and a lack of self-indulgence. What communicates itself strongly is the Coens' love of their creation in Walsh's character, their residual affection for him is very evident, that he is their favourite amongst the ensemble upon the basis that the glitter of evil is far more interesting and compelling than small-town treachery. The baddie is frequently the heroic manqué of many films, in almost all of Hitchcock, and especially *Strangers on a Train* (1951), and notably in George Sluizer's original version of *The Vanishing* (1988), whose shocking buried-alive dénouement was surely grave-robbed from the earlier *Blood Simple*.

The nightmarish quality of the film functions like a bad recurring dream, underwritten by the illogic of dreams and their fatalistic quality. The hallucinatory texture of noir is thereby induced in *Blood Simple*, but with assurance, flair and originality. Flashback structures are frequently the storytelling method of many film noirs. The flashbacks themselves operate like opaque memory film and reflect the subconscious emotions and confusions of the narrator. Often, as in the Edward Dmytryk 1944 version of Chandler's *Farewell, My Lovely*, flashback recollections are employed as Kafkaesque dream-sequences, expressive of the lead character's unstable psyche.

Without using them specifically as a storytelling device, the Coens cannily introduce nightmare sequences aligned to the characters experiencing them, but do so in a way which make these sequences initially appear to be real and a part of the film's narrative. Only after the sequence has horrifically climaxed are we disabused of its reality and realise that the experience was lived only in the psyched-up paranoias of the characters. This effect is superbly achieved, notably the imagined resurrection of the buried-alive husband, timed incisively to shock but also to amuse. We laugh own over-active imaginations and are made to feel as foolish as the characters. It is a devilish device and one to realised with greater emphasis upon surrealism by the Coens in *Barton Fink* (1991).

The dreadful summit climax of *Blood Simple* is rich in resonance. It combines tension and terror with black humour and the farce of violent events. Walsh's deeply sinister gumshoe victimises McDormand's frenzied femme, in sequences which are as ludicrously accidental as they are frighteningly credible. The sardonic edge of the movie is empowered in its fulsomness in these closing sequences, with the death of the barn-like Walsh and McDormand's rebirth, following her torturous trial-by-fire. Yet her successful emergence at the close of the film is not celebrated with golden cloud heroics. Only exhaustion and the dead left around her are featured. Relief, yes, but no sense of victory.

The verisimilitudes of *Blood Simple* are greatly dependent upon the Coens' ironic sense of the absurd. Yet the humour is very carefully controlled and never permitted to become overtly satirical or fun-poking. The Brothers Coen , chuckling quietly with delight, keep their tongues very firmly in their cheeks.

BLOOD SIMPLE

Dir: Ethan Coen Dist: Electric Pictures. Cert: 18.
Dur: 99 mins. Released: 1983.

JOEL AND ETHAN COEN

by Richard Armstrong

TAKE A CLOSE LOOK at a good large-scale map of the American mid-west and you will see a landscape black with small towns. Drive through this landscape and you will be subjected to the garish hopes and pinched dreams of a million truck-stops, loan companies and car-dealerships. Midwesterners like to think that this is where the real work of America is done. Indeed, fast-talking Easterners and laid-back Californians both believe that Midwesterners don't know how to enjoy themselves. But what they often do not realise is that, behind the industrious Midwestern facade, a lot of thought and energy is being used up in the perpetration of murder.

(Re)released in cinemas and on video, in time to (roughly) coincide with each other, The Coen Brothers' *Blood Simple* (1983) and *Fargo* (1995) are two of the best observed and most engrossing examinations of violent crime ever to have been set among the plain and dead-straight roads of the American heartland. Yet, in mood and treatment, their Texas and their Minnesota are worlds apart.

"There's more to life than a little money, you know!", Police-chief Gunderson (Frances McDormand) of Brainerd, Minnesota, tells Gaear Grimsrud (Peter Stormare), after he has shot a state trooper and two passers-by, permanently silenced his hostage and fed his partner into a wood-chipper. If the inhabitants of the tiny Texan town of *Blood Simple* seem surly, already wise to the iniquities of their fellow men and women, those of Brainerd and Fargo actually believe in those pinched dreams behind the tawdry neons. It may seem that you are on your own in these snow-covered grasslands, but Minnesotans still reckon that God, love and an honest day's work will pull them through every time.

Looking every bit as dark as a fifties B *noir*, *Blood Simple* is suffused with a mood of fear and loathing which the folksy humour of *Fargo* constantly checks when it threatens to erupt in Minnesota. The scene where Abby's (McDormand again) lover Ray (John Getz) tries to dispose of her dead husband Marty (Dan Hedaya) in a ploughed field, seems to occupy that filmic twilight where the grubby sticksville homicide of, say, Robert

RAISING MINNESOTA

Siodmak's *The Killers* grazes against George A. Romero's zombie cycle. In *Fargo*, the snow-swept field where Grimsrud and Showalter (the ubiquitous Steve Buscemi) leave the dead trooper and witnesses, is investigated, by contrast, on a pristine morning with nothing to hide. Both films may be set in communities far from the main urban drag of contemporary American crime cinema, but *Blood Simple* and *Fargo* part company over the tiny matter of how they interpret those pinched dreams.

As Marge Gundersen drives Grimsrud away, she chatters gaily *"And here ya are, and it's a beautiful day."* No matter how many car dealers lay plans to kidnap their wives for profit, and how many poor souls are thereby murdered, in Fargo you can always bounce back with an optimistic word and a smile. But *"Down here in Texas, you're on your own"* private dick Visser (M. Emmet Walsh) drones in *Blood Simple*.

If Abby cannot stop dreaming of the bloody corpse of her husband; offsetting the dangerous doings of Grimsrud and Showalter are the warm and dorkish locals. Their taciturn monosyllables inflected with the sing-song nuances of a Scandinavian heritage, there is a plain and simple pragmatism to the folk of Fargo which undermines the horror which violent outsiders bring to these little towns. Significantly, there are a wealth of real Minnesota communities seen or mentioned in *Fargo*, adding to the overdetermined integrity of this society. Conversely, in the ineffable darkness of *Blood Simple*, nowhere is named.

Jerry (William H. Macy) Lundegaard's dream may be so pinched as to prompt him to desperate measures, but he is totally unprepared for first degree murder. These Minnesotans clearly do not speak the same language as the 'funny-looking' Showalter, whose demand for some 'action' is met with stupefaction by the locals. But Minnesotans communicate well with one another. Mired in darkness and suspicion, *Blood Simple* has no equivalent of the supportive rapport between Marge and Norm Gunderson (John Carroll Lynch). While he plies his pregnant wife with fried eggs and ham, she gives solace when his mallard painting fails to make it onto the 29¢ stamp. And when she arrives at the scene of the crime, her colleague scurries over with hot coffee. In precious few police procedurals are cops as cosy as this.

In *Fargo*, lengthy conversations are punctuated by shots of cars cruising through the snowy landscape, its inhabitants, in their padded jackets and ear-muffs, looking for all the world like amiable penguins in some contemporary ice-age. There is no more forlorn a moment in the film than the overhead shot, seemingly taken from miles away, where Jerry trudges back towards his car, parked in a whited-out lot, spindly saplings all around him.

Uniting *Blood Simple* and *Fargo* is the sheer desperation which marks their protagonist's desire to overreach themselves. It is as though, without a desperate act on these creeping plains, the boredom and inertia will destroy even those with the strength to dream. In *Blood Simple*, every object seems charged, poised to take part in a bad night in hell. Notice how Barry Sonnenfeld's camera lingers on Visser's lighter at his last meeting with Marty. While, every time Abby's phone rings, it brings the promise of violent death. Indeed, *Blood Simple* is full of images of the dead or apparently dead, as though to ironise the deadly pace of life here. Arguably, the choice facing Abby and Ray is between the possibilities unleashed by a single irrevocable act, or the ennui of a straitened life in a Texan town. The Coens are great story-tellers, and, as Marge and Norm snuggle down in bed, the story of the bad guys who disrupted the calm of Brainerd seems as remote as Texas is from Minnesota.

BLOOD SIMPLE
Dir: Ethan Coen Dist: Electric Pictures. Cert: 18.
Dur: 99 mins. Released: 1983.

FARGO
Dir: Ethan Coen Dist: Polygram. Cert: 18.
Dur: 98 mins. Released: 1996.

BRIAN DE PALMA

by John Ashbrook

Memo found screwed up in a skip on the Paramount Studios backlot:

Good morning Mr De Palma,

The photo is of a known Scientologist called **Thomas Cruise**, he has something of a reputation for being a talented actor, although evidence for this is largely anecdotal. In recent years he has become a recluse, allegedly refusing to get out of bed for less than twenty million dollars (paid into numbered Swiss bank accounts).

This much is known: whenever he breaks cover, a media storm rages around him, fuelled, no doubt, by his elusiveness at all other times. He is married to an Australian Oscar-nominee whose career is rising in profile faster than his. Although he has made many successful films, none have yet spawned the series of sequel*s* that have maintained the careers of Sean Connery, Clint Eastwood, Harrison Ford and, of course, Macauley Culkin.

Your mission, Brian, should you choose to accept it, is to spare no expense in adapting yet another 1960s TV show into a spectacular event-movie which will secure Mr Cruise's seat on the gravy train for life. No, we aren't referring to 'The Munsters'.

Needless to say, if the film is a flop, the producers will disavow any knowledge of your activities.

Good luck, Brian, this memo will self-destruct in ... no it won't, this is a no-smoking country these days. Damn.

THE MAN WHO KNEW TOO MUCH

IN THE PRE-TITLE SEQUENCE of *Mission:Impossible*, we are introduced to star/icon Tom Cruise when he tears off a disguising rubber mask, revealing the fresh-faced all-American we have come to know and expect. Brian De Palma has recently torn away a similar mask to reveal an inner person, simpler but arguably more attractive than before.

The old De Palma would not have been capable of steering a simplistic big-budget extravaganza to the screen, he would have darkened and deepened it as a matter of course. But maintaining artistic integrity is obviously not enough, after all, he lives in the land of opportunity and can't help but notice that it hasn't knocked as loud as on his friends' doors: *"It's frustrating to have a success and not a blockbuster. I'm surrounded by associates who have monster hits"* † Since his associates include Spielberg, Lucas and Scorsese, this comment is truer now than when it was made in 1979!

It seems that the new De Palma is determined to at long-last compete on an equal footing with the men who emerged from film-school beside him, but soon lost sight of him in their career-view mirrors. Spielberg, Lucas, even Coppola have eclipsed De Palma in terms of success and bankability, yet their films are rarely as fascinating. Having decided that enough is enough, he is suddenly playing the game by their rules. The question is whether or not the newly unleashed De Palma personality is for real, or is the discarded one merely being suppressed?

Traditionally, Brian De Palma doesn't feel, he thinks. This is an attribute which has become increasingly uncommon in film-makers as post-modernism and the influence of Messrs Spielberg and Lucas take ever greater hold. Films no longer tell, they just show, they are proud to evoke emotion over cognition every time, yet this isn't and has never been enough for De Palma. Whereas the Lucasfilm and Amblin empires have been built on a bedrock of Saturday morning matinees and pulp fictions, De Palma (who has always resisted the temptation of creating a corporate vanity label under which to umbrella his films) always drew inspiration from 'higher' art - initially the audacity of Welles and the new-wave verité of Godard, then increasingly and more blatantly from the manipulative mastery of Hitchcock.

The practical upshot of this clinical precision has been films that are not about people (save in so far as the people who function within the world contrived by De Palma) but are about set-pieces. Strings of high gloss pearls separated but held together by thin threads of plot. Certainly, the movies of his more successful contemporaries build to their spectacular highs - what are the T-Rex attack in *Jurassic Park* or the Death-Star trench in *Star Wars* if they aren't set-pieces to which the films have carefully steered us? The difference is that the techniques employed in family films are simpler and the tension more reliant on the audience's empathy for the characters. Until *Mission:Impossible* this has been a consideration beyond De Palma's grasp.

Film is not a passive medium for him, he doesn't want the audience to sit there, munching popcorn, brain idling, eyes wide; he wants active involvement and appreciation, and wishes more directors would refrain from taking the easy and populist way out: *"Do you really want to go to work each day and shoot two-shots of people talking to each other? ... that's not directing, it's being asleep at the switch. When you can put the camera anywhere and you can make it do anything, it's like you can put anything on that canvas. Well, why not think about it a bit?"* ††

This is why his early films are among the handful made in America to feature sparkling use of split-screen. Multiple perspectives on the same screen in *Sisters, Phantom of the Paradise* and most famously (though least effectively) in *Carrie*, serve to give the audience more information than the characters have (one of the techniques identified by Hitch for generating suspense) as well as pushing the compliant viewers back into their seat and reminding them that they are watching a movie. In *Sisters* it is used to heighten one of those *two-shots of people talking to each other* by rounding off a tense race to hide a corpse with a conversation in a doorway - the left hand side of the screen shows it from over the police officer's shoulder, the right side is over Margot Kidder's, their respective motivations reflected by their opposition on the screen. That is how to make the ordinary extraordinary!

Never satisfied to merely grab an audience, De Palma will throw in distancing devices right at the height of the tension - such as the climactic burial sequence in *Body Double* when Craig Wasson, fighting for his life as the villain attempts to plant him six feet under, suddenly segues in his mind (but on our screen) to the pretend burial scene we saw on a movie set earlier. Here Wasson decides to face up to his crippling claustrophobia and, with that decision, suddenly cuts back to the real confrontation. Another way of deliberately interrupting the suspension of disbelief is through the blatant allusion to another film. Why else does De Palma cut away from Margot Kidder's knife-murder of her boyfriend in *Sisters* to watch the shadow of the knife stabbing the wall, as Bernard Herrmann re-works his *Psycho* strings? Why else does he interrupt the climactic shoot-out in *The Untouchables* with a slo-mo retread of *Battleship Potemkin's* Odessa Steps scene? He cannot take pride in getting the audience excited about the incident, they have to get excited about the technique, or *the visual grammar* as he prefers to call it.

"Audiences are very much used to being told what they are going to see and feel, so they're very comfortable with that. Any movie that makes you a little uncomfortable is good news to me, because it means you are experiencing things you are not familiar with. But when you make a film that plays with form it throws a lot of people off. They're not used to playing with form the way we did in the '60s and '70s with Godard or Antonioni." ††

In interview, De Palma comes across as humourless and evasive, he obviously does not enjoy explaining himself, but is constantly required to do so because it is almost unprecedented in cinema for a credible and talented professional to have based so much of his work around that of another. Although he perpetually rejects claims that he has built his career on plagiarising Hitchcock, he cannot and indeed does not deny the obvious and deliberate debt he owes: *"I wanted to make films based on visual grammar, and Hitchcock is the master of visual grammar, so I made a whole bunch of films based on Hitchcock story ideas, Hitchcock visual ideas, and basically learned the grammar."* †††

Of course, this alone doesn't explain why *a whole bunch* should have kept him busy from *Sisters* in '71 through to *Raising Cain* over twenty years later but, as ever, he has a rehearsed answer ready for anyone who thinks to bring this up: *"Hitchcock made fifty movies and explored every kind of visual grammar of suspense and action. So somewhere, if you're working with this type of visual storytelling, you're going to be using material Hitchcock has used before ... It's almost impossible not to fall into his grammar, which is, of course, the best."* ††

Thanks largely to De Palma's influence, the POV - point of view - shot is a mainstay of cheap horror films, serving to focus the audience's attention on whatever atrocity the viewpoint character is committing, as well as disguising said character's identity. For De Palma it is, inevitably, far more than a stylistic conceit. By cutting the character out of the frame and simply allowing you to see what they see, you can temporarily inhabit their space *"... instead of just using the camera as an objective recording device for dramatic action. Voyeurism is a direct link with a point-of-view shot."* †

It is one of the few trademark techniques that survives into *Mission:Impossible*, when Phelps sits at mission control and watches three images play across his computer screen - one from each of the mini-cameras embedded in his agents' spectacles. This neatly combines POV with split screen and, for that matter, voyeurism. However, it is achieved electronically and is an effect reproducible on any reasonably sophisticated desk-top computer. This sounds the death-knell for split-screen, a motif which can no longer be considered stylistically startling. Technology has caught up with and surpassed his vision, time then to move on.

In common with his absent father Hitchcock, De Palma is unrepentant about his fascination with the theme of voyeurism. It opens *Sisters*, with the bizarre *Candid Camera* type game-show *Peeping Toms*, then, half an hour later, when the evolving love-story suddenly hangs a left into horror territory, the new direction is heralded by a split-screen of the dying boyfriend crawling across Margot Kidder's carpet, while the journalist in the opposite building watches him clawing at the window with bloody fingers. This is clearly a reference to *Rear Window*, taken several steps further. He uses an identical set up in *Body Double* when Craig Wasson lasciviously uses a telescope initially to spy on his masturbating neighbour, then later to see an armed attacker waiting for her upstairs.

A twist on the voyeur theme is the sightless eaves-dropping that the sound engineer practices in *Blow Out*, where a rifle-mike hears a Chappaquiddick-like assassination take place, and propels John Travolta (what ever happened to him?) into a political scandal and murder mystery.

Sound, and by extension, silence are integral to De Palma's technique. The voyeurism scenes in *Body Double*, along with the impossibly long chase which fills the middle act of that movie, are performed without any significant dialogue. The stand out moment in *Mission:Impossible* is the CIA Secure Room scene, where ten of the tensest possible minutes are played out without dialogue, and largely without music:

"It all flows from visual form, which I think is a very important aspect of cinema and which no one practices anymore ... Because a whole generation of film directors have been brought up on television, on MTV essentially, they've lost the ability to work in the silent medium, which is the purest form of cinema and something, of course, that all the directors of Hitchcock's generation made films in." †††

The flaw in this argument is simply that music-videos are inherently visual above all other considerations. Narrative in music videos is as rare as it is in songs, but when it is employed it has to be communicated without dialogue - giving directors a visual sense comparable, I would say, to that of the silent directors. It is only when it is unsupported by a script that visual precocity becomes hollow and cheap. Again, fashion has caught up with De Palma, and he will soon have to contend with directors like Marco Brambilla (*Demolition Man*), David Fincher (*Seven*) and Michael Bay (*Bad Boys, The Rock*) should they be fortunate enough to find a script the equal of their visual sense.

De Palma sees the job of directing as epitomising both the voyeuristic side to his work, and the dualistic side: *"Directing is standing behind the camera and watching what other people do ... You have to make things happen and then you have to sit back and see what you have created in order to make it effective, you have to be detached. So it's a schizophrenic profession."* ††

Conflicting identities in a single body has been a perpetual theme of De Palma's work and, it seems, his working practice. It is a theme lifted from *Psycho* but explored more fully in the mordant mistaken-identity melodrama of *Vertigo*. In *Sisters*, guilt over living when her Siamese twin died has fractured Margot Kidder's personality into both Danielle and Dominique. In *Phantom of the Paradise*, William Finley is scarred for life and withdraws into the guise of The Phantom. In *Obsession*, Cliff Robertson courts the image of his lost wife, only to find that she is in fact his daughter. In *Dressed To Kill*, Michael Caine plays a *Psycho*logist by day and a *Psycho*-sexual sociopath by night. In *Body Double*, Melanie Griffith is hired to pretend to be a murder victim. In *Raising Cain*, John Lithgow was systematically traumatised by his scientist father into developing multiple personalities.

There have, one hardly need add, been two strands to De Palma's career, two strings of pearls, two personalities at the helm. The first and longest serving turns out sophisticated thrillers in the Hitchcockian mode, the second uses the same techniques, but applies them to stories with entirely different concerns. This is the De Palma of the gangster epics *Scarface, The Untouchables*, and *Carlito's Way*, of the alleged comedies *Wise Guys* and *Bonfire of the Vanities* and even of the Viet-Nam crime drama *Casualties of War*.

These are De Palma's mainstream movies and they as critically and financially mixed as any of the thrillers which are so obviously closer to his heart. The undercurrents are still there, of course, though buried deeper than usual. The theme of suppressed duality is at its most subtle in the place you least expect to find it - in *Scarface*. Pacino's deeply buried love for his own sister, and for his best and only friend Manny-Boy, finally manifests itself as self-destructive *Psycho*tic jealousy, with him brutally and impulsively executing Manny mere hours after refusing to blow up a car full of children because it was unethical.

As immortalised by Pacino, Tony Montana is an illiterate savage, barely civilised yet highly ambitious. He is the antithesis of the *Godfather* style gangster, he has no belief in anything save himself, and no concept of politics. Early on he states that in America *"... you gotta get the money first. When you get the money then you get the power. When you get the power, then you get the girls."* But when he has the money, the power and the girl of his dreams, he finds himself isolated behind security patrolled walls, his natural paranoia honed to a science. He achieves omniscience through having a closed-circuit TV system installed, so he can watch split-screen images of his world. In his hall a gaudy neon sculpture declares 'The World Is Yours.' His irresponsible power over those around him results in all of their deaths. His own is a mirror of the assassination he himself conducted to get himself on the ladder of success. Montana is a virulent disease, fatal to all who contract it.

In *The Untouchables* (De Palma's first adaptation of a TV series) violence is also a disease, a social disease, spread by another Scarface - Robert De Niro's Capone. Kevin Costner under the tutelage of his surrogate father Sean Connery is transformed by the disease from the clean cut upstanding man who saw wrong and knew how to right it, to a soldier who *"... violated every law I have sworn to uphold; I have become what I beheld and I believe I have done right."* He has been absorbed into The Chicago Way, he has become that which he despises, and only in this way can he exert any control over his city. The transformation is painful and permanent.

In *Bonfire of the Vanities*, Tom Hanks' Sherman McCoy is transformed from a showy, arrogant success to a lowlife disaster, drowning in his own ignorance. He is dragged from the polished granite penthouses of Manhattan to the desolation of Brooklyn through being involved in an accident when out with his mistress. Being of low moral integrity is the key to success on Wall St, but on most other streets it is not a way to make friends. The duality of these characters, the dilemma they must fight through, is the opposition between integrity and success. The message of these movies is simple and clear - transformation is painful but essential.

Slowly, torturously, the realisation must have dawned on De Palma that no one was interested in perpetual re-runs of fifties thrillers. No one shared his fascination with visual grammar of suspense and action. If he ever wanted to enjoy the accolades and financial achievements of his contemporaries it was time to put away childish things.

Raising Cain was De Palma's last word on his great love. It is replete with references to his own previous references to Hitchcock, as well as drawing on the other great paean to voyeurism and manipulation *Peeping Tom.* As Carter Nix (a name which means 'nothing' and yet is also an allusion to mid-seventies American politics) John Lithgow, who has been an easily-overlooked but constant collaborator with De Palma over the years, not only contains the personalities of himself and his brother, he is also the ghost of his own father. As the trauma develops, he assumes the identity of Margo (as in Kidder!) and becomes a homicidal woman. When he needs to hide a body, he locks it into a car which he sinks into a lake. It is, for all the world, the coda to De Palma's first career, his way of saying good-bye to his obsessions. Clearing the decks for him to devote himself to a concerted effort at achieving once and for all that mainstream blockbuster which has always eluded him.

And now we have *Mission:Impossible*, as obvious and visceral as any summer movie could hope to be, and as such it has earned more money than any other bearing De Palma's name: tickling $400 million in receipts as I write this, with the bonanza of video rentals and sales still ahead of it.

He has achieved his goal and earned the kind of money that all his old college friends (save Scorsese - who never makes money, but no one seems to mind) have long been accustomed to. Certainly *Mission:Impossible* contains moments that are ubiquitous De Palma, but the short-hand grammar for a multiple or transformative personalities is no longer the split-screen, it is the computer generated morph - as when Jon Voight tears off his face to reveal Tom Cruise beneath. Computer effects and star names are the currency of big-budget movies, Scripts are prepared methodically and minutely not as a step to creating something intellectually challenging, but because there can be no room for unnecessary shooting when your star is being paid $20 million for twelve weeks' work.

Characters are still ciphers, but their significance is not decided upon in the director's mind, that is the responsibility of financier's board meetings. The control that De Palma typically exerts over a production is now the Hollywood norm, but the director is not the one in control - that is now the task of a phalanx of producers. De Palma is part of the machine which has itself transformed over the last twenty years. The successes of Amblin and Lucasfilm (and their good right arm Industrial Light and Magic) have produced an environment where riches beyond the dream of avarice can be won, providing the product conforms to the pre-set pattern.

Ever the pessimist, De Palma must be writhing in agony at the cost of his new-found success: *"The problem is that by even dealing with the devil, you become devilish to a certain extent. You need the machine. And once you use it you are a tainted human being."* † This is surely the message of *Phantom of the Paradise.*

His outlook is unremittingly bleak, he sees the fate of the artist as a choice between being absorbed or being rejected: *"Look at Welles, he [was] the greatest director in the world and he [couldn't] get a job and he sold out. Orson Welles on the Johnny Carson show doesn't give us much to hope for. That is the story of this business. It's right there for you to see. Beware. Be aware of what you're getting into."* †

In the mighty battle between integrity and success over the soul of Brian De Palma, success has won. For now.

† ***De Palma quoted in* The Movie Brats *by Michael Pye and Lynda Myles. Faber and Faber, 1979.***

†† ***De Palma quoted in* Out Of The Ashes *by Peter Keough in* Sight and Sound *Vol. 2 # 8, 1992.***

††† ***De Palma quoted in the* Bonfire of the Vanities *edition of* The South Bank Show*, 1990.***

JOE ESZTERHAS

...presided over by Steve Holland.

SPOILER WARNING: The following feature reveals a lot of movie endings. If you really hate that sort of thing, skip onto the next article.

Originally written for Crime Time #4's Pulp Fictions *column, the introduction refers to an earlier interview with author Joe Lansdale, whose novels (*Savage Season, Mucho Mojo*, etc) were referred to as modern day pulp. For those of you who know Pulp solely through the Tarantino movie, the pulps were popular in the early-to-mid 1900s, mass produced magazines printed on pulp paper. The pulps produced writers like Raymond Chandler, Max Brand and Lester Dent, and pulp writing is often used as a synonym for crime noir in the Sam Spade/Philip Marlowe sense, or for larger than life heroes like Doc Savage or The Shadow. See also Graham Barnfield's* Hard Boiled Cities *interview for more explanation.*

PULP FICTION DIDN'T DIE with the magazine industry's switch to digest size. Take Joe Lansdale as an example of a now sorta mainstream writer with an attitude who was a direct descendant of the pulps, via the likes of Mike Shayne and the hardcover mid-list. But if Lansdale has risen over the past few years to writing for the modern equivalent of *Argosy* or *All-Story Magazine*, where are all the descendants of the other magazines? Where in the mainstream can you go to find the descendants of *Dime Mystery Magazine* and the other weird-menace pulps?

OK, so you've lost the thread of the analogy already because you don't know what the hell *Dime Mystery Magazine* was. Here I have to turn to my old friend Mike Ashley for a definition of the weird-menace, or terror, pulps. "*The basic idea of the terror tale,*" Mike writes, "*was that of a bizarre mystery where our hero, and more often our heroine, is menaced by some character with a warped sense of justice. As the field 'developed,' or perhaps degenerated, there was an increasing emphasis on sex and sadism ... The dénouement, however, no matter how bizarre the mystery, usually had a mundane explanation.*"

Which set me thinking about the glossy, modern Hollywood sex thriller. I applied the definition to *Jagged Edge*, which has Teddy Barnes (Glenn Close)

ASSESSING ESZTERHAS

defending Jack Forrester (Jeff Bridges) when he is accused of savagely slaughtering his wife. She is being 'stalked', if you like, by an anonymous tipster who supplies leads which eventually get Jack released. She herself has a warped sense of justice, taking the case as a way of redeeming herself from the knowledge that years earlier she helped send an innocent man to jail, a man who has recently hung himself. The dénouement was, to say the least, more mundane, the twist in the tail being that Jack really was the murderer but had plotted the murder years before and laid a false trail leading to his wife's lover. Hardly a surprise.

You can apply the same definition to *Basic Instinct*: in this case Detective Nick Curran (Michael Douglas) is stalked by might-be murderess Catherine Tramell (Sharon Stone) whom he is investigating for the savage slaughter of her boyfriend. His career is on the rocks, she has a Psychology degree and is able to twist him around her little finger. Suspicion falls on a few people, but at the end of the day she did it.

Which, in turn, set me thinking about the guy who wrote both the above movies, Joe Eszterhas.

What is it about Eszterhas that bends people so out of shape? He's become the whipping boy of Hollywood scriptwriters, too outspoken, too aggressive, too successful. A couple of flop movies has made Eszterhas a legitimate target of comments: *"You've read one script, you've read them all,"* said one anonymous Hollywood executive last year. Sorry? An executive in Hollywood complaining about derivative stories? Did this guy remain anonymous because he'd just ordered *Die Hard 4* or maybe *Nightmare on Elm Street 9*? Or maybe he was one of the execs begging for an Eszterhas script after *Basic Instinct* took over $350 million world-wide, pushing the price of an Eszterhas story to $4 million, and post-*Showgirls* was thinking he may have bought a pooch instead of a thoroughbred. Hollywood isn't just chiding a successful man for going belly-up on a couple of projects: they've got their teeth into him and they are tearing at his flesh.

So, we're going to play Pulp Fiction Crown Court. I'm acting for the prosecution (and the defence), and it's up to you to decide: Is Joe Eszterhas the Weird Terror Pulp Writer of the Nineties?

OPENING REMARKS FOR THE DEFENCE:

"I grew up in a blue-collar, working neighbourhood and had a lot of juvenile scrapes." - Joe Eszterhas, 1995.

Joe Eszterhas was born during an air raid in a barn in Csakany Doroszlo, Hungary, on November 23, 1944, with the aid of a local midwife. His parents were fleeing Hungary and eventually moved to America when he was six where he attended Cathedral Latin High School in Cleveland on a scholarship, the poor kid whose clothes came from the Salvation Army shop. Even the brothers who taught at the school would make fun of his clothes.

Eszterhas' mother was diagnosed a schizophrenic when he was thirteen, and remained so until her death ten years later. In Hungary, his father had been a writer, and it was into journalism that Joe moved after college, taking reporting jobs on Dayton and Cleveland newspapers. In 1971, he was fired from his job on the Cleveland Plain Dealer for fabricating an interview, but a week later was snapped up by *Rolling Stone* as a feature writer during its 'gonzo journalism' heyday. Eszterhas was writing about bikers and narcs, and making his point at editorial meetings by stabbing the conference table with a hunting knife.

Eszterhas' first novel was published in 1974; *Charlie Simpson's Apocalypse* was nominated for the *National Book Award.* After two more forgotten novels, he penned his first screenplay, *F.I.S.T.*, at the suggestion of a Hollywood executive. The film was picked up by producer Norman Jewison who approached stars like Al Pacino and Jack Nicholson without success. The script kicked around for a while until Sylvester Stallone (hot off the back of *Rocky*) agreed to take the rôle. In *Stallone: A Heroes Story*, a lick-arse biography by Jeff Rovin, Jewison is quoted as saying *"[Stallone] called me the next day and told me it was one of the best scripts he had ever read and he wanted to do it."* He wanted to play Johnny Kovak, head of the powerful Federated Inter-State Truckers union, but...

"Johnny Kovak was a dastardly guy, the most rotten human being to walk the earth. At the end, when he gets killed, we would all cheer. I said I would do the picture if I could tailor the part to me." Which Stallone did, under Jewison's supervision, to make Kovak a man *"who made deals under duress, but who in the end rectified all of it with intelligent business handling. The labor leader I portray brings dignity to working men."* Stallone's rewrite reduced the movie to a *Rocky* rehash, even writing an ending in which Kovak throws up his clenched fist at the Senate buildings where he has been under trial. Jewison went with a Hoffa-style ending in which he disappeared.

Only in the novelisation by Eszterhas does he die. *"To have Kovak die is a total downer,"* said Stallone at the time. The film stank. Read the book instead. It's fiery and unsentimental and a damn sight more powerful than the prettied-up movie. Eszterhas' public fighting with Stallone (claiming Stallone was stealing his script and wanting credit to feed his ego) was a sign of things to come.

OPENING REMARKS FOR THE PROSECUTION:

"I see myself as a gentle and kind man." - Joe Eszterhas, 1995.

So he had a rough upbringing? So what? Does that give the man the right to make bad movies? Just look at his early career...

It took six years for Eszterhas to hit the major league with *Basic Instinct*, but he'd had a couple of milestones along the way. His second movie, *Flashdance* -

an inane feel-good movie about a steel-worker who becomes a dancer - was a big hit. *Variety* commented that the film had *"more crotch shots than [the muscle movie]* Personal Best*"* although that's down to (1) the attractiveness of 18-year-old Jennifer Beals' body, (2) Adrian Lyne's fascination with sexual matters - he went on to make *9 1/2 Weeks, Fatal Attraction* and *Indecent Proposal*, (3) that wasn't Jennifer Beals - it was her body double, or (4) all the above, rather than Eszterhas' script or Tom Hedley's story. If it wasn't for Tom Hedley's draft script, you might think that Eszterhas was already hitting the formula of strong, female characters. *Jagged Edge* took him into courtroom drama, with its motivated and well-performed female lead, Teddy Barnes, falling for her client. *Hearts of Fire* was another musical number, which uncomfortably cast Bob Dylan and stank; *Big Shots* (which I've not seen) is described as a *"so-so juvenile adventure"*; *Betrayed* was a full-blown and prescient drama about the white supremacist movement in the rural Midwest with Debra Winger as an undercover cop working as a combine girl who becomes ensnared by Tom Berenger's widowed farmer; *Checking Out* was an unsuccessful Jeff Daniels black comedy about hypochondria; *Music Box* was a far more successful return to courtroom drama in which a Chicago defence lawyer, Ann Talbot, is forced to defend her own father, a Hungarian immigrant accused of Nazi war crimes. Of these early movies, the best are the three which strongly feature female leads - *Jagged Edge* (Glenn Close), *Betrayed* (Debra Winger) and *Music Box* (Jessica Lange, nominated for an Oscar).

It's a mixed bag of work (his CV included executive producer on both *Betrayed* and *Music Box*, both directed by Constantin Costa-Gavras) which was already making Joe Eszterhas a name. He was also making tabloid news including a major bust-up with Michael Ovitz who threatened *"My footsoldiers who go up and down Wiltshire Boulevard each day will blow your brains out,"* if he quit Creative Artists Agency. Eszterhas countered the threat of blackballing with a letter that ended *"do what you must do, Mike, and fuck you,"* which somehow found its way into Variety.

You can understand why Ovitz, 'the super-agent', wanted Eszterhas to stay: his first script was picked up for $80,000 (the novelisation earned him $400,000), *Jagged Edge* pushed up the price to $250,000, and by 1989, Eszterhas was earning $1.25 million a script. Footsoldiers or not, Eszterhas moved to ICM, and his next script was auctioned off in the summer of 1990: the 120 page *Basic Instinct* was picked up by Carolco for $3 million.

FIRST WITNESS FOR THE DEFENCE

"This movie is already a very erotic mystery. The focus has to go on subtlety and on acting. If you hype the sex, the whole apple-cart gets upset." - Joe Eszterhas.

There can't be many people who haven't seen *Basic Instinct*. It sold on Sharon

Stone's sex. In fact, Paul Verhoeven wanted to up the content of lesbian sex 'to balance out' the hetero sex. Eszterhas left, and after six months Verhoeven had to admit that the film didn't need spicing up any further.

Slow-burning and, yes, highly erotic, *Basic Instinct* succeeds where many others have failed despite its very basic plot: cop-with-a-drink-problem Nick Curran investigates the murder of a rock star in which the sole suspect is the icy-but-beautiful Catherine Tramell. What lifts the movie out of the muddy weave of clichés is the controlled building of their relationship. Catherine, as irresistible as a Siren, toys with Nick's emotions with skill and subtlety, pressing buttons (his drinking, his habit of shooting first and asking questions later, his being investigated by Internal Affairs for same). She's in control. There's that much discussed leg-crossing scene where the physical reality of it (Is she wearing anything? Does she show anything?) has buried the meaning of it: a row of hard-bitten cops line up to intimidate a confession out of her; in one simple move she turns the tables on them (yeah, but how many cigarettes does she light?). The leg-crossing scene is the perfect example of where the apple-cart gets tipped over. You forget that the film's well paced, well shot and well acted because Sharon Stone happens to have nice legs. In that moment, Sharon Stone became a star (and her price rose from the $250,000 she got for *Basic Instinct* by a factor of ten for *Sliver*) and Joe Eszterhas and Paul Verhoeven became invisible.

But not for long.

FIRST WITNESS FOR THE PROSECUTION:
"We live in a town where you don't root for your friends to fail; you root for your friends to die." - Joe Eszterhas, 1995.

Sliver the screenplay and *Sliver* the Ira Levin novel are almost completely different works. In the book, the heroine is Kay Norris, in the film Cally Norris (Sharon Stone). The William Baldwin character Zeke Hawkins was Pete Henderson in the book - in fact, very few of the major players survive without a name change, a personality change, or a circumstances change. The plot of the novel is simplified down to one very plain theme: voyeurism. In the movie, Zeke's Oedipal fascination with his mother (whom he only ever saw on TV) is hinted at; in the novel it's central to the plot, down to a contrived blinding at the end.

In fact, if you've seen the film you've not seen it all. There was a completely different ending which involves Cally and Zeke flying out to Hawaii. But test audiences didn't like the fact that he was the murderer and got away with it, so the ending was rewritten by Eszterhas in three days and reshot. That pretty much sums up the movie, which is a mess of 'can't quite figure it out' scenes that sort of relate but don't get you anywhere. The film has none of the pacing, tension and sexual chemistry between stars that *Basic Instinct* had: Billy Baldwin looks like a hick and you cannot believe that he's a walking Orgasmatron who could snare Sharon Stone and fuck her into wanting to share his dirty secrets.

This has been described as Eszterhas' *Rear Window*. But stripping the plot of all its other elements and concentrating on the peepshow aspects of Levin's plot has caused a major flaw in how we perceive the whole movie. As Hitchcock noted, one of his reviewers complained *"that Rear Window was a horrible film because the hero spent all of his time peeping out of the window. What's so horrible about that. Sure, he's a snooper, but aren't we all?"* If *Sliver* intended playing on our guilt, it failed. Who wouldn't want a six million dollar surveillance system and be able to check out the neighbours at will? Lucky Zeke, the *Peeping Tom* who gets the girl; you don't so much dislike him - which, as he's being set up as the killer, you're supposed to - as feel jealous of him, an entirely different emotional response. You almost wish Cally would pull the trigger of the revolver she has aimed at Zeke's head near the end of the movie.

The fault isn't just with the actors. The script strips them of character and emotion and concentrates on the sexually voyeuristic. Book in hand, it's possible to compare scenes. After Kay's first sex with Pete, she goes back to her apartment where, in Ira Levin's version: *"[Kay] had gushed to Roxie on the phone the night before, 'He has those vivid blue eyes and I swear to God he sees right into me!... You can't believe how perceptive he is! And funny, and sweet, and wild about me ...'"*

In the movie's similar pivotal (she's just been sexually reawakened after a boring marriage - I rate that as pivotal) scene:

JUDY (on the answerphone) Something's going on, I can smell it. You've probably been having multiple orgasms. You've probably been fucking your brains out.

CALLY (sleepily) I have.

This is writing without dignity. Get a life, as Cally says later on.

SECOND WITNESS FOR THE DEFENCE:

"Eszterhas is one of the most limited talents in Hollywood. He simply identified a formula." - anonymous Hollywood executive, 1995.

If *Sliver* was a *Rear Window* for the nineties, *Nowhere To Run* was an updated *Shane*, with Jean-Claude Van Damme in the Alan Ladd rôle and Kieran Culkin in place of Brandon de Wilde. The major plot change is that Van Damme's Sam Gillen is not trying to set down roots: he's on the run, an escaped prisoner. The film moves quickly to isolate Van Damme and get him into position to become the white knight in a fracas between Franklin Hale (Joss Ackland), the real estate developer (ex-cattle baron), and Clydie (Rosanna Arquette), the widow whose land he needs (homesteader; I'm sure her widowhood was intended to make her more vulnerable, but my cynical streak tells me it was to get Sam and Clydie into bed without complications).

Other than updating the setting, this is Shane-by-numbers, with young Mookie (Culkin) the wide-eyed hero worshipper who finds the strength in Sam that he lost with his father's death. If anything, it's too oversimplified for its Van Damme fan-base audience: to signify that Sam has reached a cross-roads, wondering whether to return and fight or ride-on, he...er ... reaches a cross-roads, grunts *"Clydie,"* and turns his Triumph (the bike standing in for Alan Ladd's horse).

The script, from a story by Eszterhas and Richard Marquand (the director of both *Jagged Edge* and *Hearts Of Fire* who died in 1987), was credited to three writers - one or both the others (Leslie Bohem, Randy Feldman) almost certainly brought in once Van Damme had been cast to add a little kick-boxing action (Feldman, for instance, had previously written *Tango & Cash* which shamelessly lifted scenes from Jackie Chan's *Police Story* and was no doubt thought the perfect writer to add a little chop socky). While it does not have the purity of a *Basic Instinct* (or even a *Sliver*), *Nowhere To Run* does however still have a fascination with voyeurism, with two scenes dedicated to having characters spy Van Damme naked: Mookie and his sister Bree see him bathing in a lake, and Clydie and her boyfriend see him in the shower. There then follows a hilarious breakfast scene where Bree comments on his penis size (she's all of six years of age). Whether this is character development or not is open to debate.

Unfortunately for the film, which - by blatantly lifting it from elsewhere - at least had a serviceable plot, Van Damme just does not have the ability to carry off the rôle of romantic lead. Whatever tension develops between Sam and Clydie is constantly interrupted by action where Van Damme can strut his stuff and the film fails to work as either an action movie or romantic drama with this constant swinging from one to the other.

SECOND WITNESS FOR THE PROSECUTION:

"With every movie the level lowers." - anonymous Hollywood executive, 1995.

And so to *Showgirls*. *Showgirls* wasn't just given a hostile reception. It was tied down and ice-picked to death in a savage frenzy. Since it's not particularly a crime movie, I can pretty much skip over its paper-thin plot which involves a young drifter, Nomi, arriving in Las Vegas to become a dancer. She does, lap-dancing her way into the Cheetah Club and then clawing her way into a big, glitzy review style dance club where she cat fights with the show's lead, Crystal. In the end she triumphs, takes over the lead, then - a tacked on plot thread - karate kicks her way to revenge against a rock star who rapes her friend. End of story. It's tacky. So tacky it can't quite go the full 360 degrees to so-bad-it's-good. But it somehow makes it in places: non-titillating T&A sequences apart, there are some wonderfully gross lines, none better than Nomi's bewildered ex-manager's visit and his gasp: *"Must be weird, not having anybody come on ya."* If this is what it takes to get an NC-17 rating, no wonder Hollywood is terrified. In its defence - sad, sick little man that I am - it's too awful to be offensive; the nudity isn't gratuitous for once - the story takes place in strip joints so it's necessary to the plot; and I guess lap-dancing is as legitimate a subject as any to get the Hollywood treatment. It won awards (for worst film, worst actress, worst script, etc, for which director Verhoeven had the humour and grace to actually show up to receive his 'accolades'), it's not controversial outside of being a wall-to-wall titfest, and it bombed because it stank.

THIRD WITNESS FOR THE PROSECUTION:
"We all do belly flops, but few of us clear the water out of the pool." - Joe Eszterhas, 1995.

His next thriller, *Jade*, also flopped big time on bad word of mouth. It was hardly in the cinemas long enough to generate any heat. As an attempt to recapture some of the glory days of ice-cold maidens, it struggled. It begins, as does *Basic Instinct*, with the murder, but develops its own story. Linda Fiorentino plays a husky-voiced socialite who becomes a high-class hooker not for the cash but for her own personal pleasure since her husband cannot satisfy her. Trina Gavin hasn't the vulnerability of *Sliver*'s Cally, nor the ice-pick manipulating coldness of a Catherine Tremell. She falls somewhere in between. Again, the stumbling block is a lack of heat generated between her and David Corelli (poorly played by David Caruso), an impoverished man's Nick Curran. In fact, there is not one character developed throughout the whole movie. The threads that lead to the conclusion are not tightly knit, and unravel shamefully at the end. It is not a great movie; at best it's a B-movie dressed in an Armani suit. It is, however, a guilty pleasure for me to see William Friedkin produce a corker of a car chase which in a completely ludicrous way manages to generate the one moment of surprise in the whole predictable tableau.

SUMMING UP FOR THE PROSECUTION:

How, then, can you assess Eszterhas? His work is derided, his plots derivative, his characterisation at best thin, at worst a porn mag male-fantasy, his dialogue crude (in both senses) and his view of women as bitch-goddesses who use sex as power overstated and bludgeoned through, a hammer to break an egg. Eszterhas' weird-menace stories found themselves an audience in *Basic Instinct*, but, like the pulps they were derivative of, they degenerated. The editors, and the producers years later, thought they'd identified the selling factor, sex and sadism, only to find that the lowest common denominator only attracted a fraction of the potential audience, and nowadays we're not talking about a dime magazine but a $40 million plus movie. Eszterhas should hang for degrading the medium and giving Bob Dole so much ammunition.

SUMMING UP FOR THE DEFENCE:

There has been too much made of Eszterhas' limitations. Put simply, his profile has been limited by the media: he is Joe Eszterhas who wrote the movie where Sharon Stone crossed her legs and *Showgirls* and nobody remembers *Jagged Edge*, or that *Basic Instinct* had more to it than one scene. His plots are derivative? Quentin Tarantino's are rip-offs, and nobody slams him the same way. His characters are shallow? What about Teddy Barnes or Catherine Tremell? He's sexist? Not so. More often than not, they have a deeply rooted strength ... even Nomi Malone.

But it was inevitable that Eszterhas would be knocked. Eszterhas was paid $3.7 million for *Showgirls*, and while sleaze was selling, he clocked up sales of at least three more erotic thrillers for between $3-4 million, amongst them the forthcoming *Original Sin, One Night Stand* and *Reliable Sources*. Hollywood created the market for sexy, sleazy movies, and writers only filled the demand. Eszterhas was the leader of the pack: he was expected to go further and deeper than anyone and his fall from grace was so much greater because of it.

Future movies will prove that Eszterhas has a much wider range: recent sales have included the comedy *An Alan Smithee Film*, crime thriller *Evil Empire* (about Russia's crime lords), an Otis Reading bio, *Blaze of Glory*, and the semi-autobiographical *Telling Lies in America*. Time will prove his talent.

JUDGE'S SUMMING UP:

Can Eszterhas adapt to the changing mood of Hollywood, or is he a one-trick pony who risks going the way of the pulps? Only you, ladies and gentlemen of the jury, can decide.

The quotes presented here come from two features:* J-Pegged: Joe Eszterhas *by Michael Fleming and* The Industry Still Raking It In *by Steven Gaines.

WILLIAM GIBSON

By John Ashbrook

***JOHNNY MNEMONIC* OPENS** with a slow crawl of text, explaining, for the benefit of those who've never read Gibson's novels, that, in the foreseeable future, the populations of the West will be cut down by a successor to AIDS, an electronically-transmitted brain disease called NAS, Nerve Attenuation Syndrome. As hardware and software are progressively replaced with 'wetware' - wiring that is woven into the tissue of muscle, organic chips which replace selected matter in the brain, computers which are, in other words, worn under the skin - NAS has become a trans-national epidemic, symptomatic of the human organism's rejection of the artificial implants.

It is a world of new flesh, where no one has to be how nature made them, where rôles are constantly being re-negotiated. This is the future, and it doesn't work. Welcome to 2021, some eighteen months after the setting of *Blade Runner*, the original science-fiction noirmare and spiritual father of Cyberpunkculture. This slow-crawl of information is designed to evoke the opening moments of *Blade Runner*, the swooping flight over a virtual landscape that follows reminds you of the apocalyptic LA skyline of 2019.

There are several reasons for writer William Gibson and director Robert Longo to evoke *Blade Runner*, partially, I expect, because comparisons were always going to be inevitable, so why not acknowledge the fact; more significantly, Gibson has never hidden the fact that his seminal creations of The Sprawl and Cyberspace came out of the early eighties, a time when popular culture was swamped with *Blade Runner* references, from fashion fads (such as the re-birth of the padded shoulder) to the grandiosity of Russell Mulcahy's *Duran Duran* videos (particularly *Union of the Snake* and *The Wild Boys*). By return, nineties dance culture and 'net' culture have heralded Gibson as some notional messiah, and appended the modifier 'cyber' to any number of nouns and verbs:

When asked about this, Gibson is nothing if not philosophical: "*Well, considering the way that I quite consciously appropriated the visual aspect of my work, if you can call it that, from pop culture at large and particularly from rock culture, it seems only appropriate. It's the sort of thing that goes around and around - y'know, I appropriate, they re-appropriate, then the whole thing gets re-commodified and goes around again to sell another batch of magazines, games, bands or whatever. It's the nature of late-stage capitalism, it's what we do. So I can scarcely complain if they do to me what I did to them.*"

Unlike many SF writers who seem to write their first best-sellers in their early twenties, promptly going on to win the *Hugo* and *Nebula* awards, and then embark on sickeningly successful careers as research physicists and SF. novelists, Gibson approached writing more steadily, engaging first in what he likes to refer to as 'some sort of life'.

"Of course, the real classic career for a science fiction writer in America is to be a child prodigy, twenty or twenty-one is quite a late start. A lot of them, especially the last couple of generations, would start in their late teens; but that wasn't my experience at all. I forget the actual ages involved, but if you look at Isaac Asimov or Robert Silverberg, people like that, they started really young. Silverberg put himself through college in high style by writing and selling lots and lots of pulp SF.

"Coming at it late just gave me a different kind of aesthetic agenda. I started writing science-fiction after having been exposed to literature of various kinds, and after having had some adult experiences. That just made me a different sort of animal as far as writing this stuff goes."

Having read a lot of his work, I always imagined him to be a keen science-watcher, with expertise in many areas, but he denies this with, I might add, just as much grace as he deflects compliments:

"No, no, quite the opposite; it's just that, in order to do my job, I had to leave that impression! An important thing to remember when you read science fiction, is that it is the work of a charlatan, possibly a benevolent charlatan, but a charlatan none the less. No, science fiction writers are not the God-Priests of high-technology they're credited with being, far from it. We are, by and large, a delightfully shabby lot, particularly intellectually. We are not necessarily your hot ticket to the future. If you're interested in what the future's really gonna be like, you should temper a little more serious thought. Go and see what professional futurists are doing, not just the kind who try to write best-selling books."

So what was it he saw in his late twenties, in the early eighties, bumming around the West coast of his adopted Canada, that led to formation of the great urban cage of The Sprawl, where mutated people are kept in technological bondage by unbelievably vast *zhiabatsu* corporations? What led him to explore the conceptual space inside a computer, now universally known by his term 'Cyberspace'?

"It wasn't really that I knew about Virtual Reality before other people did, I still deny that what I did was predictive. Besides, my real ability in what appears to be a predictive function, is really nothing more than a kind of trend spotter, if you will. I'd never heard the term 'Virtual Reality' then, I'm not even sure it existed, but there were enough bits of nascent VR technology around in 1981 to put it all together. There were things you could look at - such as the rumours floating about, about various pilot/aircraft interfaces the American Airforce was working on. Fighter planes to be flown by computers, where the computer would fly the plane, while the pilot interfaced with the computer. And I'd heard various stories about pilots sitting at the hearts of windowless aircraft, which were covered with television cameras. The

pilot's head was inside a huge helmet with all these screens inside, so the plane, in effect, became transparent and he was looking through it, except he was looking at television pictures. So, just from that image, from about 1980, you can infer the kind of VR technology we have today."

However, the idea of total immersion experiences (more real than real, to coin a phrase) is hardly a new one, Aldous Huxley called it 'The Feelies' in *Brave New World*, where a combination of drugs and recreational technology kept a whole society docile, functional and at peace. In The Sprawl, the drugs are digital and flight into the non-dimension inside the computer is the only escape from a cracked and leaking real-life society. Never the less, Gibson was more likely to take his inspiration from *The Scientific American* than the literature section.

Thus, the ideas of VR and telepresence had been around in a larval form for quite a while, but never before had their use and popularisation afforded their author the chance to influence a technology's development as it happened. Most of the ex-hippie scientists we see in documentaries working out on the virtual cutting edge, insist on referring to VR as 'Cyberspace'.

"I'm quite pleased, my hopes for 'Cyberspace' are coming true, in so far as it is my baby. Y'know, when I produced this neologism, it was hollow; it kinda came out of the oven empty. And since then various people, including myself, have attempted to fill it with meaning. But my real ambition for it is that it will wind up in the dictionary. I've been watching the updates on the new OED with some interest.

"'Cyberpunk' has already appeared in some dictionaries specialising in American contemporary language, but that's not my word, and I'm not particularly fond of it. But I would love to contribute a word to the language, that would be a great coup! I think the only other science-fiction writer who's done that is Robert Heinleinwith the term 'waldo' for those remote control robot hands they use for handling isotopes. I suspect that in laboratories, even now, people are referring to those things as waldos, never knowing where it came from or why they're calling 'em that."

And so it came to pass. The Cyberpunk Movement was a product of the early eighties, a metaphor for the cold, dark hole western society was being propelled towards. Now, in the late nineties, we're so far down the hole it is hard to see Gibson's work as fiction. And now, finally, his vision hits the screen.

"Johnny Mnemonic *was only the second work of fiction I ever wrote, it would be about 1980, and it was the start of it all for me, got the creative juices flowing, and led right on to* Neuromancer[his immensely influential debut novel]. *That's why I wanted to write the script for the movie-version myself, I wanted to see how well it stands up after all these years, and it stands up pretty well."*

Gibson's previous experiences with Hollywood had been abortive: a rejected script for *Alien3*("I think the only thing of mine that remained in the film was a barcode on the back of someone's neck"), several futile attempts to hang on to his vision with adaptations of *Burning Chrome* and *New Rose Hotel* (both

Sprawl stories from the collection *Burning Chrome*) which slowly suffocated in development hell. Consequently the plan for *Johnny* (originally hatched in 1989) was to do it small - to be filmed in Toronto and directed by Gibson's very good friend, sculptor and painter Robert Longo. "*This is his first feature after working on things like REM videos, so for Robert and for me, it's a sort of shot in the dark. 'Cos I've never had a screenplay produced before, and he's never directed a film before.*"

Unfortunately, making it small and personal proved difficult: "*We weren't asking for enough money. We were going to financiers and asking for one millions dollars, which is nothing for a movie. They didn't take us seriously. So we re-worked it, made it bigger, more complex, more expansive, then Robert went to Hollywood, took the script and his design sketches and asked for 30 million dollars. Suddenly they were impressed.*"

The end result book-ends Gibson's career thus far. His first Sprawl story, the foundation-stone for so many disparate dystopias (including aspects of the one we all now live in) has become the first grown-up science-fiction movie in a decade, and an amalgam of all his works. The opening swoop through infospace is taken from *Burning Chrome* (via Steven Lisberger 's still-cutting-edge *Tron* from 1982). The law has broken down (or been privatised ... which is pretty much the same thing) leaving life-support to be the task of vigilantes (as in his latest novel, *Idoru*, published in the UK by Viking Books). The tough underbelly of society - the lo-teks - don't just live in a giant scaffolding web, as in the original story, but have woven their habitat between the high-tension cables of a suspension bridge - as in *Virtual Light* .

The obvious way to go would have been for the spastic lighting and ragged editing of Cyberpunk à la MTV, but they deliberately rejected that direction. "*If we'd filmed the story as-is, it would have seemed passé, the 'cyberpunk look', if you will, has been very hip, but for how much longer? Billy Idol has taken it (with his* Cyberpunk *album) and killed it dead, as far as I'm concerned. That aesthetic will now forever be identified with a particular movement of the mid-90s, which is already as good as over. If we'd followed that style, our film would have been born old.*"

"Johnny Mnemonic *isn't about flashy graphics and rock music, although we've used 'em when appropriate, it's about The Politics Of Information . It's about a strange, but consistent world, not quite like our own, but similar.*"

It's a world swamped with devices, technologies machines that surround us and even penetrate us (the whole plot of the movie concerns the hard-drive Johnny has wired into his brain) yet that technology consistently fails to make the human condition happier.

"*My response to this stuff is one of the deepest ambivalence, I'm inclined to think that that's the only sane response. I wouldn't want to be a luddite, but by the same token, I wouldn't want to be a technophiliac sucker who's just waiting for the next new medium to come down the pike, and who believes that science always makes it all better."* How do the Americans, who are notorious for their love of a happy ending, take to his dystopic vision? *"Well, y'know, I sell more copies overall in the United States, but I think I've probably always done better proportionally in the UK. And certainly there was recognition early on over here of a certain kind of irony and comic content which is remarkably rare with American critics when they look at my work. They just don't see that grimness can co-exist with comedy. They don't see that extremes, the very, very, very deadly grim, can co-exist with humour, so, with my work, they just ignore it.*

"It's like when they were looking at Terry Gilliam 's Brazil *, it just baffled them, they said 'My God, it's neither fish nor fowl'. But with my work they don't even see the humour, so they think, 'Wow, this guy's great, he's deadly serious about this stuff, let's go and build these machines right now'!"*

One of my favourite examples of 'technophiliac suckerdom' from *Mnemonic* is the character Ralfi Face, as presented in the original story (he's portrayed quite differently by Udo Kier in the film), who has had his face altered through plastic surgery so he is forever a living quote - a representation of his favourite pop-star. He evokes, for me, images of sad worshippers wandering around Graceland, wearing Elvis' face. *"Well, actually, that was kinda predictive for me, because, when I wrote it, I hadn't spent much time in Hollywood. I now sometimes think of Ralfi Face sauntering around Melrose looking at these technically very, very beautiful women who have lost any degree of individuality to the knife. Because something like that is actually happening. If plastic surgery became something you could get at the Seven-Eleven, or your local gas station, people would wind up with these rather unoriginal jobs that were a composite of three or four people; y'know Alicia Silverstone and Cameron Diaz and the ubiquitous Madonna, and by the time you've loaded six on, you've got a generic face. There are a lot of people around who wanna be actresses in Hollywood, who have generic faces, and if enough of them get into movies and become role-models, well ..."*

Finally then, accepting that he claims his fiction isn't predictive, I was curious to know what one of literature's more celebrated prophets of gloom really expected the future to hold in store.

"Well, on the whole, I'm as hopeful as I can be. There's an American philosopher named Frederic Jameson , who's the guy who brought the idea of post-modernism to literary criticism, and he said that the characteristic emotion of our era is something he called 'The Post Modern Sublime', which consists of an equal admixture of ecstasy and dread. And I think that comes pretty close to describing what I really feel, when I look at the future!"

ALFRED HITCHCOCK

Notes From A Work-In-Progress by Paul Duncan

I HAD A DREAM once. I'm at LAX (Los Angeles airport) and I'm waiting for my case to slide down the chute. There are lots and lots of people milling about. They are nondescript. I see my case on the carousel, pick it up and roll it towards Customs. I've got drink to declare but, before I get there, I trip on my laces. A customs man walks towards me, asks if everything is okay. I'm fine. I crouch to tie my laces. He picks up my case and dusts it off. As he does so, I look at my case and realise it is not mine. My heart misses a beat.

Looking at my face, the customs man realises something's wrong. He asks me to accompany him to his desk. I pause, then get up. Slowly, I walk towards his table, watching him unlock the case, open it. I can only see his eyes look down, then look up at me. *Is this your case sir?* he asks me. I wake up in dread. What was in that case? I knew it was something bad.

Alfred Hitchcock pervades our consciousness. There is no doubt in my mind that virtually everyone in the Western world has seen at least one of his movies. We have see the world through his eyes and we find it frightening. Alfred Hitchcock was afraid, and he was able to communicate his fear through the use of situation.

His films are scary, not because the people are scary, but because they are nice, even attractive. Awkward, shy, gawky Norman Bates - he wouldn't hurt a fly.

His films are scary, not because they take place in the dark shadows of the night, but because they are situated in bright sunlight, in plain sight, amongst the crowd.

His films are scary, not because he is explicit, direct, but because his worldview is coded in abstraction. *The Birds* ends with the world in chaos, and the people having to tiptoe through the rest of their lives, because, at any moment, the world will turn on the humans. At the end of *Vertigo*, a man possessed of obsession for a woman, sees the thing he loves killed all over again - life not only puts the knife in, it twists it as well.

The reason why people are uneasy about watching Hitchcock is because they know he may actually kill people off. He knows that their experiences in the story may damage or cripple them forever. Janet Leigh is killed in *Psycho*! Mrs Thorwald is killed and chopped up in *Rear Window*! Vera Miles ends up in a sanatorium at the end of *The Wrong Man*! People are killed in virtually every movie he made. Worse than that, Hitchcock shows you the killing and the killers but you do not avert your eyes - you want to see it all.

Hitchcock is not *Hitchcockian*. When people describe a Brian De Palma or Richard Franklin or whoever film as being *Hitchcockian* they are usually referring to certain camera movements and angles. They refer to the visual language that Hitchcock used. People are then confused when they see Hitchcock's movies, because they're never quite the same as the modern movies. The reason for this is because Hitchcock's visual language is developed from story, and the story is one of suspense.

Suspense is the art of telling you that something bad is going to happen in a specific timeframe, but you do not want the bad thing to happen. This tension is held by Hitchcock, who strings you along, plays you like a fiddle. His most ambitious, sustained and, it must be said, successful attempt was *Psycho* - after Janet Leigh is killed we are not let off the hook until the end of the film, over an hour later. However, the Hitchcockian directors mostly concentrate on the shock aspects of *Psycho* rather than the suspense elements.

After looking at quite a few films, I began to develop a view of Hitchcock as a cubist filmmaker. What I mean by this is that he places the characters within an imaginary cube and moves the camera along the sides of the cube. This gives his films a uniquely formal quality. Think of the following angles:

When seen from the back, we are discovering, seeing the world from the protagonist's point of view.

When seen from the front, we are seeing the protagonist's reaction to the world they are seeing.

When seen from above, we are seeing the ironical, detached point of view, without emotion.

When seen from the side, we are seeing someone else's point of view of the character, usually sinister because there is no eye contact, then the character turns to look at us and we are afraid of them. This is used to great effect when Joseph Cotten is at the dinner table talking about rich widows and strangling, Teresa Wright looking at him, seeing the side of his face.

CONTROL

Hitchcock controlled his life with obsessive detail. He never liked to leave his office during working hours. He wore the same type of suit and tie so that he didn't have to think about clothes. He took the same suites in hotels around the world, so that he knew where he was, felt comfortable, safe.

He controlled his films in the same way. Trained as an artist, he drew the film before filming. Film is a visual medium after all. Just as an artist collects fruit or models to paint, Hitchcock collected actors. Does an artist depict the feelings of the model, or does the artist project the sympathetic part of themselves upon the model? I think the later is the case.

To Hitchcock, actors represented a style of person, in the way that buildings represented a style of architecture. A balanced and directed combination of elements result in a whole vision. To Hitchcock, the actors were part of both the image, the story, and the subtext.

Although critics tend to lump the James Stewart films together, or the Cary Grant films, and imply obsessions with actors and actresses, they forget to tell you that Hitchcock constantly switched from one actor to another as the style and content of the stories dictated. James Stewart appeared in films in 1948, 1954, 1956 and 1958. Cary Grant appeared in films in 1941, 1946, 1955 and 1959. This is not obsessive behaviour from a man who made 21 films between 1941 and 1959.

All the evidence seems to point to Hitchcock being obsessed with the main female protagonists in his films. Whatever the truth, it has to be said that most of his films feature very strong female leads or, at least, the stories are about troubled women. *Blackmail* (1929) is about what we now call date rape, where the woman kills the guy who attacked her. The Blackmailer gets killed and the woman walks off scot free, which doesn't seem quite fair when you stop to think about it. There are many Hitchcock films from a female perspective: *Sabotage*, *Rebecca*, *Spellbound*, *Suspicion*, *Shadow Of A Doubt*, *Marnie*... And the female characters in the others are more than a match for any man. In his films, women are independent, opinionated, qualified and often quite aware of their sexuality.

EXPERIMENTATION

It is something of an understatement to say that Hitchcock was an accomplished storyteller. One can see that after, say, twenty films or so, it could get boring unless you stretched yourself every now and again. Hitchcock stretched himself with some amazingly minimalist films. *Lifeboat* was a film about a group of people in a lifeboat. That's it. That's all the production designer had to do - a few bits of wreckage, the odd hull, a sky, some choppy water; sorted. *Rope* is a series of eight 10 minute takes set in one apartment room. *Rear Window*'s set is James Stewart, in a wheelchair, leg in plaster, in a room, watching and listening to people in and around a courtyard.

(It may seem bizarre as a comparison, but have you ever considered the way Stephen King has occasionally restricted his books in order to stretch himself? *Cujo* is mostly set in a car; *Misery* takes place in one room, *Gerald's Game* likewise. *Dolores Claiborne* is essentially a conversation.)

Hitchcock was constantly striving to tell stories in as imaginative a way as possible. The phenomenal number of visual ideas he had in his work, especially in his early films, are heavily influenced by the German expressionistic films of the Twenties, which used trick photography and symbolic images to tell stories. Add to this the rhythmic editing of Sergei Eisenstein, D W Griffith and others.

As his style and confidence grew, Hitchcock abandoned the symbolic images, and only used trick photography and special editing techniques for key moments in his films. Another reason for this is because a lot more fact and emotion could be conveyed through the use of sound and music without the need for obvious symbolism.

Also, the occasional camera movement in the early films is noticeable because the rest of the films are static. By, for example, *Suspicion* (1941) Hitchcock had wholly integrated camera movement into his style and the thing was flying about all over the place. The movement, I hasten to add, is not gratuitous but completely serves the telling of the story.

STORY

Much is made of Hitchcock's acute visual sense, and the spectacular set pieces he concocts. Yet, they must have plot, and they must have characters, although the measure of each varies depending on the type of film Hitchcock made.

The best writers in the world wrote for Hitchcock: Dorothy Parker, Ben Hecht, Raymond Chandler, John Steinbeck, Thornton Wilder, Brian Moore.

Although not bad, the source material was never brilliant. It is significant that Hitchcock never adapted a literary masterpiece to the screen. This was because he believed, quite rightly, that a genuine masterpiece had found its definitive form as a book. Hitchcock only adapted those stories which leant themselves to visual interpretation. Furthermore, he had no hesitation in completely jettisoning scenes and characters from his source material in order to service the film. Raymond Chandler, when working on the script for *Strangers On A Train*, complained that Hitchcock had already visualised the film in his head, so Chandler couldn't add anything.

For Hitchcock, the film was a continuous series of images which resulted in a physical and/or emotional response. His rollercoaster ride of *The Man Who Knew Too Much* is repeated in *The 39 Steps*, *Young And Innocent*, *Foreign Correspondent*, *Saboteur*, etc, right up until *North By Northwest*. He left the field open for action heroes from James Bond to Arnold Schwarzenegger to exploit.

He rearranged the plot to set up either surprise or suspense situations - mostly he selected suspense. The novel *The Living & The Dead* by Boileau & Narcejac, the basis for Hitchcock's movie *Vertigo*, tells two stories concurrently, one in flashback, which reveals in its closing passages that the woman in both stories is one and the same. That is a surprise saved for the end. Hitchcock rearranged the structure, telling one after the other, so that the first story is about the dead woman and the second is about the living. Early on in the second story, he reveals to the audience, but not to James Stewart's character, that the woman is one and the same. This has two effects. Firstly, the woman and her motives become real and understandable. Secondly, we are held in suspense for an hour, waiting for James Stewart to find out the secret, and wondering what he'll do next.

It should be recognised that Hitchcock did more than one type of film. People talk as thought they are all the same, as though they were supposed to elicit the same emotions from people all the time. This is blatantly untrue, although it is true to say he did make similar films, as the following list makes clear:

Man-On-The-Run (*The 39 Steps, Saboteur, North By Northwest*) Spy Thriller (*Secret Agent, Notorious, Torn Curtain, Topaz*) Horror Suspense (*The Lodger, Blackmail, Psycho, The Birds*) The Wrong Man (*The Wrong Man, I Confess, Frenzy*) Psychological (*Spellbound, Strangers On A Train, Vertigo, Marnie*) Murder Mystery (*Murder!, Dial M For Murder, Rear Window*) Black Comedy (*The Trouble With Harry, Family Plot*).

The problem with doing such a list, of course, is that everyone is going to disagree about placing the film in a certain category. I sympathise, because many of Hitchcock's films can be placed in several categories, depending on your point of view. For example, *Frenzy* lurks somewhere between horror suspense, the wrong man, the man on the run and black comedy, depending upon whether your point of view is the killer, the man accused of the killing or the policeman investigating the case.

HORROR

Suspense is the feeling of being afraid for one or more characters in the movie. Ooh-err, that boy is going to get blown up in *Sabotage*. Crikey, Teresa Wright is going to get offed by Uncle Joe Cotten in *Shadow Of A Doubt*.

Horror is a kettle of a different colour. Horror is being afraid for yourself as much as for other people. In film, the horror moments are often triggered by surprise or by images which are unacceptable to society.

I suggest that a horror film, by definition, is one with a supernatural basis. Who can forget *Nosferatu, Frankenstein* and *The Haunting*? They, and most horror films, are great fun, they give you a fright, you release lots of pent up emotions and then you forget them. These films use distorted views of reality (light and sound), but they always return to reality in the end. Horror tales are moral tales - they are adult versions of children's fairy tales. Far from being disruptive and a bad influence, they reinforce a white, Christian view of the world.

Hitchcock marked a change of approach to the suspense thriller film, by turning it into a horror thriller film. He did this with *Psycho*, financially his most successful film. Significantly, it was made as a cheap little experiment by Hitchcock's TV crew, not his usual film crew. It is also much more like his TV series, the Roald Dahl, *Tales Of The Unexpected*, sting-in-the-tail type of story. The texture of the film is grainy, realistic, almost documentary, like *The Wrong Man*, as opposed to the smooth, luxurious images of his big-budget films.

The surprising and unacceptable images? Well, showing people in vests/underwear, sweating, going to the toilet, Janet Leigh getting killed off a half hour into the movie. Take your pick.

Two other films must be mentioned here. Two years earlier, Dennis Weaver appeared as a thin, nerdy motel man who menaced Janet Leigh in Orson Welles' *Touch Of Evil*. *Peeping Tom*, written and directed by Michael Powell, dealt with the viewer's relationship with the filmmaker. Basically, in *Peeping Tom*, the central character is a nice boy, whom everyone thinks is a little strange but likes him anyway. Our hero goes out and kills women, as a sort of revenge for his mother not being around as a child. Worse than that, this monster films the women as they die. Worse still, he makes them watch themselves die. The subtext seems to be 'Why do you like watching other people die?' with the extrapolation being 'If you like watching other people die, then you'd like to see your own death even more.'

Hitchcock has been having a dialogue with the viewer from very early on in his career. As often as possible, he has put them in the position of his characters. You see a character on the screen looking at something, you see what they see (you in their position), then you see the character react to that something. It's simple.

In *The Lodger*, the Bunting family look up at their ceiling to see the light fittings shake, then we are looking up at the ceiling, at the light fittings shaking, the ceiling made of glass and watching the lodger walking up and down. That's in 1927.

In *Rear Window*, we are in the position of James Stewart, realising something is wrong, but not being able to do anything about it, being helpless in the wheelchair, as we are helpless in our cinema seats.

In *Psycho*, we are Norman Bates, looking through a hole in the wall, at Janet Leigh undressing (the beautiful, forbidden, pure Janet Leigh!) In this film, more than any other, we are both the villain and the hero, able to switch sides, to satisfy both our civilised and uncouth instincts.

GLASS HALF EMPTY

Ultimately, Hitchcock's world view was more pessimistic than optimistic. His films give a satisfying physical resolution (the baddie dies, the accused man does not get put in jail) but the mental anguish and consequences continue (the mastermind is still at large, the central character has to live with their mistakes, people are dead). Fry falls off The Statue Of Liberty at the end of *Saboteur*, yet the upper class mastermind and his associates remains free to plot against the US Government. At the end of *Blackmail*, the girl and her detective boyfriend walk off into the distance, but they do not embrace, hold hands or show any affection, connection. Their trust in each other has gone, and may never be repaired. The same can be said of Cary Grant and Joan Fontaine in *Suspicion*.

This is why Hitchcock's films will survive, because they give food for thought. They unsettle us and we don't know why. They do not assume we are morons, they let us work things out for ourselves. Eventually, we work out that Hitchcock is telling us that there are no pat solutions to life, that things don't necessarily work out right in the end.

I am at the Greyhound bus station in San Diego, reading a magazine. I'm engrossed in an article. I glance at my watch and, shit, I'm late. I run towards my stop. I'm knocking people aside, people looking at me, shouting, angry. I bump hard, straight on, into a middle-aged man. He falls back, hits his head on the tiled floor. People stop, stare, surround. They look down on the man and see two roses of blood, one around his head and the other on his stomach - he's been stabbed. They look up to my hands, my red hands. They accuse me. They surround me.

I don't wake up.

I'm not dreaming.

It's not a movie.

CRIME FILMOGRAPHY

UPTO 1936

The Lodger *(1927)*

Blonde Virgin: June Tripp

Story: The Avenger kills blondes every Tuesday. A mysterious stranger takes lodgings at the Buntings' house. Their girl Daisy takes a shine to him. The lodger leaves the house late Tuesday, and the next murder occurs. Daisy's boyfriend, a Scotland Yard detective, suspects the lodger and arrests him. The lodger escapes with Daisy, is chased by a crowd and almost killed by them. Based on the novel by Mrs Belloc Lowndes.

Visual Ideas: A man's face is distorted in a tea urn, looking just like the feared Avenger. Seeing two men delivering newspapers, their heads in the windows are like the pupils of eyes. The lodger is seen walking up and down his room through a glass ceiling. Looking straight down a stairwell, we see a hand holding the rail, circling as a character descends the stairs.

Recurring Motif: The flashing neon sign 'To-Night Golden Curls' is repeated throughout the movie, as a sign of the constant presence of The Avenger. At the end, the Avenger imprisoned, the hero and heroine kiss in the bright light, whilst the neon sign still flashes in the black night behind them.

Recurring Ideas: The Kiss (pure, close-up, slow, white). The Handcuffs (as a sign of a man being marked as being outside society). The Switch (For the first half of the movie, the lodger is dressed in black and placed in shadows, so we don't trust/like him. After the murder, and the family suspect him of being The Avenger, the lodger is dressed in nice, light clothes and his room is bright, so we like/trust him). The Hanging Man (at the end, the villain hanging, to be saved by the hero, if that is their rôles).

Paul Duncan says: If you can watch silent movies, you'll love this one. 4 out of 5.

Blackmail (*1929*)

Blonde Virgin: Alice White.

The MacGuffin: A glove left by Alice at the scene of the murder.

Story: Alice two-times her Scotland Yard detective boyfriend by going with an artist. The artist tries it on in his garret, and Alice knifes him. Shocked, distraught, she makes it home. Her detective boyfriend finds her glove at the murder scene but covers up for her, only to find out Tracy, who has the other glove, wants to *Blackmail* them. Our fearless detective bluffs Tracy into making a run for it, chase ensues through the British Museum. Alice racked with guilt tries to confess, but events contrive to let to go free with boyfriend. Based on a play by Charles Bennett.

Visual Ideas: As the cops silently enter a room, a man is on the bed, reading the paper, oblivious to the cops. The camera pans from his face, to a mirror, then zooms into the mirror, where we can see the faces of the cops. Time passing shown by the number of cigarette butts in the ashtray. As Alice and the artist mount the stairs, from side-on, the camera travels up. This is not done for any discernible plot/emotional effect and I suspect Hitchcock did it on a whim. As the artist is about to attack Alice, he pauses and the light and shadow of the lamp falls on his face, distorting half his face, as though revealing an inner demon. That's the effect it had on me, although Hitchcock maintains he just wanted an old-fashioned villain's moustache to fall on the artist's face. When Alice is in the artist's garret, she sees a policeman walk by in the street, so she thinks she's safe but, as she's being attacked, the policeman walks by and can do nothing to help her. When a description of the Blackmailer is circulated by the police, a montage of mugshots and the various books slide in and out of the frame, until the Blackmailer's face looms large. When Alice decides to give herself up, she writes a confession letter and rises - as she rises the shadow of a noose falls around her neck. When she enters the artist's room, Alice laughs at the funny clown painting laughing and pointing at her, but after the murder, the clown is laughing at her and later, when her confession is not heard, the picture is there again, laughing at her.

Audio Ideas: Every possible sound is used - music, whistling, horns, birds, cars - to show off. At one stage, our detective hero whistles *Sonny Boy*, a cheeky reference to *The Jazz Singer* of the previous year - the first talkie. Some of the dialogue is well-written, natural like, when Alice and the detective are discussing going to the movies, the detective wants to see the film *Fingerprints* because *"They're bound to get all the details wrong." "I don't see why,"* says Alice, *"They got a real criminal to direct it, just to be on the safe side."* The high-pitched twittering of the bird in Alice's room annoys her. The doorbell of Alice's tobacconists shop is loud and distorted, creating an unsettling effect when people enter. At breakfast, Alice is asked to cut the bread - the knife and bread are like the knife and bread beside the dead artist's bed. As Alice picks up the knife, a neighbour babbles on about the murder using the word knife all the time, her words getting softer and lower, but the word knife staying loud, so all Alice hears is KNIFE. Surprisingly, the slimy Blackmailer has a posh voice, a sign of villains to come.

Recurring Ideas: The Procedure (The apprehension and processing of the criminal is shown from police van to lock-up). The Double Scene (Hitchcock shows a scene at the beginning, the hunting of the criminal, and then repeats it later on, our expectations of the outcome conflicting with our desire - we want the villain to be caught and he probably will, but he'll blow the gaffe on Alice, who we like). The Outstretched Hand (When the artist tries to kill Alice, her hand stretches out from behind the curtain, desperately flailing, before falling upon a knife with which she kills him.The outstretched arm of the dead man also reoccurs throughout.) Handcuffs (Seen briefly in the police station, shining). The Switch (At the beginning we don't like Alice because she's two-timing the detective but, after she kills the artist, perversely, we sympathise with her and don't want her caught).The Public Finale (The Blackmailer is chased through the British Museum, clambers down a ladder by a giant face, ends up on the roof, and falls through the skylight). Never The Same Again (At the end, Alice and Frank leave the police station. They do not hold hands, or embrace. A distance has entered their relationship.)

And Another Thing: The film was shot silent then, when sound was introduced, Hitchcock had Alice, played by German Anny Ondra, dubbed live by Joan Barry. Michael Powell, later of famous film partnership Powell & Pressburger, was the stills photographer on *Blackmail* and later directed *Peeping Tom* (1960).

Paul Duncan Says: Mr Hitchcock would have done well to leave this one silent. The pacing is atrocious, mainly because of lengthy static dialogue sequences. 3 out of 5.

Murder! *(1930)*

Blonde Virgin: None

Story: An actress is found guilty of murder and is sentenced to hang. One of the jury, Sir John Menier, an acting impresario à la Noel Coward, regrets his decision and decides to investigate the actors, scene of crime etc. with the help of the acting troupe. Sir John tries to trap the villain by auditioning him for a murder mystery, based on the real murder, where the villain plays the murderer... and must fill in the missing clues. By jiminey, the villain doesn't fall for it. Later, when cornered, the villain commits suicide. Based on the play *Enter Sir John* by Clemence Dane & Helen Simpson.

Visual Ideas: Opens with two tracking shots. The first is looking into the upper windows of a street, as people look out the window, in response to screams. The second is a murder tableau - a crowd is looking at the murdered woman on the floor. Everyone is standing stone still. The camera, slowly, painfully moves from one face/body to the other, eventually following the arm/hand of the murderess to the poker and the dead body. A seminal shot -used by Martin Scorsese, David

Lynch, Brian De Palma etc. When a stage manager walks across the office of Sir John Menier, the floor is made of sponge. As time runs out, looking for Fane, a vane is shown because they are looking in all directions, as the accused woman is circling her cell, as the shadow of the hanging rope rises up a wall.

Audio Ideas: During the jury's deliberation, they pressure Herbert Marshall to vote 'guilty' in rhyme/rhythm - don't ask me to explain it further. The rhyme/rhythm idea is repeated over the Fane/vane visual sequence described above. Herbert Marshall's thoughts are spoken to us in a stream of consciousness manner. Music is used as background rhythm to his thoughts. Hitchcock tried to improvise with the actors, to explain the scene to them before they acted it - the result is a lot of stammers and silences and no rhythm.

Subtext: Throughout the movie, great emphasis is made of people putting on and taking off clothes. The opening shot is people putting on clothes. The actors exchanging costumes whilst performing. The Markham's putting on their Sunday best to meet Sir John. This changing of identity/rôle is further confused by women in male rôles: the female barrister; the jury women as experts on psychology. Identity, specifically sexual identity, is the theme of the movie. The villain turns out to be an effeminate man who lets his fiancé take the rap for his murder - he's an actor who falls back on his old drag trapeze artist act to make money. The reason, in the movie, for the killing is because he is a half-caste, which is a bit weak. Saying he was gay would have made more sense of his actions/rôle throughout the picture, and have been more interesting psychologically.

Recurring Ideas: The Hanging Man & The Public Finale (at the end, the villain, a drag trapeze artiste, hangs himself in front of the circus crowd).

Paul Duncan says: Despite experiments, boring, overacted, static, stilted. In two words: a dog. 2 out of 5.

Number Seventeen *(1932)*

Blonde Virgin: None

The MacGuffin: A jewelled necklace

Story: It's difficult to describe this one because almost all the characters don't have names. Anyway, the man who later is revealed as The Detective, goes into a darkened house where he discovers a salty seaman, a dead body, the dead body's daughter, three villains looking over the house, and a villain in the back room. There's a couple of fights, gunplay, and the girl and detective get tied up. Eventually, they all end up on a train or chasing the train in a bus. It's totally ludicrous, but eminently watchable. Based on a play based on a book by J Jefferson Farjeon.

Visual Ideas: Starts with long tracking shot of a hat rolling in the wind and leaves (later borrowed by The Coen Brothers for *Miller's Crossing*), stopping at a garden gate, man, his back to us, picks up the hat, looks up, sees a light flickering in the dark house, walks up to the door, tries it, it opens, walks in, walks up to the stairs and quickly looks up. Shadows appear and move along the walls: a giant hand, a web, a shadow hand grabbing a doorknob. Several times, the swish of the wind is accompanied by a shot of a window, an extremely fast pan, as if the camera were following the wind, to a candle being extinguished by the gust. We look down the centre of the stairs as a hand on the rail slides around and around, coming up towards us. The fight is hand to hand, very close in, silent - looking from above a hand is on a chin, pushing the head back. The bodies switch around during the fight, so that the wrong man is hit.

Audio Ideas: When a dead body is discovered, the wide open mouth and distorted face of a scream is covered by the screaming whistle of a train going by. The dialogue is very good, very sharp, very natural - the first well written Hitchcock.

Subtext: None. There is no thought behind this one.

Recurring Ideas: The Hanging Man (When tied to the banister, it breaks, and detective and the girl are left dangling between the stairs). The Mute Woman (The brunette Nora is introduced as being deaf and dumb, for no apparent reason, but then turns out not to be so). The Great Train Race (The train carrying the villains must get to the night ferry to the continent. On the train, there is a fight for the jewels, a pursuit, hanging from the side of the train, as the train races neck and neck with the hero in the hijacked bus.) Handcuffs (Called bracelets in this one, the brunette Nora is cuffed and drowning at the end, but is saved by our hero).

And Another Thing: Hitchcock did not want to direct this one, and conceived it as a burlesque - the mute woman (the heroine is always dumb, why not literally?), the villains calling to see the house after midnight, the train chase using models (meant to be derisory but is actually quite effective). To make this more obvious, he tried to film sequences involving stray cats running all over the house, but the cats would not comply. It all backfired, and moves along splendidly although, it must be admitted, the characters are not sympathetic.

Paul Duncan Says: A fast-moving, running-about-a-deserted-house, adding-a-character-every-five-minutes type of movie that works because it twists and turns before we have time to think. 3 out of 5.

The Man Who Knew Too Much *(1934)*

Damn and blast, I haven't seen this one. Someone - ANYONE - get me a copy.

The 39 Steps *(1935)*

Blonde Virgin: Madeleine Carroll.

The MacGuffin: A silent aeroplane engine.

Story: Hannay picks up a woman during a fight at a London music hall, but she ends up dead and Hannay is the only one in the frame for the blame. Whilst being hunted, he follows the clues to a place in Scotland near Killin (nice pun) and finds the villain of the piece, who promptly shoots Hannay. Saved by a very thick Bible, Hannay goes to the police and ends up on the run again, back to London. This time, he's picked up by the villains and accompanied by a disbelieving Madeleine Carroll - they end up handcuffed together and on the run from the villains. Ensconced in a pub, Madeleine discovers Hannay is telling the truth and they track down the villain to the Palladium. Mr Memory turns up on the bill, Hannay asks what are the 39 steps, *"...a secret organisation of spies for..."*, Mr Memory is shot by the villain, the villain is caught, Mr Memory dies and the Hannay and Carroll hold hands. Based on the novel by John Buchan.

Visual Ideas: Where to start? The film starts by following the feet of a man into a music hall (neon sign) whom we later find out is our 'ero. As 'annay escapes on the train, his pursuers' legs run after the shadow of the train. A woman screams as she discovers the dead woman's body, which turns into the train whistle as it passes through a tunnel - not seen that one often. As Hannay and Carroll are being escorted in a car by the villains, dialogue flowing, there's a great pan from the front of the car around to the back that cuts seamlessly into a shot of the back of the car driving off down the winding Scottish Highland roads.

Audio Ideas: The body of the woman is discovered, the cleaner (who looks like the screaming woman from Eisenstein's Odessa Steps sequence in *Battleship Potemkin*) turns to scream, but her wide open mouth turns into a railway tunnel and the train coming out of the tunnel is whistling/screaming for her. At the crofter's hut, the suspicious crofter goes outside, looks back through a window and sees his wife and Hannay talking animatedly, and thinks them lovers because he cannot hear their words - the irony, of course, is that silence is being used in the talkies. As Hannay escapes from the Sheriff, he jumps through a window and into a crowd - Hannay is afraid and trapped in the jeering crowd, the jeering could almost be for Hannay. When Mr Memory is dying, his words are accompanied by cheerful music as the chorus girls dance in the background.

Subtext: This film is about betrayal and the lack of trust, and the reasons why people do what they do. At every stage of the chase, Hannay is betrayed or trusted by everyone, depending upon their prejudices and assumptions, not on his word or appearance. A milkman doesn't believe that a woman has been killed in Hannay's apartment and spies are after him, but helps Hannay because the milkman understands the idea of Hannay having an illicit affair and wanting to dodge the husband and brother. On the train, Hannay on the run from police, kisses Carroll to hide his face - she takes umbrage and promptly tells the police *"this is the man you want."* The crofter only takes Hannay in for money and, when the police come, will turn him in for a reward. The man Hannay tracks down to prove his innocence turns out to be the villain, who promptly shoots Hannay. The Sheriff turns Hannay in because he trusts the villain, a respected local man. The publican wife and husband protect Hannay and Carroll from the villains because again, they believe them to be a love couple eloping because they always hold hands (because of the handcuffs). There are people who say they are police, when they are not - people trust the police. Hannay is assumed to be a politician, when he is not. Mr Memory remembered all the details of the silent engine both for money, and also for the professional challenge - his professionalism was his undoing because he cannot refuse to answer a question and he was asked what were the 39 steps.

Recurring Ideas: The Public Place (It starts at the Music Hall, where there is a fight, there is a political meeting where Hannay speaks in plain sight waiting for the police to capture him, and it ends at the Palladium). The Smart-Aleck Crowd (At the Music Hall, political rally and the Palladium there are lots of one-liners and a sense of community). The Psychological Explanation (Hannay says that the woman he picks up at the beginning suffers from 'persecution mania'). The Defect (Hannay knows that the man with a top of his little finger missing is the villain). The Shock Twist (The woman Hannay meets and we have grown to like and know, is killed, a knife in the back, in Hannay's apartment - killers in his apartment who don't then kill him is never adequately explained, by the way. This is a real shock, we thought she was going to be the romantic interest. A precursor to *Psycho?*) The Wrong Man & The Man On The Run (Hannay is accused of a murder he didn't commit, hunted by the authorities from London to Scotland). The Train Chase (On the train, Hannay listens to a pair of lingerie salesmen talking shop in front of a priest. He runs through the train, kisses Carroll, goes out the door to the outside of the train, ends up hanging off the Forth bridge, looking down). Technology (Hitchcock, bizarrely, has a shot of an autogiro scouring the Highlands in search of Hannay). The Cultured Villain (Professor Jordan is a respected figure in Scottish life, has a cultured voice, a simple, matter-of-fact way of explaining things and is always calm, fatherly). The Family Of Villains (The villain's wife, servants and probably children know the villain is a villain, and support him. They carry on with a normal family life - a chilling view of life if you think about it). Handcuffs (End on them holding hands). The Recurring Tune (Hannay hears the entrance music for Mr Memory, whistles it occasionally throughout the film and, at The Palladium, recognises it from the music hall at beginning of the film. Although never stated, it gives the reason why all the spies were in the music hall in the first place).

Paul Duncan Says: A sparkling script, engaging characters and razorsharp editing makes this just as enjoyable today as when it was first shown over 60 years ago. 5 out of 5.

Secret Agent *(1936)*

Blonde Virgin: Madeleine Carroll, although, if she still had it, she loses her virginity to Gielgud about halfway through the picture. Strangely, her voice and looks in this one reminded me of Miranda Richardson.

The MacGuffin: I don't care what it is.

Story: Novelist and soldier Brodie is dead, his coffin attended by a one-armed veteran. But lo, Brodie (played by John Gielgud) is alive, reinvented as Ashenden, and embarks on a mission to assassinate a German spy in Switzerland. He is accompanied by gorgeous Madeleine Carroll as Mrs A, and a crap Peter Lorre as The General, an assassin with an earring and a frazzled perm. First they kill the wrong bloke - an innocent tourist! - then the villain gets killed by accident in a train crash. What pathetic people they are. Based on the play by Campbell Dixon which was based on the *Ashenden* stories of W. Somerset Maugham.

Visual Ideas: There's a lovely transition of a car roaring off and the exhaust fumes dissolving into a sauna scene. The German spies use Swiss chocolate to pass on their messages, so they buy the bars, unwrap them and throw the chocolate into the dustbins. Later, there is even a chase in a chocolate factory.

Audio Ideas: As the innocent man is about to die, his dog, miles away, senses something is about to happen and whines uncontrollably, scratching on the door to get out, eventually howling when his master dies. David Lean used a similar idea 12 years later in his adaptation of *Oliver Twist* when Sykes is killing Nancy and the dog tries to escape. After the death, Hitchcock uses a wall of irritating noise - the local folk performing by rolling coins in dishes - to create a feeling of unease. Another time, in the church, there is a steady, loud note on the organ, because the organist is dead, which is disconcerting because of its insistence.

Recurring Ideas: The Charming Villain (Robert Young plays an American who woos Carroll throughout the movie and even gives her a picture of himself with a inked-in dastardly moustache, signed 'to the heroine, from the villain'). The church bell tower (Gielgud and Lorre are trapped in the church tower, the bell ringing, a dead body below them, leads to Lorre's immortal line: 'I'm still blind in this ear.'). The Train (switching compartments, trapped, attacked and crashes).

And Another Thing: Lorre's look, with moustache, earring, flower in his lapel, is very reminiscent of his rôle, five years later, in *The Maltese Falcon*.

Paul Duncan says: A huge misfire. Unbalanced characters and plot fail to create the right atmosphere. How can you sympathise with people who clown about whilst preparing to commit cold-blooded murder? No, no Mr Hitchcock. Doesn't even look as though Hitchcock was even trying with this one. 1 out of 5.

... to be continued...

(My thanks to John Ashbrook, John Kennedy Melling, Ellen Cheshire and others for supplying me with information and food for thought whilst compiling this article.)

PHIL JOANOU

by John Ashbrook

PHILLIP JOANOU is not an independent film-maker, in the commonly-held sense; because he works deliberately within the Hollywood mainstream. He commands large budgets and works with big stars, on both sides of the camera. Yet he seems to avoid making typically mainstream movies. His films are about BIG themes: sin, redemption and the Damoclean rite of confession.

Joanou earned his spurs by directing episodes of *Steven Spielberg's Amazing Stories* TV series - including one for which John Lithgow won an Emmy. This was followed by the 'comedy' *Three O'Clock High*, a teen version of *High Noon*. This really needed John Hughes and John Cusack to make it work. Not great.

Next up came his cross-over movie, *The Joshua Tree*, the semi-pop-video/semi-documentary chronicle of U2's tour of America. Shot in black and white apart from concert sequence at the end, this film has proven heavily influential on subsequent pop-videos and music documentaries. Appreciation depends on your opinion of U2!

His first foray into the crime genre was 1990's bleak and affective *State of Grace*, giving centre-stage to a still-little-known Gary Oldman, some three-years before Francis Ford Coppola 'discovered' him with *Bram Stoker's Dracula*. A modern noir featuring Sean Penn's best performance since *At Close Range*, ably supported by the ever-reliable Ed Harris; this film sets up many of the concerns which Joanou continues to explore.

Even 1992's glossy Hitchcockian *Psycho*-drama *Final Analysis*, Joanou's lightest and, probably not co-incidentally, most successful film to date, is a good deal smarter than the typical Hollywood thriller - requiring a nodding acquaintance with Freud from its audience. Most nineties mainstream films are pushing it to require an acquaintance with the alphabet. Richard Gere plays his usual spoiled brattish character, getting his come-uppance from the diabolic duo of Kim Basinger and Uma Thurman, both of whom show that they can act when they try! The devilish cunning script more than makes up for the predictable set-piece show-down (which is unnecessary enough to feel tacked-on as an afterthought, and can therefore be ignored).

HOLLYWOOD'S PRISONER

1993 brought the piece which Joanou seems to hold greatest fondness for: *Dead End For Delia*. Made as part of the *Fallen Angels* US TV series, this thirty-minute period-noir simply and efficiently tells of how Gary Oldman investigates the murder of his wife Gabrielle Anwar. Given an economical but excellent script, Oldman quite rightly talked his way into a *Cable Ace* Award. The episode has been screened at least once by BBC2 as part of a celebration of noir, but, to the best of this author's knowledge, it remains unavailable on video in this country.

And so to *Heaven's Prisoners*. Less overtly stylish than its predecessors, but following naturally on from them. It brings James Lee Burke's character Dave Robicheaux to the screen - in the form of the underplaying Alec Baldwin, who gives a committed performance as a haunted ex-cop, out to protect his wife and newly-adopted daughter from the dangers lurking in his past. The film is notable also for its confidently slow pace (or 'deliberate pace' as film-makers seem to prefer it) and surprisingly good support work from Eric Roberts and Teri Hatcher.

Unfortunately, *Heaven's Prisoners* enjoyed neither a smooth nor a pleasant journey to our screens. The industry press had carried various, often contradictory stories over the years, concerning the film's mysterious on/off production. Soon after the film's American release (where it was practically buried beneath Summer Blockbusters), I found Joanou to be happy, even keen, to lay to rest a few rumours and, in the process, exorcise some ghosts.

"I gather that Heaven's Prisoners has been on the back burner for a while, why was this?"

"Well it was filmed in 1994 and completed in 1995. It was scheduled for release in the early fall of '95, but the company which financed the film, Savoy Pictures ... let's just say they left the film business. They ran out of funding, so couldn't afford to release, market and distribute not only my film but seven or eight others which they had in various stages of completion.

"So my film, along with the other completed movies, were held up until they could arrange another form of distribution. Ultimately, New Line Pictures stepped in and released it this year. I suppose it could have been much worse; for instance, when Orion Pictures went bankrupt, some of their films sat for years before they got a chance to come out.

"The delay had nothing to do with the making of the film, it was just a situation where the studio was financially no longer able to release movies. During the post-production period we were all aware that the studio was in trouble, which also caused a series of delays in terms of them giving us the money to finishes stages such as sound and music. So the post-production process got drawn out a few months longer than it needed to but, when a company is scrambling for money, you just have to wait for them to come up with some. I guess it was kinda hand to mouth for a while there ... it was a very frustrating experience and *the* most difficult professional experience I've ever had.

"When I got involved with Savoy they had only released two pictures: Robert De Niro's *A Bronx Tale* and Richard Attenborough's *Shadowlands*, both quality films which had wide releases and were well-supported, so there was no reason for anyone to suspect that, a year later when my film was finished, the company would be in any trouble. But the movie business is very fickle, it's a giant gamble with an awful lot of money involved - if you're making eight or nine movies a year you're looking at investing several hundreds of millions of dollars - and the films they released in the year I was with them weren't performing, so they ended up losing their money. Of course, they lost their confidence as well, naturally, when you're running out of money you become more tense and more difficult to work with and these people were very difficult to work with."

"In that kind of environment it must be very difficult to remain an artist!"

"I'd say about twenty percent of my time was spent being creative on *Heaven's Prisoners*. the rest was spent fighting political and financial battles. Normally it's more like 60-40 or 70-30 in terms of creativity to politics, but here I spent the overwhelming amount of my time dealing with, in my opinion, ridiculous situations where they were just being very tough with me.

"This company was formed by investment bankers out of Wall St, not by film-makers or people who know anything about producing motion pictures. It was unfortunate that I got involved with them and, in retrospect, if I got my time again, I wouldn't, but, y'know, hindsight is twenty-twenty!"

"Bearing all that in mind, is Heaven's Prisoners the film you wanted to make?"

"Oh I'd say it's about 70% there. The process was complex, James Lee Burke's novels are very dense and complicated and I feel that we really needed to do more work at the script stage but, again, the studio would not pay Scott Frank *[who also wrote* Get Shorty, *the adaptation of Elmore Leonard's novel]* to continue working on the project, so we shot what was essentially a first draft script, which is highly unusual. I think that the film suffers structurally in places for there having not been more work done on the script.

"I'm very proud of the performances in the film and the work that George Fenton (who is English and works out of London) did musically for me. I'm not so satisfied with the length of the film because the studio insisted on certain cuts and trims just to reduce the length, and I feel that the film would have been more whole with only about five more minutes of scenes I wish we could have included, but length is just such a huge issue with these people that that wasn't possible, contractually I didn't have the control or power to make that happen. So, overall, it's a kinda bittersweet conclusion for me."

"Has this made you stronger for when it happens next time?"

"I could bend your ear for four or five hours telling you horror stories people have told me, but people I know who've been in the business forty years or more and have, you would think, seen it all, are unanimous that the experience I went through is unheard of. *Unheard of* in feature film making in Hollywood, and I don't see how it's possible for me to go through anything similar again. I feel like I've seen the worst that Hollywood can dish out in terms of distracting all of us from the actual job of making the film. So, yes, I do feel more confident than I did two years ago, but I certainly wouldn't want to have to go through that again.

"When you go through something like this, you obviously learn a tremendous amount. It tests your desire on a very, very deep level, you have to question if all the struggles and battles are worth it. At a certain point I had to put quite a bit of my own money into the film, as did Alec Baldwin, in order to get it completed. Then you really have to question the reasons why you got into this process when you wanted to be a film-maker and, at the end of the day, you end up being a politician, which isn't what I became a director for. I think I've learned a tremendous amount about the corporate side and what can go wrong in that area, the necessity of having strong and supportive producers, the need to have more time to work, re-work and work again the screenplay, because we really were short-changed on that front. Also, I've learned several things about myself as a film-maker, but then you learn every single time you go out, this time however was particularly ... testing.

"Many times I felt that the film was at risk and many times I considered leaving the project in all three phases - pre-production, production and post-production - and in fact I tendered my resignation several times, more, I must admit, as a ploy to get them to realise that they were not addressing the concerns and needs I had on the film, not really with the intention of leaving the project, just to point out to them that if I left they would have nothing. "The producers were all fired off the film during production, I completed the film on my own with no producers, the head of the studio was fired, the head of marketing was fired. At the end of the day, the only individuals who were left standing were myself and my editing staff, the entire regime at Savoy had changed over. It was a really strange experience.

"But, I was determined to complete what I had started and to do the best I could for the film, and particularly for James Lee Burke's book because he's an author who's work I love, and indeed I love the man himself, he's one of the most wonderful individuals one could have the opportunity to deal with.

"I opened here in America the week after *Twister* and four days before *Mission:Impossible*, sandwiched between those two monsters *[In Britain he was similarly sandwiched between* The Rock *and* Mission:Impossible*!]*. We were given minimal support in terms of marketing, publicity and distribution by New Line who had, after all, a very, very minor investment in the project. So, I liken the whole experience to the Indy 500, and you can't win the Indy 500 driving a Volkswagen Beetle. In fact, if you even *finish* the Indy 500 in a Volkswagen Bug then that's something to be proud of. So, to some extent I'm just amazed that *Heaven's Prisoners* even reached the finish line."

"It often amuses me to see which films the companies will put money behind and which ones they won't, some films aren't so much released as allowed to escape."

"Well, I think we performed The Great Escape! We had to dig tunnels for ten months and then we finally burst out only to find that we were in the middle of the desert with no food or water for a hundred miles. But at least we got out!

"What it boils down to is marketing. They take films out and test-market them again and again and again, then they take the market research scores and put them through computers which tell them whether the film has a high degree of commerciality, and if the computer says yes, then they support that film. This is why, other than in independent low-budget film-making, you find very few dramas being made any more, very few films that are about anything, very few films that explore serious subject matter. Sure, film-makers like Martin Scorsese and Kubrick (when he decides every decade to make a film) can go out and explore that territory; but for film-makers such as myself and the rest of us mere mortals, the opportunity to dig in and do something really interesting through Hollywood is becoming more and more difficult, if not impossible.

"I'm sure I'd have a great time directing something like *The Rock* or *Independence Day*, I'm not putting down those big pictures, I'm just saying that that's what gets the studios excited because that's what has the greatest commercial potential. A film about an ex-homicide cop who is a struggling recovered alcoholic and who steps into a lot of trouble and, instead of doing the right thing and walking away, pursues the trouble and brings a lot of heat down on himself and his family; that's not the kind of story you're gonna see a major studio get behind."

"Maybe not at the moment, but who's to say that that won't be big box-office in, say, five years time. I think timing is crucial, Final Analysis *[1992] was a product of the self-doubts of middle-class, middle-aged people which emerged out of the late eighties and was a success, I think, because it was released at the right time."*

"You can never predict the winds of cultural change but, what I can say fairly confidently is that, when there's a lot of money to be made or a little money to be made, the studios will always choose the obvious!

"More and more the budgets of films are sky-rocketing; *Final Analysis* was a very expensive movie at the time, costing thirty million dollars. Now, you have to understand that the budget for the making of the film was only 13 million, what we call below the line; above the line was 17 million in star salaries. But now, a thirty million dollar movie is slightly below average. The Hollywood average is thirty-four million dollars. Schwarzenegger's *Eraser* had over 100 million dollars budget, the same with *Batman Forever* last summer; *Mission:Impossible* was sixty million dollars but that was because Tom Cruise didn't take his twenty million dollar fee up front, instead he's in for a slice of the profits and will do much better than just twenty million! With these big budgets it doesn't necessarily mean you have more money to make the film. *Heaven's Prisoners* was a 25 million dollar movie but the below the line cost was just nine million.

"Now, as the stakes get higher and higher due to star salaries and huge special effects requirements, the gamble is like going to Las Vegas, they're putting a lot more money on the table and they wanna make sure that their bet is insured as best they can. So there's a very cautious, safe approach to mainstream film making currently.

"Something else to remember about *Final Analysis* is that Warner Bros. released it and they decided right from the outset that they were going to support it, which they did and I had a wonderful experience with them. That film was only complicated because Richard Gere was also executive producer on the film and he and I had disagreements about the direction of the movie. Other than that, the production company is a multi-billion dollar power-house who could support that film world-wide.

"When I made *State of Grace*, ironically enough, Orion was also going out of business, and that film suffered a virtually identical fate to the one *Heaven's Prisoners* has suffered here in America; which is somewhat tragic, but that's the way the business is. It's a lot about the attitude of the studio toward the project even before you make it, which determines whether it will be given a proper release or if it will just be allowed to escape.

"Unfortunately I've had two experiences now where the studio went out of the business literally as my film was ready for release. I was five weeks away from *Heaven's Prisoners* release when they pulled the plug, and there was a huge headline in the trade papers 'Savoy Leaves Film Business', which was news to me! I wasn't shocked but, at the same time, I was surprised to realise that my film wasn't going to come out and I had no idea what was going to happen to it for many months.

"Unfortunately, ten years ago, when I was lucky enough to get the chance to work in this business, I didn't realise that it was so full of political and financial and business-driven problems which can severely affect the creative outcome of a film. I thought that you took a script, hired some actors and went out and made the best movie you could and, it seemed to me, in the interest of making the best possible movie, that the studio would be supportive. Little did I know that, quite often, that's not the case.

"I've always believed that if you try to do good work which you believe in and you work as hard and as passionately as I do on my films (that's not to say that other people don't) then, hopefully, people someday will notice, even if those films don't get a lot of publicity and don't make a lot of money during the time in which they were released. Never the less, I still feel very frustrated by the process and by my career currently and by the fact that I feel I could be doing even better work.

My films could be more successful - I don't mean hundred million dollar hits, but they could reach an audience. I always knew when we were making *Heaven's Prisoners*, that the mystery genre has a very narrow and specific audience. It's not a psycho-sexual action thriller like *Final Analysis*, it's not the MTV licketty-split *Bad Boys* kind of film making which is the rage today. I knew that a slow, moody film noir story would have a limited audience. What's frustrating is that, at the time of release, it doesn't even have a chance to reach those people because you're swarmed by these massive blitzkriegs like *Twister* and *Mission:Impossible*. If I was in a more supportive environment both creatively and particularly professionally, then I could excel and do better work."

*"But I think it's worth sticking to your guns because you can never predict how things will change; after all, who would have said twelve months ago that a no-budget movie made on 16mm [*Leaving Las Vegas*] would have been nominated for all the big Oscars, and that its lead actor [Nicholas Cage] would win!?"*

"Absolutely, and that is of course extremely heartening, and my hat's off to Mike Figgis *[the director]* and to everyone involved in that terrific movie."

"And it all came about because he had a similar experience to you [with studio interference on his film Mr Jones*, starring Richard Gere] so just turned his back on Hollywood and went off to do something else!"*

"And I'm looking into doing that! I'm continuing on the path I'm on with Hollywood features and big studios, but at the same time, I'm reading unsolicited scripts and first-time writers and I'm reading obscure novels that might be appropriate for low-budget adaptation. But, frankly, the press over here likes to put a lot of hype behind the *Leaving Las Vegases* of this world, ignoring that for every low-budget film that gets released, there's fifteen that never saw the light of day.

"I sat on a panel which mixed studio film-makers and independent film-makers, and the five Indie film-makers were talking about the wonderful freedom of making your own vision at a low-budget. Over the two-hours of the session I spent with them, I realised that four out of the five films they had made had no distribution. They had made their films for an audience, but no one was getting to see these visions they were so proud of, that they had made with such freedom. So independent film-making is not quite the paradise that the successful films make it appear to be.

"At least with a major studio (Savoy notwithstanding) you have a certain amount of assurance that your film will get out to the public, by hook or by crook. Miramax release forty to forty-five movies a year, something insane like that; yet you could probably only name four or five of 'em off the top of your head. So it's still very tough to get noticed, it's still risky, and it's very difficult to find material to adapt - like Mike Figgis did with *Leaving Las Vegas* - which isn't already owned.

"Everything in the world is owned! It's unbelievable. You think you have found the most obscure, out-of-print book, no one must have heard of it - you check with the publisher and sure enough a producer or studio or a financial company owns the film-rights. You have to deal with them and, suddenly, you've got partners, and not partners of your own choosing. As was the case with *Heaven's Prisoners*. I wanted to do the book, Alec wanted to do the book, unfortunately it was owned by a studio and that's who we had to team with. It all becomes so terribly complicated!"

"I'm glad that you mentioned two of my favourite words earlier: film and noir. I've often had arguments with friends about whether or not you can do noir properly in colour. Now, looking at State Of Grace *which is the noirest of your films, the palette is almost exclusively blue, grey and black, which makes the film seem very cold. Did you film it in winter?"*

"Actually we shot that thing in the middle of a hot New York summer, from June to September of 1989. But the cinematographer Jordan Cronenweth *[who shot* Blade Runner *among many, many other films]* and I talked extensively about this: we wanted to use a lot of cool colours even in the daylight scenes and we timed the scenes cooler, to take it in the direction of the original film noir, to make it as monochromatic as possible. Naturally, today it's extremely difficult to get a studio to make a black and white film, so that option was neither here nor there.

"But I would say there has been good colour noir. *Chinatown* is an excellent example of a noir detective story that works that way. Needless to say, I'd love to make a noir in black and white, it's just not possible. Even on *Heaven's Prisoners* we did our best to pull down the colours, especially in the scenes in New Orleans which is a very colourful city. When you're in a city, you're able to control the look more carefully than in the green, lush swamps of Louisiana which is, put simply, uncontrollable."

"Just to run with this idea of your films being 'chilly', for a moment. The characters, especially the women, are often emotionally very cold in your films. Kathleen in State Of Grace *almost seems content to stand around and allow members of her family set-to and kill each other."*

"There's actually a line in the film where Sean Penn says directly to her *"You're cold, Kate!"* and she agrees. Her only way to protect herself is to numb herself to the violence and the insanity of her brothers, she had to separate herself from her family otherwise her life would be a disaster too. She doesn't wanna get sucked into their world, yet at the end of the film she's the real victim. All the guys have gone down the road to violence and death and retribution, she's the only one who has attempted on any level to fight against it and consequently she's left with nothing, no family, no lover, isolated in the middle of the St Patrick's Day parade.

"I think the two women in Final Analysis *are kinda diabolical too, they're more than happy to throw each other to the lions. In* Heaven's Prisoners, *Kelly Lynch [who plays Baldwin's wife] has some warmth and compassion, as does Mary Stuart Masterson [who plays the hooker-with-a-heart-of-gold type]. But Teri Hatcher [yes the 'Lois Lane' Teri Hatcher] is certainly the femme fatale.*

"I don't know why I gravitate towards these stories and this material, but it really is part of the genre to have characters who are not necessarily emotive people. They are, generally speaking, in violent situations, surrounded by death and some form of intrigue. They have to live by their wits and by there ability to handle the dark things that are thrown at them. It is something that's always been there and consequently surfaces in my films."

"There is another feature in this book [Graham Barnfield's Hard Boiled Cities *article] which looks at* Devil in a Blue Dress *and contrasts it with* Seven, *saying that the former is traditional noir in that bad things happen to innocent people, but redemption is available to those prepared to earn it. Yet, in* Seven *there is no possibility of redemption, which is a much more cynical, nineties notion."*

"It's very nihilistic isn't it! Yeah, I completely agree with both of those readings; and my films side more with *Devil in a Blue Dress*. For example, Dave Robicheaux *[Baldwin's character in Heaven's Prisoners]* suffers great loss and almost loses himself in the process, yet at the end of the film he is intact, although emotional pieces of him are missing, so he puts down his gun and goes home and decides to try to move on and find some form of redemption. Redemption isn't actually offered to him in the film, except maybe symbolically in the form of the little girl he has adopted, but it's not dramatically offered. It also suggests that there is some form of justice, in that both Eric Roberts' and Teri Hatcher's characters *[the man-and-wife villains of the piece]* are doomed for their actions, physically, Psychologically and in terms of Eric Roberts' soul, they are finished; while Dave has the chance to move on.

"The question on *Heaven's Prisoners* was always made clear by Mary Stuart Masterson for me, when she says *"Sooner or later you've gotta decide who you wanna be; do you wanna be a pissed-off guy trying to right every wrong in the world or do you wanna be alive?"* That's really the choice he makes at the end of the film - the choice to be alive.

"I find those themes and questions very interesting, particularly in today's age when we are confronted with a daily barrage of some very dark and difficult issues. Maybe movies should be an escape from those issues, a lotta people think that that's what they should be, but I enjoy going to films that confront those issue, and I also enjoy making 'em. Unfortunately it's not the most popular form of film-making on the planet.

"There's a lot more room for these kinds of films in Europe, my films have always been much more successful in Europe than over here, and I think that's because there's a greater tolerance for exploring the inner workings of the soul. For centuries Europeans have been doing great work in all forms of art with that kind of theme, which makes for a more patient and insightful audience. Americans want a rollercoaster ride, they wanna go to Disneyland. A European audience is generally more analytical than over here, which means you encounter a harsher group of critics, but I prefer to go in with an intelligent audience that has the patience and wants to look at what's working and not working both on the surface and in terms of the subtext, as opposed to simply saying *Wow, good special effects*."

"Are you Catholic?"

"Noooo. I was actually raised Episcopalian, which is kind of a watered-down version of Catholicism."

"But your films are very Catholic."

"Yes I know, and it's very funny! I don't put it there, I just kinda find it there. I don't have the Martin Scorsese story - 'Gee, I wanted to be a priest or a film-maker and I couldn't decide' ... My story's much less interesting than that.

"Obviously *State of Grace* was filled with that influence, and there's odd moralistic reverberations of it in *Final Analysis*, with the sense of guilt and confession. *Heaven's Prisoners* clearly demonstrates the same concerns given that it opens in a Confessional. You know, I keep finding myself shooting scenes in churches and I really don't understand why, it's not something I seek out, it's not something that I was raised with, obviously something about it attracts me. Maybe it's the moral dilemmas presented by Catholicism, and presented by religion in general.

"I've been fascinated by religion since I was young and, although I'm not a deeply religious person I find it fascinating to watch people from any denomination or any faith trying to find some moral, spiritual ground upon which they can feel solid in this crazy world which seems like it's spinning out of control. That, to me, is a real issue we face today as human beings in the very late twentieth century. Where do we stand morally, ethically, spiritually and what do we do when presented with choices? I think that's interesting dramatic fodder, so the films naturally link up with some form of that, and in the case of a couple of the films Catholicism has been the conduit for that exploration.

"Even with something as simplistic as *Final Analysis*, you've got a guy with a moral dilemma. He falls for a patient's sister and what does he do? He does the wrong thing, he pursues the relationship and finds himself paying a price for it. Well, that's a page straight out of the Catholic book. The same thing happens with Dave Robicheaux, he finds himself in trouble and, instead of letting it go and protecting his family, he deludes himself into believing he's protecting his family be going out to pursue that which he shouldn't, and consequently he too has to pay a price. This is also true of Sean Penn's character in *State of Grace* and Gary Oldman's character in *Dead End For Delia*. Maybe I just have some morbid fascination with the price you pay. In fact I made a movie when I was in film school called *The Price You Pay*, about how the choices you make in life affect you negatively or positively. Of course, because conflict is drama, it's more interesting to explore the choices that affect your life dramatically, as opposed to the ones that make life easier and happy."

"And you get the feeling that your characters, Sean Penn particularly, are being drawn back into the abyss, back to somewhere from which they escaped ..."

"That's right, and it's also true of Alec's character in *Heaven's Prisoners*, and Gary's in *Dead End For Delia*. And even with Isaac Barr, the character in *Final Analysis*, he's drawn into a whole new situation, but you kinda get the feeling from Richard Gere that he's been through some shady dealings in the past anyway. That's just kinda natural in his presence. In fact, in the original version of that script, the character was much darker and it was more obvious that he too was being drawn back into that abyss. It was a much, much darker film, more noir, as opposed to *Hitchcockian*, but it drifted and became much lighter when Mr. Gere became involved."

"Was that the difference of opinion you mentioned earlier, he wanted Hitchcock, you wanted noir?"

"Well we didn't describe it as *Hitchcock versus* noir, it was *more romantic versus edgy*. I wanted to be tougher on his character, I felt that he needed to pay that price for what he did, that we needed to call a spade a spade. He does something immoral and now he's screwed because of it and we've gotta watch him wiggle. Now, Gere was already attached to the film when I came on, and I thought that watching Richard Gere wiggling and getting yanked around by these women would be really entertaining. Unfortunately Mr Gere wanted to soften that up and make him a much more likeable guy who just happened to stumble into this situation which is beyond his control. For me though, that's not a very interesting character, I don't like characters who are out of control. I thought the character was weakened and deluded by his desire to create a more romanticised version of this environment, and naturally, if we were gonna go in that direction, we ended up heading towards *Vertigo* as opposed to *The Postman Always Rings Twice*."

"Well obviously I can't speak for the man, but I think it's possible that, on reflection, he may have changed his mind, since he's just effectively re-made the film as Primal Fear *and he's certainly gone the other way in that one."*

"Yes he has. You see, in *Mr Jones*, he tried to take a paranoid schizophrenic and make him loveable, make him a cuddly teddy even though he was crazy, and in *Intersection* he played an architect who is a negative situation, but is still a likeable guy. I think he's realised that he's most successful when he plays rôles like he did in *Internal Affairs [Gere's comeback film, where he gives a chilling performance as a bent cop]* rôles that are edgier, that do explore the darker side of the game of life; and actually he's more enjoyable to watch in that environment.

"It's funny, but you're not the first person who's suggested that he's re-made a version of *Final Analysis* in which he plays the guy I wanted him to play! Which is quite annoying to me! But we all evolve.

"I can't really blame him, after all, he was coming off the back of *Pretty Woman*, which was clearly the greatest success of his career, and it was a romantic comedy where he played a very likeable character, even if he is an investment banker - one of the slimiest forms of life you could ever wish to meet - who buys a woman for a week because he can't have a relationship of his own. That's really a pretty dark character, but the tone of the piece was very glossy and fun and he understandably wanted to stay on that track because that was working for him. Now he's maybe realised that other elements in that film were what was working - namely Julia Roberts - and that he is actually more suited to playing someone who has more of a burn and an edge, which is more like Richard's real nature in my opinion, Buddhism aside. So, good for him, that he has come to that realisation ... I just wish that he and I had been more in that zone, in synch, when we made *Final Analysis*."

"I think it's consistent with your obvious aim to create a body of related work, that you work with the same people over and again. Scott Frank wrote Delia *and* Heaven's Prisoners, *Gary Oldman and Eric Roberts have shown up a couple of times ..."*

"And I have the same costume designer three films in a row, Jordan Cronenweth has shot three of my movies, and, incidentally, Scott also did an uncredited final re-write on *Final Analysis*. Yeah, you try to work with people who share a vision with you and who are gonna support the choices you make when you're out shooting. I try to keep as much consistency as I can but it's difficult because everyone in this business is a free agent and so I can't have the same people every single time because they get booked. If I have to find replacements, I look for people with a similar style and taste, because that'll help me see my vision through, and also elevate the vision."

"You also work with leading men who've got themselves something of an off-screen reputation."

"Yes, but I think, particularly in the cases of Sean, Gary and Alec ... and Eric, they're very passionate, committed, intelligent men; and I relate to them personally and creatively exactly because of that. They're willing to fight for what they believe in, which sometimes means fighting with me ... thankfully not very often because we're pretty much in synch. But I like that. I like people who have a strong point of view, they know what they want, they come in with the intention to work, fight, scrape and scrap to the death to get it out of themselves and on the screen. I relate to that, because to survive the war of making a movie - and it is very much like fighting a little mini war for a year or so - you have to surround yourself with people who have a similar passion to yourself."

"In Heaven's Prisoners, Baldwin actually plays against type for the first half of the movie, he comes across as very vulnerable, almost helpless in a family situation. But as soon as he enters New Orleans everything changes, even his walk is different!"

"We called it the detective walk. He put on the detective suit, the detective attitude and the detective walk. I'm pleased you noticed that, because we deliberately chose a completely different physical attitude for him when he's away from the bayou. When he hits the city, he's a cop again, *Psycho*logically; and as a guy going through AA, he's looking for that negative excitement to fill the void where the booze used to be.

"The film was not really noticed here as much as I wish it had been, because of the big movies coming out around it, I don't think it was looked at very closely when it came out here, but Alec took a real risk with this rôle, by showing sides of himself as an actor and as a person that I've never seen him show on screen before, and that really differentiated this performance from others we have seen from him. I think he's done some of the better work of his career, I'm very proud of his work, in fact it's probably the part of this film I'm most proud of, and I had a tremendous working relationship with him. I speak to him quite often and I know he remains proud of the film, regardless of the financial outcome."

"And Eric Roberts is taking a bit of risk too, here. It's certainly not the one-dimensional character he too-often has to play. He's obviously paid the rent now, so can afford to be a bit more choosy about the rôles he takes."

"That's actually one hundred percent true, he went through a very expensive divorce and, as you say, needed to pay the rent; but that's done with and he feels that he can take some risks and get back to the kind of acting that began his career in such an exciting way. He is definitely one of the most underrated actors in the world today. I think something to bear in mind about Eric's career is to compare it to Tommy Lee Jones'. He was out there doing films which were way below his talent and potential for many, many years, but the last five years or so have put him right where he should be. Now, you keep an eye on Eric and I think you find he has the same sort of career, he'll build himself right back up to where he began in *Star 80*, and even exceed it. When Eric is in a film he brings humanity even to the most absurd of situations. Alec and I had to fight very hard to get him in *Heaven's Prisoners*, but he was worth all the effort because he brings so much to a rôle, and he's really something to watch when you're on set making the film."

"It's interesting that you feature such powerful men in your films, because one of the conventions of noir *is to have dominant females, who are often the motivators of the action, and can easily eclipse the men if you don't have men who are sufficiently charismatic."*

"And certainly that exists in *Heavens Prisoners*, although the three women each have their own third of the movie, so no single one of them dominates the film. With *State of Grace*, Robin Wright's rôle as Kathleen was larger than it now appears, quite a bit of footage was shot with her and Sean Penn, developing their relationship, but that didn't make it into the final cut simply again because of length.

"The same is true of Mary Stuart Masterson's rôle in *Heaven's Prisoners*, there was a seven minute sequence where Alec goes down to visit her, in a drunken stupor, and she helps sober him up and get him together before sending him back to New Orleans to track down the badguys. It's a sequence I'm really sorry isn't in the film, but that was part of the fight that I lost. *[Hopefully it'll surface one day in the Director's Cut video!]* These were very emotional scenes and actually very hard to watch because Alec was really way out on that limb, but they slowed the pace so had to go. So the cutting room has diminished the dominance of the women, and the simple fact that there are three of 'em thins out each characters screen-time."

"But aren't they all aspects of the same character? We're back to Catholicism and the virgin/whore thing. Kelly Lynch is the virgin 'cos she and Alec have no kids, Mary Stuart is the whore and Teri Hatcher is ... ehm ..."

"Teri is the devil! She's literally dancing on Dave's shoulder taunting him back into Hell. She carries a flask of booze with her all the time, and all the time it's *Would you like to have a drink? Would you care for a drink, Dave?* In fact, when he walks into the final confrontation, what are the first words out of her mouth? *"Can I fix you a drink?"*! So, I saw the women as working in a triangle in that regard."

"Talking of drink. Alcoholism is another common thread in your films, and I noticed that the only two times in Heaven's Prisoners *where you use the classic noirish beam of light through a window type lighting, are in the church and the bar."*

"Hmm. It's not conscious, y'know, but whenever I'm making a movie I end up in a bar or a church. Or both. I know how those scenes should look ... I feel very confident in those two environments ... and straight away I know how it should look. I think there is a thematic similarity between the two, they're both places people tend to go to deal with their sorrows, their sins, their problems, either to drown 'em in a drink, confess to a priest or pray to God. In fact, in *Delia*, the very first time Pat and Delia meet, they're sitting in a bar and talking about church. She says: *"Going to a bar just to drink is like going to church just to pray"*. So I think that there are parallels to what these people in these *film* noir stories use these locations for. Alec goes into a bar to purge himself, whether it be to drink or beat up the bartender, and he goes to church to purge himself in Confession."

MICHAEL MANN

by John Ashbrook

MICHAEL MANN'S FAVOURITE COLOURS are blue and white, his films shine with them. *Miami Vice*, the TV show he executive produced, made white suits and white-painted walls with electric blue neon lights the necessity for conspicuous consumption in the eighties. *Manhunter*, his last foray into crime and punishment, is all about the evil that lurks in a brightly-lit world. Its characters are all caged in a world of clean white surfaces, splashed with blood.

There are relatively few mirrors in Mann's world, which is curious given that the key defining concept in all of his crime stories is that of the reflection or the double. In *Miami Vice*, Crockett and Tubbs battle against drug pushers by looking and acting like them, wearing the same suits, driving the same cars. In *Manhunter*, Graham tracks down the *Psycho* by retracing his steps, both physically and *Psycho*logically. In *Crime Story*, his paean to the fifties 'n' sixties, Turillo and Luca are dark twins, eventually bonded in annihilation. *Made in LA*, a one-off TV movie from 1989, is a bright, tight companion-piece to these earlier renderings, and shows the doubling more starkly, it suggests that the leader of a criminal force, and the leader of a police force, are really just the same animal. *Made In LA* is, for several reasons, most of them, I suspect, financial, the least of Mann's full-length works, but it is fascinating now for what it came to be. It became half of the ultimate double.

Check out any biography of Michael Mann, any article about him, any interview with him, you will find no mention of *Made in LA* The film is cheap and simple, with no stars and an editing style that cuts it to the bone. It feels incomplete. Possibly this is why it became the bastard son he refused to acknowledge. An embarrassment. Possibly this is why it became *Heat*. *Made In LA*'s primary point of interest now is that it was a rehearsal for *Heat*, a dry-run that maybe we weren't supposed to see. Masquerading under the pseudonym *LA Crimewave*, the film was briefly available on video in this country, few people noticed. Now MIA have re-released it as *LA Takedown* and, along with Warners Home Video's release of *Heat*, it provides an opportunity for the first time of evaluating both films properly. When I saw the film upon its unheralded screening on satellite TV back in 1990, it was called *Made In LA*, to avoid confusion in my own feeble mind (and make the most of my punning title) this is the name by which I shall refer to it.

RE-MADE IN LA

Made In LA/Heat is set in a cold, clinical LA, where even the sunlight is bled of all warming yellows and reds. Alex MacArthur plays Patrick McLaren, whilst Robert De Niro plays Neil Macauley, both are very slick, very professional leaders of break-in crews. They are also the only significant character in the two films who's name has been totally altered. In common with Will Graham, Mann's manhunter, they live in a cavernous white-walled house with no furniture but a spectacular glass-wall overlooking the clear blue sea. Their house is the metaphor for the state of their singular soul - elegant, cold and empty. The defining principle of Mclaren's life is the simple and matter-of-fact principle *"Have nothing in your life you can't walk away from in ten seconds flat"*. For Macauley and *Heat*, painted on a far wider canvas, the principle is more elaborate: *"Have no attachments, allow nothing into your life that you cannot walk away from in thirty seconds flat if you see the heat coming round the corner."*

Their nemesis, the heat around that corner, is Lieutenant Vincent Hanna, played respectively by Scott Plank and Al Pacino, He is messier, but is possessed of razor-sharp faculties. Fuelled by nervous energy, Pacino, given much more dialogue, and the screen-time to deliver it, proclaims that rage *"... keeps me sharp, on the edge, where I gotta be!"* He is as much a professional as Neil, but his life is far less streamlined: his marriage is floundering, his-step daughter is deeply disturbed, his house is a warren of corners and corridors and domestic clutter. When he dons the badge, however, he leaves this all behind, he can switch off his life in order to do his job; unfortunately he can't reverse the process. *"Ferocious, aren't I!?"* he jokes; the answer is unequivocally 'yes'!

Dialogue is disjointed and likely to end suddenly. The editing is similarly uncompromising, keeping you on your toes. In *Made In LA*, this succeeds in pushing the viewer away from the film, emphasising that you aren't being given enough time to know the characters. *Heat*, being almost twice the length and stitched together by *four* credited editors, gets the pace about right. The first act is shot almost entirely in close-up, bringing you claustrophobically close to the characters, but lit or cut or framed to confuse the eye and keep the mind working. Scenes are short, often without establishing shot, and are generally unlinked, causing the viewer to play a constant game of catch-up. *Where the hell are we now?*

To some extent this is a question the characters themselves are forced to ask. Most live in houses with picture windows, which look down on the oceanic mass of LA, a vast panorama of tiny lights against an ink-black background. Repeatedly people are framed by these vistas, reminding us that Mann's characters are, after all, just figures in a landscape. And they look down upon this landscape like malevolent gods, MacArthur/De Niro from the window of his girlfriend's warm russet apartment, Plank/Pacino from a helicopter, and both when spying on each other. They keep their distance from each other, giving the viewer the room to get in close.

Even with its choppy storytelling techniques, the plot proceeds almost imperceptibly through *Heat* for more than an hour, elaborating on character and plot developments which *Made In LA* polished off functionally in twenty minutes flat, Working in chapters, layering initially disconnected details and performances, providing glimpses of subplots, only some of which will be brought back into the light later on, Mann builds his second-draft version like a novel, slowly, carefully, demanding and rewarding close attention.

Pacino consistently proves that he is the only one who can live without love. He abandons his wife, and leaves his child, to obsessively pursue De Niro. Although we don't get the glimpse into his nightmares, *Made In LA* tells us about Hanna's self loathing in a way that *Heat* significantly doesn't - because it is done in the form of a confession to his wife, not his 'brother'. He lies on a sun lounger, gazing vacantly at an empty sky and bemoans *"I like to think I make a difference. Even if you need an electronic microscope to measure it, I make a difference. Tonight I made no difference."* Yet McLaren/Macauley himself, despite insisting that being alone doesn't make him lonely, has formed an attachment with Eady (Laura Harrington/Amy Brenneman). *"I am"* he confesses *"a double blank"*, a man with no relevant past and no future save that which he decides upon. He decides upon relocating to New Zealand. But this relationship is based on confession rather than love. He loves the crew. Michael Cerrito/Cherrito (Vincent Guastaferro/Tom Sizemore) is a crew-member with a wife and family which console him when he can't get the adrenaline buzz of working with the people he really loves: *"For me the action is half the juice!"* Chris Sheherlis/Shiherlis (Peter Dobson/Val Kilmer) is constantly at war with his wife, yet desolate without her, a victim of his own weaknesses and supported only by his 'brothers'.

This emotional need beneath the most fearsome of surfaces has been a constant in crime thrillers since the days of Cagney and Edward G. Gangsters, it suggests, are romantics, in love with the glamour and excitement of their violent careers, but deeply in need of an anchor, craving like children the approval of a woman. Most tellingly like James Caan in Mann's *Thief* (aka. *Violent Streets*) who carries around a composite picture of all the things he wants in life: a wife, a child, a house and his mentor/father (played effectively by Willie Nelson) by his side. By contrast, Pacino's rage won't allow a woman to get close, he cares more for the prey, they are his focus and his passion, for without them he cannot rescue their victims and confound his nightmare.

All building towards the core scene when MacArthur/De Niro and Plank/Pacino finally meet. In *Heat*, this confrontation is foreshadowed when Pacino gets his first good look at his prey, picked out in cold tones of blue and white on a monitor screen, seen through the eye of a thermal camera, seen only as shades of heat, presented as shades of cold. By return, Neil's first good look at Vincent is through a powerful telephoto lens. It is time for them to forgo technology and meet eye-to-eye.

The scene which, no doubt, sold the project to its two leads, comes when they finally do meet, in a restaurant. Like Graham and the notional red dragon in *Manhunter*. It is a scene where the light and dark aspects of their shared character come together and, rather like matter and antimatter, their proximity is likely to produce sparks. A word oft-used in this film is 'brother', and this scene is why. Throughout, Pacino is a flask of ill-restrained rage, yet De Niro, who rarely raises his voice, calms and placates him. MacArthur and Plank are more akin, neither man is given to passionate outbursts or rash decisions, yet, in both films, their dialogue is essentially the same.

In *Heat*, given space to embellish, they discuss their nightmares: Pacino fears the judgement of the victims he failed, whilst De Niro fears losing the drive to stay ahead, to keep his head above the water he sees through his living-room window. This is a very Catholic moment, an epiphany for both of them and a calm, admiring Confessional. They see each other in clear, bright light, empathising with and understanding each other in a way no one else can. *"Did you ever want a real-type life?" "I don't wanna do anything else." "Neither do I."* In the absence of redemption from any other source, they can at least offer it to each other.

Then they remind each other of their chosen paths. *"I'm not going back. I do what I do best, I don't know how to do anything else." "Neither do I".* They assure each other that, when the time comes to pull the trigger, they will. This isn't a threat, it is a statement of conviction, a confirmation of their belief in the order of things. *"That's the discipline!"*

And thus the films shift gear; the editing is just as frantic, but the scenes are less placid, the incidents more kinetic.

The crew waste no time in expediting their final bank job, proving that they are industrial strength and deadly serious. Forswearing the automatic pistols so beloved of Tarantino's men in black, they wield automatic rifles, and the inevitable shoot-out is correspondingly up-scale. Trained and ready, their reaction to the police presence is instantaneous and indefatigable, a running gun battle over streets and shopping plazas. Making the most of his expanded resources, Mann orchestrates the re-make of this scene into something unparalleled by anything mainstream cinema has ever had to offer, save the parodic excesses of early Landis. It comes as no surprise that McLaren/Macauley's loyalty to his crew, and his inherent loneliness, drive him to confound his avowed philosophy. The heat are swarming around him, but he can't leave everything in thirty seconds. Foolishly and heroically, he blasts his way out, carrying the wounded Chris Sheherlis/Shiherlis he should, by rights, have left to die. Hanna, on the other hand, is untroubled by such qualms. When Michael Cerrito/Cherrito (the family man), holding a little girl as hostage, is in his sights, he doesn't hesitate. He will struggle with the repercussions of a bad decision after he has acted upon it, not before.

As with any good novel, as the pace quickens, so does your reading, you turn the pages faster and faster; disparate plot threads come shockingly together, the tight close-ups become prowling tracking shots; and so the film enters its third act, a race against time with McLaren/Macauley attempting to escape, and Hanna, not surprisingly, determined to stop him. It is now that his wife Lilian/Justine chooses to hammer the last nails into the coffin of their marriage. Having attempted to gain his attention and affection without success, she pushes him out of her life and into the solace of a cold hotel room (with picture window). It is now that the traitor to Patrick/Neil's crew resurfaces to drag them down. It is now that Patrick/Neil's ethics draw him out of hiding into the light. It is now that *Made in LA* and *Heat* separate to pursue their different closures.

Momentarily Neil is free - he drives to the airport, passes out of the dark into an impossibly brightly-lit tunnel - his passage through cleansing white into the welcoming embrace of neon blue. Then his honour, his desire to avenge his fallen 'brothers', pulls him back into the dark and propels him towards the classic, inevitable and entirely necessary showdown. Vincent is dogged by no such honour; where Neil cannot allow a debt to go unpaid, Vincent can enthusiastically abandon his wife, still reeling from the attempted suicide of their daughter, in pursuit of the game. This is why they are so perfectly matched, entirely balanced in the scales of justice.

Made In LA makes the bold move of confounding their showdown, it shows McLaren arriving at the hotel, intent on killing the traitor Waingro, and, momentarily distracted by the timely arrival of Hanna, dying ignominiously from a lucky shot through a door. No one-on-one shoot-out between the 'brothers'. No redemption. Indeed, as Hanna holds Maclaren in his arms, he demands to know why he came back: *"You were as free as a bird!"* The whispered response: *"Nowhere to go"*. You are left, like Hanna, feeling cheated and desolate. Although McLaren's inherent nobility has brought him down, it has not done so in a significant and satisfying manner. As the eighties drew to a close, the reassuring conventions of symmetrical plot structure were fractured. In the final episode of *Miami Vice*, broadcast the same year, the heroes don't win, they don't ride off into the sunset in glory, and they don't get to carry on fighting the good fight. Disillusioned by the darkness and corruption all around them, they turn their backs and walk away. They leave the battle unwon.

For *Heat*, six years on, the history and legendary status brought to the production by De Niro and Pacino, and particularly in view of it being their first on-screen meeting, needs a bolder, more spectacular finale. So, after successfully enacting revenge on Waingro, Neil walks away free into the night. But there, in the darkness, Vincent reminds Neil of his convictions, of his thirty seconds rule - and so, now it is too late, he flees, abandoning his confessor and redeemer, Eady, severing the connection with what made him pure. With that decision and at that moment, his fate is sealed. It is only a matter of time before he and Vincent are engaged in battle, caught in the glare of the incriminating white landing lights of a runway. Judgement is passed as Neil's shadow betrays him, cast by the pure white light which he has literally turned his back on. So Vincent brings their relationship to an end. In the diner he had promised that he would and now he is bound by his bravado.

He has prevailed, he has killed the only sibling he truly had. He is finally, truly and profoundly alone. Silhouetted against a dark background, alone in an unlit landscape. Overwhelmed with empathy, he reaches out and touches Neil for the first time, the first human contact of any kind he has had, since making love with his wife in the opening scene. The classic Hollywood ending to a classical tale of fragile male relationships in a hostile male world. It's a helluva lot of trouble to go to, for two men to hold hands.

Although this more traditional ending is more satisfying on an emotional level (and doubtless appeased the two leads' egos) it holds up less well to consideration. What *Made In LA* lacks in class, it makes up for in energy. It is messy and sudden and sharp, *Heat* perforce carries a sheen of professional contrivance which makes it cleaner and easier to take.

Subjectively, *Heat* is far and away the better movie, it looks, sounds, feels and plays better. Better cast, better locations, better script. But *Made In LA*, its ignored elder brother, less sophisticated, more down-to-earth, is no less fascinating. They contribute to each other, both are made greater by the existence of the other, neither should be seen in isolation.

Grateful acknowledgement to Val Hill for leaving her essay *Tonight I Made No Difference* (co-authored with Yvonne Tasker) unlocked and unattended long enough for me to nick the best bits. It is the only work in print I have been able to find which even admits to the existence of *Made In LA* - John Ashbrook

A GOOD CAST IS WORTH REPEATING

NOT ONLY DOES Michael Mann recycle the same ideas, incidents and lines of dialogue he does pretty well at re-using all those old character names as well. Waste not, want not.

Actor in Made In LA	Character	Actor in Heat
Alex MacArthur	Patrick McLaren/Neil Macauley	Robert De Niro
Scott Plank	Vincent Hanna	Al Pacino
Peter Dobson	Chris Sheherlis/Shiherlis	Val Kilmer
Vincent Guastaferro	Michael Cerrito/Cherrito	Tom Sizemore
Robert Winley	Nate	Jon Voight
Xander Berkeley	Waingro	Kevin Gage
R.D. Call	Lilian/Justine	Diane Venora
Laura Harrington	Eady	Amy Brenneman
Richard Chaves	Officer Casals	Wes Studi
Michael Rooker	Officer Bosko	Ted Levine
Victor Rivers	Officer Drucker/Ariega	Mykelti Williamson

MARTIN SCORSESE

by John Foster

YOU BEEN AXIN' FOR IT, Marty! You been gettin' too famous an' too damn fat, bruvver. You forgettin' who y'r real buddies are! Alla dis classy crap, you becomin' a - wachyacallit - a dilettante, man. I tellya, y'r gettin' above yo'sel' wiv dat arthouse shit. Next you'll be buyin' a fuckin' dinner-suit for alla dem 'wards ceremonies, 'steada hirin' one out like da resta da schmucks. It's gettin' ta dat time, Marty; someone's gonna hafta take yous outside 'n' 'splain it to ya. Yous knows it ain't nuffin' pers'nal, bruvver ...

The general critical opinion regarding Martin Scorsese's *Casino* reduced it to some kind of less-effective *Goodfellas Revisited*, *Goodfellas Two*, or *Badfellas*; whatever trite convenience allowed this deeply passionate and reflective work to be shrugged off by media-ites who had, in all probability, already come to this vacuous conclusion before the film was lensed or even penned. Being too successful, both aesthetically and commercially, which combined to become the deadliest of sins in the eyes of some movie commentators, Scorsese has become a prime target, and also rather a soft one. He has produced some of the world's most profound and disturbing cinema and, as such, has placed himself right in line for a mugging from critics who can't get up in the morning.

It was predictable that *Casino* would be compared unfavourably to its famous gangland predecessor, *Goodfellas* (1990), a very powerful and deeply uncomfortable film, but also a low-life bleed-off from Scorsese's breakthrough picture *Mean Streets* (1973). In the book *Scorsese on Scorsese*, (Faber and Faber, 1989) the director ruefully admits to censure from his mentor, John Cassavetes, concerning his formulaic movie, *Boxcar Bertha*, (*"I've got to tell you Marty, you've just spent the last year making a piece of shit!"*) As a response, Scorsese began to direct the kind of picture he really wanted to make: *Mean Streets*.

Although the chronically overrated *Taxi Driver* (1976) represented an unproductive cul-de-sac of trend-conscious artifice; these early films proved quite narrow and introverted. They dealt with the psyche of trash-can gangsters and gruesome, bar-brawl, *Psycho*tic violence, often with deftness and veracity, but also lacking the sweep and majesty of *Casino*, for which its forebears were clearly dry-runs.

NEUROTIC CITIES

Casino could only be made by a man wholly in touch with his dark side. It is the kind of movie which will, in time, be seen as seminal of the period it reflects, of the period in which it was made, and late twentieth century cinema in general. It is so dense and complex that immediate journalistic response to it was inevitably going to be fast-food criticism, and it became a field day for the tired hacks of received opinion, wallowing in their easy dismissiveness. Scorsese's magnificent remake of *Cape Fear* (1991) was similarly bad-mouthed by critics; a film which, despite shortfalls, is far superior to the dreary hackdom of J. Lee Thompson's 1961 original, to which it was unfavourably compared. It is a film which drips with delicious melodrama and moral ambiguity, exhibiting more than any movie in the Scorsese canon the influence of the greatly admired Michael Powell, and particularly his incisive essay in cinematic voyeurism, *Peeping Tom* (1960).

Casino opens audaciously with the projected death of its lead character, Ace, played by Robert De Niro, that consummate actor, indelibly aligned with Scorsese and whose utterly egocentric and selflessly committed performances provide the definitive persona of the ambiguous anti-hero, subtly evoking the ethos of ruthless personal pragmatism in the post Thatcher-Reagan eras. No other actor has provided a greater sense of late twentieth century mores and how we live now. As Raymond Chandler said of Humphrey Bogart *"All he has to do to dominate a scene is enter it"*.

Inaugurating a complex pattern of interior monologue, De Niro's voice-over tells us that during the course of the past-tense narrative about to unfold, he dies violently, having been blown apart by a car bomb. À la *Sunset Boulevard*, the deceased is talking to us from his grave. Or so we are to believe. This is, of course, all a canny cheat and, admittedly, the revelation of how it pans out, is the weakest moment in the movie in terms of credibility. In effect, the mirror of his magic broken, finally stripped of his fame and fortune, De Niro does symbolically die, but few openings have presented us with the panache, wit and confidence of the first few minutes of *Casino*, a stubbornly long and discursive movie which, following this arresting, cardsharp opening, moves into a dense flashback structure.

The celebrated French novelist, playwright, poet, screenwriter and film-maker, the late Marguerite Duras, was the most distinguished innovator of the art of interior monologue, especially with her screenplay for *Hiroshima Mon Amour*, Alain Resnais' 1959 French New Wave masterpiece. Duras demonstrated not only the power of poetic language in voice-over, but how complex layers of narrative and characterisation may be deployed through its use, with time and space manipulated in support of thematic, character-led story-telling. In *Casino*, Scorsese and his screen writing partner Pileggi utilise this same technique, employing three narrators during the movie, in monologues which are ambiguous and frequently redefine or contradict what is witnessed on the screen.

The unreliable narrator, where we are invited to question or to distrust what we are being told in voice-over, is a well-established *film-noir* technique, from

Chandler in *Double Indemnity* (1944) to Terrence Malick in his mould-breaking *noir* road-movie *Badlands*(1974). In *Casino*, as in *Goodfellas*, Scorsese employs this frisson of visual and verbal counter-point, so that De Niro's cool in the voice-over is contrasted with the turmoil of his on-screen image.

Like the Bob Dylan song *Jack of Hearts*, itself possessing formidable wit, pathos and narrative power, and once described by Quentin Tarantino as 'a little movie', *Casino* proceeds like a game of cards, with many judicious and artful sleights-of-hand. We are presented with a fastidiously detailed depiction of the world of the gambling casino, and the lives of those who populate it, their attitudes and values. The corrupt universe the film occupies is unquestionably accepted by its characters, so their casual immorality bounces back upon the audience when the violence erupts in all its bestiality.

Chinese boxes of lives in moments of imagery requiring no further elucidation, are presented: such as Sharon Stone's praying mantis destruction of hickville Romeos who are stitched-up, bled of their wealth, then returned to the little woman and hapless penury. Not only do these scenes define the soulless philistine backdrop of Ginger (Stone) and Ace's lives, but they provide the movie with its elegant broad-brush-stroke canvass.

Casino is a big picture, which achieves its power through the small change of experience rather than portentous thematics, large-scale locales or worn-on-the-sleeve production values. Some of the casino scenes sustain a visual virtuosity almost Hogarthian in detail, bursting with energy and atmosphere. They are freshly-minted without any sense of self-admiration, unmannered and without self-consciousness. The unforced breadth and scope of the film suggests a major development for Scorsese and his cinema.

With the delicately feline skill of Patricia Highsmith, he shocks us with deliberately underplayed violence. The comparatively slow pace of the first half of the film gradually ameliorates into some stomach-churning sequences, far more affecting, yet equally less gratuitous than the notorious Ear Scene in *Reservoir Dogs*. Some commentators found the level of violence - particularly the ritual clubbing to death of Joe Pesci - too much to take.

Yet the graphic mayhem in *Casino* is the epitome of responsible and honest depictions of screen violence; it is 'good' violence precisely because it is uncomfortable, relentless and disturbing. Unlike Tarantino, Scorsese does not disingenously pan away to the sound of an echoing scream, his camera stays with the thuggery and forces you to confront the mindlessness of it. He shows us the consequences of such sordid behaviour and dramatises the pornography of violence without himself indulging exploitatively in it.. More importantly, the violence emerges explicitly from the characters themselves, from the extremity of their natures and that of the dangerous world they inhabit. The violence is meant to be shocking but is never there for its own sake, and employed to underwrite the neuroses of the ensemble.

But it is the complexity of the character relationships which make the film such an advance for Scorsese. This is a morality tale of mythic proportions, a classic tragedy about human weaknesses and failings, with enviable dramatic foreshadowing, a downward spiral where the audience know from the first that things will inevitably end badly, as if pre-ordained. These are real people with histories, not cardboard cut-outs made to dance to the director's tune. Ace's blind and mutually destructive love for Ginger disabuses our perception of the manipulative, laid-back wise-guy, and invests in him an Achilles Heel about which the wheel of misfortune spins.

Until *Casino*, Sharon Stone appeared desperate to prove herself a real thespian and move away from the synthetic sado-masochistic *femme* of *Basic Instinct*. However, in Scorsese's hands, she produces a rich and rewarding performance. Her giddy downfall in *Casino* deconstructs the stereotype of the mantrap *femme fatale* by showing the user used, the wrecker wrecked. Not since Isabella Rossellini's performance in David Lynch's *Blue Velvet* (1986) has the screen witnessed a fatal beauty expose the frailty behind her deadly nightshade allure.

One of the many achievements of *Casino* is to present characters who evolve, who have embraced altered states by the end of the movie. They are very different people from when we first meet them. Because of the film's detail, we are able to look down the tunnel of their experiences and see where they made the wrong turns. They are characters in action, brought low by the incidents which overtake them. Hitchcock was one of the few directors of international significance who committed the in-depth *Psycho*logical manifestations of his characters to celluloid. Here, with *Casino*, Scorsese finally joins the ranks of this rare genius.

A novelist is able, through the power of language, to describe the inner mental verisimilitudes of fictional characters. It is much more difficult for the what-you-see-is-what-you-get medium of film to do this. The contours of mental and emotional character switch-back is more problematic to depict, which is one of the reasons for employing interior monologue, where such private thoughts sand feelings can be voiced. *Casino* is vibrant in its multifarious portrayal of characters and their variegated secret orchards.

Each persona is indefinable, refusing to be pigeon-holed, and subject to continual update. You are never quite sure where you are with anyone, and the effect of this is quite unsettling. One of the underlying themes of *Casino* is the power of obsession, in this case the drug of gambling and its undying compulsiveness for the main characters, a psychological bind far more tellingly teased-out than in, for instance Karel Reisz's tedious 1974 piece on gambling, cunningly entitled *The Gambler*. In the final sequences of *Casino* we witness a sad-eyed De Niro, now eternally confined to a small-time existence, still possessed by the gambling bug.

With the intimidating line-up of raw talent assembled for this picture, it is difficult, given its collaborative nature, to say that *Casino* belongs to any one individual. Yet, partly because of De Niro's gently self-effacing performance, Pesci's

'Nicky' finally steals the show, and De Niro, with a true actor's generosity, lets him.

Nicky is a character of Dickensian depth and unease. Again, Scorsese builds upon Pesci's psychopath in *Goodfellas*, but rounds him into an unforgettably disturbing personality who threatens to explode off the screen and attack the viewer in person. It is a performance of gripping intensity and passion, twinned brilliantly with De Niro's nonchalance, and underwritten by brilliant black humour. Nicky is also very likeable, a man of charm and good humour and a doting, compassionate father; yet he constantly threatens to boil over and commit grossly sadistic acts of violence.

Because he is so empathetic, you will Pesci not to lose his cool, you want him to stay in control; which creates an extraordinary tension between actor and audience, a genuine engagement with the man's turbulent psyche. The likeableness is the principle evolution of this recurring character in Scorsese's cinema, and it's a killer. Nicky's decline into self-betrayal, climaxing with his succumbing to Ginger's seductions - the most personal and irredeemable betrayal of De Niro - is convincingly seeded in his wayward instability. Nicky becomes one of the great tragic figures in modern cinema.

What strongly communicates itself is Scorsese's love of his characters, despite - and partly because of - all their flaws and failings. They are as they are and he does not judge them, even though he may regret their self-destructive actions. It is clear that Scorsese sustains a particular affection for the Joe Pesci characters.

And there is a way in which Nicky and Scorsese seem related. They appear to be very similar personalities: the public face of the film-maker is one of geniality, personableness and good humour, with that shy smile only relatively recently brought out from behind a masking beard. Yet he makes dark, violent movies about deeply ambiguous killers; disturbed characters in neurotic cities. There is a rage in his male-orientated pictures which echoes the emotional duality of this auteur, and which is best represented in the characters portrayed by Joe Pesci. Joe Pesci is Martin Scorsese's screen alter-ego.

BILLY WILDER

by Richard Armstrong

***VETERAN DIRECTOR BILLY WILDER** reached his ninetieth birthday in 1996, and the lifetime achievement awards keep rolling in. Yet, considering that a handful of his films are reckoned to be classics, sell steadily on video, and feature regularly on TV-schedules world-wide, a closely-argued study of his work has not appeared since video copies of his work allowed easy reassessment.*

Keen to challenge both the image of Wilder as a cocky little Viennese of dining table legend, and his closet romantic reputation of the '70s, Richard Armstrong's *forthcoming book sees Wilder as a hardworking Hollywood craftsman and rigorous commentator on the American scene. Focusing on such examinations of his adopted society as* Sunset Boulevard, The Apartment *and* The Fortune Cookie, *along with neglected works like the Wilder-scripted* Ball of Fire, *and his final film* Buddy Buddy, *Armstrong attempts to chart the chronicle which Wilder offered of American life in the middle years of an 'American' century which was born with him.*

What follows is an extract from his chapter on the seminal 1944 thriller Double Indemnity. *Despite the interest of a wide range of British and American publishing houses in this project, the author's search for a mutually satisfactory deal continues...*

Double Indemnity is one of Wilder's finest films and is widely acknowledged to be one of the greatest American films ever made. In it, the director's preoccupation with the underside of American enterprise is most fully articulated. As supple as a well-crafted sentence, the film has all the elegance and efficiency of the best mainstream Hollywood product. In *Double Indemnity*, there is thorough harmony between plot, theme, space and time, and each word and gesture has its place.

In the novella by James M. Cain which formed the basis for Wilder and Raymond Chandler's screenplay, morbid, grasping Phyllis Nirdlinger lures lover, insurance salesman Walter Huff, into selling her husband a 'double indemnity' accident policy before both murder him and elope with the proceeds. The screenplay is said to have been influenced by the Snyder-Gray murder case in the '20s, and it is easy to imagine its appeal for the young Wilder immersed in coarse narratives from the American undergrowth.

So coarse was it that the patrician Charles Brackett, Wilder's collaborator since 1938, refused to work on the project. Casting around for a suitable

AN AMERICAN TRAGEDY

partner, in Cain's absence, led the film's Associate Producer Joseph Sistrom to a novelist whose work oozed with the Southern Californian social climate which permeates the novella. Chandler, a tweedy and reclusive English-educated writer of the 'tough school' of pre-war American crime fiction, was signed to co-write *Double Indemnity*'s screenplay in 1943. The collaboration between the workaholic Wilder and the alcoholic Chandler was fraught. Suffice to say that Chandler hated Hollywood, did not understand scriptwriting techniques, was unused to the regime at Paramount's Writers' Building, and didn't like Billy Wilder. Yet their two views on the story meshed.

Chandler's fiction is a brand of fatalistic realism. His characters inhabit a word where morality is almost entirely relative. But, if their laconic conversation was considered 'modern' when it appeared in the pulps of the 1930s, Chandler's detectives bore the honourable stamp of medieval knights. Chandler could also write dialogue which rings out as it is read, being spoken by real American urban types who eat, breathe, love and die.

The dialogue in *Double Indemnity* is some of the richest in any Wilder film. It does not waste a word, is setting scenes and fashioning them to the motion of the plot. Indeed, the screenplay's power lies in a punchy mélange of Chandler's deft descriptions, Cain's California rootlessness and the vigour of Widerean storytelling.

When bored housewife Phyllis Dietrichson (Barbara Stanwyck) and confident young insurance salesman Walter Neff (Fred MacMurray) meet, they discuss her husband's risky work as an oil executive. Their talk of falling crown blocks and snapping casing lines owes much to Chandler's 13-year stint with an oil company. Later, in the office of President Norton at Walter's employer Pacific All-Risk, Claims Manager Keyes (Edward G. Robinson) offers a breathtaking exposition of the workings of an actuarial table which conceivably derived from Chandler's experience as an accountant, as must have the officialese in Walter's Dictaphone confession to Keyes. When Phyllis offers Walter iced tea, he asks whether she is English. This would also suggest the hand of Chandler, an anglophile whose work betrays an obsession with the genteel habits of 'English roses'. Walter's voice-over, as he leaves, *"How could I know that murder sometimes smells like honeysuckle?"* contains a forlorn romanticismwhich suffuses both Chandler's fiction and Wilder's films.

If Cain's novella seems overwrought and tends to read better than it would play, the screenplay blends coherence and irony in a concise and pungent way. Written in the vein of a stylised realism, as Richard Schickel put it, *"Their dialogue is just a little jazzier than we are likely to hear in life,"*[1] While, in Bernard Dick's words *"Neff talks ... in units of thought, where the ideas generate their own rhythm and their own grammar,"* [2] resulting in a heady mix of raciness and realism. Neff talks in images tautly cut to fit an atmosphere of dread. *"We have a guy in our office named Keyes. For him, a set-up like that would be like a slice of rare roast beef. In three minutes he'd know it wasn't an accident. In ten minutes you'd be sitting under the hot lights. In half an hour, you'd be signing your name to a confession."* When Walter and Phyllis banter in her lounge, they use a traffic violation as a metaphor for his pursuit of her, creating a lively 'American' subtext which translates longing into a combative exchange in a universal clash of wills. Indeed, *Double Indemnity* is one of the most cutting examinations Wilder ever offered of a society bent upon verbal and political one-upmanship.

However, the world of *Double Indemnity* is a mixed economy, and its characters are also implicated in a network of chance and circumstance over which they have little control. When Walter's jaunty Dodge Coupé - so like him in character - runs the stop light on a downtown intersection, we are compelled into a one-way journey into paranoia and despair. *"Straight down the line"* is an incantation which Walter and Phyllis swap throughout the film. The 'machinery' of their conspiracy motivates conversations which are riddled with references to implacable mechanisms. But, in a meta-narrational sense, it could just as easily refer to the seamless plotting of Wilder's film. Few Hollywood films of the classical period are as compelling as *Double Indemnity*. If the novel flashback structure of the screenplay creates the impression of a fixed set of fortunes which can only go one way, Wilder's editing methods are significant too. His technique was to 'cut in the camera' or only shoot as much film as was necessary for the scene, a tendency which was also facilitated by his close rapport with editor Doane Harrison. As Steve Seidman writes *"Action is usually played out in medium shot and relatively long takes ... The editing here is not to provide symbolic effect but to break master scenes into a variety of set-ups. This 'invisible editing' maintains a narrative flow and also anticipates the viewer's conception of the action taking place on the screen. Dissolves are used to establish even the shortest passage of time."* [3]

Before Walter leaves his apartment to meet Phyllis and murder Dietrichson, there is a series of dissolves in which he places cards in the doorbell and phone exchange box, which will drop if they ring. He then leaves, using the service stairs, having made a point of asking the garage attendant to clean his car. If asked, Charlie will say that Walter was working in his apartment all night. Such attention to detail has seldom been reflected in so thoroughgoing a fashion as in Wilder's own methods. At the close of the film there was to have been a scene in which Walter goes to the gas chamber. Typically, Wilder set it up, taking the minutest care to authenticate the execution. Such realism, considered shocking when the film was previewed, represents one the most pungent aesthetic currents in Wilder's '40s films, forcing the audience to look into, as well as at his masterpieces of narrative cinema.

The extent of *Double Indemnity*'s sense of tragic inevitability seems to occur in the final scene when Walter, dying from a gunshot wound inflicted by Phyllis, asks Keyes whether he is to be nursed back to health so that he can walk into the gas chamber on his own two feet. His assumption that Dietrichson's and Phyllis' deaths will result in his own, is not only the result of stringent plotting, but seems to make redundant the moral distinction between illegal murder and judicial execution. With the pall of death, a legacy of the novella, hanging over the film, *Double Indemnity* here becomes one of the most searing indictments of capital punishment prior to Tim Robbins' *Dead Man Walking*.

Other than that necessary to move the plot along, the film offers little information about its characters' pasts. But, when Lola Dietrichson, Phyllis' step-daughter, reveals to Walter that Phyllis caused the death of the first Mrs Dietrichson some years previously, it hints at much about Phyllis.

If Walter was " *... trying to think with your brains, Keyes*", Phyllis must co-opt Walter's expertise in order to attempt release from a buried existence. The critical line on Phyllis Dietrichson has traditionally been that she is an alluring and treacherous woman who cynically uses Walter as an escape-route from her marital responsibilities and in order to earn a fast hundred grand.

Seen through Walter's eyes, Phyllis is a woman of moments and parts; her perfume, her gold anklet, her silky blonde hair, her fawning appeal to his professionalism. For many critics, she is an up-market slut. But perhaps Phyllis simply lacks direction, having, at some point, been corrupted in her search for a purpose in life. It is significant that we can only ever see Phyllis in terms of Walter's voice-over or Keyes' account of her actions. In the light of the progressive examinations of neurotic women offered by Woody Allen in recent years, it is perhaps time to re-examine the character and a Wilder ending which has been the subject of critical debate for over forty years.

Dolores Paley, in Allen's *Crimes And Misdemeanours*, recalls the libidinous woman of *film noir*, of whom Phyllis is the prototype. Like Phyllis, Dolores has a shady past and, in both films, revelations about their pasts trigger these characters' downfalls, each death emerging as a result of scrupulously refined schemes. Like Dolores, Phyllis is a tragic figure. If loneliness and insecurity hasten Dolores' death, Phyllis' desperate need for security has driven her into marriage to a drunken slob twice her age - *"I wanted a home. Why not?"*

In keeping with both films' tight structures, both characters are defined by the unscrupulous liaisons which compel them. Phyllis married someone with the temperament of Wallace Beery's ringside failure, a father whose twisted attitude towards his daughter consists of the opinion: *"A great little fighter for her weight!"* Then she has an affair with someone who will eventually murder her. Phyllis lacks the discourses of self-discovery which feminism offers characters of Dolores' generation. Consequently, she is unable to determine her own future and must have a man to steer her, a situation resulting in him discarding her when her crude self-assertion becomes problematic.

Rather than acting to avert a predestined future, Phyllis can only react to a hellish past and present. Having swapped uncertainty for a comfortable home and a two-car garage, she finds herself married to a workaholic who drinks in bed and beats her up. Phyllis tells Walter that once Dietrichson came home from a party and sat in the garage with the motor running. Arguably, straitened dynamics operate throughout the screenplay, this marriage making victims of both characters.

Male critics tend to harp on the fact that Phyllis is guilty for using her sexuality to ensnare Walter. But, reared in a pre-feminist culture in which women were the appendages of men, Phyllis lacks the know-how to be anything more than an accessory to Walter's imagination. Her inability to start her own car without his help illustrates the extent of her helplessness. Since Phyllis' story comes to us via Walter's voice-over, we are made to go along with his judgement of her. In Keyes' opinion, she murdered Dietrichson with Nino Zachetti, Lola's boyfriend, and what is good enough for Keyes is good enough for Walter. Phyllis must attempt to function in a world in which the paternalistic Keyes, the husband Dietrichson, and the lovers Walter and Nino, take moral precedence over her, even while this patriarchal order is being challenged by the prodigal Walter. In the warlike universe of the film, Walter challenges the husband and the 'father' Keyes with the object of installing another man - himself - in their places.

As a woman, Phyllis is not only untrustworthy, according to the misogynist Keyes, but unable to act without copious instructions from Walter. His handing her a drink with the words *"See if you can carry this as far as the living room"* and her *"I never know what's in the ice-box"* state her redundancy and her sense of discontinuity, even in her own home. Given the critical emphasis on Phyllis' manipulation of Walter, it seems ironic that it she who complains that his scheme to kill her husband, claim the insurance and be together, is actually tearing them apart. As emotionally confused as she may be, Phyllis is more in touch with her feelings than the hard-boiled Walter, as her demonstrations of affection suggest. In their final scene, it seems more likely that Phyllis lacks the maturity to know the difference between love and like, than that she is feigning affection. Her admission *"No, I never loved you Walter, not you or anyone else"* is not so much a confession to insincerity as to stunted emotional development. *"I used you, just as you said"* again borrows his words as a sign of her helplessness. When she embraces him for the last time, she is emotionally as well as physically hurt when he puts the gun against her and fires, this scene being one of the most romantically forlorn in all Wilder, for its grotesque parody of meaningful verbal and sexual intercourse. Phyllis' confession of love is sad because it contrasts so poignantly with such exchanges as when he asks her the name of her perfume. *"I don't know, I bought it in Ensenada"*, she replies, unable to even find a scent which is her own and could be theirs. A fundamental part of their romantic currency thus remains a mere purchase in a cheap border town.

Walter rejects her confession in favour of Keyes' suspicion. His "*Save it; I'm telling this*" obliquely calls to mind his voice over, but also embodies the masculine attempt to control feminine wiles. The overriding tragedy of Phyllis' existence is that she may only have discovered herself at the point at which she is about to die. Her giving Walter the gun effectively enables him to 'execute' her for her crimes against the patriarchal order. Even if we read Phyllis as insecure and unchanged by events, she is still tragic for having failed to realise just how buried her existence has been. If not, her confession is her first and final moment of truth.

Apparent transformations of character often occur in Wilder. But this final scene between Walter and Phyllis is one of his most equivocal closures. We are left with the possibility of Phyllis' redemption without needing the obligatory happy ending which mars *The Fortune Cookie*, another of Wilder's insurance scams. As far as the patriarchal order is concerned, it is enough that Walter finds redemption by confessing, while Lola is left to settle down with Nino and assume the conventional feminine rôle. What Phyllis' death suggests is, as a character in *Crimes And Misdemeanours* reflects, that wisdom comes to some suddenly.

Phyllis has been read as a cautionary screen reflection of the self-sufficient American woman of the war-years. Newly independent and with money to spare, such an individual could enjoy her freedom and might even frequent bars alone. The implications for fidelity to absent husbands and lovers are clear. The patriarchal order which Phyllis disrupts supports a system of property relations which defines a woman as the property of a man's estate. Phyllis' acquiescence in the system's logic: Money = Fulfilment, renders her the docile vector of attitudes which neither she nor any of her sex have instituted. In stressing her allure so as to ensnare a breadwinner, she has blindly complied with the rules of a game which she did not invent but must play in order to merely exist. Far from relieving her plight, Walter has simply added to her perennial despair.

Weltered in the phoney claims which pile up on his desk, Barton Keyes is steeped in a conviction that humans are infinitely deceitful. *"You wouldn't even say today's Tuesday without you looked at the calendar ... and then you would find out what company printed the calendar, then find out if their calendar checks with The World Almanac calendar"*, Walter teases. Keyes was almost married once, but 'the little man' inside who tells him when a claim is crooked led him to have his fiancée investigated.

Aside from his ravenous enthusiasm for the job, the only fellow feeling which Keyes allows himself is his fondness for Walter, the son he never had. Beneath the heterosexual drama of *Double Indemnity*, a touching father-son dynamic is tersely expressed through the ritual in which Walter lights the matchless Keyes' cigar. Poignantly reversed in the final scene, the dying Walter takes out a bloodstained cigarette and Keyes lights it for him. *"You know why you didn't figure this one, Keyes? The guy you were looking for was too close, he was right across the desk from you." "Closer than that, Walter!"* Keyes corrects. In a film in which one couple's rapport feels more like warfare than love, this scene recalls those battlefield clinches in war movies in which dying buddies can be hugged by their comrades. Indeed, Parker Tyler argues for Keyes as symbolic of the Allied 'claim adjuster' who was to preside over Germany's war-guilt in 1945 [4]. If his matches always ignite in Keyes' pocket, the Claims Manager's ferreting talent has blown up in his face. As much a victim of the plot's mechanical logic as Walter, the hard-headed rationalist finds that his rationality leads straight back to the one chink in his armour. In a film in which all the characters are trapped with each other and none can escape being hurt, the 'machinery' denies the individual the will to evade being crushed. Keyes is therefore bound to lose the 'son' whom he cultivated and who now lays dying at the hand of a woman. As Andrew Sarris writes, *"For all its deadpan stoicism,* Double Indemnity *strikes uncommonly sweet chords of male camaraderie in its final confrontation."*[5] Keyes feels that Walter should steer clear of women, at one point offering him a martini with two olives, in a Freudian allusion by Wilder which, for once, does not mock psychoanalysis.

Double Indemnity's is a grim screenplay, but there is humour, particularly in the first half of the film. Keyes' scene with Norton deftly announces who the real brains behind Pacific All-Risk are, reinforcing the film's portrait of a deeply competitive universe, and revealing Wilder's slangy touch: *"Nice going Mr Norton. You sure carried that ball. Only, you fumbled on the goal line, then you heaved an illegal forward pass and got thrown for a 40-yard loss. Now you can't pick yourself up because you haven't got a leg to stand on."* Much of the dialogue's colour stems from its ease with mid-century American vernacular. As Schickel noted, Wilder *"... heard something wild and strange ... what sounded like clichés to the native born, sounded like fresh metaphors to a wry spirit listening closely."*

Double Indemnity was released in America in September 1944, its bleak vision a truer reflection of a long and bloody world war than many films of that year. With its scenario of redemption through violence, the film now seems more in touch with the times than such as *Meet Me In St. Louis* and *Going My Way*. For Tyler, *Double Indemnity* seems to be the expression of a latent public perception that war, whatever the motive, is murder, and murder represents a *Psycho*logical kink. (Hence the wartime perception of Hitler as either crazy or barmy, depending on which side of the Atlantic one was). Without doubt, the film brought moral and physical carnage onto American screens as an aggressive analogy of real warfare. It is not tenderness but murderous frustration when Walter seizes and kisses Phyllis. Never before had apparently decent suburbanites been portrayed as killers.

In this tragedy, all are on the make. Tyler writes of Walter: *"Neff's pathological illusion is one of the diseases of American culture: that salesmanship can be aesthetic value."* Phyllis' last words are: *"I'm not asking you to buy, just hold me tight."* For once, she is attempting to escape the trading of even one's words, in favour of a status quo based upon love and personal value. *Double Indemnity*'s suburbia could be seen as the prototype of the social consensus whose values Presidents Nixon and Reagan represented in the '70s and '80s; one endorsing the Watergate cover-up and the other the culture of insider trading. Arguably, Walter engages in a little insider trading in a Wilderean universe in which the best-laid plan is often a lonely fist shaking at God. Ultimately, the poetry of *Double Indemnity* is the poetry of failure.

NOTES

[1] ***Richard Schickel,* Double Indemnity. *BFI Film Classics, 1992.***

[2] ***Bernard F. Dick,* Anatomy of Film, *St Martin's Press, 1990.***

[3] ***Steve Seidman,* Billy Wilder, *G.K. Hall and Co, 1977.***

[4] ***Parker Tyler,* Myth and Magic of the Movies, *Secker and Warburg, 1971.***

[5] ***Andrew Sarris, 'Billy Wilder - Closet Romanticist',* Film Comment, *July - August 1976.***

REFERENCE WAS ALSO MADE TO:

Ann Kaplan (Ed),* Women in Film Noir, *British Film Institute, 1978.
Dudley Nichols and John Gassner (Eds),* Double Indemnity *screenplay from* Best Film Plays of 1944, *© Paramount Pictures.

WONG KAR-WAI AND CHRIS DOYLE

by John Ashbrook

WONG KAR-WAI was born in Shanghai in 1958, but moved to Hong Kong when his parents relocated there in 1962. His memories of this period form the backdrop to *Days of Being Wild* (made in 1990) the film that first brought him together with cameraman Christopher Doyle, and got him noticed as a director of note over here.

During the mid-eighties he worked in Hong Kong script factories, turning out ten produced scripts between 1982 and 1987, ranging in style from romantic comedies to Hong Kong's trademark action dramas. Promoted to director, he made his first movie in 1988 - *As Tears Go By*. Modelled on Scorsese's *Mean Streets*, it tells the story of two gang-land debt-collectors in Kowloon (the mainland half of Hong Kong), who look upon each other as brothers. Little brother Fly's constant posturing to prove that he's a man means that big brother Ah Wah, is forever bailing him out. Eventually the resentment between different 'families' within the gang come to a head in a brutal torture scene which, in typical Hong Kong fashion, manages to be as nasty as it is stylish.

All the motifs which would become Wong's calling card are here - love-lorn loners; a claustrophobic urban jungle, lit in strongly contrasting shades of red and blue; a popular music background; sudden explosions of extreme violence shot in a time-distorted blur known now as 'smudge motion'. Similarly, his leading man Andy Lau, in common with many Hong Kong stars (including Jackie Cheung who played Fly), is not just an actor but also a million-selling recording artist and movie producer. Wong loves taking huge celebrities and presenting them as average, every day people. Of course, this aspect is rather lost on us here, where most people haven't heard of any of 'em. It is worth remembering, however, that both Lau and Cheung won Best Actor awards for their performances in *As Tears Go By*.

Wong's next two films *Days Of Being Wild* and *Ashes of Time* (1992-4) were something of a departure, being respectively a historical romance and a martial arts epic.

Days of Being Wild tells the story of a disappointed and debauched young man, Yuddi, who's life seems meaningless to him because he doesn't know who is parents are. Women fall at his feet and he does nothing more than abuse them, not caring for anyone who has the bad taste to care for him. As with *As Tears Go By*, this tale is about a person's need for family, and what the cost of that can be. It features Wong's first use of voice-over and multiple story-lines, which he uses to jump from perspective to perspective, and from location to location, usually without warning.

This a much calmer film than its predecessor, allowing its historical setting (1960) to show a peaceful and uncluttered side of Hong Kong (both mainland half and island half) which is ignored by the action movie mainstream. Indeed, it isn't until the story re-locates to the Philippines that Yuddi encounters the kind of gangsters such films are usually full of.

Ashes of Time became the crucible in which Wong Kar-Wai's film making concerns were burnt down to the very basics. In this elaborate two-year production, he and Chris Doyle learned once and for all what they didn't like about Hong Kong cinema. It remains unreleased in this country.

Chris Doyle is Australian, although at the age of eighteen, somewhere in the early seventies, he left Sydney to join the Norwegian Navy - presumably because a Norwegian ship was the first one to come along. After that he pursued various 'career options' including selling quack medicine in Thailand and digging wells in the Indian desert, before being 'reincarnated' by a poetry and language teacher at the Hong Kong University in the late seventies. She gave him his now notorious pseudonym Du Kefong, under which he still directs the occasional movie.

As well as running theatre workshops, publishing books of his behind-the-scenes photographs (a few of which he has generously sent over to illustrate our interview), producing television documentaries and creating collages, he directs pop videos for the stars of the movies he works on ... oh, and in his spare time he is Chinese cinema's most in-demand director of photography.

After their exhausting experience on *Ashes of Time*, Wong and Doyle decided to do something completely different, something fast and cheap and improvisational: they made *Chungking Express*. This film and it's sort-of sequel *Fallen Angels* bring together everything that Wong had been experimenting with: a huge cast of dysfunctional characters, several plots, lots of voice-over, sudden punches of violence (to keep the distributors happy) shot in that trademark 'smudge motion' style, claustrophobia, glaring artificial light and Doyle's energetic hand-held camera-work.

The end result is as emotional as it is exhausting. It is a quantum leap away from the mainstream action movies of John Woo and the like, whilst bearing all the artistic and stylistic hallmarks that Hong Kong films uniquely bring with them.

Ever restless, there is nothing to say that their next film together will bear any resemblance to anything that came before, all that can be said for sure is that it will be worth watching, if for no other reason than because Wong Kar-Wai's influence is already being felt in Hollywood, and if he won't go there himself, someone else will appropriate his techniques for their own use.

I was late for my interview with Wong Kar-Wai. Something to do with a miscalculation about the time difference between Britain and Hong Kong. I was exactly one hour late. Never the less, Mr Wong was still sitting in his office, waiting for me to call. He mentioned that I was late, but didn't seem to mind, in fact he found my inability to add seven to twelve quite amusing. He finds many things amusing. This unnerved me a little, he's supposed to be a serious artist whose films are highly regarded and have won him many fans and many awards around the festival circuit. He's the respectable face of Hong Kong action cinema. He can't have a sense of humour as well, surely!?

He talks calmly and quite slowly, thinking about his answers; this may be because his excellent English isn't as effortless as it seems, but it is more likely a sign of a methodical intelligence at work. He is happy to make light of his achievements, keen to demystify the process of movie-making but, at the same time, careful not to let too much of his guard down.

The Yin to his Yang (or should that be the other way round?) is Director of Photography and Australian emigreé Christopher Doyle. My talk with him was quite a different experience: on one level he is a dream to interview because you hardly need to ask him any questions, on another level, his wit, knowledge and enthusiasm are quite exhausting. Sparkling with nervous energy, he couldn't just sit quietly and be interviewed; so our conversation was recorded firstly in the back of a taxi, then as he elbowed his way through the markets and subways of downtown Hong Kong, his mobile phone stuck to one ear.

Together, Wong Kar-Wai and Christopher Doyle are the epitome of Strategy and Tactics, the former being a carefully considered long-term plan of action, the latter being the short-term tenacity and improvisational skill to bring those long-term plans to life. Chungking Express *and* Fallen Angels *could not have been made without the perfect balance of both. Shot illegally on the streets of their neighbourhood in the Chungking district of Hong Kong, they set off, with a band of enthusiastic actors and no script, to re-energise the moribund Hong Kong film industry. Filming what they felt like, where they could, while the life of Britain's busiest principality spun and hustled blithely around them, they have brought a new spontaneity and vigour to the East.*

Firstly, to ease you into the topsy-turvy world of Chungking Mansions, the calm and modulated words of director Wong Kar-Wai: I mentioned to him that I had seen Chungking Express *and* Fallen Angels *on the same day, and felt that that was a particularly good way to see them!*

"I think of *Chungking Express* as half and *Fallen Angels* as half." *He explained,* "Together they are one film. I had three short stories originally for *Chungking Express* but, because we filmed it in chronological order, I found that I was making it too long, so I skipped the third story. Then afterwards I thought *well, maybe I can do another one.* Not as a sequel but as a counterpart, so one character in *Chungking Express* can be projected into another character in *Fallen Angels.* Also, some of the smaller details, such as the uniform and the number 223."

"And the all-night fast-food joint, that was the same one wasn't it!"

"Yes, that is the Chungking Express take-away, where I got the title. It is part of Chungking Mansions, where the stories are set, so I had to re-use it in *Fallen Angels.* In fact, to me, the main character of these two films is Hong Kong itself, and the place never changes, but the stories change all the time. A different story happens in the same background. So we work like a closed-circuit camera, watching people going in and coming out, and the story just happens. They can be the same people or different people, it doesn't matter."

"These films are very cinema verité: you seem to just shoot what's there, using available light."

"Yeah, that's because we have to work that way. It's the same situation as with the French New Wave in the sixties, we don't have much money, we have to finish the film very quickly, and normally we don't have street permits. The shops have their own lighting so, yes, we shoot what we find.

"We shot like this because I wanted a holiday after spending two years on *Ashes of Time.* I *needed* a holiday but, instead of going someplace else, I decided to make a quick film. I didn't want a big cast or a big budget, I wanted to move around a lot and have fun. Everything was by instinct, I didn't have to consider and consider and consider a lot of elements like budget and scheduling. I wrote it and shot it in chronological order, usually writing in the daytime and shooting at night.

"Hong Kong is a very crowded place, so it would be quite impossible to make a film in that way in daytime. And I'm a night person anyway, that's when I'm at my best. The problem is that people have complained that I make Hong Kong look too quiet. Normally I have only one or two actors hanging around, it's a very quiet set. Except Hong Kong isn't like that."

"You do show the contrast though: there's the crowded chaos of the opening scene of Chungking Express *with everybody elbowing everybody else out of the way, compared to the shot out of the Killer's bedroom window in* Fallen Angels, *when you have acres of open concrete with nothing happening save the occasional elevated train rumbling past."*

"This is my wish. I want to make Hong Kong seem bigger and quieter than it is. Really it's just like any other city. You'll see the quotes, *MacDonalds, Circle K,*

Seven-Eleven, this city has that, but every big city has that, so this story doesn't have to be in Hong Kong, it could as easily be in America or England.

"It is true that Hong Kong is maybe more cosmopolitan than most, that's why I chose Chungking Mansions as my location: there's over two-hundred guest houses in one single block, and something like five thousand tourists from all over the world live in that space. It's very much like a small Hong Kong world, with a lot of people from many backgrounds living in a very limited space."

"Why do you use the so-called 'smudge-motion' technique of shooting fewer frames per second so the action blurs?"

"It's because I want to stop things down so that the things I want to concentrate on don't move while everything around them moves fast. Sometimes it's like trapping time. This is the magic of cinema, and the fun of being the director. You can change the time, you can play with time, but you can't in real life. You can be more real than real."

"In a place that's so crowded, you're films are full of lonely people. Is this your take on night in the city, or just people in the city?"

"I think most people in a big city have a problem like this. Everyone is moving too fast, concentrating on their own business. And nowadays we have so many ways to communicate - we have phone, we have fax, pagers, e-mail, we have everything to make human contact more and more distant. It's like people would rather talk to a stranger over the phone in another city, than to meet that person personally."

"So that is why Faye in Chungking Express *engages in time-share relationship, only visiting her lover's house when he's out!?"*

"People are becoming more and more insecure, they don't want to get hurt. They want to protect themselves so they keep themselves to themselves. To avoid getting too lonely you have to know how to entertain yourself, even without a partner. My characters think they're communicating with each other, but they're not; so finally they decide that the most direct way to touch people or get hold of people is to share their houses."

"It's a very pressurised environment, with a lot of stress. But the two gun-toting characters, who relieve their stress by shooting people - which are the two characters we in the West would most readily identify as being from a Hong Kong film - are as good as irrelevant to the main thrust of the plot."

"That's because I'm playing with the genre. The reason I originally wanted to have three short-stories in *Chungking Express* is because I wanted to include the cop, the gangster and the contract killer; which are three of the main archetypes in Hong Kong film. So we have cops, but they're not supercops like Jackie Chan would play (so he doesn't have to worry about the competition). As for the killer in *Fallen Angels*, I wanted to introduce him in a way that makes you expect a John Woo film, with a big shoot out. But it was only interesting to me if I could follow it up with having him go home on the bus and meet an old school friend who tries to sell him insurance. What an anticlimax.

"Of course, it was important that the school-friend be played by the action director, who'd choreographed the shoot out and rigged all the special effects. You see, I'm trying to give you a surprise. It's like I'd given you a MacDonalds but when you unwrap it you realise its really a Chinese dumpling! It's good to put your crew in your films because in years to come you can look at it say 'My God, you look so young! Where did it all go?' It's a punishment.

"This isn't just me being difficult though, it's a strategy to get the film seen. Normally the distributors here in South East Asia will ask 'Do you have action in your film?' And I can say 'Yes'. 'Do you have cops?' Of course I have a cop, but my cop is quite different. 'Do you have gangsters and gun fights?' Yes I do, but it's done differently.

"Sometimes the audience goes along with it, sometimes it fails. In *Fallen Angels* the audience is usually laughing when the killer gets on the bus, because they've been watching shoot-outs like that for so many years it has almost become a ceremony; when the killer meets his school friend, it tells them that he is real, a human being.

"Lately, of course, for the last two years or so, the two hundred action films that the Hong Kong studios produce each year have been less popular than the big-budget Hollywood films, with their bigger special effects and bigger explosions; but I think this is because films like the *Die Hard* series are more and more like Hong Kong films."

"And many of your contemporaries - like Ringo Lam and John Woo - have moved to the States to make those bigger films. Are you planning to join them?"

"No. You must remember that Ringo and John have always dreamed of working in Hollywood, I've known them since I worked in the script factory and they've always wanted to make at least one big Hollywood film. But that's not my dream.

"To be able to work I have to know the place, and know the people I am working with. My crew is like my family, Chris Doyle and I have worked together since my second film, so we know each other very well. Sometimes Chris says we're not like film-makers, we're like musicians at a jam session, I'm the band leader and everyone is jamming. I don't know enough musicians in the States. And can you imagine it, if they tried to re-make *Chungking Express* in America. They'd spend millions building Chungking Mansions again so they could light it properly, and then cast Tom Hanks as Tony Leung."

"How do you respond to the parodies that are made of your films, like Days of Being Dumb*?"*

"We had to stop shooting *Ashes of Time* for a few months so the cast could go off and film a parody of it, even before we'd finished. You have to be philosophical about it; I don't mind them, but I don't want to see them, that's all. I'm not against them, but I don't like them so I won't buy a ticket."

"In the resumé they sent me, it mentions that you are perpetually wearing widescreen shades, in order to see the world through a cinema screen ..."

"Well that's only when I work, it's kind of my uniform. I'm not normally used to public speaking, so it's comforting to have dark glasses to hide behind; but also, on set, it means that I can sleep and nobody notices. I just sit in my chair and people think I'm considering something, deep in thought. Just so long as I don't snore."

"So when are you next likely to don the shades and sleep on set?"

"Well I'm leaving for Argentina in four days to shoot *The Buenos Aires Affair* there. It's based on an American novel I admire very much."

"Well this one might sell in America, since you've made it on the American continent!"

"Yes, but it's the South American continent. And the cast will be speaking Cantonese. I'm filming there because it's as far from Hong Kong as you can get. It's exactly the opposite side of the world, it's winter there and summer here and it'll be daytime there when it's night-time here."

"You're just out to have a good time, aren't you; and here are all these critics making high claims for the seriousness of your films!"

"Well, don't trust critics .... or newspapers .... no offence. In my career, I'm having a full-course meal, you know, I have the entrée, the main dish and the dessert together."

"Well, I'll try to track down your director of photography now. I rang him before you but, since I was running behind schedule I think he must have gone to bed."

"No, I don't think so, the night is yet young for him!"

Indeed, when I rang him, he wasn't sitting fretting by the phone, he'd gone out. However, he had left an answer-phone message, in English: "Hello anyone calling, I have to go out for a moment but please try my mobile phone number .... byyyeee." *This I dutifully did.*

"Ah, you got my message then, good. I had to go out 'cos I'm late for a whole load of things; but I'm in a cab, so we can talk."

"I gather you're heading off to Argentina very soon ..."

"Yes, I'm taking a cab to Argentina right now! No, okay, we're setting off in about three days."

"And what techniques are you planning to use in this new f -"

"Aaah, good question. I won't know until we get there. You know, when we shot *Days of Being Wild*, I did ten camera tests to find this nostalgic look we wanted. We didn't wanna use sepia, so I tried everything. First of all that sent the producer crazy because no one's ever done so many tests before in Hong Kong, and secondly Wong Kar-Wai would always say "*...yeah, it's good, but this is still missing, and that is missing.*" So, after ten tests they wouldn't let me do any more, but we knew exactly what we *didn't* want. It wasn't until the first day of shooting that we found the right mix and got exactly what we did want and it was a great relief.

"It's the same thing this time; we can't use step printing, the so-called smudge-motion technique, because that's been done to death now by everybody. Every film released here looks like a homage to Wong Kar-Wai, even the music videos look like my assistant shot them ... it's horrible. So, for now, the look will rely on what the location gives us.

"I do like to hand-hold the camera, and he likes to just see what happens, so why work against it if it's working for you!? I dunno why, but it's extremely comfortable for me to hand-hold a camera, it gets things done quicker and more directly and gives you more time for an extra take without having to stop and re-lay the tracks and move the dolly, I just adapt my footwork. So that aspect, I don't see any need to change, but how that works within the whole context of how we use colour or processing or lighting, that will be determined by the space itself.

"As far as I'm concerned, that's what has become more and more evident the more we make films together. We trust each other more now, and we both trust that our choice of location will give us a direction on the look of the movie. It's what Buenos Aires gives us, not what we take to Buenos Aires. Unfortunately Buenos Aires hasn't given me much so far, it's so bloody grey and European, and they still haven't worked out what happened after the tango. So I think we'll have to put a bit of energy in there to get anything out of the place.

"Have you ever been there?"

"No, I ne -"

"It's very weird, that's for sure. Everyone seems to have an identity crisis, they still think they're Italians or Spaniards or Nazis. Still, it doesn't matter, we'll all speak such beautiful Spanish by the time we've finished; that's why we're going really, for Spanish lessons, not to make a film! Hey, that's what we'll do, we'll structure the film like a Spanish language lesson. That's it, you've found the direction.

"In *Ashes of Time*, we spent a year in the desert, I had three assistants carried back to civilisation in hospital chairs, it was extremely gruelling and yet, when we found the right space ... after something like eight months of shooting ... well that makes up something like sixty percent of what we see. It's amazing and very intuitive and inspires the horribly poetical metaphor that Wong Kar-Wai's films are really like sculpting, always taking away instead of adding.

"I'm always running around in circles all the time and he's so slow and analytical, and then you add-in William Chang's design and editing, looking at it from an art-director's point of view but also having a great complicity with me. I think it's a wonderful triad. A real triad. If you want me to sit down and watch the monitors I'd go crazy, I have to be up and running around with the camera.

"That was the problem when I first started shooting Chen Kaige's *Temptress Moon*. He's used to standing beside the monitor and being very analytical, I can't do that, I have to have the camera in my hand because then, when I'm exhausted enough, something interesting happens. And that's when Wong Kar-Wai, sitting there with his dark glasses on says *"Is that all you can do, Chris?"*

"For me it's very much a process based on the energy of the place. More and more the locations determine what we film. After all, I never know the story, so I can concentrate on other things. I think our 'greatest contribution' if you will, to local film making is coherence of space, which is such a classic thing, a simple thing. But now everyone shoots around my neighbourhood - you know I live in the apartment where we shot *Chungking Express* - and everyone uses it because they think it's a coherent space, which is true, but only once you've discovered it. They should go off and discover somewhere else.

"Look at *Fallen Angels* and all those confined spaces. No matter how much you theorise about things like 'oh, there's a distance between these people therefore we'll use a wide-angle lens to make them seem further apart than they really are', which is a great thing to write in a film journal and teach film students at the London Film School; but the reality is that we didn't have much space, we wanted to try something different, wide-angle lenses looked okay, so we went with it. That's it! Then the film evolves day-by-day because you make stylistic choices about the acting style, the directorial style, the mise-en-scene etc, as you go along. At least between the three of us, the Wong Kar-Wai Triad, that's very much how it works, and it's a very comfortable way of working."

"And so -"

"You know, you start from day one and it becomes a process. I'm terrified when western film-makers say 'we'd really like you to shoot our film but we only have six weeks, two weeks of prep ... oh, and a storyboard!' And I'm thinking: 'Shit, what am I gonna do? I don't even know you, how are we going to make a film together?'

"I get approximately a script a month now that I'm flavour-of-the-month Chris Doyle, and they all expect another *Chungking Express*. But *Chungking Express* can only happen because of that collaboration, because of that space, because of that energy, because of that working style. Now, if you want me to imitate it, first of all I don't see the interest and secondly, why? Why do you want to do it? So I've been getting a lot of offers lately, and I hesitate because I'm not sure what they think I am, and secondly I'm not sure what they think I'm going to give them, and thirdly I don't know them, so I always say, 'well at least let's meet each other'.

"For me, for example, Chen Kaige or Stanley Kwan or any of the people

I've worked with have been friends first before they became collaborators. Maybe I should test myself, but I'm a little hesitant because it's always been the people who have been the motivating force for me to take on a project, rather than a script. To be honest, I can't tell the difference between a good script and a bad script, it all looks horrible on paper, but hopefully it'll be a wonderful experience on film. For me the key has always been the experience and the process, and that means the people.

"I will be taking some western projects, even a Hollywood project next year, but that's also with people I've known for a long time. The script is totally secondary. That's the good ... or bad ... affect of working with Wong Kar-Wai. It's not planned, it's not an academic exercise, which, of course, has its great dangers in terms of Hong Kong film-making. I assume we should move on, work out a more disciplined process, maybe, or we could just keep the costs down and continue working like this, where it takes a year to finish a film but it's gonna be something interesting. I'm torn between the two! I'm getting old, so I'd prefer the shoots to be shorter, but my experience and personality are more of the 'let's just go for it' school."

"It'll be interesting to see if you can hang on to that in Hollywood."

"Oh, impossible. But then, the other day my agent rang me and said *"Hollywood is asking how much you want"* and about a week before Jackie Chan had announced (whether it was true or not, I dunno) that he was asking something like twenty-five million dollars. Well my agent just happens to be Jackie's partner so I said *"Don't I get the same as Jackie!?"* That's my basic attitude to Hollywood at the moment - if they don't pay the cameraman what Jackie gets, I don't go." *[Pause for laughter].*

"I know there's an exhibition of your photographs being arranged in Rotterdam, and they're mostly taken behind-the-scenes while you're filming ..."

"Let me try to explain. I'm kind of hyper, in case you hadn't noticed yet, and I have to have something to do otherwise I'm gonna jerk off five times a day. I have my wonderful team to work with, you know, I tell my lighting people what I want and they arrange it all, so I have a little time on my hands. I carry this little SLR camera in my pocket and I just wander around and if anything catches my eye I take pictures of it. It's become a wonderful obsession actually, so much so that last month I had a book released in Taiwan, this month I have one released here, I have two in Japan ... it's all becoming a little overwhelming. The problem is it's very easy to take the photographs but extremely difficult to organise them afterwards.

"I take them because, first of all, a lot of people don't know what goes on on a film set, secondly there's a lot of stuff that catches my eye, and I think I should train my eye as I go along, thirdly, it just keeps me occupied while I'm waiting for other people to catch me up."

"And -"

"I've got this incredible accumulation of images now, which I've just got to get out of the house, because I'm using up an incredible amount of my energy just editing these photographs for exhibition."

"I was wondering if they were just snaps of your friends from work."

"Oh very much so! They are just snaps, but they're useful because they're practice. It's like language, you practice, practice, practice and suddenly you say something that you didn't know you knew how to say. You realise that you can do something that you couldn't do before. I hope that the photography is the same, after all, it's not the machinery that's important, it's the atmosphere. I guess I've always self-trained, but that's because I think it's important to see where you're going, and how far you've come.

"Then, of course, it's a film making situation, and a lot of people are involved that the public seem to be interested in, and you can see strange things happening that most people have never witnessed before; so it's an exciting experience to be able to share this kind of stuff.

"But yeah, they're snaps of the family, it just happens that my family is a film family, they just happen to be superstars. My family album is full of superstars, so, of course people are interested. Then maybe some of the images will be seen as human documents. I get trapped between deciding whether to release only the arty-farty stuff, or show people the superstars and the process, I'm always in two minds. Problem is, if I let someone else edit them, then I might find out that neither of them are intrinsically interesting.

"Actually I do much more collage work than photography. It's sort of Post Withdrawal Syndrome Therapy. After twenty hours of filming, having to take care of thirty people who are directly answerable to me, and a hundred extras, and listening to Wong Kar-Wai moaning "Is that all you can do?"; to just go home and cut up pieces of a magazine and put it with other pieces of another magazine to see what works, that's a great therapy."

"Some people go out and get drunk, you make collages!"

"Oh I get drunk while I'm making collages. Or I get drunk first."

"Tell me about Du Kefong."

"Du Kefong has no ID card, thank God, otherwise he'd have been in jail long ago. Du Kefong is a wonderful alter-ego, 'cos, first of all, his mother doesn't know what the hell he's doing. My mother's a raving Catholic, if she knew half of the shit Du Kefong gets up to ... I'm convinced she still thinks I'm a virgin, by the way. He makes a total ass of himself on stage, and wins all these awards, which is really strange, you know. But at least he doesn't take the awards home, because he usually loses it in the cab because he's so drunk. So, when she visits, his mother isn't going to ask where it is, because she doesn't even know what it is.

"So Du Kefong is either a great burden, a great responsibility or a great liberation. It's great having him around. I'm very proud of him sometimes, and he gives me a great freedom that a lot of film-makers don't have, to just sit back and laugh.

"After several forays into the drug and esoteric religious cultures of the world, I ended up in Hong Kong, studying Chinese, and my teacher was a wonderful, wonderful very beautiful poet, who knew I was in love with her and responded by giving me this beautiful name. 'Du' comes from Doyle, because it's traditional to make it sound like your English name, 'Ke means 'like' and 'fong' means 'the wind'. So, supposedly this guy is like the wind, which is appropriate since I'm all over the place anyway, but also it comes from a classical expression which goes 'a gentleman is like the wind'. So it implies that this guy has an incredible amount of culture. *[There is a pause here as Chris is gripped by hysterics for a few moments, before regaining - for want of a better term - composure]*

"It's a very Chinese name. It's been something almost to live up to, also it protects me from any prejudice that he might face if people really knew who the hell he is. He used to just go around making films, and people were used to the fact that some of the stuff he did was okay, and very Chinese, because they didn't know that he wasn't.

"He's wonderful for me because he has aspirations that Christopher Doyle would never have, and he's not a Catholic - that's the *great* thing! He can do what he wants because he has no ID, no passport, no wife, he's a very free person, and it's just been great to encourage him along the way."

"Was Christopher Doyle the well-digger, also the photographer?"

"I dunno. Christopher Doyle is definitely the collage-maker. The well-digger ... yeah, he's probably the one character who is, because my form of camera-work is a great deal of physical effort, and a little bit of intellectual effort. That's the perfect balance for me. You want me sitting at home writing a book, no way, but you want me running around doing crazy things and thinking on my feet, yes, that's extremely appropriate. That's true to what I am and what I can do. That's where the focal style and camera-work comes from, the fact that I like to dance has a much more direct relationship to the stylistic choices that I have made than any intellectualisation.

"I think I've done what I have done because I can, more than because we wanted to. The problem is that maybe we don't want to sometimes, but we can, so what are we gonna do? Are we gonna negate the idea because we can, or because other people are imitating it? This is the question that has come up over the last couple of months as we prepare the next film.

"We've talked a lot about this, now that *everyone* is imitating our style. Then I did a short film with Wong Kar-Wai recently, just for Japanese release, and I've realised that it's okay; firstly because we do it better than they do, because we know that it's not about the movement, it's about the pauses. I hope it's like music, I hope it's like poetry, the rhythm is there, the spaces between the notes are there. I hope that's what we're doing. I think we know more about the spaces between the notes than the people who just see our rhythms and try to imitate them. So I've become more reassured about that over the last few weeks, so what we do now is work on the other areas of the collaborations, which is the colour, the texture, the decoupage, how the thing fits together, how we react to the actors, things like that.

"Having said that, the smudge motion is something that we have to avoid as much as possible, it really is over-worked here. But then, if it's appropriate ... what are you going to do? Did Picasso stop using blue? What's the expression ... *"if I don't have the red, I take the blue."* Okay, I am being facetious by comparing us to Picasso ... maybe David Hockney But we are fore-warned, too many people are using the technique in inappropriate ways, but that's par for the course.

"Sometimes I think that we should apologise to the Producers' Organisation, because, if the box-office goes down, we are partly to blame.

"The real problem is that I don't have anyone pushing me, I don't feel that there's a new generation coming behind me, doing eye-opening work. I don't see people saying *"Fuck you, Chris. Fuck you Du Kefong, I can do better."* I just see people saying, *"that was a good idea, now I'll do it."*

"*Why do you think that is?*"

"Well don't forget '97. I have assistants who are extremely devoted to what they are doing, there is no question that they believe what we're doing is important, but they have families, they have kids, they have parents who want to emigrate and so they have to make money. They can't turn up one day because they're trying to make extra money.

"It's interesting that they have the Mercedes Benz and the great apartments, I don't, but that's fair enough. Given the present socio-political situation I don't blame them what-so-ever. But it means there is an artistic gap, and I believe that gap will definitely be filled by mainland Chinese film-makers.

"My attitude is that I'm just delaying my emigration to Shanghai, it's inevitable. Firstly because my Chinese is not too good, but it's better than my Cantonese, secondly I know a lot of film-makers there. After '97 the impetus will be to push Shanghai as a centre of film-making, and I've made three films there already.

"The whole thrust of Chinese film-making, whether it be the money, the politics, the infra-structural support will gravitate more and more towards Shanghai. But not all of my assistants appreciate this. Sometimes they don't have the language skills, but mostly they have to take care of finances while they can because the future is so ambiguous."

"*Yet Wong Kar-Wai has said that he won't leave because he wants to keep on telling stories about Hong Kong.*"

"And we are telling stories about Hong Kong, but Hong Kong is going to change, there's no question about that, and he is Shanghaiese himself. Half the important film-makers here are.

"But when I say I have to leave, I don't mean tomorrow, it will be after '97. But the difference will be like living in San Francisco instead of Los Angles. For the level-headed film-maker, the obvious thing to do over the next three years or so is go to Shanghai. Now, maybe what that means is that only the money will be coming from Shanghai and Wong Kar-Wai and I will stay. Providing my landlady lets me.

"Because my apartment has become quite famous, and other people have shot in the building since we did, in fact everyone seems to know that this is *the* apartment. Well, about two months ago we were renewing the lease; I was busy running around so my assistant was taking care of negotiations with the landlady and I could only hear his side of the conversation, but he was saying *"No, no, no, he's not a director, he's just a cameraman!"* [*Pause for more hilarity*] So obviously the landlady was hiking the price: *"Yeah, yeah, yeah, he can afford it, he's the famous director!"*

"Oh my God. While the film crew were there I lost half my CDs and half my books. I used to have a coffee machine but I've no idea where that is now. I suppose it's my own fault, I wasn't there half the time. So the moral is: never let a film crew into your house, what ever you do."

"And your downstairs neighbours must have been so pleased when you had the place flooded."

"Oh I didn't know until a couple of months ago, but downstairs is a computer software library. There was a leaky pipe somewhere, it wasn't ours, thank God, but they came upstairs hammering on the door: *"It's you again!"* It turns out that we'd flooded out their library when we were making the film. [*Hilarity - Composure*] They weren't too happy."

"I gather the action movies that we know so well in the west are a dead art-form in Hong Kong now."

"Well that's 'cos everyone's moving to Hollywood, isn't it. No, it's not a dead art-form, it can't be, it's rejuvenated itself many, many, many times over the last fifty years, since the war. It's interesting that Shanghai used to be the centre, and now it's Hong Kong, and soon it'll be Shanghai again. I think it's basically just the same people moving back and forth across the border.

"What's popular locally is teenage gang stories, it's an evolution of the martial-arts genre, with young people who don't necessarily have much martial-arts training going round doing a similar thing. In *Ashes of Time* we tried very hard to evolve the genre, but I think that, until there's new blood, there won't be any surprises.

"I was kind of like a guerrilla, running both the A and B units. So I was shooting the main story elements, with Wong Kar-Wai directing then, as much as possible, I was directing the action sequences, supervised by the action director.

"That's always a difficult collaboration when it came to making stylistic choices because, as far as an action director is concerned, it's all about content. Person X delivers a punch which connects and it looks beautiful, it's about martial-arts style, but not about cinematic style *per se*. So it was interesting for me to work almost like a documentary film-maker, I had to take what we needed from what they were doing. I think that's why Jackie Chan directs himself, because he can balance making cinematic choices with the demands of action."

"*Well since* Chungking Express *and* Fallen Angels *remind me of nothing so much as* Au Bout de Soufflé, *which led to the French New Wave, maybe it's time for a Hong Kong New Wave.*"

"Hmm. I don't know if we were as reactionary as Godard. Maybe conceptually, but I don't think the local industry is anything like as strong as the French industry was at that time, not so entrenched in its own ways. A lot of our industry was already falling apart before we came on the scene. I think we were more intuitive than reactionary, which is a very Chinese way. I don't think Wong Kar-Wai is as aggressive as Godard, he's very discreet about the way he's doing things. When we work it is obvious that there's no holds barred, there's no question about that. While we were shooting our first film together, I thought that either it would be great or neither of us would make a film again. It really was intellectual guerrilla tactics. He is extremely driven and that's contagious. That's why his favourite saying to me is *"Is that all you can do, Chris?"*

"When you've been working thirty-six hours straight and you're exhausted because you've been running around with thirty kilograms of camera on your shoulder, and you've been hanging upside down suspended from a rope out of a window in order to get that shot, to have him say *"Is that all you can do?"* kinda reminds you that film-making should be one hundred percent attention to one hundred percent of what's happening one hundred per cent of the time. And no excuses. Don't fuck off no matter how tired you are."

"Hard Boiled novels inherited the audience for the Western, which lost much of its power to excite the imagination once the frontiers closed. After this, you find that the spirit of adventure is transported back to the city."

Graham Barnfield

HARD BOILED CITIES

by John Ashbrook and Graham Barnfield

***FILM LECTURER, GRAHAM BARNFIELD** hosted an event at Birmingham's annual Film Festival described as:* "an exploration of what detective fiction has to say about the risks and realities of life in urban America ... from private dicks to Tarantino flicks." *After the talk, John Ashbrook invited him into an interview room, shone a light in his face and asked him a few hard boiled questions:*

"Firstly, would it be correct to assume that you are drawing a distinction between specific Hard Boiled fiction and more general Pulp Fiction?"

"Yeah, there is a difference; 'Pulp Fiction' is populated by characters like *The Shadow, The Spider, Operator No. 57*, your basic super-powered characters; there's less realism, less street-life in Pulp Fiction. However, that said, there are a lot of common elements with 'Hard Boiled': there's the low quality pulp paper it was printed on, the racy dialogue which is supposed to be the language of the streets, and the popular readership which, probably more than anything else, led to its being held in disdain among literary circles.

"I think Hard Boiled novels inherited the audience for the Western, which lost much of its power to excite the imagination once the frontiers closed. After this, you find that the spirit of adventure is transported back to the city."

"They're urban westerns then?"

"Well, there's a big debate going on at the moment about whether Hard Boiled is a break with the English detective story - like *Sherlock Holmes* - or whether it's just a re-located Western. I fall somewhere between the two stools. But the important thing is that for the first time ordinary people were appearing in fiction in ways that didn't make them appear to be idiots, or use them for comedy. It rehabilitated ordinary people. Also, don't forget that city-dwellers in the 1920s were made out to be lowlifes and in need of prohibition, but in the 'thirties they were the people whose votes politicians needed to secure."

"What changed after that to make the genre peter away?"

"Some of it actually continued in a bastardised form into the fifties with writers like Mickey Spillane, albeit in a rabidly anti-Communist, extremely violent form. But the most creative strain was cut short, partly because of The Cold War, when people like Hammett were penalised by the authorities for the political views they demonstrated anything up to twenty years earlier. This led to blacklisting in publishing as well as in Hollywood, where, of course, a lot of the Hard Boiled writers had stopped writing novels to become scriptwriters."

"*So it fell victim to evolution. Why, then, has it suddenly re-emerged?*"

"It's interesting how much of the genre has carried-over, but the democratic impulse about empowering the populous has gone, leaving a down-beat, pessimistic view of the city. It's no longer glamorous because it's dangerous. It's just dangerous. If you look at the film *Seven*, you just get a picture of a nameless city where petty criminals nick your bag, then come back and scoop your eyes out. It's lost the forward-looking optimism of Hammett and Chandler."

"*Maybe that's just because we're not so naïve these days.*"

"Sure, to an extent; but I think we also have a streak of masochism which encourages us to look for the worst in people. Go to the big city, and you'll find it!"

"*But the ubiquitous Tarantino is more positive than that, and he uses Hard Boiled motifs!*"

"Absolutely. He's certainly mastered the snappy dialogue, I never cease to be impressed by the number of ways he finds to put someone down or make an every-day experience seem extraordinary. Of course, the violence is there, and so are the wise-cracks, which were always a pivotal ingredient in Hard Boiled fiction. In some ways though, his pre-occupation with the seventies is his most interesting facet; because he's not simply using the city as a vehicle for putting people down as *Seven* does, but rather as an opportunity for revisiting his childhood."

"*Back in the seventies there were various attempts to kick-start the detective movie again, with the likes of Elliot Gould and Robert Mitchum following in Bogey's footsteps. But it didn't work. Why are we susceptible to it now, all of a sudden?*"

"Funny old world, innit! If you look at everyday life, it does look more and more like *Blade Runner* every time you step out of the house. We're also very aware of risk these days, which is usually exaggerated and often non-existent, but it's still a concern. Every time there's a health scare, be it The Pill or Mad Cow Disease, there's usually a panic of some sort.

"So people are already feeling insecure, and these films tap into that in a way that wasn't possible in the seventies when people were more concerned about political corruption and big issues like The Bomb. The, if you like, *urban western* can chime with our every-day fears and feed off them . So, even though *Seven* is a magnificent film, it also has an underlying anti-humanism which makes it a rather dark and cynical depiction of how things fit together in the world today."

"*Pessimism can't last forever though, so do you think Hard Boiled will evolve again and change into something else?*"

"I think we can expect more of the same, at least in the short term. The Walter Mosley film *Devil In A Blue Dress* is a return to *noir* in quite an up-front way. Even though it is informed by the politics of race, it is a very deliberate attempt to get back to the forties. But I don't think it speaks for the whole genre; instead we'll see it spinning off in all sorts of directions. James Ellroy is a good example, in his world it's harder to find a redeemable human than it was in, say, *Dirty Harry*. Also significant are issues of identity, and the more fragmentary dynamic in society, where everyone wants to have a unique hook on which they can hang their hat and say 'This is who I am'. This is seemingly reproduced in modern detective fiction: we have women detectives, Hispanic detectives, Ellroy even has an Italian/American accordion-playing detective."

"*So we can find an infinite variety of ways of enjoying being miserable.*"

"Absolutely. What an offer."

SEVEN UP

by John Foster

ENTREATED TO DO SO friends by and other strangers, I hired out the video of the movie *Seven* the other day. Some very intelligent people had commended it to me, one or two had even described it as the best movie ever made. Admittedly, this was later amended to 'the best movie ever made in colour'. More importantly, the movie got a five-star rating in *Empire Magazine*: the final accolade.

Clearly, this film would have to be viewed without benefit of popcorn, in due homage to the best movie ever made in colour. This was something I couldn't afford to miss, even though the High Concept formula of seven murders committed upon the basis of the Seven Deadly Sins sounded like the product of a coke-induced Hollywood think-tank on a very bad day.

As a farcical comedy, *Se7en* is entirely amusing, if low on Keystone capers and really good jokes. As a post-*Silence Of The Lambs* urban policier dealing with the dark psyche of the mass murderer, it is entirely risible. I giggled so much that several members of my family looked like they might take up serial killing as a career too.

Se?en is not only a bad movie, it is also a very dishonest one, and immoral, if I can be so uncool as to bring matters of morality into a discussion of popular entertainment these days. It also commits the worst crime of all: serial boredom. It is better to be bad than boring, *Se#en*, however, manages to do both. It is a spectacular achievement in dullness and predictability.

It seems that admirers of the film have been seduced by its style and production values, if deeply derivative, it is well acted, designed and directed. Director David Fincher did pretty well in convincing otherwise reasonably well-adjusted people that they were not having their intelligence insulted by this movie. Sustaining a moody, mean-streets look, its urban locales convince, even if the film noir rain, graffiti, dark places and sounds of the city are not exactly new to the screen. They have been executed with greater flair and frisson in earlier works, over a number of decades in European as well as American movies.

Here the gritty realism is laid on with a dragline, as if Fincher had just completed a short course in forties American cinema. It looks as if he received a banal, contrived, designer screenplay, cooked up by some wannabes from UCLA, and wondered how on Earth he could make such a hoked-up, unconvincing hotchpotch look remotely real.

However, the film might have been more credible if it had been set, as with

Roman Polanski's *Chinatown*, in sunny LA, with its pseudo-smartness, stucco patios and archways. Then at least it would be possible to perceive *Se*en* as just a fairground ghost-train of cheap ghoulish thrills.

What little tension there is, relies entirely upon a mawkish squeamishness of response in the audience. This is the most tawdry aspect of the film: What Deadly Sin comes next, Who's in line for The Chop and How will they Get It? The movie deals in lip-smacking snuff-movie pornography, inviting the audience to savour the anticipated torture and slow death of victims who are kept at arms length throughout, anonymous characters we are deliberately prevented from identifying with.

This tackiness of approach plays insidiously upon our own moral failings, yet trivialises the tragedy of violent death in our society by reducing it to style cross-word puzzle speculation. How appropriate is the brutal punishment meted out to each Deadly Sinner on the agenda? What constructed niceties of terror and pain will the next Sinner be put through? The camera sweeps down corridors and through Chinese-boxes of rooms, press-ganging us into ameliorating scenes of wretched horror.

The film plays dishonestly upon a voyeuristic fascination with the details of torture and cruelty, both to wind-up the audience and to satisfy its morbidity in a vertigo which combines revulsion with sleazy allure: I don't want to know, but ... okay, tell me anyway.

Unlike, say, Hitchcock, the film does not confront the audience with its own collusion, culpability and own residual sadism. It simply exploits the darkside in the audience, whilst posing as a serious examination of contemporary themes, and therefore renders itself spurious and immoral. *Se@en* wears its deluded thematics on its sleeve with mindless solemnity and portentousness.

Of course, all this is taking the film more seriously than it deserves. Basically, it is a piece of gaudy melodrama with two familiar stereotypes as its protagonists. Morgan Freeman's characterisation is mildly racist, although I doubt if the brainpadded casting executives will have realised it: a worldly-wise, world-weary *Uncle Tom* figure, a bachelor once in love, it didn't work out, that's Life, Death and the American Dream, poor melancholy mister. As Marx Brothers' writer SJ Perelman put it: *I'm sorry I made me sad*. Oh, and, of course, Morgan's going to retire in just SEVEN DAYS! Except we know he won't really. After all, someone's got to do the job, go down those filthy mean city streets with that grizzled 'I've-seen-it-all-before' countenance of Bogarts's compassionate cynic. Who else is there, Morgan? Hopefully a cop more interested in crime-prevention than pontification.

Se$en naïvely teases us with the idea that Morgan or Brad Pitt could be the killer. Brad's your bog-standard rookie, bit of a loose cannon, likeably wild, a bit naff: in sweaty undershirt. He and Morgan are reluctantly teamed. Recognise the duo? It's not unfamiliar to viewers of *Lethal Weapon* or, more properly,

Don Siegel's *Dirty Harry*, as well as countless movies in-between.

Brad has a nice little wifey, sweet smile, teaches grade five in High School, of course, hates the Big Bad City, naturally, is pregnant, surprise-surprise. 'I need to talk to you, Morgan' she treens; after one TV-dinner Morgan is her coffee-bar confidant; but then he's black and wise, remember, a man of Few Words and Hidden Depths.

What does she want? Morgan's worldly advice, when all the time we thought she was going to come onto him. Luckily, Morgan has a Secret Past and the platitudinous homilies abound. She's grateful, butter wouldn't melt, shy little smile. Come back Madonna, we do need you after all.

Mrs Pitt is so coy, sweet and Apple-Pie-ish that the least the killer is do is cut her head off and do us all a favour. Especially Brad. The ultimate punishment for him would have been the long-term purgatory of continued marriage to this mutant. It isn't difficult to spot wifey as being lined up for the big sleep. She's very much in evidence, yet insufficiently developed to be dramatically significant. She's a marked lady, and the film-makers have my wholehearted support and sympathy. My only criticism is that we have to wait too long for the axe to drop.

Meanwhile, detectives Brad and Morgan don't do much in the way of detecting, instead they ride around the gloomy streets piously ruminating on urban alienation, as if this is news. TS Eliot has a lot to answer for! Nobody cares anymore, its a city of lost souls, and so on and so forth. If the killings were based on the Seven Deadly Truisms, Morgan and Brad would top his hitlist on several counts.

It is also curious that these two inappropriate gumshoes are left alone to solve these bizarre murders, with all their attendant newsroom publicity. No criminal psychologist on board, no specialist murder squad, no FBI. But get this: the killer has been borrowing books from the library, no less. He has a private income, the hackneyed get-out clause of movies like this, in case we ask the awkward question: 'How does anyone have the time and resources to conduct such an exhaustive, elaborate and painstaking series of killings?' Despite evidence of dusty leather-bound Sadean tomes lining the walls of his apartment, the killer regularly nips down the library to pay his overdue fines.

This fastidious, meticulous murderer, planning everything down the finest of fine detail, deploying a torturous trail of brainteasing clues, leaves himself open to discovery over the cost of a second-hand paperback. Believable, huh? And the breakthrough comes from a paid informant who has access to FBI files denied to the cops. A one-page computer print-out locates the killer straight away, who then turns up with his shopping while Morgan and Brad are outside his apartment. He presumably failed to notice the cop-car parked in the street outside.

Granted, the movie is fleet-of-foot in covering up its very many holes, mostly through its pretentious and pious air of fatuous Significance, which dares us to ask such banal questions as; 'Why does the killer cut off his fingertips?' The film-makers hope that the gruesomness of the act will distract us from wondering why on Earth the man does such a silly thing.

To stop the police identifying him from his fingerprints, you say? Yes, of course, sorry. Ever heard of gloves, mate? Of course, this ignores the fact that fingerprint specialists have problems in establishing identification from good prints, and if you have no criminal record, they've got no chance. Fingerprints are meaningless.

Never-the-less, our guy cuts off his fingertips. 'He's been doing it for some time', a cop mutters ominously. We obediently cower back, the horror, the horror; just imagine that! He cuts off his fingertips, he must be nuts! But not as nutty as those who leave their brainpower in the powder-room and swallow this asinine nonsense whole.

We are being asked to believe that a man with mutilated hands can kidnap, torture, maim and murder seven people over a seven day period, engage in a high-speed chase through a tenement block, make good his escape, mount a conveniently situated truck in the pouring rain outside and beat then hold at gun point a younger, fitter, trained police-officer. He wouldn't be able to hold a gun, let alone fire it. He wouldn't even be able to take down a book from a library shelf, nuts or not.

There are holes in the best thrillers. Melodrama is dependent on our willing suspension of disbelief, but there is hardly a scene in *Se%en* which sustains any credibility at all. In a movie which postulates contemplation of contemporary life, this matters. If the raw dramatic material is so dishonestly constructed in pursuit of gratuitous horror, then its pretty certain that we have a deeply flawed and fraudulent movie.

Fat Boy is the first victim. Never mind that, given his immensity, he was probably carbohydratedly challenged through neurosis or glandular illness rather than gluttony; there he is, face down in his spaghetti hoops and serve him right. It is an image of such grotesque absurdity that a belly laugh is all that's possible. Morgan returns to the scene of the crime, acting on a hunch, and finds the word *Gluttony* scrawled in grease across a wall. Don't the film-makers know that, in a murder investigation, the forensic teams even take the floorboards apart? Its fine-toothcomb time. There's simply no way that this clue would have gone undetected.

An intense (two-man) round-the-clock, race-against-time murder investigation concerning daily killings, gives way to pseudo-philosophising over glasses of red wine. The cops, busy with navel-gazing, don't seem to feel it important to interview those acquainted with the victims, a line of enquiry which might offer leads, until the killer himself points them in the direction of the lawyer's wife.

The sole one-dimensional purpose of her one scene is to reveal A Vital Clue. which actually leads nowhere save to provide further bouts of calculated if unconvincing nastiness along the storyline's circular switchback of grubby malevolence. Although distressed and traumatised, she still manages to notice, through her tears, in an average sized photograph, with a post-it note covering-up the eviscerated remains of her husband, the momentous fact that a painting on the wall is upside down. A surprising and fortuitous presence of mind, given her grief-stricken state, especially when the eagle-eyed cops, trained in observational skills, failed to notice it themselves, but then, they're police officers, what do they know about art? Even though Morgan frequents the library, reads literature, and listens to classical music, he still can't pronounce 'De Sade' correctly.

None of the other victims seem to have had lives worth taking. A man is held hostage for a year, tied to a bed, even though the killings were agendaised within seven days. Nobody misses him. His hand is cut off (by a surgeon with no fingertips), no noise, no screams, the killer can function with apparent impunity. In the most hilarious moment of the film, Sloth awakens from the dead and rises. He should have been dead for yonks, but manages to survive just long-enough to cash-in during the contrived seven-day pattern.

Can anyone really take this seriously? Apparently most people can.

Raymond Chandler said that the kind of murder which really bothers the cops is the one that happens at the bottom of the street, unmotivated, just for kicks, violence which is spontaneous. The murderer who has been very cute, very smart and too-clever-by-half is dead easy to detect. Not for these potato-brains.

Much has been made of the way that the violence occurs off-screen. This supposed subtlety permits us to imagine the process of slow-death and torture for ourselves. Thank you very much. I'm glad these film-makers have such a high opinion of our ability to re-enact the psychopathic propensities of serial killers. In actual fact, this film leaves very little to the imagination: the murders are graphically described, aided and abetted by those grim scene-of-crime snapshots (borrowed, along with the film's music score, from *Silence of the Lambs*) and peeks at the squalid aftermath of murder. Again, the appeal is to the mordantly salacious, whilst failing to turn this around upon the audience.

But what would be the effect of showing the killings? The entire artifice of the movie would collapse in an instant. The guy is going to kill you anyway. How do you choose, a quick bullet in the head or slowly and painfully being force-fed until your stomach explodes? How do you choose, a quick bullet in the head or cut out a pound of your own flesh and bleed to death? But the last thing this movie wants you to do is think!

In a blatant cop-out, the killer gives himself up to the police. He seems to know exactly where Morgan and Brad will be (except when they're at his apartment) but their lacklustre police routine wouldn't make that difficult. He's covered in blood. He's just gotten out of a taxi, having taken a cardboard box down to a courier company, whilst dripping with blood. 'Good afternoon, sir. Had a bit of an accident have we? Would we like a band-aid or two?' But why, for that matter, razor off your fingertips for years if you're intending to give yourself up? He can't be famous and get his point across if he doesn't give himself up, so doing so must have always been an integral part of his plan.

So we arrive in the home-straight, the build-up to The Great Un-Hollywood Climax. The police strike a deeply unlikely deal with the killer, who has mountains of evidence stacked against him, but nevermind, anything goes in this picture. Wifey's head turns up in the cardboard box, courtesy of Red Star. Her head has been hanging around the depot all afternoon, but there's been no leakage, no blood, no brain-fluid, the box is not wet, or dampened, or even stained. There appears to have been no physical decomposition either, hence no smell. The decapitated head arrives as if from Betterwear.

It isn't clear precisely what Deadly Sin wifey has committed. Being too perfect, maybe? Breathing with intent? The film-makers remain stubbornly silent on this matter.

The shallowness of *Se▲en* is finally confirmed by this synthetic twist-in-the-trail climax: the killer himself will be the seventh victim, his sin that of Envy. Except, since he's done away with wifey, there's nothing left to be envious of. For all their sociological pretensions, the film-makers throw in their hand with this totally implausible, concocted finale.

The killer has positioned Brad as his executioner, which is fine by me. Shooting's too good for him anyway, even though he has provided us with all manner of inventive diversions and, despite the slip-up over the library books, has a brilliant sense of timing. He can even get Red Star to deliver on the dot. However, the problem seems to be that if Brad shoots him, despite all mitigating circumstances, he will end up as bad as the killer. As *Evil* as the killer. Hmm.

Consequently, Morgan wants to save Brad from himself. So he throws down his gun in the hope that Brad will follow suit. Morgan's time-stained knowledge of human nature seems temporarily to have deserted him; but the ways of Morgan are passing strange. Where he less witless, or less a prisoner of his screenwriter's gauche manipulations, he would have fired a bullet (for the first time ever) into Brad's leg and immobilised him. But that would spoil The Great Un-Hollywood ending. Brad goes through a well-acted trauma of some duration, during which Morgan does ... what? Pick up your gun, Morgan, put Brad out of action. Rush him, ground him. Save his soul!

But Morgan just stands there and does nothing. The camera cannily keeps him out of shot, in case we realise that Brad, in his weakened, distressed and confused state, could easily be contained by any cop trained in unarmed combat, even the hapless Morgan.

And so the film delivers the most traditional of all Hollywood endings. Brad kills the bastard.

But what if he hadn't? What if he'd let him live? That would induce the most dreadful mental torture in the killer: an unrequited living-death for his Deadly Sin of Envy. That would confound the killer and cheat the audience's expectations. Now *that* would be Un-Hollywood!

But Fincher, et al, know what the public want: blood, revenge and violent death. And pretty-boy Brad must do it. That lets everyone off the hook; mostly the audience, who remain unconfronted with their own rabid and violent impulses. His action is perfectly understandable, even given the unlikelihood of the circumstances, so what's all the fuss about? Poor Brad leaves the film carted off in the back of a cop-car, symbolically replacing the killer.

Se™en disingenuously links Brad with the killer in a half-baked dopplegänger motif. Certain movies, such as Michael Mann's *Manhunter* and Sidney Lumet's *The Offence*, have disturbingly themed the idea that the capacity for violence and murder resides within us all and that this brutalisation most particularly affects the cop in pursuit of the killer. Whatever his shortcomings, the callow Brad cannot be equated with the man who has patiently committed such a bestial string of calculated murders. Brad responds with the unpremeditated emotional upheaval of a guy who has just lost a loved one, in a brutal fashion, by ritual beheading. The film's desperate and transparent quest for meaningfulness is illustrated by this token alignment between Brad and the killer.

Se♥en is a fake, needing to conceal its counterfeit content under the King's New Clothes of apparent depth and seeming meaning. Now; how about a serial killer who murders the film-makers of crass serial-killer movies? That's a helluva cute concept which no-one has yet exploited. But it's going to have to be smart, so lets brainstorm ... What about motive, is that important? No, but I guess we ought to have one. How about toe-nail curling tedium induced by fraudulent and contrived serial killer movies? The first victim? The overpaid screenwriter who chokes to death beside his swimming pool. The killer, a failed writer, makes him eat the pages of his very bad serial-killer screenplay. Victim two: the rip-off director who thinks he's a born-again Jean-Pierre Melville.

Will it work? Sure it will, run it past 'em fast enough and the suckers will think they've seen a profound movie.

SEVEN

Dir.: David Fincher Dist.: Entertainment Films. Cert.: 18.
Dur.: 125 Min. Released: 22/09/95. US Box-office: $100.25 million.

GOOD COP, BAD COP

by Richard Luck

THERE IS A BRILLIANT moment mid-way through John Carpenter's action drama *Assault on Precinct 13* (1976), where one of the besieged cop shop's receptionists exclaims *"Why would anyone want to shoot at a police station?"* Why indeed? In the majority of Hollywood movies, the police have been portrayed as a force for good. This was particularly the case in the films of the '50s and early '60s, where the image of the straight-laced, law-abiding copper was so strong, it filtered over into people's perceptions of the real-life United States police force.

Of course, now, we are well aware of the police's darker side, a side that Hollywood has reflected in pictures like *Dirty Harry* (1971), *Prince of the City* (1981) and *Bad Lieutenant* (1992). Now, Lee Tamahori's period police picture *Mulholland Falls* suggests that, rather than being a modern phenomenon, there has always been something ambiguous about the behaviour of the police.

With his coffee, doughnuts and flat cap, the Hollywood policeman of the 1950s was rather an endearing figure. In a never-ending stream of B-movies, the police were depicted as either upholders of the law or comic characters who always come good in the end. While the politically aware Roger Corman might have intended some criticism of the police in his pictures, it never rose above the level of some teenager whining *"Lousy cops! You guys are so-oo-oo square."*

In the mainstream movies of the time, the image of the police was even more clean-cut. The paranoia of the age, together with the powerful Hays Office, insisted that the police be shown in a decent light. In films like Richard Fleischer's *The Narrow Margin* (1952), the policeman was the modern day equivalent of the Western sheriff. If he was tough, it was because that was part of his job. If he slapped a woman, it was because she deserved to get slapped. Come the end of the day, the policeman would go home, hang up his badge, kiss his wife and play with his children. Lantern-jawed and hard as nails he might have been; nevertheless, the '50s policeman remained kind and polite to the extent that it was perfectly okay to ask him for directions.

The real shady characters of '40s and '50s crime movies were the private detectives, the Philip Marlowes, Mike Hammers and Sam Spades of this world. Although they operated on the right side of the law, the private dick was a very different creature to the cop, liable to hit women and perform break-ins. The anti-heroes of a hundred film *noirs*, dicks did do good. It just so happened that their brand of good was often indistinguishable from the bad done by their adversaries.

The move towards depicting the police as an ambiguous force on-screen began in the 1950s. In Fritz Lang's *The Big Heat* (1953), Glen Ford plays an honest cop who quits the police force in order to pursue his wife's killer in the manner he wants. One imagines this portrayal of a policeman as vigilante must have been quite distressing to '50s audiences. It certainly wasn't a hit with other film-makers. Although there were a few exceptions to the rule (Orson Welles' bent cop Quinlan in 1958's excellent *Touch of Evil*) cops on-screen remained squeaky clean right up until the end of the 1960s. The image was brought under attack by films like *Bonnie and Clyde* (1967) and John Milius' *Dillinger* (1973) with their glamorous depiction of the gangster life. Such pictures did much to blur the line between good and evil.

In Sam Peckinpah's epic western *The Wild Bunch* (1969), the line between law man and law breaker was almost completely indistinct, with William Holden's band of mercenaries (dressed, incidentally, in US army uniforms) being chased to their deaths by a group of government sponsored, morally bankrupt bounty hunters. The new morality that was emerging in Hollywood had direct implications for the cop movie.

In the 1960s and '70s, Don Siegel made three land-mark cop movies. The first of these was 1968's *Madigan*. A distinguished TV director (he shot a few early episodes of Rod Serling's *The Twilight Zone*), Siegel came to shoot *Madigan* after turning down offers to direct episodes of popular cop shows like *Dragnet* and *Arrest and Trial*. Written by blacklisted screenwriter/director Abraham Polonsky, *Madigan* starred Richard Widmark as a cop who has his gun stolen by a suspect. When the thief murders two cops with Madigan's revolver, the uncompromising cop gives chases, killing the wanted man but losing his life in the process.

With its tough, law-flouting anti-hero and suffocating bureaucracy (as represented by Henry Fonda's officious chief), *Madigan* was a blueprint for two later Siegel movies. 1969's *Coogan's Bluff* starred Clint Eastwood as a Stetson-wearing, Arizona cop who comes to New York to pick up a wanted man. Arrogant and aloof, Coogan upsets the New York authorities (namely the pork-pie hatted Lee J Cobb) when he goes to pick up the villain (Don Stroud) unaccompanied. Stroud then escapes, forces Coogan to break every procedural rule in the book. He rifles files, visits crack houses, sleeps with and then beats up Stroud's girlfriend to find out where he's hiding. The methods are uncompromising, but they work, Coogan eventually capturing Stroud after a lengthy motorbike chase.

Like *Madigan*, *Coogan's Bluff* showed police officers operating in a way that the public were largely unfamiliar with. The brutal beatings dished out by Coogan were a million miles away from the one punch knock-outs movie cops usually scored. While they might have been alarmed by the method, crowds liked the fact that Coogan got results. At the time the film was released in America, an awful lot of people appeared to be getting away with murder. The Kennedy brothers, Malcolm X, civil rights leader Medgar Evers; all had died at the hands of unknown assassins. Whatever you said about Coogan, he made sure justice was served. Tough as he was, Eastwood's cowboy law-man couldn't prepare audiences for the next on-screen incarnation of the American law-man. A cad and a brute, Coogan was nothing compared to the protagonist in Siegel's 1971 thriller *Dirty Harry*.

In many ways, *Dirty Harry* was a re-make of Siegel's earlier cop movies. Besides re-presenting Clint Eastwood in the title rôle, the film featured the same stifling authority figures and savage, no-good criminals as had appeared in *Madigan* and *Coogan's Bluff*. What was so interesting about *Dirty Harry* were the contradictions apparent in the title character. Like his forerunners, Harry was a brute, liable to blow away bank robbers and torture suspects. He also didn't give a shit about authority figures. When questioned about his decision to shoot a rapist, he replies *"When I see a woman being chased by a naked man with a butcher's knife and a hard-on, I figure he ain't out collecting for the Red Cross."*

Beneath the brutality, there was another layer to Callahan. A widower (his wife was murdered), Harry is neither the racist or misogynist critics usually assume him to be (check out the scene with the black doctor). He is, instead, the prototype of what we have now come to know as the dysfunctional cop. A wretched private life has forced Harry to throw himself into his work. When he is denied this escape (the mayor believes his methods to be unsound), Harry has no choice other than to throw his badge away. Rather like John Wayne's Ethan Edwards in *The Searchers* (1956), Callahan is a man who no longer has a place in society.

Dirty Harry was Siegel's last great crime movie. Although he would continue to pursue the genre in *Telefon* (1977) and *Escape From Alcatraz* (1979), he never matched the intensity of his three break-through movies. It was these films that were tò shape the evolution of the cop movie throughout the '70s, '80s and '90s.

Arguably the most shocking character to come from this period, was not Harry Callahan, but Gordon Parks' *Shaft* (released the same year as *Dirty Harry*: 1971). By far the best of the blaxploitation movies, *Shaft* subverted the innate racism of the genre by casting a black man (Richard Roundtree) as a cop. And not just any old cop, either. Roundtree wasn't some sidekick who could be killed off to provide his white superior with a revenge motive - he was the main man, the boss nigger.

During the '70s and '80s, the police were portrayed in an increasingly ambiguous light. While out-and-out good cops were still to be found in films like *The New Centurions* (1972), and *The Taking of Pelham* 123 (1974), the police, while still being depicted as upholding the law, were now often shown as uncompromising and brutish. William Friedkin's *The French Connection* (1971 again) has as its hero the brawling, foul-mouthed 'Popeye' Doyle. Likewise, Sidney Lumet's superb *Prince of the City* (based upon Robert Daley's non-fiction novel) told the story of a good cop (Treat Williams) shopping his drug-dealing colleagues. More recently, law-bending policeman have included Samuel Jackson's detective in *Kiss of Death* and Chazz Palminteri's Dave Kujan in *The Usual Suspects*. Perversely, the character that had started this trend, Harry Callahan, lost his maverick tag and became a regular 'good' cop in the sequels to *Dirty Harry*. While Callahan might have changed his stripes, the image of the Hollywood law man has become increasingly tarnished, reaching its apotheosis in the ravaged form of Harvey Keitel in the appropriately entitled *Bad Lieutenant*.

This said, there have been very few out-and-out 'bad' cops in the movies. Sure, there was Joe Don Baker's C.O.P. in the Chevy Chase comedy *Fletch* (1985), Peter Greene's cartoonish Zed in *Pulp Fiction* and Gary Oldman's homicid(al) detective in *Leon*; none of these were 'real' people, however. The only incidence of a life-like policeman behaving unethically which actually lingers in my memory is when the ageing black cop menaces Cuba Gooding Jnr with his revolver in John Singleton's *Boyz 'n' The Hood* (1991). While they might bend the law, by and large, the Hollywood policeman doesn't break it outright.

Lee Tamahori's *Mulholland Falls* marks another important step in the depiction of the police in Hollywood movies. Many people have compared *Mulholland Falls* with the Roman Polanski noir classic *Chinatown*. There are certainly similarities; both films feature excellent casts, subtle direction and superb period detail. Thematically, however, the films couldn't be more different: *Chinatown* tells the story of Jake Gittes, a law flouting, woman-slapping, LA private eye. *Mulholland Falls*, meanwhile, is about The Hat Squad, a bunch of law-flouting, woman-slapping, 1950s LA policemen.

Led by Max Hoover the Hats intimidate, brutalise, vandalise; in other words, absolutely anything to get the job done. While Gittes comes straight out of the pages of classic crime fiction, Tamahori's Hats are a real shock for the system, a bunch of real-life period coppers who use tactics not unlike the modern LAPD.

The fact that we've seen this sort of violence a hundred times before means that it isn't particularly shocking in itself. What is somewhat more disturbing is to see this sort of modern-day brutality in a period setting. Instead of conforming to past Hollywood portrayals of the police, Tamahori shows his officers acting just like modern day cops. It is this that makes *Mulholland Falls* so important; the film shows that the image of the police on film has come full circle.

Not only are we now able to look at the police of today for what they are, we are also able to look back and see that the law-enforcers of the past weren't quite the angels they were painted as being. And, if nothing else, the real-life brutality of the police in previous decades helps us to understand why there might be people today who would want to shoot at a police station.

ASSASSINS

by Stephen Christian

TWILIGHT. A glint from a window, an anonymous man walks down the street, a nobody. From behind the window, skilful hands silently fix together a rifle in near pitch-dark, eyes never leaving the man in the street. The window opens, followed by a soft pop, a breath of smoke, and the man walks no more. The one who took his life away never knew him ... those skilful hands disassemble the weapon and he slips away into the shadows to collect payment.

Film-makers such as Oliver Stone would have us believe that utopias that seemed so tantalisingly attainable in the fifties and sixties, were subsequently thwarted by the trigger finger of such assassins. One man, or multiple figures entwined in conspiracy, seem to be the very model of popular modern history. The Kennedys, King, Lennon, victims of seemingly unguided acts of random violence, or of callous design, perpetrated by a stream of desperate men in lonely rooms.

Film like *Suddenly* and *The Parallax View* and *JFK* touch on the paranoia of this era, following, as it did, the feelings of powerlessness that shaped *film noir*. Where the gangster film grew out of The Depression and Prohibition and represented the distorted search for some kind of American Dream by immigrant outsiders; the assassin is the paranoia-inducing reflection of untouchable powers and shadowy governments, beyond whose reach no one can hide.

In his 1948 essay *The Gangster as Tragic Hero*, Robert Warshow explains that, from as early as Fritz Lang's German films of the '30s, the gangster has been cast in the shadow of the dreadful city which he cannot do without. The same goes for their antagonist, the hard-boiled detective, who is scarred by the city, yet draws strength from it as if through an umbilical. The assassin is tied to nothing, he is merely found in the cities because he hunts humans, and the city is the whereabouts of his prey.

Luc Besson's *Leon* begins over water, from the point of view of a great bird of prey travelling at speed towards an unsuspecting New York. Yet Besson's predators are children: the naïve Leon (essentially reprising his rôle from Besson's previous outing *La Femme Nikita*) and the waif Matilda whom he

WHO ARE THESE 'GOD'S LONELY MEN'?

adopts. Leon meets his father figure Tony in his Italian restaurant and is given jobs whilst slurping down the milk which seems to comprise his entire diet. He never progresses to solids.

Leon is a blank slate on which are drawn many motifs from a long tradition of assassins in films, from *Le Samouraï*'s 'lonely tiger' Jef Costello via the '80s über-warrior John Rambo to Besson's own *Nikita*. The firepower of the innumerable body-guards of the first 'mark' is useless against Leon's skill and stealth, leaving the target as isolated as *First Blood*'s police chief. Leon's features float out of the dark, accompanied by the most simple and personal of weapons - a knife. Message delivered, he melts back into the shadows leaving the target as Rambo leaves Brian Dennehy, broken and afraid and very alone.

When the manchild encounters the young Matilda, she takes the adult initiative. It is she who smokes, hides coyly behind sultry hair and generally wears the demeanour of the *femme fatale*, yet, whenever real adults are around, she swaps the cigarette for a lollipop. The clutter, crowding and noise of her home-life contrast with the bare, minimal surroundings he lives in - echoing as much with the ghost of Travis Bickle as of Jef Costello - with the single concession to companionship, his potted plant. There are no comforts, nothing to make the apartment a home, nothing to tie him to a particular life.

Gary Oldman inadvertently sees into the substance of Leon and Matilda's relationship when, standing over her, ready to blow her into the next world, he comments: *"It's only when you start to become afraid of death that you really appreciate life."* Leon is given a taste of life by Matilda, and it kills him.

Glancing through his filmography, you notice how Besson doesn't associate home with traditional happy endings, for him happinesses are fleeting momentary things. Leon watches *Singing in the Rain* and aspires to the Hollywood ideal, the gloriously happy ending, but such aspirations can be dangerous. In their dressing-up game, he can only think to emulate the simple innocence of John Wayne, where she immediately selects the slut/mother Madonna.

When her family is butchered by Oldman's Stanfield, he hesitates for a moment, then opens his door, flooding her with light and admitting the possibility of friendship, love and domestic happiness. Later, realising the change she represents could be dangerous he makes to execute her in her sleep, but his credo is 'no women, no children' so, next morning, he attempts to reject her, their one-night stand over, after all, as Tony reminds him, he arrived in America " ... *in deep shit because of a woman!"*

Never the less, he becomes her tutor and together they live like Steinbeck's Lenny and George, rôles reversed so the innocent has become the teacher. He instructs her that the high-velocity rifle is a weapon for beginners, children, and talks her through a mock presidential assassination, mixing *Day of the Jackal* with Lee Harvey Oswald and Clinton the jogger. After the target has fallen to the floor, spattered with a paint-ball, she asks *"Can we use real bullets now?"*

Our culture, our film history, recounts the exploits of individuals who live by a strict code of honour, who have the attractive face of Alain Delon but are the victims of circumstance; yet they are completely in control of their fates in a way that most people aren't. Alone, alienated from emotion, human contact and trust, the foibles that can kill, they are free to act.

John Woo describes his masterpiece *The Killer* as a homage to *Le Samouraï*. Melville's French noir had Delon obsessing about the witness to his last hit, as does *The Killer*. Woo emphasises the mythical status of the solo warrior in whom we place so much stock, seeing Jef as *" ... a tragic hero, a lonely tiger."* In *The Killer*, this murderous nobility is such as to earn the admiration even of its binary opposite: the police sergeant, culminating in their side-by-side battle against a common foe.

Woo positions such men within the Bushido code, the Japanese tradition of The Samurai which is still fundamental to Eastern ideals of masculinity, and particularly attractive to the Americans who like to think of the same code informing their frontiersmen's lives, most obviously in the iconic forms of John Wayne, Charlton Heston and Clint Eastwood. We don't have to be at war to admire the warrior, film gives us a safe distance from which we can do it any time.

Besson first explored the notion of children being made into killers in *Nikita*. That too opens with a tracking-shot, this time over damp tarmac which initially seems like water. The shot widens to watch a gang of drug addicts rob the pharmacy run by their leader's parents. He, not without symbolism, kills his father, then leads the assault against the authorities. Nikita herself, physically little more than a child and mentally hardly more than an infant, becomes an offshoot of the traditional assassin; the state-sanctioned killer, most oft seen in conspiracy thrillers such as *The Parallax View* or Peckinpah's *The Killer Elite* and even in the person of John Rambo in *Rambo II* and *III*. The sanctioned killer gone-wrong is the core of *In The Line of Fire*, as personified by John Malkovitch's Mitch. Here assassins have achieved omnipotence, thanks to their extensive (un)official support networks.

It is an unacknowledged agency of the government which gives young Nikita her second chance, in their assassin factory where she is taught to put away childish things by her imperious 'father', Bob (Tcheky Caryo). It is figures such as he who Mitch blames for his existence, when explaining himself to Clint Eastwood.

Nikita fetishises the woman's body as weapon, as does Richard Donner with Mel Gibson's body in the first *Lethal Weapon*. This is the overt influence of the homo-erotic imagery of all those Scwarzenegger and (particularly) Stallone muscle movies which Reaganite paramilitary culture popularised. Such individuals are energised as modern myths, unstoppable weapons of flesh and bone, dependent only on themselves, able to battle even without armaments. For a country built on still-recent violence, the frontiersman has returned, not as the monstrous Vietnam vet of the '70s and '80s, but as the lonesome warrior of *Die Hard* and his dark reflection: the silent assassin.

The assassin is our modern wish-dream, uncluttered by the complexities of the rat-race, he has the perfect cure for urban angst. To be completely in control of our destiny, untroubled by enforced values, combined with a subjective sense of stark morality. Travis Bickle was born of such visions of warped masculinity, living the life of his writer Paul Schrader, fascinated with guns and too much pornography and living in the big city where there be monsters.

Yet directors like Besson will continue to create poetic figures, lonely tigers who remain our paranoid delusions of a romantic life. In the dark, captivated by those images, we will always love fallen angels and we will always secretly admire those figures in the window, waiting patiently in the shadows, still all save for their cold and empty heartbeats.

LEON

Dir. Luc Besson Dist. Touchstone Home Video. Cert. 18, Dur. 106 Min. Released: (France) 28/09/94, (US) 08/11/94. US Box-office: $32.25 million. A 'Version Integrale' Director's Cut was released in France 26/06/96 with some 25 minutes of additional footage.

LEON

By John Foster

THE PROBLEM WITH *LEON*, apart from its rampant sentimentality and the unwholesome tinge of paedophilia, is not dissimilar to that which has so-far affected John Woo's sadly impotent American excursions. Like *Leon*, Woo's new movies are culturally displaced.

Hollywood has succeeded in emasculating Woo's pulp cinema, simply because it lacks the indigenous uniqueness of Hong Kong, which allowed him to produce high-octane yet deeply personal movies like *Hard Boiled* (1991). In the States, the Catherine Wheel of his balletic violence is toned down and his vigorous camera grows lacklustre. The very panache Hollywood bought, it systematically undermines, making his work a pale parody of its former glory which pleases no one including, judging from recent interviews, the director himself.

Leon is similarly asset-stripped of energy in favour a pragmatic, slow-motion narrative, paying patronising lip-service to the Hollywood mainstream, whilst replacing vulgar exuberance with worthiness. Luc Besson continually nudges his audience, reminding us that this isn't any old piece of Hollywood hokum, it's made by a cult director, it's art, and it matters. This is deep, existential even, and although it may be dull, it's good for you.

Leon contains appropriate helpings of empty symbolism and ponderous pretence, emulating that perception of European cinema which Besson himself has done so much to disabuse: of whimsical characters, consumed by abstraction, walking slowly across rooms and staring pensively into sunlit spaces. This is Universal Truth time, and even the movie's poster, featuring a rueful Jean Reno staring loftily into the distance like a constipated Inspector Clouseau contemplating Life, dares us to challenge its solemnity and self-importance.

Yet, sadly, the only truth revealed by *Leon* is that constant posturing towards the meaningful ends in tedious self-regard and indulgent cinema. Besson's film isn't deep and profound, it's just leaden.

Over the years, many directors have come to America and producing movies of flair and originality, from Sergio Leone's *Once Upon A Time In America*, to Louis Malle's *Atlantic City* and Wim Wenders' *Paris, Texas*; from *Cathy Come Home*-producer Tony Garnett's impactive *Handgun*, to *The War-Game*'s writer-director Peter Watkins' ferocious *Punishment Park*. During the thirties a clutch of directors such as Fritz

GLORIA IN DRAG

Lang, Billy Wilder and Otto Preminger fled Hitler by seeking sanctuary in LA. They prosecuted a major influence on Hollywood cinema, especially in the rising movement of *film noir*.

Such directors brought a fresh eye and a new voice to Uncle Sam. Many mainstream American movies are extremely parochial, despite their publicity-saturated international appeal and premeditated destabilisation of other national cinemas; they invariably take as their setting downtown New York, mid-town LA, or an American city-scape of the mind, a genre USA. Foreign directors come along and produce new images, even of the familiar, which force us to see America in a startlingly new way.

Unfortunately, *Leon* looks and sounds like a French film in a New York setting. This lock, stock and barrel transfer, from the croissant continent to sunny-side-up South-Side, sits gauchely on the screen. It is the work of a pious itinerant, straining to be hip but carrying too much old-world baggage to pull it off.

The art which conceals art is absent from this movie, leaving only publicity-still style. Following *Nikita* (1990), it is a disappointing betrayal of genuine grass-roots popularism. Like *Le Samourai* set in San Francisco, or *Diva* in downtown Dallas, the mix lacks conviction, and the bemused characters look parachuted in.

Riding high on the international wave of *Nikita*, Besson didn't want his first American movie to be too much of a pot-boiler. He obviously had one eye on those reviews in the film quarterlies, the *auteur* status, the BFI study guide and the undergraduate dissertations which might be written about him. He forgot that vulgarity breeds panache.

Nikita is brazen and audacious, with a narrative rich in irony and pathos and well-delineated characters. It takes pleasure in gripping and unusual set-pieces, fastidiously mounted and executed with aplomb. It has a dangerous edge, flirting with sado-masochism in the person of its, by turns, chilling, sensual and vulnerable lead. She is an ugly beauty, steaming through her half-lit world like a crucified lemming, controlled yet out-of-control.

The narrative neatly balances its erotic imagery with a keen sense of Nikita's wantonness and despair, rage and instability. More honest than the lateral sexual duplicities of Truffaut's *The Bride Wore Black* (1967), less ambiguous and penetrating than Jean Becker's *One Deadly Summer* (1983), the film nevertheless flies, storming its way through a plot less dependent on logic than adrenaline. It thinks on its feet and the compulsiveness of pace is all.

Hollywood's anaemic and subtly-entitled remake, *The Assassin* (also known as *The Return of No Point* ... or something like that), and more especially George Sluizer's embarrassing 1993 revamp of his 1988 masterpiece, *The Vanishing* (for which even the performance of the usually engaging Jeff Bridges was risible); should have warned foreign directors like Woo and Besson to stay at home, where they can be nasty, decadent and disturbing, without straight-jacketed restraints. If you have nothing to say about America, then leave the Americans to say nothing.

They're better at it!

Nikita is a racy caricature from a graphic novel, screaming her own thought bubbles. Indeed, Frank Miller's assassin, *Electra* very much comes to mind. Leon is Hamlet without the poetry, tragic only because of the absurdity of his earnestness. *Nikita* is the real thing, a genuine movie experience where you emerge buzzing. *Leon* is a dud, counterfeiting significance and making you feel, through its over-insistence, that you ought to like it really.

More significantly, *Leon* is also an uncredited re-make of John Cassavetes' 1980 masterwork, *Gloria*, which is a barnstormer of a movie with the same basic plotline: An adult of dubious morals and criminal background protects the life of a minor whose family has been murdered by cold-hearted gangsterism, which then proceeds to hunt down the fleeing duo. *Leon* merely reverses the genders, making the protector a male hitman instead of a female call-girl, and the protectee is a sexually precocious girl instead of a petulant brat. *Leon* is, in fact, *Gloria* in drag.

Actor, screenwriter, producer, editor, songwriter and director, Cassavetes, who died in 1989, was virtually a one-man American New Wave when, at the time of new waves in France, Italy and Britain, he made his first movie - *Shadows* (1959). This was to be followed by *Too Late Blues*(1961), *A Child is Waiting* (1963), *Faces* (1968) and *Husbands* (1970) and a whole series of deeply personal, low-budget films which challenged the primacy of the commercial mainstream and spoke with a different voice, even though Cassavetes was not especially *avant-garde* nor surrealist. Vehemently anti-Hollywood and anti-mainstream, Cassavetes provided an alternative, popularist cinema, independently funded and distributed, in opposition to it. *"The only art America appreciates,"* he once stated, *"Is the art of making money!"* (1)

Cassavetes was more interested in the process of making a film, than in the finished product; consequently, niceties such as composition and technical virtuosity were not a primary concern. Often film equipment, caught in the frame, was left in the final cut because he felt that *"The technical quality of a film doesn't have much to do with whether it's a good film or not."* (2)

It was the interpersonal experience of making a movie which preoccupied him, producing a raw, edgy cinema of formidable innovative range, diversity and originality, yet which remained accessible to popular audiences. He reversed the dominant production process, so to make technicians the servants of the actors; indeed, the cameraman was often excluded from rehearsals until the actors were ready. This evolved into a performance-led cinema, employing Cassavetes' company of improvisational actors, and producing some of the most disturbing human-drama ever witnessed on the big screen. As *Columbo*'s Peter Falk (one of the company) put it *"He established a spontaneity in acting never achieved before or since."* (3)

More than anything else, Cassavetes produced non-judgmental cinema. His characters were not hung on crosses of pre-ordained thematic, but permitted to live and breath and sustain all the complexities and complications of ordinary people. *Gloria*, whilst functioning on a much lighter and playful level, still embraces the themes, concerns and production methods which forced him to exclude himself from mainstream American cinema.

The one favour *Leon* offers us, is an excuse to reconsider Cassavetes' vastly superior, yet relatively unknown movie. Recently re-issued in the UK by Tartan Video, we can now see *Gloria* as a film of great charm, humour, wit and excitement, even if it was made for commercial reasons. The director had run up large debts from making his more experimental films, notably his idiosyncratic noir thriller *The Killing of a Chinese Bookie* (1976) and the rarefied *Opening Night* (1977). He had no intention of directing *Gloria* but *"... wrote the story to sell, strictly to sell!"* [(4)]

Commissioned initially by MGM, the project was sold to Columbia, who wished to produce it with Cassavetes' wife Gena Rowlands in the title rôle. Rowlands is an actress whose performances - particularly under her husband's direction in his masterpiece *A Woman Under the Influence* (1974) - are second to none in the whole of cinema. Surprising, especially given his maverick reputation, Columbia also wished to have him on board. *"The bad news is they want you to direct it"* [(5)] his agent explained.

Cassavetes didn't rate the script, which he clearly regarded as hackwork, but was used to working on television and film projects he disliked (usually as actor, but also as uncredited script-writer), in order to finance his own productions. Of course, artists are rarely best-positioned to judge their own work and *Gloria* is, in fact, a very well-written screenplay. It is a mean streets chase thriller, set in the director's beloved New York City.

However, there was a feeling among some Cassavetes admirers that he had betrayed his deep commitment to alternative, independent film-making. Analytical studies of his 'oeuvre' barely touch upon *Gloria*, perhaps because it is just too much fun for glum-faced academia. A film which can bring an embarrassing tear to the eye and a lump to the throat, cannot possibly be a serious work of art, now can it!?

Unlike *Leon*, *Gloria* offers no overt pretence to seriousness; it refrains from sledge-hammering you with needless significance because Cassavetes isn't setting out to prove how profound he is. He delights in his characters and their world, and in telling a good yarn; the impassioned thematics emerge naturally through moments of pathos during the fast-moving and exceptionally tense narrative. You can watch this immensely enjoyable entertainment, and absorb its meaning as a parable of change without having to take a evening class in Film Studies.

The difference between *Gloria* and mainstream Hollywood cinema, on the surface, doesn't seem that great, it being an unashamedly populist film and also deeply emotional; but it maintains a hard edge and refuses sentimentality. As such, the movie stirs the feelings and raws the nerves. It raises the barometer of our emotions without resorting, as in *Leon*, to easy appeals to our compassion. But

Gloria's superiority to Besson's film lies primarily in its non-patronising, sympathetic investigation of its characters, and in the way it charts their changing state as they are battered against the ragged rocks of experience.

Gloria is not an immediately likeable person, there is no artificial mystique constructed around her, unlike Leon. Phil, her charge, apes Cagney and is basically an obnoxious handful. In fact, Cassavetes makes us work hard to latch on to either of them, having introduced them late in the film. Initially it is Phil's beautiful young mother who seems to be the film's focus, until she is murdered.

Before being killed, Phil's father entrusts him with a book of incriminating evidence, the book for which the whole family is soon executed. *"You are the man,"* he tells his son, and this line reverberates through the film, underlining its false bravado and Cagneyesque heroics; for Phil is not a man, he is a vulnerable child, soon to be orphaned.

Cassavetes makes us feel for Phil's family, his parents, his elder sister and his grandmother, when they are coldly machine-gunned down, even though we hardly know them. Which is, of course, entirely the point: don't judge people, feel for them. Indeed, the film works hard to make us emotional, too disturbingly emotional for it to sit with total ease in the mainstream.

Unlike Besson, Cassavetes is restrained in his depiction of violence and refrains from showing us torture and cruelty. He leaves it to our imagination, because he knows that will be far more potent than anything he can show us. At once we are engaged both emotionally and imaginatively with the film. A lesson Besson would have done well to apply to the gunnings in *Leon*.

Gloria is hard, ruthless and violent, the very casualness of which is itself shocking. To quote Raymond Chandler: *"It is not funny that a man should die, but it is sometimes funny that he should die for so little."* [(6)] In Gloria's world, people die for nothing, over a notebook containing information which is, as she points out, 'no big deal'!

Cassavetes fought against rigid social structures, which inhibited the true expression of the personality and the possibility for change for reasons which he considered to be 'no big deal'. His cinema allowed the free flow of natural expression, however gauchely that may sometimes manifest itself. His theme was the need to live life intuitively, instinctively, Lawrentially, in opposition to the constructed life-systems which deaden and entrap. To Cassavetes, spontaneity was all.

There are no bad guys in *Gloria*, Cassavetes' underworld is more credible and less simplistic than even Scorsese's. There's no De Niro here, no colourful wise-cracks, only hoodlums distinguished by their ordinary drabness. Not evil, they are commonplace men caught up in a crime syndicate's rules and plebiscites. They function like businessmen, the job has to be done and it is simple as that; they have forgotten how to feel and that is how they are able to do what they do.

Gloria is initially a part of this dehumanising strata, but events force her to act impulsively. Her fury at the hoods seems disproportionate to what they are: simple, hapless hirelings. But it is a fury against herself, of course, against her own cowardice and complicity, therefore, in the zeal of her escape from her personal prison, she explodes upon the streets.

We learn little about her, as always with Cassavetes, his characters remain oblique, corners of life are left unexplored or unexplained. He is teasing us to ask how well, in truth, do we know anyone, including ourselves? Gloria cannot be the subject of synopsis, one of those potted biographies, so beloved of screenwriters. Indeed, he fastidiously gives us glimpses of all the people in his city. They all matter, they all have inner lives and their own uniqueness and individuality. Either all lives are worth living, or none are.

Gloria has been to prison and has Mafia connections, she is, literally, a broad. She has a second, much more modish apartment uptown, its purpose remaining unclear, suggesting a double-life, that maybe she earns her living as a high-class call-girl; but the director leaves this deliberately unclear. All we really know is that her best friend is her cat.

Violence is no stranger to her, and she can use a gun. There is something lonely and unfilled about her, as if, in Lillian Hellman's phrase, she is an 'unfinished woman'. Smart and funny, stylish yet curiously vulnerable, it is as she is hiding from something, in hiding from herself. Circumstances force her to make an instant choice: to feed the kid to the Mafia or save him and risk her own neck. She chooses instinctively, irrationally, and on behalf of life.

All the talk and rationalisations are blown away in an instant when her so-called friends are prepared to condemn and murder her. Thinking on her feet, reacting spontaneously to the vagaries of life, her existence becomes increasingly personalised; Gloria comes through and begins to find out who she really is.

Ultimately, this film, as with all Cassavetes films, is about love. Not romantic love necessarily, but the intuitive, spontaneous love felt between people. Both Gloria and the kid break free, by the force of circumstance, from their personal traps. They are made to learn empathy through mutual tolerance, flexibility through the needs of survival, and that there are no absolutes in life except life. Consequently, an extraordinary bond grows between them as their personas develop and they, finally, become 'family'. But it is not easy; there is the question of trust and loyalty, the resentment of dependence and, the biggest obstacle of all: pride.

The action is played out against a real world, not a Hollywood backlot, as if the camera were a natural part of the world. Real streets. A real bar. A real tenement block. This nerve-jangling action is constantly character-led, never just there for thrills; the dynamic of the story is always related directly to the feelings of Gloria and Phil and their insecurities.

Gloria is frequently contrasted with the gangsters, whose lack of passion makes them dangerous; whilst she is dangerous precisely because of her rebirth, her coming alive. *"Give me your hand"* she says to a taxi-driver who has aided their escape. It is a fleeting moment of empathy towards someone who had instinctively trusted her when he had no reason to. What little he had, he stood to lose, yet still he risked it all for a stranger. Risk and lose everything, Cassavetes is saying, rather than protect yourself. It is better to trust and to bleed than be deadened by defensive armour.

This is his most commercial film, yet he still takes several swipes at mainstream clichés. In the post-title sequence, he mocks the film-makers who open their films with bland panoramic city-scapes, as epitomised by the London of Hitchcock's *Frenzy*. He counterpoints this convention by bringing us down into the streets, into the real lives lived by real people. Luc Besson, aping Cassavetes' superb montage with swooping shots across the New York skyline, merely subscribes to the stereotype and entirely misses the point.

The tongue is rarely far from the cheek with Cassavetes. Gloria and Phil need to escape New York; their destination: Pittsburgh. A convention of the mainstream thriller is the flight to safety - usually across the border to Mexico, or some other Eldorado But Pittsburgh? *"Maybe there are gangsters in Pittsburgh too"* muses Gloria, with uncharacteristic naïveté. One can almost hear Cassavetes chuckling.

Then there is the closing sequence, with the two protagonists united in slow motion against a background of swelling music. This cliché is not, unsurprisingly, the ending Cassavetes intended: he wanted it shot in black and white, which would have evoked Phil's dream and therefore left the audience uncertain as to the outcome of the story. In the event, the studio wouldn't wear it and forced a more conventional ending on him, which he satirised in order to ridicule the system which so constrained him.

Yet it actually works as a haunting reaffirmation of the film's thematics. Ironic, yet deeply affecting. As always, Cassavetes succeeds in making us laugh, whilst making us feel. His ironic, shark-like grin, employed in so-many mainstream acting jobs, is the face watching you watching his oddball, independent cinema.

NOTES:

(1) The Films of John Cassavetes: Pragmatism, Modernism and the Movies. *by Ray Carney. Cambridge Books. 1994.*

(2) *ibid.*

(3) *Peter Falk speaking in* Cinefile On John Cassavetes. *Channel 4. 1992.*

(4) *Sleeve notes.* Gloria. *Tartan Video. Released in the UK in 1996.*

(5) *ibid.*

(6) The Simple Art of Murder. *Raymond Chandler.* Atlantic Magazine. *1944.*

LEON

Dir. Luc Besson Dist. Touchstone Home Video. Cert. 18, Dur.: 106 Min. Released: (France) 28/09/94, (US) 08/11/94. US Box-office: $32.25 million. A 'Version Integrale' Director's Cut was released in France 26/06/96 with some 25 minutes of additional footage.

ROAD RAPE

By John Costello

WITH THE MEDIA OUTRAGE and scare-mongering which was whipped-up following the London Film Festival screening of David Cronenberg's latest feature, you might be forgiven for suspecting him to be none other than Satan himself. However, if you're familiar with the Canadian director's portfolio you will realise that *Crash* shares similar devices, themes and concerns with his previous work. The word 'auteur' has become somewhat devalued by overuse, but few filmmakers better suit the term than Cronenberg, who since the mid-70s has consistently explored 'difficult' territory, confronting his own psyche unflinchingly and creating a unique celluloid body of personal visions.

So, what is it about *Crash* that has so powerfully incited the media machine to take arms against it? Why is this film seen as so much more of a threat to the nation's well-being than, say, *Shivers* (1974), *Scanners* (1980) or *Videodrome* (1982)?

Pre-election political posturing, the collective closed-minded terror of exposure to issues requiring the application of criteria outside of pure black or white and the desperate desire to blame the power of the image for our increasingly dysfunctional society all play a part. However, a comprehensive study of the complex issues surrounding censorship today would require several volumes, so I'll just sketch in the background:

At the Cannes film festival, *Crash* won the Special Jury Prize for its *"originality and daring"*.

On June 6th, the London Evening Standard carried a full-page attack on the film by respected critic Alexander Walker, who considered it *"...beyond depravity"*. This brought it to the attention of our moral guardians, who without having seen a frame of the film itself, began to denounce it from every available soapbox. This in turn led to a mention in the House of Commons and the very real possibility of a ban in this country. To date, it has been screened four times by the BBFC and once under special licence at the London Film Festival. As I write, Westminster council has just banned the film from West End cinemas unless substantial cuts are made, and the media circus around this 'Sex and Wrecks' movie gains impetus.

Crash is not a 'normal' film. It cannot be judged using the usual popcorn criteria. It is a highly-stylised exercise in existential film-making which is designed to challenge our comfortable assumptions of what a film is supposed to be. Its market

DAVID CRONENBERG'S CRASH

is limited to art house/cult devotees and genuine film buffs. The extensive tabloid publicity will only serve to draw titillation-seekers who will be utterly disappointed by the film. It's like asking a Take That fan to appreciate musique concrete or Karlheinz Stockhausen.

A synopsis reveals the extent of the problems the film poses: Well-to-do middle-class couple James and Catherine Ballard (James Spader and Deborah Unger) indulge in casual sex with various partners and then recount their exploits to each other while engaged in clinical, almost passionless coupling. When he is involved in a fatal freeway head-on, a new plane of experience is opened up for them both. The passenger in the other car, the now-widowed Dr. Helen Remington (Holly Hunter), has sex with Ballard and then leads him into the crazed world of ultimate hedonist Vaughan (Elias Koteas), who re-enacts famous car-crash scenes from history (Albert Camus, James Dean, Jayne Mansfield) with the aid of the motliest crew of characters since Frank Booth's bunch of misfits in *Blue Velvet*. He also prowls the airport perimeter roads in his huge, battered black Lincoln in search of accidents to photograph, and of the last word in sexual highs - his own final fusion of man and machine. Ballard and Catherine are drawn into this surreal netherworld and are propelled almost involuntarily toward their own cerebral and physical ca(r)tharsis.

J.G. Ballard's 1973 novel must have seemed a model of narrative cohesion for Cronenberg after adapting William Burroughs' notoriously difficult, almost abstract *Naked Lunch* in 1991. Ballard has since become a more establishment author and has described *Crash* as *"...a cautionary tale from the eye of the hurricane"*, although he still has a great deal of affection for the book and loves the film, which he thinks is more extreme than the novel and is unlike any other film he's seen. This has pleased Cronenberg, who always brings his own creative processes to the material he adapts, and also tries to let the material alter him somehow, in much the same way as many of his central characters become altered in a fusion with something outside themselves, however bizarre.

Cronenberg's concern with altered states of being informs most of his films, but with *Crash* the experiment has stretched to the assembly of the film itself. Narrative obeys few conventions - the film opens with a series of three sex scenes, one after another - yet it has a recognisable structure. It is sexually explicit but unerotic. It intensely examines its characters' search for new levels of experience but remains curiously detached. The viewer is given no sense of 'normality' which is then deviated from. The car is as much a central figure as any of the human characters.

The sex is presented as almost disembodied; certainly unsatisfactory in the most fundamental sense for the participants. The missionary position is not used; indeed, the man is usually behind the woman so they cannot see each other's faces. In one scene, Ballard seduces Vaughan in his car; in another, he has sex with a healed-up crash-wound in Gabrielle's (Rosanna Arquette's) rear thigh.

This is an experiment in style, not subversion; film-making pared to its essentials, right down to the base metal. The film as a whole is unlike anything else, and its parts are only reminiscent of other Cronenberg films.

In *Videodrome* we are unsure if James Woods' nightmarish reincarnation is taking place in the 'real' world or an induced video-hallucination (*"long live the new flesh"*); in *The Fly*, Jeff Goldblum's experiments cause his molecular fusion with both the physical and behavioural traits of a common house-fly; in *Scanners*, people with heightened mental capacity have to learn to live with their own superhuman powers as if they were an incapacitating disability; in *Crash*, Vaughan sees his death in a crash as a liberation of sexual energy on a level more intense than any other, and Ballard reclaims Vaughan's car and resumes his activities as if his own personality has been eclipsed by the more powerful Vaughan.

The detachment from events taking place in *Crash* is not confined to the audience; most of the cast seem to wander aimlessly through situations in a sort of robotic limbo which is as much a comment on the surface values of the '90s as George Romero's shopping mall zombies in *Dawn of the Dead* were an indictment of the shallowness of capitalist society. The only exception is Koteas, who plays Vaughan as if he is breathing not oxygen, but a potent concoction part petrol fumes and part pheromones.

At the recent Guardian lecture at the NFT, I asked Cronenberg if this detachment was a deliberately stylised approach. He replied that the film somehow evolved that way, it was a subconscious interpretation by the actors to play their rôles with this sense of spiritual unease and aloofness, adding another layer of subtext to the film.

Cronenberg also says he feels *Crash* is a surprisingly emotional film. I found it more cerebral than emotional and a far less devastating experience than my first viewing of *Videodrome*. That said, *Crash* is in my opinion his best film since then and requires more than one visit to attune yourself to its unique vision of a search for a metaphysical catharsis in the absence of Meaning.

David Cronenberg has taken up the challenge of examining the areas at the borders of existence and treating what he finds with dispassionate curiosity. His method of film-making is not bombastic or prone to emotional rant; it is quite formal, almost antiseptic in its approach. As the bandwidth of what we are allowed to see by our repressed and repressive system narrows further, directors like Cronenberg are our last defence against the moral majority who, rather than be asked to consider films requiring thoughtful analysis, run screaming to hide behind the nearest pillar of society. If I prefer to have my intellect stimulated and display no irrational fear of being corrupted, does that make me a menace to society? If I am fully aware that what I see on the screen is not the same as real life, am I somehow abnormal?

If I reach the conclusion that the answer to these questions is 'yes', I have only one thing left to say:

"Long live the Immoral Minority".

THE YEAR IN REVIEW

"Don't Trust Critics"

WONG KAR-WAI

ASSASSINS (DAY OF RECKONING)

Dir. Richard Donner Dist. Warner Bros. Cert. 15, Dur. 106 Min. Released: 06/10/96 US Box-office: $30.25 million

AS THE TITLE INDICATES, this is not a film about social workers, instead, despite popular demand, it's about Sylvester Stallone effectively reprising his rôle from *The Specialist*.

It begins promisingly, with Sly escorting a hitman out into rainy swampland, in order to kill him. No explanations, it's just the way it is. The hitman endeavours to offer some defence - *"Someone has to do the jobs you won't. You and your damned morality."* A-ha, so Sly is the hitman with the heart of gold. How delightful. In fact, in assassination circles he is regarded as *numero uno*.

Then, along comes a giggling and wide-eyed Antonio Banderas, the new chip off the block, tired of being *numero dos*. So the film develops into a race, as the two professionals attempt to stop each other fulfilling their respective contracts, whilst trying to air each other out in the process.

Enter Julianne Moore and her cat. She is a computer hacker who makes some serious enemies (well, they're silly enemies really, but you know what I mean) and thusly earns a contract on her head. Sly, in a radical departure from the usual Hollywood plot, decides not to execute her, as he is being paid extremely well to do, because he has taken a liking to her and her pussy.

Shot through with contrived set-pieces and hammy dialogue-delivery (I hesitate to call it acting), *Assassins* fails on so many levels, it's hard to credit that director Donner has been doing this sort of stuff for decades - most recently with the *Lethal Weapon* series.

The potential packed into this plot is such that it took real cowardice and incompetence on behalf of the producers and scriptwriters to turn it into a dull and disinteresting turkey. But with diligence and determination they managed it; proving once more that Hollywood-at-large has learned nothing from Woo and Tarantino about how to make shoot-'em-ups exhilarating again.

Amazingly, Banderas won this rôle on the back of, and directly because of, the sterling work he put into *Desperado*. If Donner had seen so much as a promo of Rodriguez's movie, he would have closed up production and put *Assassins* back where it belongs - on the shelf.

JA ▼

BAD BOYS

Dir. Michael Bay Dist. Columbia Tri-Star Cert. 18. Dur. 114 Min. Released: 07/04/95. US Box-office: $65.75 million.

THIS FILM SHOULD have been tedious in the extreme. A buddy movie about two black cops who squabble like man and wife. Yawn. A sexy young witness they have to protect. Big deal. An evil foreign badguy who's masterminded a hundred-million dollar crime. Seen it all before. Mix in some Miami sky-lines, some rock music, a few car chases and a lot of explosions and what've you got? Surprisingly, you've got a damn fine movie.

For director Michael Bay this was his first time out of the gate on anything other than a pop video. So, obviously, he brings with him a pop-video director's eye for colour and composition. Nothing special there, most films look good these days. As was shown by his second film *The Rock*, swirling cameras do not a movie make. The script about the big heist and two cops' attempts to track the bad guys down is similarly par for the course. It's efficient but hardly inspirational. What this film has which lifts it, and the work of everyone involved, way above anything that could have been anticipated - is the interaction of stars Martin Lawrence and Will Smith.

Apparently they improvised much of their dialogue, and the bug was caught by Teã Leoni, who plays the only eye-witness and therefore next logical target. The electricity that flies between these three characters is a delight to watch, and, because you're enjoying their company so much, because you care about them, you find yourself forgiving and even appreciating the film's more contrived moments. *Independence Day* director Roland Emmerich must have noticed what a natural Smith is, and cast him as the man who saves the world.

Now on video, the energy and enthusiasm of the *Bad Boys* beams straight through the TV screen and works its magic on the most jaded of old curmudgeons. And I speak with some experience! Consequently, what could have been just any old shoot 'em up, turns into one of the stand-out Hollywood actioners of recent years. Presented in widescreen format, it recaptures as much of the sparkle of the cinema experience as possible.

Whatcha gonna do? You're gonna buy the damn film, that's what!

JA ▼▼▼▼▼

THE BAIT (L'APPAT)

Dir. Bertrand Tavernier Dist. Artificial Eye. Cert. 18. Dur. 115 Min. Released: September 1995

THIS IS SOMETHING of a thematic sequel to Tavernier's gritty semi-documentary *L627.* It follows the *travails* of young Natalie (Marie Gillian) who claims to be eighteen but looks worryingly younger. She lives with her boyfriend Eric and his best friend. This *menage â trois* are *naïve* drop-outs with big ideas, but no clue. In her unfocused quest to become a model and actress, she has cultivated an address book full of interesting contacts, which Eric decides could be their ticket to the big time.

Using her not inconsiderable charms, the *petite* Natalie persuades one of her affluent contacts to take her home for the night, where the dim-witted duo duly break in, rob the safe and steal off into the night to divvy up their ill-gotten gains. Well, that's the plan. But in a Tavernier film, as in life, things rarely go according to plan; so a needlessly complex burglary becomes a slow, lingering murder.

Albeit it full colour and French, there are distinct similarities with *Man Bites Dog*: not least in the fractured editing style which cuts you into a scene after it has started, then cuts you out again before it has finished. Modishly *verité* use of shaky hand-held camera, and the stark amorality of the players as they bumble through their reign of error, make this a late entry in the '90s as moral wasteland' stakes.

Tavernier is attempting to make an anti-film here, constantly digging at French cinema-going habits by using everything from posters on walls to a throwaway line in a video store: *"It can't be any good, it's French!"* Rather in the way that Ken Loach and Mike Leigh cut across the grain of British film, he is attempting to shake up a bored and self-indulgent industry. He wants to inspire a new New Wave, in other words.

Ultimately though, this minor tragedy with major aspirations isn't much good either. It suffers because of the sheer idiocy of its three key players, particularly the short-tempered *chauvinist* Eric, whose ambition succeeds in destroying not only his own worthless life, but also those of the only two people he loves. *C'est la vie.*

JA ▼▼

BATMAN FOREVER

Dir. Joel Schumacher Dist. Warner Bros, Cert. PG. Dur. 120 Min. Released: 16/06/95 US Box-office: $184 million

I'M IN A MINORITY with regards the 1995 summer sci-fi punch-up - I thought *Judge Dredd* was better than *Batman.* Why? Well, not really because *Dredd* was a shining example of how best to use $70 million and a much-loved comic character, but more because, by comparison, *Batman Forever* so sorely lacked focus, plot, characterisation, tension, credibility, wit, originality or flair. Other than that, I thought it was dull.

Director Schumacker's photography is delicious (though no more so than in *The Lost Boys* or *Flatliners*) making the most of the computer-generated city-scapes and outlandish costumes. Where he keeps falling down however, is in trying to juggle a cast which is, plainly, too large. Jim Carrey strides about Gotham as if to the manner born, Michael Gough's Alfred gets all the best lines ... again, but no one else (Bats included) gets chance to make much of an impression.

Harvey Two Face (no longer played, as in the first film, by Billy Dee Williams, but hey, most everyone else is different, so why not!?) owns the first half-hour of the film, and allows Tommy Lee Jones a rare opportunity to show a different, more exuberant side to his personality (because, let's face it, since that Oscar, he's been taking himself just a little too seriously!). This results in a performance which makes Jack Nicholson's Joker seems subtle. Jones' sole function, it eventually transpires, is to orphan Dick Grayson and thereby inflict Robin on the world. This done, he evaporates, until it's time for him to plunge to his doom several reels later.

Meanwhile, the Riddler has rigged up some green doo-hickey that sits on your TV and sort-of sucks your brain out, type of thing, turning you into some kind of mindless zombie. Wow, now there's a subtle metaphor. Of course, this preposterous contrivance is neither explained nor pursued.

On the plus side, although he is finest mahogany as Bruce Wayne, Val Kilmer makes an effortlessly impressive Batman, whilst Chris O'Donnell confounds all expectation by turning out an enjoyable Robin - not that it was all that hard to improve on Burt Ward's rendition. Similarly, Elliot Goldenthal's contribution succeeds where it shouldn't, it almost ties this incoherent mish-mash together. Indeed, as a soundtrack album, his score is marvellous. Maybe you ought to buy that and leave the movie well alone.

Did I mention the new Batmobile? It looks like a pile of lacquered spare ribs on wheels and it can now drive up walls, apparently. Unfortunately, its ominous profile is rather besmirched by the way that its tail fins inadvertently flap every time it hits a bump. Personally I was glad when Carrey torched it.

Ultimately, then, this is a clinically-designed fashion-accessory, with a limited shelf life, tooled to travel at great speed from stock-room to megastore in the hope that they'll be sold out before too many people realise that, compacted onto even the finest 28 inch pro-logic box, all its sound and fury signifies nothing.

JA ▼

BULLETS OVER BROADWAY

Dir. Woody Allen Dist. Miramax (BVI). Cert. 15. Dur. 102 Min. Released: 21/10/94. US Box-office: $4.75 million

1920S NEWYORK, and the city is in the grip of prohibition. With the gangsters growing fat, struggling playwright David (John Cusack) approaches a bootlegger with an eye to financing his production. The Mafioso agrees on one condition, that his girlfriend gets a starring rôle. Cusack complies, only to be lumbered with the helium voiced Olive (Jennifer Tilly) and her body-guard Cheech (Chazz Palminteri), a thug whose unrealised genius for theatre eventually sees him turn David's pretentious melodrama into a modern masterpiece.

It sounds fun, and it is for the first twenty minutes. After that, *Bullets Over Broadway* goes the way of so many of Woody's recent pictures. The things that made *Manhattan Murder Mystery* and *Mighty Aphrodite* minor Allen movies are at work here, too: overwritten dialogue (*"the world will open up to you like ... a magnificent vagina."*), irritating, shrieking female leads, the director's contempt for the working classes. The character development is also piss poor, with Harvey Fierstein's theatrical agent and Rob Reiner's adulterous intellectual never making it beyond first base.

In the midst of this mediocrity, Palminteri stands out like a lighthouse. As Tilly, Tracey Ullman and Jim Broadbent over-act like billyo, Palminteri plays the butch, brutal Cheech with a perfect blend of menace and dead-pan. He is so good, you really wish the whole film was about him. As it is, Allen focuses his attention on Cusack's Woodyesque David, a man about whom the only mystery is why he would rather sleep with Diane Wiest's ageing drama queen than Penelope Anne Miller.

For all its period touches and warm, glowing camera-work, *Bullets Over Broadway* is just another in a worryingly long line of recent so-so Allen movies. Next up for Woody - a musical starring Tim Roth. I can hardly wait.

RL ▼▼

THE CABLE GUY

Dir. Ben Stiller Dist. Columbia Tri-Star. Cert. 15. Dur. 97 Min. Released: 14/06/96. US Box-office: $60 million.

I WAS VERY SURPRISED to learn that Jim Carrey's latest foray out of the rubber room is in fact a crime movie. He plays a nameless cable-installer who takes a shine to customer Matthew Broderick and begins to invade and finally ruin his life. The only background we have on Mr Cable Guy is that, as a child, his mother would leave him in front of the electric baby-sitter watching films like - not insignificantly - *Play Misty For Me*.

But such subplots are merely dark veins beneath the surface of visually sharp, edgy movie which isn't shot or edited like a comedy and isn't meant to be untroublingly funny. Carrey is just as loud and extraordinarily physical as ever, but because he's not smiling, suddenly his mania is scary. He makes a convincingly obsessive stalker! Yet, against this dark background, when the jokes do let rip, they seem all the funnier. Not since the great days of John Landis (that's from *The Blues Brothers* to *Coming To America* if you really must know) has a mere barrel of laughs been so lavishly and stylishly decorated.

The richest lode is exposed when Carrey takes his hapless victim to Medieval Nights, a restaurant which, worryingly, actually does exist. Herein the punters eat with their fingers, quaff from goblets, and watch knights whack hell out of each other over dessert. Needless to add, the dynamic duo soon find themselves on horseback, battling to the death (complete with unnervingly accurate *Star Trek* sound effects from the impossible-to-embarrass Carrey).

A sub-plot left far enough in the background to attract the attention of only the most suspicious viewer, concerns the murder by TV star Sam Sweet of his twin brother. In his television cameos, Sweet is played by director Stiller, unable to resist the chance to do a Hitch. What this has to do with the main plot is wisely never made clear, making it all the more fascinating.

Unfortunately, the film loses it's way about an hour in, because the thriller plot and comedy characterisations actually work against each other. It isn't really incisive enough to be satire, not critical enough to be pastiche and not funny enough to be parody. It is the first film Carrey has made since the first *Ace Ventura* which wasn't a guaranteed hit and, now that he has more money than South America and can afford to relax a little, I suspect it is an example of the braver direction his career will go in. Stay tuned for more info on this late breaking story after these important messages ...

JA ▼▼▼

CASINO

Dir. Martin Scorsese Dist. Universal (UIP), Cert. 18, Dur. 178 Min., Released: 24/11/95. US Box-office: $42.25 million.

CASINO IS REALLY *Goodfellas* 2, and don't let anyone tell you otherwise! It stars Robert De Niro and Joe Pesci playing substantially the same rôles as last time - De Niro's 'Ace' is Mr Cool-and-in-control whilst Pesci's 'Nicky' is Mr Short-psycho-on-a-stick.

Like *Goodfellas* the film's narrative is largely communicated via voice-over, which guides us through the labyrinthine complexities of sixties and seventies gangsterdom. Indeed, the film's first forty-five minutes is a fascinating roller-coaster ride through the ABC of running a casino, introducing the hard-men, hustlers and hookers who inhabit its darkened auditoria.

This all makes for scintillating viewing, stitched together with trademark Scorsese panache, the only problem is ... it's the same as *Goodfellas*.

When Nicky invades Ace's empire and starts to cut away at its roots by knifing, beating, torturing and killing his way into his own seedy little empire, you cannot shake the image of Tommy De Vito from your mind, standing foursquare, effing and blinding his way to an Oscar. The only problem is that Pesci was genuinely scary in *Goodfellas*, but five years of light comedies and *Home Alone* movies have rather sucked the marrow from his menace.

As you would expect, the photography, editing and music mix is flawless. Scorsese is quite simply the most effortlessly excellent director Hollywood currently has. But lighting and editing do not a movie make. Performances do. Characters. The human element. Yet these characters seem spookily familiar.

Sharon Stone received the film's only Oscar nom for her supporting rôle as Ginger the fucked-up floozy; however, this is not in recognition of the excellence of her performance (she gave a much better 'straight' show in the unfairly ignored *Intersection*) but of her ability to remain cute whilst crying profusely. After all, she isn't exactly forging new ground, given that her rôle is scarcely distinguishable from Michelle Pfeiffer's in *Scarface* or Lorraine Bracco's in ... you guessed it ... *Goodfellas*.

True, the film has a mythical subtext, concerning the fall of Sodom and Gomorra, but this aspect only really dawns on you about the time that *Sight and Sound* or *The Guardian* point it out to you, it certainly isn't self-evident from the film. If you haven't picked it up by the time the closing *Apocalypse Now*-type montage shows the city being consumed in flames, you never will.

Over all then, a worthy film in it's own right, but I can only whole-heartedly recommend it to those who haven't seen and been overwhelmed by ... oh, what was it called again?

***JA* ▼▼▼**

THE CEREMONY (LA CEREMONIE)

Dir. Claude Chabrol Dist. Tartan Video. Cert. 15. Dur. 108 Min. Released (France) 30/07/95. US Box-office: $76, 750

WEALTHY EX-MODEL Mme Lelievre (Jacqueline Bisset) engages the odd but hard-working Sophie (Sandrine Bonnaire) as live-in maid for the rural Brittany home she shares with a husband and their two children. Much to the family's dismay however, the new help forges a rapport with Jeanne (Isabelle Huppert), the skittish local post-mistress with a reputation for opening mail.

Gradually, dark stories emerge, implicating both women in violent death, while Sophie's carefully concealed illiteracy leads her further into trouble. Things can only end in tragedy.

Darling of English crime Ruth Rendell is not the most obvious of targets for a French New Wave veteran like Chabrol, but in co-adapting (with Caroline Eliacheff) *A Judgement in Stone* he has made his best film in a years. Like his most celebrated thriller, 1968's *Le Boucher*, it's a complex slow-burner, built not so much on event as on character. On such occasions the casting is all-important, and here it is immaculate.

Bonnaire is mousy and taciturn, smiles rarely and walks with a deliberate, shuffling gait. From the outset she is a closed-book, able to turn-up at the station with her whole life in a single suitcase. When not working she sits and stares at the TV in her room.

Huppert - 1996 Best Actress *Cesar* winner - is brash and tomboyish by comparison. Hair in pigtails, she skips through much of the picture like an excitable child, insulting those who dare venture into her Post Office, abusive when she collects old clothes for the local church. Jeanne is ticklish and capricious, a dangerous and unpredictable catalyst for the timid maid.

It is clear, however, where their director's sympathy lies. Bisset is terrific as the snobbish employer, supposedly enlightened but incapable of seeing hired help as anything but subordinate. Virginie Ledoyen is particularly good as grown-up daughter Melinda, clearly cut from the same cloth. To them the new maid is initially problematic, later someone to be ignored, like a well-trained dog. Bisset's dignified tantrum when Sophie takes-off on the day of Melinda's birthday-bash, is a volcano of class resentment.

The women watch trashy TV, giggle in corners, get ticked out by the pompous local priest. The Lelievres are refined and haughty in their privilege; they dress specially for opera on their television. They are, Chabrol is saying, asking for it.

The end is significant for its restraint, executed with cold, deliberate detachment. The final resolution, even as the credits roll, completes a circle but seems almost redundant, like a second punchline.

Coldly shot and simply scored, *La Ceremonie* is less melodramatic, less heated and even better than Chabrol's last, 1994's delirious psycho-horror *L'Enfer*. After a decade in which much of his output never even reached this country, this goes a long a way to restoring a reputation as rightful heir to the Hitchcock mantle.

***GH* ▼▼▼▼**

CITY HALL

Dir. Harold Becker Dist. Columbia Tri-Star. Cert. 15. Dur. 111 Min. Released: 16/02/96. US Box-office: $20.25 million

WHEN A DECORATED COP, a Mob-connected drug-dealer and a six year-old black child are shot dead in Brooklyn, the incident triggers an investigation which unravels all the way to City Hall.

Giving another intense and focusing performance as Mayor John Pappas, is Al Pacino, whilst John Cusack essays Kevin Calhoun, his smart deputy, assigned to get out in front of the press over *The Incident at Broadway and Marcy*.

Meanwhile, Marybeth Cogan (Bridget Fonda), a dedicated Detective's Endowment Association lawyer, involves herself on behalf of her client's widow, and the duo begin to lift the lid on the city.

As he did in *The Godfather Part II* and, to a lesser extent, *Heat*, Pacino plays a character with buried extremes to his character. At the centre of *City Hall* is the 'son' Calhoun's discovery of those extremes. Yet it is the dissection of Pappas from flamboyant man of the people to quietly-spoken political dealer which holds the gaze.

City Hall is an efficient, if unoriginal, political drama, snappily wrought in a smoke-filled room by screenwriters including Paul Schrader and Scorsese-regular Nicholas Pileggi. While the effort to ground its events with copious references to past Democrat figure-heads begins to sound like a history-lesson, community leader Frank Anselmo (Danny Aiello) and his passion for Rodgers and Hammerstein tunes threatens to moulder into cliché.

The course of American big-city politics since the Civil War and Hollywood's penchant for its darker alleys, has set up certain expectations involving romanticised city-scapes, shady utility deals and public assassinations. It is no serious criticism of this enjoyable film to say that it fails to do anything new with these conventions. But then, it isn't much of a commendation to call its achievement merely workmanlike.

RA ▼▼▼

CITY ON FIRE

Dir. Ringo Lam Dist. Made In Hong Kong. Cert. 18. Dur. 101 Min. Released: (Hong Kong) 1987.

IT WAS ORIGINALLY made in 1987 but, until now has remained unavailable in this country. Amongst those of us who watch Hong Kong films with interest, Ringo Lam's *City On Fire* has achieved near-mythical status. Since 1992 it has been known as *the film which inspired Reservoir Dogs* (translation:'the film Quentin ripped off to make *Reservoir Dogs*!') It would be both more accurate and more generous to label it as 'the film which inspired John Woo'.

City On Fire lays down many of the motifs later Hong Kong action movies would emulate - particularly Woo's triumvirate *A Better Tomorrow*, *The Killer* and *Hard Boiled*. As with these films, its concerns are those of violent men, trying to maintain a spirit of brotherhood-under-fire in a teeming, crime-choked metropolis. As it becomes increasingly difficult to tell the gangsters from the police, who can we turn to for help? No one. We have to help ourselves by - as the saying goes - any means necessary!

It is interesting that both Woo, and Hong Kong's Jerry Lewis with attitude, Jackie Chan, have preceded Lam into the American market, as each has, in turn, fled the Chinese assimilation of Hong Kong. Woo has stamped his mark with *Broken Arrow*, whilst Chan has unobtrusively spent six-months in the US chart, mopping-up financially with *Rumble In The Bronx*. Now Lam has scored big, with the Jean-Claude Van-Damme vehicle *Maximum Risk*. A week in the number one spot in the US chart is a very respectable way of introducing yourself to the Americas! Already, it seems, he's determined to set LA on fire ...

Meanwhile, back in 1987 ... Chow Yun Fat - South East Asia's answer to Melvester Cruisneggerllis - plays Chow, a disgraced and disgruntled cop, who has been so far under cover for so long there's no one left, barring his immediate superior (who also happens to be his uncle), knows he carries a badge. He even forgets himself occasionally. Being the typical *noir* anti-hero, he steadfastly refuses to demonstrate emotions. Whenever he is upset, challenged, in pain or in shock he sparks up - a drag on a cancer stick being an all-purpose alternative to feelings.

His uncle, on the other hand, hits the bottle whenever life deals him a dodgy hand. His authority has been undermined and a much younger man has been brought in to head the task-force dedicated to bringing down a new, highly polished gang of jewel-thieves. Chow decides that unk deserves support, so takes it upon himself to bring the gang down single-handedly.

Playing against this decidedly chilly plot line is Chow's negotiations with his best girl as she tries to pin him down to a wedding date. Finally she insists *"Be at the registry office tomorrow morning at 10.30 or forget it. I'm leaving for Canada!"*

Meanwhile. he has made contact with the leader of the bad guys - Fu (Nice Guy Eddie), who believes Chow is a gun-runner and will keep them equipped for their next heist. (Uncle has authorised this so as to monitor the villains' activities by picking traceable bullets out of the corpses they leave behind them - a curiously *laissez faire* attitude to policing). Unfortunately, so deep under cover is he, the police also believe he is a gun-runner. So he spends a morning haring around the city, trying to avoid the police, pick up a consignment of illegal guns, deliver them to the villains, and all the while he's supposed to be getting married.

You may be thinking that this doesn't sound much like the *Res Dogs* you know and love. You're right, it doesn't. That comes when Chow gets roped into joining the gang on their next job. The last twenty minutes or so of *City On Fire* are a hectic, messy and pessimistic rendering of the tale Q.T. presented in a far more leisurely fashion four years later.

Ranging in styles from the slickly *noir*ish to the cluttered documentary style of The New Wave, *City On Fire* is a film which ultimately suffers from its own ambition. Later Chow Yun Fat films are far more focused, with smaller roll-calls and simpler plots. This film could have easily been expanded into a trilogy (and if Tarantino gets his way, probably will) but Lam obviously wanted to make something that was hectic and instant and reflected the million stories available in the naked peninsula.

***JA* ▼▼▼▼**

CLOCKERS

Dir. Spike Lee Dist. Universal (CIC) Cert. 18. Dur. 128 Min.
Released: 15/09/95. US Box-office: $13 million

THE FIRST IMAGE is a scene-of-crime photograph of a young black man: all livid wounds, a puddle of drying gore. It's followed by more of the same - all black men ripped apart by bullets - as the titles roll. This is a film about street crack-dealers, uneasy diplomacy and violence. It is also the best 'hood movie to date.

Martin Scorsese co-produces, Lee's mentor and the man originally slated to bring Richard Price's monumental novel to the screen. In the event, he was green-lighted for *Casino* and his doubts over this material allowed him pass. In turn, Robert De Niro went with Scorsese to Vegas, and his old sparring-partner Harvey Keitel slipped easily into the shoes of homicide detective Rocco Klein; investigating a drug-execution in The Projects.

The police have arrested Victor (Isaiah Washington), a model citizen with two jobs and a family, but Klein sees the handiwork of Victor's dealing 16-year-old brother Strike (first-timer Mekhi Phifer) all over the crime, and determines to right a wrong.

The whodunit structure of Lee's film (adapted by himself and Price) is both flaw and saving grace. They tinker with the novel to the extent where any mystery has been effectively drained away; it gives more impetus to the picture than other 'hood movies. but feels lightweight, almost perfunctory. What it provides is much needed shape. The result is: we avoid the all-too-familiar 'hood fatigue.

The performances are uniformly strong. Keitel is playing a familiar game (a sort of photo-negative of his *Bad Lieutenant*), but he didn't get to be the value-for-money actor of choice without consistently coming up with the goods. His partner, Larry Mazilli, is the equally-reliable John Turturro, once again doing some of his best work for Lee (see also *Do The Right Thing* and *Jungle Fever*). Delroy Lindo's sinister, paternal head-dealer is a subtle, cruel, malevolent performance. But the real star is the debuting Phifer. His Strike is wise-ass smart, but troubled by a vicious and humiliating stomach-ulcer; a youth who feels deeply the desperation of his contemporaries, but sees no way out. It is a long, difficult rôle which Phifer handles with grace. Lee has discovered a new black star here.

Malik Hassan Sayeed shoots all of this with more grit than we've come to expect from a Spike Lee joint. There is no gloss on this claustrophobic, ugly little neighbourhood, yet the director lets fly with all manner of jittery, impatient, circling camerawork, to carefully detail the micro-size of Strike's world. In the police-station, interrogations are harsh, bleached, over-lit. Towards the end, Lee piles on all manner of hallucinogenic effects - floating Keitel through the air, restaging events as drama; it's a gamble that just about pays-off.

Not so the climax. Price had 4 years and 600-pages; Lee is dramatically forced to the same conclusion, but has to bring it about in a couple of hours, consequently the denouement rings false. That, and Terence Blanchard's striking but over-cranked score, work against what some are calling the director's best film. It's not that (the masterly *Do The Right Thing* is), but it crosses the line a credible second.

GH ▼▼▼▼

THE CONFESSIONAL (LE CONFESSIONAL)
Dir. Robert Lepage Dist. Artificial Eye. Cert. 15 Dur. 100 min

THIS FILM TAKES as its inspiration (and framework) the only exciting thing that ever seems to have happened in Quebec - the filming of Alfred Hitchcock's *I Confess*. Although far less (melo)dramatic than the 1953 original, this film explores, in its own dark and deliberate way, many of the same themes. Don't get me wrong - this is no re-make, but a complex homage to and re-evaluation of one of Hitch's densest works.

In 1989, Pierre (Lothaire Bluteau) returns home for the funeral of his father and to take possession of the family home. The house is lit only through the windows, casting gloom throughout - so, he sets to and redecorates, pulling all the family photos off the wall and painting it a vivid, bloody red. As the paint dries, he notices that the ghostly outlines of the photos, the tell-tale remainders of where they used to hang, can still be seen through the paint. So he slaps on another coat after which, if anything, they are even more pronounced. This house won't let him forget the past, he can't cover it up and pretend it isn't there.

In response, Pierre begins to look into the past of his brother Marc, with whom he has only recently been reunited. More precisely, he investigates the curious and seemingly seedy relationship that exists between his brother and a much older, very rich man.

Fading backwards and forwards from 1952 (when Hitch was in town) to 1989 with a shift of focus or a pan of the camera or, even more cunningly, through reference to a motif (such as the painting and decorating Montgomery Clift's Father Logan was also busy with in the original movie); Lepage shows a studied, patient control of his art, deliberately reminiscent of his fellow Quebecois Denys Arcand (*Jesus of Montreal*).

Footage from *I Confess* is interwoven with reconstructed footage of the production process (Englishman Ron Burrage giving a delightful turn as The Big Man himself) and then compared and contrasted with modern Canada. Far more than just walking the same ground as Hitch, *The Confessional* looks at the way that the past lives on in the hearts and mind of its survivors, and explores how guilt in the nineties is a more complex, subtler, yet equally pernicious as back in the fifties.

The imagery is a delight, relying heavily on the colour palette Hitch's movie could only hint at in shades of grey. The walls of Pierre's house shift through primary colours, as he tries time and again to over-paint those marks. Pierre's assignation with his brother in a gay sauna, filmed slowly and silently from overhead, is a warm, dark labyrinth of threat, choked with stinging yellow steam. Pierre's chess game with his brother's mysterious benefactor, played-out with different sized shot-glasses, filled with white or red wine on an underlit glass board, evokes *The Thomas Crown Affair*, whilst skilfully re-deploying the sexual tension.

The Confessional is the first film from a director who, whilst not seeming to be saying a great deal, plants ideas and images in your head with timers attached, set to explode into your imagination hours or even days after you've seen them. Certainly it won't be to all tastes, being far too deliberate in its pacing and too cerebral in its themes, but it is a thrilling and rejuvenating experience and left this viewer eager to see Lepage's next experiment come to life.

▼▼▼▼▼

COPYCAT Dir. Jon Amiel Dist. Warner Bros Cert. 18 Dur. 123 Min. Released: 27/10/95. US Box-office: $32 million.

HOLLYWOOD JUST CAN'T get enough of those serial killers, they're big bucks at the box office, and no mistake. Anthony Hopkins chilled your marrow, Kevin Spacey cooked your goose, now quake in abject terror at the awesome prospect of ... Harry Connick Jnr.

No, you didn't read that wrong, Mr Recipe-of-Love plays homicidal maniac Daryll Lee Cullum in this high-gloss late entry in the psycho-babble stakes. He is stalking criminal psychologist Helen Hudson - played by Sigourney Weaver who has, lets face it, been hunted by more than her fair share of nasties in her time.

She is brought in (unwillingly) by ambitious young investigator Monahan (Holly Hunter, to advise on a bizarre and grisly new series of murders, and so she finds herself hunting a devilish opponent who knows every detail of every famous serial killing - and is determined to re-enact them all. When he learns that Sigs is hot on his heels, he decides on a particularly special fate for her.

The potential for suspense with this vehicle was considerable, and, to his credit, director Amiel does bring out many of the creepier aspects. But the film is also hobbled by the familiarity of the material. Siggey, traumatised by Connick's attack of her in the film's opening moments, is agoraphobic. House-bound. Or rather, palatial, no-expense-spared-apartment-bound.

The problem here is one of plausibility - Ms Weaver carries neither the demeanour nor the reputation of a woman who would be freaked out by the attack. She wouldn't get mad, she would get even. In 1995's overlooked Polanski pic *Death and the Maiden*, she played a victim who became empowered (if a little deranged) by the presence of her ex-persecutor. This she did convincingly; but the rôle of a woman who daren't step through her front door, and who communicates with the big wide world through Hollywood's new wonder-drug The Internet, isn't suited to her. It is also far too reminiscent of Polanski's *Repulsion*. Now Catherine Deneuve, she could do vulnerable and make you believe it completely.

Certainly *Copycat* lives up to its name, as it lifts liberally from Hitchcock, Thomas Harris and, of course, Polanski before descending, disappointingly, into expensive stalk 'n' slash, the type of movie that Jamie Leigh Curtis made far too many of in the early eighties. In those days they were cheap quickies featuring motiveless psychos, nowadays they are big-budget star-vehicles with Serial Killers. What with that and the Internet in the same film, one can't help but wonder if there is a band-wagon being jumped upon.

JA ▼▼

CRIME TIME

Dir. George Sluizer Dist. First Independent. Cert. TBA. Dur. anyone's guess. Unreleased at time of writing.

FOLLOWING THE PRESS-SHOWING of George Sluizer's new film, a representative from the distributors announced that, owing to the projectionist having kicked it under the table during preparation, *Crime Time* had been screened with a twenty-minute reel missing.

It is a measure of the film's inadequacy that a sparky individual amongst the press corps replied that he hadn't noticed, and received a big laugh.

Crime Time is a mess, an incoherent, poorly written and badly acted mess. In it, unemployed actor Bobby Mahon (Stephen Baldwin) shoots to fame when he is given the rôle of the serial killer in crime-re-enactment show of the title. While he becomes dangerously engrossed in the rôle, the real serial-killer, mild-mannered Sidney (Pete Postlethwaite) becomes seriously enamoured of his new-found screen status. Both become increasingly addicted until, until one terrible night ...

Proclaiming itself an examination of the downside of the *Crimewatch/999* television aesthetic, it is unfortunate that this project stinks. In a culture where too many read TV as reality, and acres of column-inches are devoted admiringly to actors' rôle-research, we need a state-of-the-art offering on this late-century phenomenon.

The main problem with *Crime Time* is that Baldwin's limited talent and charisma are dwarfed by Postlethwaite and by Geraldine Chaplin, in the limited but telling rôle of Sidney's myopic wife. While Postlethwaite wrestles with a lack-lustre and, at times, laughable script, the movie loses its centre. Indeed, *Crime Time* resembles one of those British flicks of the '50s, featuring an audience-alluring second-tier American player in place of literate dialogue and competent performances. It is a dishonest and tacky strategy.

At one point, the cynical director of 'Crime Time' (the show) tells the fastidious Bobby to *"Just slice the bitch up, then we can all get some pizza and go home."* It is the film's best line, and in some perverse way, I suspect it captured precisely how the projectionist felt that day.

***RA* NIL**

THE CROW - CITY OF ANGELS

Dir. Tim Pope Dist. Miramax Films Cert. 18. Dur. 83 Min.
Released 30/08/96 US Box-office: $17.5 million to date

"SOMETIMES LOVE IS STRONGER THAN DEATH!" *Oh, wow, man, that's like, just so totally profound, y'know. Dude.* "Life is but a dream on the way to death." *Oh yeah, I know what you're sayin' ... it's, like, so totally rad, man.*

I'm sorry, but, if you're trying to tell me that Californians have anything profound to say you better be either a) Michael Mann or b) taking the piss. *The Crow - City of Angels* doesn't actually tell you where it's set, but it doesn't leave much doubt. A near-future LA, ruled by the crime-lord Tudor Earl, who employs the usual selection of slobbering psychopaths as his henchmen. One such is Iggy Pop - yes, really - whose gang of lower-than-low-lives are witnessed beating someone senseless for ... well, no reason at all, really. Ashe (new-boy, Vincent Perez) and his son are the hapless witnesses and, as such, become the next victims of the Iggster and gang.

We know all this only because Ashe tells it to Sarah, after the fact. He's dead, she's a tattooist. Sarah (although, again, this isn't made clear) is the little girl from the first *Crow* movie, now grown up. Consequently, she knows that Ashe is back to get payback from those who killed him. Slap on the old pan-stick, a few black lines to give him that 'interesting' Goth look, and off he jolly well goes. A pound of flesh? That'll do nicely.

Donkey's years ago, director Tim Pope was the master of the no-budget pop-video, mostly featuring *The Cure* (remember the one in the wardrobe? That was Tim's!). Unfortunately, now the big time has finally beckoned, he has made the usual pact with Hollywood and swapped his talent for a fat pay-check. Here he has money, all the toys he could ever want ... but no ideas.

City of Angels is almost a shot-for-shot remake of *The Crow*, only without the gravitas the young Brandon Lee managed to bring to the rôle. In attempting to put on screen a nightmare Andrew Eldritch would be proud of, Pope has completely forgotten a few basic ingredients - such as plot, acting and suspense.

As with *The Craft*, this is a puerile attempt by a woefully out-of-touch Hollywood to pounce on a yoof-culture band-wagon (the band in question being *Nine Inch Nails*, of course). The sad thing is, said yoofs probably love it.

JA ▼

CURDLED

Dir. Reb Braddock Dist. Miramax. Cert. TBA. Dur. 90 Min.
Released: 27/09/96. US Box-office: $16 000 (opening weekend only)

***CURDLED* BEGINS** with a close-up of a dancing zoetrope skeleton, a marriage of movie and the macabre and a foreshadow of what is to come. The zoetrope is a child's toy and said child's fascination is piqued when she sees a man gunned down out in the streets. It is 1975 in Colombia and such events are unremarkable in a nation in the grip of gang-war, but this particular shooting inspires a fascination in the young girl which takes her (via a nifty title-sequence) through twenty years to adulthood and the North American city of Miami.

As an adult, Gabriella is drawn to gory movies, and garish news-reports of The Blue-Blood Headsman, who appears to be discriminatingly working his way through the single, female members of polite high society, decapitating them with a samurai sword. Cut to young Paul Guell, played by William (Billy) Baldwin, sipping champagne and chatting, in an assumed English accent, of the delightful future he is planning for his girl and himself ... only problem is, she seems to be dying slowly of bloodloss.

In search of meaningful work, Gabriella takes a job with PFCS - Post Forensic Cleaning Service - a unit dead-icated to picking up where the police leave-off. Lodger, the compassionate bear who runs PFCS explains to Gabriella that the worst part of the job is the smell; the blood, being days if not weeks old, has curdled and the reek can make the strongest stomach puke, especially in the heat of August - their 'busy season'. Gabriella is, of course, drawn to the crime-scene of the latest Blue-Blood slaying, and slowly her path intersects Guell's.

Braddock shoots Miami with a minimum of fuss and (due, I suspect, to the budget) a minimum of exteriors, which give the all-too familiar terrain an alien feel, rather as it must seem to émigré Gabriella. The feeling that you're not quite in the real world is underscored by the TV show 'Miami DOA', a wonderful satire on tabloid TV, where the TV reporter last seen adding-up the death-toll in *From Dusk Till Dawn* (and wearing the same gruesome suit), sneaks a camera-crew into the crime-scene that Gabriella is about to set mop and bucket to.

The film is peppered with the detritus of violent crime: visual references to tape outlines, to the minutiae of mess removal (don't forget to check under the furniture for bone fragments) and to the mind-set of a woman, genuine, childlike and totally harmless, yet consumed with a morbid fascination. She bakes gingerbread-men (the recipe her mother had been preparing when that fateful shooting had re-routed her childhood) simply so she can cut their heads off. When her would-be boyfriend comes to visit, he doesn't present her with a bunch of flower or a box of chocolates, but some gory newspaper cuttings for her collection.

Did I mention that this film is, death-toll not-withstanding, actually a gentle if somewhat acerbic comedy?

Angela Jones gives an enchanting performance as Gabriella, commanding the film in this, her first substantial rôle. Eyes wide and receptive, absent-mindedly popping bubble-gum bubbles, she manages to span the seemingly unbridgeable gap between *naïveté* and *femme fatality*.

When she and Baldwin finally meet face-to-face, at the crime-scene she is supposed to be cleaning, it seems completely natural that she should be more in awe than in fear of him. If she is nervous at all, it is from attraction, not revulsion.

Also, she must feel a certain tingle of anticipation because, with the assistance of her friendly neighbourhood serial killer, she finally stands to solve the conundrum which has plagued her since childhood - can decapitated heads live on and utter a final word or two before expiring. Hmm ... now there's a science project to show teacher!

Oh, go on then ... just to keep everyone quiet. This film is also produced by Quentin Tarantino, who first saw it in short form when he was still hocking *Reservoir Dogs* around, and gave his support in getting a studio deal for it. There, and I was hoping to review it without mentioning Tarantino at all. Ho hum.

JA ▼▼▼▼

DEAD MAN WALKING

Dir. Tim Robbins Dist. Polygram. Cert. 15. Dur. 122 Min. Released: 29/12/95. US Box-office: $39.25 million

A WOMAN DRIVES ALONG a sweltering southern road to offer counsel to a young man about to be put to death for murder. As the sun sets behind some trees, the twang of a smoky guitar lament can be heard.

Dead Man Walking is one of perhaps only two of the finest studies of the rights and wrongs of capital punishment in film history (the other being the documentary *Fourteen Days*). Charting the true story of catholic nun, Sister Helen (Susan Sarandon) Prejean's attempts to offer solace to hardened Death Row prisoner Matthew Poncelet (Oscar-nominated Sean Penn). It contains performances of staggering conviction, based on one of the most thorough and coherent issue-based screenplays in a long-time.

What makes the screenplay so unexpected is its multilateral attitude to its material. Poncelet could so-easily have been, depending on the script's line on Capital Punishment, a murderous redneck or a social victim. Likewise, Sister Helen could have been the perfect angel of faith. Instead, he is, by turns, aggressive, pathetic and, occasionally, charming, while she is a well-meaning but often insensitive novice. Few issue-based movies have the guts to be this ambiguous.

Robbins clearly wants to understand what is going on inside the characters and before the lens. When the parents of Poncelet's victim react to discovering that Sister Helen is counselling Poncelet as well as them, their disgust seems thoroughly fitting on one level. When we learn that Poncelet's father drank, other movies have primed us to read this as an inevitable aspect of a poor white trash, Louisiana up-bringing. But when, in the next breath, he tells Helen that the pair used to happily drink each other under the table, we are instantly persuaded away from such cosy assumptions.

If the dialogue takes a wider view of the characters, Roger Deakins' lens wants constantly to include rather than divide the characters from each other. Notice how the focus on the grilles and perspex between Helen and Poncelet renders them the more transparent the more she 'reaches' him.

Despite its obvious anti-CP position, *Dead Man Walking* never loses sight of Poncelet's crime. But, by juxtaposing the ghastly night of the murder with the hideous details of his execution, the distinction between illegal execution and judicial murder becomes as blurred as the bars on Poncelet's cage.

***RA* ▼▼▼▼▼**

DEAD MAN

Dir. Jim Jarmusch Dist. Cert. 18. Dur. 120 Min.
Released: 10/05/96. US Box-office: $1.5 million

THE DEAD MAN IN QUESTION is one William Blake (played by Johnny Depp), an ambitious young man who goes in search of work to a community on the western fringe of America at the end of the 19th century. Failing to secure employment, Blake is badly wounded in a shoot-out with a jealous lover, and begins to drift.

Falling in with a Native American called Nobody (Gary Farmer), who thinks Blake is the renowned dead poet, he becomes a hunted man. Gradually, Blake begins to see the world anew.

Dead Man is a disappointingly violent, sometimes piquant, failure. Rejecting the cold and sunny colour palette of the big Westerns of the 50s and 60s, Jarmusch goes for the sombre monochrome 'realism' which evokes those demythologising Westerns of the 70s. The problem is, both of these traditions had the tensions of tight plotting to sustain them. As soon as our misfits leave civilisation and the colourful cameos of Gabriel Byrne, Robert Mitchum and John Hurt, which make the whole endeavour tick, the spiritual consciousness which stirs in the young man fails to engage the viewer.

The American wilderness does have a majestic profundity, but Jarmusch fails to make compelling the realisation of a man whose physical existence is slipping away to be replaced by a being in the ether. When outlaws Thelma and Louise choose death, it is because the violence of act and attitude which they encounter in their fellow human-beings pushes them over the edge. Here, we are too often left guessing where this spectacular and ambitious quest is heading. See it if you care for Depp or Jarmusch.

***RA* ▼▼**

DESPERADO

Dir: Robert Rodriguez. Dist: Columbia Tri-Star. Cert: 18. Dur: 100 mins. Released: 25/08/95. US Box-office: $25.5 million.

ROBERT RODRIGUEZ makes no secret of his love for Hong Kong film-makers, and certainly doesn't try to cover-up the joy he gets from making movies the way they do. Basically, set up a good-guy/bad-guy scenario, give everybody lots of guns then fill the screen with innocent by-standers and watch the pyrotechnics. Okay, so good HK action is more sophisticated than that, but it is this equation which makes the films popular.

Frustrated by the production-line predictability of American action movies, Rodriguez has crafted a perfectly realised celluloid confection. Profound? Not even remotely. Pretentious? Hardly. Fun? You better believe it.

Desperado is a nominal sequel to his first 'home movie' *El Mariachi*, but it is also a re-make of it. Hey, why not, far more experienced directors, working with far, far higher budgets, have fallen into the trap of making a sequel by re-making its prequel. Rarely has it been done with such panache.

El Mariachi was made in Spanish because Rodriguez (a Texan who is, in common with most Americans from the border counties, bi-lingual) reasoned that he could only sell his el cheapo movie to the Spanish exploitation market, so tailored it appropriately. This time, with Columbia Tri-Star behind him, he could work in English and afford a few real actors.

Looking at it now, Banderas was wise beyond his years to pick this as his first English-language star-vehicle, but, based on a script and a twenty-seven year-old director's enthusiasm, it was a gamble for him to sign on. Had things gone wrong, this film could have projected him right into video-only hell, along-side Rutger Hauer and Eric Roberts. Fortunately, everything went right!

The story concerns some tosh about Banderas' blood-feud with the local drug-dealing cartel, and follows-on loosely from the action in the first film (the climax of which has been re-filmed with the new cast, so to get the people who never saw *Mariachi* up to speed). But plot is not what this film is about - it is a sensory experience which confounds intellectual interrogation by forcing you to enjoy yourself. Enjoyment, the bane of all critics which, in this case, is the one thing you can't defend against.

The film is vibrant with *joie de vivre* (although, given the body-count, *joie de morte* would seem more appropriate) and entirely unrepentant about its visceral, stylish, garish over-use of loud music, bright colours and ultra-violence.

Delightful support is offered by Cheech Marin (in the rôle which has re-ignited his career) as the sleazy low-brow bar-man; the ubiquitous Steve Buscemi, there to remind you that this is a hip indie film; and last but very much not least, Salma Hayek, who radiates dark-eyed, hot-tempered sex from every pore, whilst retaining both dignity and poise. Rodriguez gave this Spanish soap-star her first English-language rôle in his first English-language film, *Road Racers* (screened by BBC2 in Autumn '96, but never made available on the big screen or, as far as I can ascertain, on video) and wisely decided that his subsequent films would benefit greatly from her mix of wit, energy and beauty.

The film lacks structure, self-restraint or any vestige of shame, and consequently serves up a dish of preposterous, unwholesome cinema that drips with imagination. Rodriguez refuses to surrender the camera to a Director of Photography, shooting every frame of film himself, and his delight at using and mis-using the camera enlightens every scene.

It was always possible that *Desperado* might have proven to be nothing more than a flash in the pan, a brief, exquisite moment of knockabout inspiration, before writer-director Rodriguez disappeared slowly in the West. Then we saw *From Dusk Till Dawn*, a very different film, with the same sparkle of energy. No, Robert Rodriguez will not go quietly into the night ... he's having far too much fun. The great thing is, his enjoyment is infectious.

JA ▼▼▼▼▼

DEVIL IN A BLUE DRESS

Dir. Carl Franklin Dist. Columbia Tri-Star Cert. 15 Dur. 110 Min.
Released: 29/09/95. US Box-office: $16 million

DENZEL WASHINGTON plays Ezekiel (Easy) Rawlins, a black ex-G.I. who (unusually for 1948) has a mortgage and isn't too particular how he pays it. Dewitt Albright (Tom Sizemore) hires Easy to trace the elusive seductress Daphne Monet (Jennifer Beals) - and pays him in advance. That money buys him a one-way ticket into L.A.'s underworld, complete with speakeasies, brutal cops, midnight shootings and a well manufactured frame for him to walk right into.

Taking to wearing his hat at a Bogartian tilt, Easy slides into the rôle of private eye as if to the manner born and, doubtless because of that stylish hat, finds he has to beat the women off with a stick (though he doesn't beat them too hard, after all, his name is Easy!) Needless to say, the plot is not long in thickening: he's hardly had time to practice his 'here's-looking-at-you-kid' sneer, when the delightful Ms Monet walks out of the shadows, wearing ... a blue dress.

In common with his first film, *One False Move*, Franklin directs this at a breakneck lick. Punchy dialogue, likeable performances and occasional brief flashes of extreme violence keep you on your toes, so you are never quite sure which way the rug will be pulled from under you next. Connoisseurs of Walter Mosley's 1990 novel won't be surprised, of course, but they may appreciate the different slant given to the story by its emphasis on the issue of race. In a literal sense, this is genuine film noir, taking as read the abuse hard-working, upstanding black people suffer at the hands and fists of white folk.

All in all then, a social and political document mixed with a traditional private eye yarn, all wrapped up in a skilfully handled, wittily performed, exciting old blue dress.

JA ▼▼▼▼

LES DIABOLIQUES (THE FIENDS)

Dir. Henri-Georges Clouzot Dist. BFI. Cert. 15.
Dur. 117 Min. Released: 1954

LES DIABOLIQUES should need no introduction. In many ways it is the archetype of modern thriller-dom. Would, for example, the lamentable *Fatal Attraction* end quite as it does without Clouzot? (Not, of course, that that's any recommendation.)

Vera Clouzot (the director's wife) and Simone Signoret respectively play the vulnerable wife and self-confident mistress of Paul Meurisse, the tyrannical, bullying headmaster of a seedy, decaying boarding-school, stocked with noisy brats and self-serving teachers. As the film opens, the women are about to enact a painstakingly-plotted revenge, luring the violent head to his death by drowning *chez* Signoret. They then hazardously transport his still-dripping corpse back to the school where they dump it in the brooding, stagnant swimming-pool, ready to be found by some innocent passer-by. But relief at a job well done slowly turns to horror, as Clouzot's unrelentingly cynical camera gazes on.

Taken from Pierre Boileau and Thomas Narcejac's novel *She Was No More*, a.k.a. *The Fiends*, this is the best film Hitchcock never made. (Reputedly Hitch wanted to option the original himself, and later made his masterpiece - *Vertigo* - from the novel *D'Entre les Morts (The Living and the Dead)* by the same pair.) The master's hands are all over this film, in the callous manipulation of its performers and audience, to the prominence of an icy blonde; even down to the *Psycho*esque coda asking viewers not to disclose its tortuous twists to their friends. The pace is deliberately slow, very slow in its second-half, loading up on a fabulous sense of monochrome doom before a humdinger of a *Grande Guignol* climax. Clouzot was a virtuoso of bleak (the prolific Claude Chabrol recently adapted an old Clouzot script to make the equally cheerless *L'Enfer*).

The acting is terrific. Holy innocent Clouzot rolls her eyes and grabs at her weak heart with silent-movie aplomb, while the hard-as-nails Signoret, all tight dresses and even tighter hair, is just sublime. Leonard Cohen-alike Meurisse spits and growls like the classic movie baddie he is. And Charles Vanel's eerie old detective, inveigling his way into the investigation of the head's disappearance, is the blueprint in every detail for Columbo.

Part suspense-thriller, part classy ghost story, this is yet another foreign classic recently mauled in the Hollywood remake machine, with, surprise surprise, Sharon Stone as The Blonde and - the horror - a happy ending. Does no one remember *The Vanishing* fiasco? Maybe the original is now too old, too creaky, too misanthropic to work for a mass popular audience without it gets radically overhauled. For sure it's a totally calculating, icy-cold one-trick pony of a movie, but it's a GREAT, scary, macabre trick all the same. European *noir* scarcely came any darker or better.

GH ▼▼▼▼

DIABOLIQUE

Dir. Jeremiah Chechik Dist. Warner Bros Cert. 18 Dur. 110 Min. Released: 22/03/96. US Box-office: $17 million.

AS SHE BENDS over her television set, zapping channels to find something undemanding, one of the minor characters in this film happens across a screening of *Who's Afraid of Virginia Woolf?* She watches Burton and Taylor snapping at each other for a moment, then decides to move on, *"I'll wait until this one's in colour!"* One can only assume that this depressingly common reaction is the reason behind a thoroughly unnecessary re-make of Henri-Georges Clouzot's not-really-as-good-as-it's-all-cracked-up-to-be *Les Diaboliques* (1954).

That was a passionless, methodical study of how a frail wife and a strident mistress coldly calculate the death of their common man. We observed distantly as they prepared then executed their plan, just as later we see how a corpse is prepared for public viewing. *Les Diaboliques* is a film about methodology. It endeavours to be scientifically objective. There is pointedly not a hint of music to emotionally heighten the proceedings, nor a trace of humanity to empathise with in either of the murderesses.

The director's wife Véra Clouzot was irritatingly docile as the sickly Cri-Cri, Simone Signore was convincingly forceful as Nicole Hunter, but the star of the show was Paul Meurisse as the thoroughly demonic Michel.

Maybe it was a mistake for me to unearth my copy of the original, before watching the remake. Maybe I would have been more impressed if I hadn't seen it all, in stark black and white, only the day before. Now, in colour, we have Isabelle Adjani as the wimpish Mia (brought aboard, no doubt, so her accent would justify their hanging on to the original French title), Sharon Stone as the scenery chewing Nicole Hunter (that name rings a bell) and Chazz Palminteri as a hardly even unpleasant let alone devilish, Guy.

Having fed the script through the usual Hollywood committee-rooms, they have felt the need to make small, barely-significant changes to the original (a more apparent lesbian attraction between the two women, a sex-change for the detective from an old-man to a middle-aged women) whilst completely re-building the film's ending from the ground up, to make it more exciting for audiences used to show-downs, not dénouements. In compliance with the original movie's request for viewers not to give the movie's ending away to friends (we are friends, aren't we?) I won't say what they've changed, but suffice it to say that you get the inevitable chase and some typically nineties blood-letting.

Even before reading the production notes, I could tell this film had been written by the same chap as *Single White Female* (turns out his name is Don Roos). Instead of a clinical movie about the process of murder, he has given us a lame-brained pseudo-feminist revenge drama, with concessions to crime fiction in that it shows us the other side of the coin: the process of detection. Kathy Bates enters proceedings late on and picks up the pace a little, as the detective determined to find Mia's vanished husband for her. She is the only vestige of the original's careful deliberation and it is symptomatic that she should be using those attributes to the good, rather than to commit murder.

Although the French original hasn't weathered well over the years, it still has an eerie, cruel air to it that the new, improved version lacks. Maybe it looked good on paper, maybe the producers just have good agents. Either way, all four principle cast members are capable of, and deserve, much better material than this.

JA ▼▼

DIE HARD WITH A VENGEANCE

Dir. John McTiernan Dist. Touchstone. Cert. 15. Dur. 128 Min. Released: 19/05/96. US Box-office: $100 million.

POP QUIZ, HOTSHOT: you've produced one of the most successful, most perfectly crafted action thrillers in recent cinema, you've followed it with an unwieldy, unsatisfying sequel; but you're still the best chance Bruce Willis has for hanging on to his superstar status. Whaddya do? Easy: you go ahead and make *Die Hard 3*.

Now the hard part: you've used two enclosed locations (a skyscraper and an airport) for the previous slug-fests, where do you set the third? Well, you make plans to set it on a ship - then Steven Seagal gets the jump on you with *Under Siege*. Bugger. Meanwhile, submarines, planes in flight, prisons, mountains, rivers, even motorways and, heaven forfend, a bus, have been employed as shoot-out locations by your imitators. So where, given the ever shortening list of public locations, do you choose? You choose all of 'em. You set it everywhere!

Thus, *Die Hard With A Vengeance* was born - partly from a trusted formula and partly from an unsolicited script, *Simon Says*, by Jonathan Hensleigh, which concerned a New York cop and a terrorist, and took very little re-writing to make that cop into John McClane.

John McTiernan is back in the director's chair (having wisely passed on the second film in order to make *The Hunt For Red October* and has brought with him a whole new bag of tricks. He has chopped the dialogue down to the bare minimum, but when characters are in discussion, they generally all talk at once. He has forsaken steadicams and dollies and glide rigs in preference of hand-held, documentary-style camera work. He makes more comprehensive use of New York locations than any film not directed by Woody Allen; and he pulls no punches. Although suffering a couple of clumsy edits which will disappoint the gore hounds, this is an extraordinarily violent 15 certificate.

The film begins with a very literal bang, then, within ten minutes all the main characters are in place, McClane is already bleeding from his first wound (of many) and the chase is on. The devilishly inscrutable scheme which always underpins the action in a *Die Hard*, is deliciously devious if rather too ambitions (after all, how would *you* spend $140 BILLION? Even with today's exchange rates, that's a helluva lotta dosh!) and Jeremy Irons seems to have fun playing the wicked Simon, Alan Rickman's equally demented and dodgy-accented German brother. Samuel Jackson is just along for the ride as the representative from the Brotherhood of Black Sidekicks, although he does prove useful at solving Simon's logic problems and hotwiring cars for the chase scenes.

Despite his screen credit (in the 'based on characters created by' category) I suspect Roderick Thorpe would be hard pressed to recognise this John McClane, as he is very definitely a product of nineties Hollywood: foul mouthed, deeply flawed, ultra-violent, high-octane, entirely devoid of subtext and back-story, but sporting a heart of purest gold.

Die Hard With A Vengeance is simply the best action movie of the decade, leaving imitators like *Bad Boys, Executive Decision, The Rock* and *Chain Reaction* in varying depths of shadow. It, at least temporarily, re-established Bruce Willis as the patron saint of working class heroes, and reaffirming John McTiernan as the master of disaster. Highly recommended, especially since the wide-screen video became available, although purists should bear in mind that the aforementioned vid has had its dialogue re-mixed to cut down the profanity count.

JA ▼▼▼▼▼

DOLORES CLAIBORNE

Dir. Taylor Hackford Dist. Rank Films Cert. 18. Dur. 131 Min. Released: 24/03/95. US Box-office: $24.25 million

CURMUDGEONLY.

Wilful.

Irascible.

Just a few of the more endearing traits of the foul mouthed Dolores Claiborne: traits she herself sums up with the homily *"Some times being a bitch is the only thing a woman has to hold onto."*

Kathy Bates won an Oscar last time she climbed aboard the Stephen King bandwagon, so she must have been more than enthusiastic when this title-rôle was offered her. Especially when she learned that she would be swapping verbal punches with the most ferociously talented young actress America has produced in a generation: Jennifer Jason Leigh, who, for reasons which continue to mystify me, has been repeatedly ignored when the Academy comes to giving out those little gold door-stops.

Meanwhile, back at the plot: this movie begins with Dolores being discovered about to bring a rolling-pin down rather violently on her employer's head. Said employer proceeds to die, which rather inevitably leads Dolores into a jail cell, by way of the front page of the local rag.

Cut to New York where big-time journalist, alcoholic and prescription drug addict Selina St George (J. J. Leigh) receives said front page through her fax machine and realises that her estranged mother is in trouble. Begrudgingly she returns to the small, bleak island of her birth, where the history of violence within the family is dragged kicking and screaming from the back of her mind, forcing mother and daughter to deal with the hither-to unspoken demons which have destroyed their lives.

There is no denying this is a wordy film, and many of the words are used to shore up the lies mother and daughter tell to themselves, as much as to each other. Gradually the characters evolve and mutate, our perspective on their lives changes as we see more and more of the pieces, undermining our initial preconceptions.

At heart this is a film about hard-working people who have suffered all their lives without complaint - because suffering was all they had ever known. It's about the reasons for being sad and for being angry. It's about how not communicating, and not caring can eventually destroy you, and those around you. It's about the power a simple bottle of whiskey can have over a normal human being, and how decisions made under its influence can be as destructive to a family as a bomb dropped into a foxhole.

So we're not looking at a sackful of laughs here, we're not dealing with the kind of people you want to be related to, or the kind of lives you want to have lived. King was in mature and contemplative mode when he wrote the novel, and it has become an unapologetically painful film - without so much as a hint of a car-chase or shoot-out to relieve the tension.

If you want to see real drama and real acting with, as we reach the heart of the darkness, some extraordinarily powerful and moving images of a total eclipse, then you're ready for two and a quarter hours in the company of *Dolores Claiborne*.

JA ▼▼▼

ERASER

Dir. Charles Russell Dist. Warner Bros. Cert. 18. Dur. 115 Min. Released: 21/06/96 US Box-office: $101.25 million

DO YOU REMEMBER those days of yore when a man's virility was measured by the length of his barrel? It was the time of *Rambo* and *Raw Deal*, of *Cobra* and *Commando*. It was a time before the influence of Hong Kong and *Die Hard* and half-way literate script-writers. It was a long time before Tarantino.

Remember the good old 1980s?

Arnie certainly does. After years of careful work getting away from the meathead movies which made his name, of sending-up his muscle-bound image, of cultivating a more cine-literate fan-base, he has pissed it all away with *Eraser*.

Eraser is his worst film since the 1987 abomination *The Running Man*.

I find it fascinating how Arnie and Sly have mirrored each other so closely in their careers: After a spectacular start (an Oscar for 1975's *Rocky*) Stallone went on to be a variable, but always interesting writer/director, whilst paying the rent with pot-boilers (the best of which were 1981's *Nighthawks* and 1982's *First Blood*). Meanwhile, Arnie had gotten his feet under the table with John Milius' strangely watchable, *Conan the Barbarian* (1981) and, of course, his definitive rôle in *The Terminator* (1984).

Then, in 1985, Arnie got his name above the title for the first time in *Commando*, whilst Stallone returned to *his* definitive rôle in *Rambo, First Blood pt 2*. They continued to slug it out as America's highest paid muscle-men (Stallone having now abandoned his directing aspirations), receiving ever-more ludicrous sums of money to make ever-more ludicrous movies.

After branching-out into unsuccessful comedies; their next step was to 'parodic' action movies - sending-up their earlier shoot-em-ups. Neither Arnie's *The Last Action Hero* nor Sly's *Demolition Man* are without their problems, but they are both so much better than anything either star had produced in years.

So where to now? Sly has led the drive right back to eighties mindlessness with *The Specialist* and *Assassins* (which are essentially the same film), and Arnie, unfortunately, has finally followed suit ...

Eraser is like a no-star, no-name, no-budget straight-to-video release. The special effects aren't, the actors don't and the writers can't. Yet, for some unfathomable reason, the whole penny-ante endeavour took the worst part of a hundred-million dollars to make. Who is responsible? I want names!

The initial scenario is a good one: Arnie works at internal espionage, arranging for people in America's witness protection program to 'die' publicly and convincingly, so that they can actually assume new identities, safe from those they testified against. So far, so not bad. However, the problems begin early ... when wicked uncle Arnie sets about 'killing' his first two clients by bringing with him a couple of corpses he prepared earlier. "Come with me!" He instructs the 'victims', *If You Want To Live* chant the audience with one voice.

Cut to the main story: singer Vanessa Williams works for a weapons manufacturer and, urged by the FBI, she sneaks into their top secret computer vault to download some illegal files ... without hanging from wires! Unfortunately, she's spotted by the cameras she obviously failed to notice protruding from the walls, and so finds herself in need of 'rubbing out'.

The bad guys set off after her, armed with the so-new-we-haven't-even-thought-of-a-snappy-name-for-it-yet electro-magnetic gun. *"You mean The Rail-Gun which fires aluminium or clay rounds at just below the speed of light?"* suggests Arnie helpfully. Yes, indeedy; and this one comes equipped with an x-ray 'scope which can see through brick, wood, metal, cloth, skin, bone and everything, in fact, except fridges. Conveniently, Arnie just happens to have an Ariston to hand, thereby saving his and Vanessa's bacon.

The most deliciously awful moment of all, however, comes when he finds himself wrestling with an unconvincing crocodile, manufactured from dodgy animatronics and dodgier computer animation When he blows it away at point blank range, it is to the accompaniment of the comment *"You're luggage!"* Well, if that isn't the pot calling the kettle black ...

As clichés jostle with product-placement close-ups for screen-time, our hero gets wounded - penetrated through the upper thigh by a steel pipe (think about it ...!) Then, shirt sleeves rent asunder by his bulging biceps, he is finally shot through the shoulder. Fortunately this doesn't stop him hanging from a crane, slugging it out with the major baddie and finally clinching with the grateful girlie.

Yes, it's another true story; which takes itself far too seriously. But then, I suppose it must do, 'cos no one else will.

JA NIL

EYE FOR AN EYE

Dir. John Schlesinger Dist. Paramount (UIP) Cert. 15 Dur. 99 Min. Released: 12/01/96. US Box-office: $26.75 million.

THIS FILM SCORES very highly on the Grishometer! Beginning with an unreasoning attack on common decent folks, who must then battle a fossilised system to win through, it is a perfect example of the reactionary right-wing of popular crime writing. Thankfully, where it deviates from form is in its refusal to sentimentalise, and in the way it gets the court-case out of the way double-quick so to concentrate on the aftermath.

Let's begin at the beginning: Sally Field is the matriarch of a happy, idyllic suburban home; heck, these folks are so nice they wouldn't even hurt a fly (or, at any rate, a moth, as the cloying opening sequence demonstrates). Then Sally's eldest daughter is raped and murdered while she, trapped in a traffic jam miles from home, has to listen on the phone. This scene is about distance, Field can't get any of the people in the cars around her to help, but she is too far from her daughter to do anything herself.

Afterwards, she is consumed with all the guilt and grief you would expect, but slowly, methodically puts her life back together. However, although the hysterics have gone, there's no process of mourning. Her daughter's killer has walked on the traditional technicality, and she is therefore consumed by the unfairness of this. She may be a typical homely, middle-aged mom, but there is no forgiveness in her soul.

A grandstand performance from Sally Field drives this film, ably supported by husband Ed Harris, rôle-reversed into the supportive but side-lined position so-often forced onto the wives in these movies. Kiefer Sutherland turns out his usual greasy heavy turn, this time modelled on *Metallica*'s James Hetfield.

Schlesinger has, rather as we've come to expect, turned what could so-easily have been a knee-jerk issue-of-the-week movie into a cunning and complicated study of rage. The attention and maturity all concerned have brought to this piece lifts it high above expectation, whilst retaining the thriller aspect, something which could so easily have been smothered by worthiness in less skilled hands.

JA ▼▼▼ ½

THE FAN

Dir. Tony Scott Dist. Columbia Tri-Star. Cert. 18. Dur. 105 Min. Released:16/08/96 US Box-office: $18.25 million

THE PROSPECT OF Robert De Niro once again assuming the mantle of psycho was an exotic one. No one can forget the first time they saw *Taxi Driver*, the first time they saw that affable face split with a grin which let the madman beneath the skin shine through. That was twenty years ago, now, in the same year that gave us two grandstand performances - *Heat* and *Casino* - *The Fan* naturally had a lot to live up to.

That it failed completely to meet with expectation is entirely due to pacing.

Strike One: Superstar Wesley Snipes has been transferred for $40 million to his home-town baseball team, the San Francisco Giants. But is he worth that kind of money? The analogies here are obvious, primarily in the way that sporting transfer fees have spiralled out of control, but also in the way that Hollywood actors can now receive more than a third of a film's budget just for turning-up on time.

De Niro, Snipes' 'biggest fan', is a knife-salesman by trade (an unfortunate occupation since the film was released in Britain in the middle of the Government's panic attack about 'combat knives'); however, he is losing his touch. Pretty soon he loses his job. Then his ex-wife serves a restraining order on him to stop him seeing their child.

Strike Two: In parallel with his fan's problems, Snipes' career starts going down the pan. In his debut game for his new team, he sprains something, and consequently plays the rest of the season below par. As the media and fans turn against him, his play worsens until, being deeply superstitious, he is forced to conclude that his run of bad luck is because someone else in the team is wearing his favourite shirt number: 11.

Caring more about Snipes' fate than his own, and somehow feeling that, if the baseball star's luck turns, so will his; De Niro determines to get that all important number back. So, one evening, he calmly waltzes into the team sauna and murders player number eleven, Benicio Del Toro (*The Usual Suspects*).

Strike Three: Snipes' game promptly improves, but De Niro's life doesn't, which finally pushes him over the edge. Problem is, we are now over seventy minutes into a film which let us know, from the out, what was going to happen.

De Niro's mental breakdown (pummelled home by the ever-present Nine Inch Nails music) is depicted far too leisurely, his psychosis grows too slowly and in too much detail. We know where we're going, a few short-cuts would have been perfectly allowable.

The kidnap drama which is crammed ignominiously into the last twenty minutes: *"Hit a home run in tomorrow's game or I kill your son"*, is a delightfully pernicious sequence, but it is far too little, far too late.

An hour of that drama rather than an hour of De Niro methodically going mad would have probably made 'Play Baseball For Me' more than just a watchable film. But, instead, you get three strikes and then the fan hits the shit.

JA ▼ (for the beautiful photography!)

FARGO

Dir. Joel Coen Dist. Polygram. Cert. 18. Dur. 98 Min.
Released: 08/03/96 US Box-office: $25.5 million

***"THIS IS A TRUE STORY.** The events depicted in this film took place in Minnesota in 1987. At the request of the survivors, the names have been changed. Out of respect for the dead, the rest has been told exactly as it occurred."*

Fargo is deceitful. Despite claims made for its authenticity, the tale of a pregnant cop's search for a couple of killers, is completely, entirely and absolutely a work of fiction. The 'true story' angle was presumably cooked up to give Messrs Joel and Ethan Coen something to talk about at film festivals.

Fargo is the tragic tale of Jerry Lundegaard (William H. Macy). He's a car salesman up to his neck in enough debt to hatch the brilliant plan of having his own wife kidnapped and her wealthy father (ghastly Harve Presnell) cough up the ransom. Unfortunately, Jerry hires petty crims Carl Showalter and Gaear Grimsrud to do the deed, and even as they flee the scene with Jean (Kristin Rudrud) trussed-up in the back, their car is stopped for a minor traffic offence. Exit in quick succession one cop and a brace of tourists. Before this is over, four more will be toe-tagged.

Fargo is the brothers' finest film since their similarly-themed debut feature *Blood Simple*, again starring Joel's wife Frances McDormund. In 1983 she made a notable debut; now Mrs. Coen is one of America's most distinctive screen actresses. She plays Marge Gunderson, police chief for the improbably named Brainerd, and wife of uncelebrated wildlife artist Norm (John Carroll Lynch). With typical Coen caprice, her being seven months pregnant passes virtually unremarked. She ushers in a decency and humanity their earlier films have been accused of neglecting, and cleverly resists the temptation to turn her cuddly character into Tyne Daly.

In point of fact, the film is littered with more terrific performances than you can shake a stick at; Macy in particular makes for a devious but heartbreaking jerk, all sculpted hair and nervous tic. That leaves the grandstanding to mouthy, 'funny-looking' Coens perennial Steve Buscemi and the monosyllabic pressure-cooker Peter Stormare as Showalter and Grimsrud. Buscemi (the new Keitel?) has seldom been better.

The brothers are here exploring something that films traditionally ignore - ordinary people. The unique qualities of the dialogue (the clotted Canadian/ Scandanavian accent, combined with every character's delightful habit of never, ever talking about anything significant) draws you in by reminding you of the messiness of real language. The script isn't really interested in what people say, but in encouraging you to listen for what they *don't* say - analysing the space around the words, while the words themselves are of almost no consequence.

An early decision not to move the camera may have been swiftly abandoned, but, while it remains recognisable, *Fargo* is by far the calmest, least baroque of the brothers' films. Instead they rely on Roger Deakins' cinematography to drink in the bleak beautiful tundra, where the horizon bleeds into an irreducible white sky. The film becomes stylistically fascinating to watch, whilst remaining almost visually mundane. Then again, blood on snow always looked good.

Fargo (which won Best Director, at *Cannes* 1996) is a violent picture. It is swift, but undeniably brutal, savagely undercutting the humour their tremendous script wrings out of the tragi-comic shenanigans. The film lurches from gut-achingly funny to chilling ferocity in a heartbeat, and, as in the *Grande Guignol* payoff, somehow pulls-off both side by side.

As ever the details are spot-on, from muzak in the anonymous bars and restaurants to the omnipresent car-door alarms, and Carter Burwell contributes his best score this side of the miraculous *Barton Fink*. Which is a good point on which to end because *Fargo*, like their other Cannes winner, is the Coens at full-stretch, at once artful and farcical, grotesque and richly resonant. Typically atypical. Peerless stuff.

RL & GH ▼▼▼▼▼

FLED

Dir. Kevin Hooks Dist. MGM (UIP). Cert. 18. Dur. 98 Min.
Released: 19/07/96. US Box-office: $17 million to date

TITLE SEQUENCES are improving. There's a mini-industry booming in Hollywood these days, with small productions companies producing high-concept title-sequences for big-budget movies. They are like little movies in themselves but, unless you wait right to the bitter dogged end of the movie's closing titles (in this case over an hour and a half later) you'll never know who's responsible for them). *Fled*'s title sequence was put together by a company called Lumeni Productions.

We find ourselves (pre-titles) in a high-security military base, where a prosecution witness under the 'protection' of the witness relocation program is being prepared for his court-appearance, during which he will bring down one of Central America's largest crime families. Enter errand-boy with a very special delivery from the local Chinese take-away - deep-fried C4. Exit one witness.

And so we ease into a montage of office-equipment burning in slo-mo close-up. It is a dreamy, eerily beautiful sequence, reminiscent of the *Dead Presidents*' burning-money title-sequence, and overplays a no-nonsense synthesiser stomp theme-tune by Graham Revell. Now that's how to make an entrance!

The film we subsequently find ourselves in initially fails to live up to this promise, telling a fairly run-of -the-mill tale of two macho meat-head convicts, chained to each other and on the run. But there are unusual details here (in-between the obligatory pointless punch-ups) such as Laurence Fishbourne's idea of playing his harmonica to provide a rhythm that he and fellow chainee Stephen Baldwin can jog to.

I know what you're thinking - Tony Curtis, Sidney Poitier, *The Defiant Ones*! I was thinking the same thing, so, imagine my surprise when, less than half an hour in, the cons are divested of their manacles, shift gear, and set about unravelling a top-flight conspiracy (involving the aforementioned Colombian crime family, the local DA's Office and the small matter of the $25 million which Baldwin hacked out of a multi-national's bank-account).

The feature which sets this film apart from the cluster of 'action' movies we are enduring nowadays, is its wit. As the escapees are running through the woods, Fishbourne insists they head for the border; *"Are you crazy?"* counters Baldwin, *"Didn't you see* The Fugitive? *The first thing Tommy Lee Jones did was seal off the border!"* Later, when they need a car, they hijack Salma Hayek's (now, why can't I have days like that?) and insist that she take them back to her house to hide-out. *"Well. okay"* She sighs, looking at their gun *"But I'm warning you, my place is really messy!"*

Progressively, you realise that these are two very decent fugitives, their heart isn't really in this 'vicious convict' lark. As the story unravels, you learn why.

The actual plot these delightful personalities find themselves gambolling through, is a regulation-issue job, replete with dogged good-cop, insidious bad-cop, South American drugs-baron, typical nineties MacGuffin (a computer disc), and equidistantly-spaced shoot-outs in public-places (which lead one to wonder if Collateral Damage may be the new sport sweeping the nation) along with more witty badinage than you can point a sharp tongue at. All the usual ingredients, in fact, but they have been whipped together to produce a soufflé which, whilst remaining insubstantial, is very satisfying while it lasts.

Fled also succeeds where so many modern Hollywood films fail - rather than beginning with a great premise and then trailing away into tedium, it actually gets better as it goes along, culminating with the funniest sign-off line I've heard in years. As with last year's *Bad Boys*, enjoy *Fled* for what it is - a superior piece of high-tech tosh - and pray they don't ruin it by making a sequel!

JA ▼▼▼▼

FROM DUSK TILL DAWN

Dir. Robert Rodriguez. Dist. Dimension (Buena Vista) Cert. 18. Dur. 107 Min. Released: 19/01/96. US Box-office: $25.75 million

WHEN ROBERT RODRIGUEZ, famed progenitor of *Desperado* and The Great *Crime Time* Headwear Scandal got together to make a film with Quentin Tarantino, who should need precisely no introduction, nails began to be chewed all over Hollywood. What exactly would these two semi-auteurmatics come up with when their full metal talents were combined?

Two of the brashest and most self-confidently throw-away films of recent cinema! Two? Oh yes!

The first film which, for simplicity's sake we'll call *Dusk*, is a finger-on-the-trigger, pedal-to-the-metal getaway from a crime we never see. Prior to a garish Russ Meyer title-sequence, we are introduced to the traditional Tarantino twosome - the men in black - Seth and Richie Gecko, played respectively by a charismatic George Clooney and a far-better-than-we-had-any-reason-to-expect Tarantino himself. They are bank-robbers on the run from several different types of law, heading for the Mexican border and in need of cover. They find it in Harvey Keitel's winnebago. Once they apply a gun-barrel to his daughter's temple (Juliette Lewis in typically evacuated form), he is more than keen to get them out of the country and out of his life (much to the chagrin of the audience I saw this film with, who kept shouting "Shoot her!").

Clooney's steely-eyed professionalism and puppeteer-like control over his brother mixes with the razor-blade dialogue and fifth-gear narrative to make this a hallmark piece of Tarantinerie. Then they cross the border and arrive at their chosen destination: the Mexican equivalent to The Conservative Club - The Titty Twister.

At this point (exactly half-way through the 107 minutes, almost to the frame) *Dusk* ends and the second movie, *Dawn* begins. This film has less dialogue than it's predecessor, less narrative, less locations and progressively less characters. However, it is more cinematic. Rodriguez, having gotten where he's going, can get on with what he enjoys most - playing with images.

The sanctuary they have so wisely chosen for their hideout is in fact the Central American branch of the Transylvanian Glee-Club, complete with table dancers, a 'live' band and a hawker selling pussy on a buy-one-and-get-one-more-for-a-penny basis. In the most unapologetically radical film tangent since Marion Crane pulled in at the Bates Motel, the small band of American tourists (aided by a couple of lovely stereotypical bikers) forget the money, forget their kidnapper/hostage relationship and set-to wading through the undead.

One of the bikers is played by Tom Savini, who earned his stripes and a lot of horror-fans' eternal admiration by single-handedly inventing the art of gore prosthetics. Back in the seventies, he redefined what could be done with latex and red corn syrup. Some of the most medieval imagery ever put on screen, was put there by him. One can only imagine what a trip down memory lane this film must have been for him, combining, as it does, the bleak savagery of *Zombies: Dawn of the Dead* and the claustrophobic mania of *Evil Dead*.

Simply put, this is the wettest, stickiest, gooiest, goriest movie to be unleashed on our screens since MP Graham Bright's moral crusade brought all that sort of thing to an end in the mid-eighties. Unlike Peter Jackson's 1993 schlocker *Braindead*, this isn't an overt comedy, although it is very funny in places. Unlike *Braindead*, it isn't a pantomime, because you've been given time to know and care for the actors. Exactly like *Braindead*, this film has been released uncut - much to the credit of the BBFC. Of course, this comes as cold comfort to British fans when they know that, the stateside laser-disc release has previously excluded footage which we in England are unlikely to see. Ho-hum.

Depending on your taste and the breadth of your mind, you'll enjoy *Dusk* and hate *Dawn*, be bored through *Dusk* and rave through *Dawn*, or you'll appreciate them both as skilful, energetic, imaginative movies created by young and talented film-makers enjoying the chance to have big-time fun. Two films for the price of one, not even Chet Pussy could turn his nose up at that bargain!

JA ▼▼▼▼▼

GET SHORTY

Dir. Barry Sonnenfeld Dist. Miramax (BVI). Cert. 15. Dur. 115 Min. Released: 20/10/95. US Box-office: $72 million

THE SUCCESS STORY CONTINUES. After the remarkable success of *Pulp Fiction*, John Travolta returns in Barry (*The Addams Family*) Sonnenfeld's *Get Shorty*, a film based upon the best selling novel by Elmore Leonard.

A slimline Travolta stars as Chili Palmer, a loan-shark with a love for the movies. In LA to call in a debt, Palmer encounters director/debtor Harry Zimm (Gene Hackman). Instead of breaking his legs, Palmer pitches the Cormanesque Harry a film idea. Next day, Chili is living out his dreams as a film producer. He and Harry think they have a hit on their hands. If only they can secure the services of diminutive leading man Martin Weir (Danny DeVito)...

Appalling pre-credit sequence, overly complicated: *Get Shorty* has all the makings of a million-dollar turkey. That it soars over its shortcomings has everything to do with its stellar cast. In a part he was born to play, Travolta oozes class and charisma from every pore. Whether he is strutting down a corridor or getting all soppy over the end of *Touch of Evil*; he just can't help but look cool. He is ably supported by Hackman, DeVito and Rene Russo (quite superb as a sharp-minded Scream Queen).

Get Shorty is by far and away the best film to be based on an Elmore Leonard novel. An ex-screenwriter himself (he wrote the superb Budd Boetticher Western

The Tall T), our Elmore has seen Hollywood bastardise virtually all of his novels, from *Cat Chaser* to *Stick*. *Get Shorty* differs from your average Leonard adaptation in that director Sonnenfeld and screenwriter Scott Franks have obviously bothered to read the novel ... and understand it. Frank, in particular, has paid close attention the subtleties of the author's style, most notably the way in which he uses the weather to mirror the mood of the characters. Apparently Quentin Tarantino has just bought the rights to four more Leonard novels. With *Kill Shot* amongst them, it looks as if Elmore's novels might just be about to receive the swell treatment they richly deserve.

At the end of the day though, this is Travolta's picture. You can forget the *Golden Globe* and the *Oscars* snub; who needs awards when you can be as cool as this?

RL ▼▼▼▼

HACKERS

Dir. Iain Softley Dist. United Artists (CIC) Cert. 15 Dur. 100 Min. Released: 15/09/95. US Box-office: $7.5 million.

A COUPLE OF years ago, science-fiction writer and (alleged) coiner of the term 'cyberpunk', Bruce Sterling, wrote a book called *The Hacker Crackdown*. It wasn't science fiction, it wasn't even fiction; it wittily explored the FBI's war against teenage computer hackers. To his credit, he doesn't take sides, he points out the inappropriate excesses of the law-enforcement agencies, but also takes time to discuss how dangerous *some* of the activities of *some* hackers can be. I mention this only because *Hackers* tells a fictional version of the same story, but does take sides.

Hackers begins with a team of heavily-armed and kevlared SWAT troops bursting into a quiet suburban house. The dangerous terrorist they are hunting ... is an eleven year-old boy called Dade. He is found guilty of orchestrating the greatest computer system crash of all time, and denied access to computers until his eighteenth birthday.

Fast forward seven years and Dade is insinuating himself once more into the digital underground, a coterie made up entirely of young, intelligent misfits. Mostly the children of screwed-up parents, they find solace in knowing that they can change the world, just with the stroke of a key.

These are the children the media is perpetually telling us we should be frightened of. They know more about us than we do about them, and therefore, since we don't trust ourselves, we can't possibly trust them. Wrong. These kids are young enough to be idealistic; consequently they are eminently qualified to repair the damage being done to the world by their elders.

Of course, as we grow older, the temptations of absolute power become irrisistible. Enter the bad guy (boo, hiss), riding a skateboard and chewing red liquorice. He is *The Plague* (*"Don't call me Eugene!"*) and he is in charge of computer security at an oil company. He's the hacker who sold out (as Sterling points out, most big companies employ ex-hackers to catch hackers nowadays). He's the guy who is prepared to generate a global oil-spillage of inconceivable proportions, just to cover-up his tedious little plan to rob the company's pay-roll. He's the guy who sets up Dade and Co to take the rap for it all.

Director Iain Softley (*Backbeat*) has brought a skilful eye to this, his first American feature. He has realised that the interface with computers is more than a matter of fingers on keys, and more than animated swoops through virtual landscapes - to have entrapped the imaginations of an entire generation, the computer must work on a much more fundamental level. To represent computer-use, he has woven hallucinatory graphics and crystalline computer interiors, with symbolic flash-frames and energetic dance-music For the first time since *Tron* (1982) someone has come up with a new way of visualising the workings of a computer, which even the computer-illiterate can follow.

Hackers is only a so-so thriller, because *The Plague* is played mostly for laughs by Fisher Stevens; but the cast of idiosyncratic Robin Hoods are a delight to spend an evening in the company of. Jonny Lee Miller (pre-*Trainspotting*) is an affable Dade (*Zero Cool/Crash Override*), the exquisite Angelina Jolie brings real balls (if you see what I mean) to the 'token' female, Kate (*Acid Burn*) but the star of the show is sixties throw-back Mathew Lillard (*Cereal Killer/Emanuel Goldstein*).

The deliberately melodramatic dialogue perfectly represents the macho-posturing that props up computer jargon ('Hard Drive', anyone? 'RAM' perchance?), whilst the sparkling visuals and euphoric soundtrack all serve to give this film an unquenchable *joie de vivre*. Mixing a pop-video aesthetic with a 'real' director's skill with actors, Softley has turned this un-promising teen-flick into, so far as this writer is concerned, the sleeper hit of the year.

JA ▼▼▼▼▼

HATE (LA HAINE)

Dir. Mathieu Kassovitz Dist. Tartan Video. Cert. 15. Dur. 97 Min. Released: Spring 1996. US Box-office: $300, 750

"NIQUE LE POLICE."

Critically lauded, damned by the fascists of the FN, and screened for the Cabinet, *La Haine* is incendiary in its native France. It represented its homeland at Cannes 1995 and fittingly took Best Director for the young Mathieu Kassovitz. This is a bold and important film.

"Fuck the police."

Kassovitz hates them and his second film makes no bones about it. Footage of riots on a Paris housing estate plays out under the extensive titles, disorder sparked by the near beating to death of a youth by the local constabulary. One officer lost his revolver in the ensuing meleé.

The following 24 hours are precisely timed. Three friends - Vinz (Vincent Cassell), Hubert (Hubert Kounde) and Said (Said Taghmaoui) - roam through the heady atmosphere of anxiety and ennui on the estate with its burned-out cars and heavy police presence. They trek into the city to collect on money owed to Said by a dealer, and tangle with both the law and a skinhead gang. Vinz carries with him the missing gun.

For precursors look to *Mean Streets* and Spike Lee's *Do The Right Thing*, but also the best (i.e. least patronising) of Ken Loach. Hubert's a black boxer, Vinz a Jew, and Said Arabic; Kassovitz's script wraps everything in one taut, expressive package, but skilfully side-steps tokenism. Right and wrong are clearly delineated even from the first frame.

And yet the film never feels moved to labour its point. The memorable moments are subtle ones: Hubert changing a billboard from 'the world belongs to you' to read 'the world belongs to us'; one of the trio snapping his fingers to 'switch off' the Eiffel Tower - a là .Eric Rochant *World Without Pity*, and Leo Carax's *Mauvais Sang* - but here it remains steadfastly ablaze.

Close-ups, fluid camera moves, a single, breathtaking helicopter track over the estate - the film belies Kassovitz's relative inexperience. It is shot in elegant monochrome, capturing at once a documentary realism and disturbing surrealism. The excursion into the city is nightmarish, the gatecrashing of a modish Parisian art gallery a notable highlight.

La Haine could stand to lose ten minutes from the city section, and has difficulties with its (all supporting) female characters, but these are merely petty quibbles. The balance of humour and drama is deft, the music inspired, and performances uniformly forceful.

Like *World Without Pity*, this is both nihilistic and aptly titled, albeit also surprisingly humane. The end is all it can be: ambiguous, fatalist, uncompromising. Kassovitz has made a outstanding picture.

***GH* ▼▼▼▼**

HALLOWEEN

Dir. John Carpenter Dist. MIA. Cert. 18. Dur. 93 Min.
Released: Halloween 1978. US Box-office: $47 million

THIS IS ONE of those films which proved so influential, who's copyists and sequelists proved so innumerable, that it is easy to forget the simple effectiveness of the original. It'll soon be coming up for its twentieth anniversary, but it is already available here in digitally remastered widescreen form. As with most people, I haven't got a clue what 'digitally remastered' actually means, but I do know that this video presentation is as crystal clear as when it was new, in fact, thanks to the improved quality of home video recorders, it has probably never looked and sounded this good.

Although very definitely a seventies film, *Halloween*'s twisted heart lies fairly and squarely in the fifties. As with all those alien invasion movies which the children sit glued to throughout the proceedings, it is a symbolic attack on the leafy white suburbs that America calls its home. It is not co-incidence that his targets are the bobby-socked children of temporarily absent parents. Unlike all those alien invasion movies, the enemy is no longer on the outside trying to get in, 'cos he's already here. He was born here.

Michael Myers came from good, decent middle-class stock; quite what drove him, at the age of six, to knife his sister to death is never revealed, neither to Donald Pleasance his psychiatrist, nor to the viewer. What drives him, fifteen years later, to break his shackles, return to his home town of Haddonfield and slaughter his neighbours, is similarly left blank.

We never see his face. We never hear his voice. With his white face-mask and laboured breathing, Michael is not meant to be looked on as a person at all, but as simply a threat, a distillation of human violence poured into one human soul. This film was made years before the phrase 'serial killer' was even coined, and so Carpenter doesn't call on clinical forensics, popular myths or handy catch-all motives such as the usual 'he was an abused kid so now he's a murder' line. Michael just is.

Showing remarkable skill for his then tender years (skill which seems more recently to have abandoned him), Carpenter moves the camera around to reveal and to disguise. This film absolutely must be seen in widescreen, as nature intended, because the flow of the camera around the streets is crucial to the pace of the movie. As night falls, Carpenter uses shadow and shape to frame the danger that Jamie Leigh Curtis and her friends are in, trapped in their little pools of light. Finally, the whole experience is underscored by that classic, shimmering soundtrack filled with stabs that Carpenter called 'cattle-prods'.

This was the first significant use of synthesisers in a soundtrack since *Forbidden Planet* in 1956, a fact which Carpenter (who also composed and performed the music himself) acknowledges when he borrows part of *FP*'s score for his own use.

More than anything else, what I find remarkable about this film, looking at it now, is it's leisurely pace. Michael is a ghost shadow passing all-but unnoticed across the face of Haddonfield for 55 of the film's 93 minutes, but when he does strike, this cumulation of suspense and expectation makes the moment all-the-more shocking.

Halloween is a great film, which remains undiminished by the decade of pale imitations that followed in its wake. The original is still the best.

JA ▼▼▼▼▼

HEAT

Dir. Michael Mann Dist. Warner Bros. Cert. 18. Dur. 164 Min. Released: 08/12/95. US Box-office: $67.25 million

***HEAT* IS A MASTERFUL FILM.** Like the greatest films of the past, its shape announces itself in every shot and gesture, and not one shot nor gesture seems out of place. It slots together like a dream.

Vincent Hanna (Al Pacino) is a dedicated man, an LAPD detective with an impeccable record, a skilled robbery/homicide team at his beck and call, and a disaster zone for a marriage. When a security truck heist alerts him to the existence of a gang of professionals on his turf, he goes on the hunt for Neil Macauley (Robert De Niro), a career thief with as much dedication and as few ties.

Heat is a film of duets. Thematically and visually, it is arranged around confrontations in which characters endlessly attempt to make contact with one another. While Justine Hanna (Diane Venora) tries to talk to her husband about their failing relationship, without really engaging his attention, the film's celebrated tête-à-tête, by contrast, has Mann editing shots of Hanna and Macauley with seamless grace; their two lifestyles ironically slotting together as only true friends can.

But Hanna must seek and Macauley avoid, in a Los Angeles with the terrain of a war movie. In keeping with the dialogue's hewn feel, in its structure and content *Heat* has an architectural splendour about it. Recalling movies like John Boorman's *Point Blank* and Ridley Scott's *Blade Runner*, the tower-blocks, freeways and municipal lots of LA have seldom been photographed so evocatively. Then, when cops and robbers collide at a midday shopping mall, the film's confrontations of thesis with antithesis erupt into a savage running battle through this architecture.

Heat is a movie which often approaches high tragedy. Few masculine dramas take the time to examine so closely the dynamics between the men and their women. If Justine and Vincent reach an uneasy truce after their daughter's suicide bid, it is Neil's hand which Vincent clutches as Macauley dies, following a pursuit which mutely recalls their evasive logic within the coffee-shop. If you buy only two videos from this year's crop, make *Heat* one of them.

JA ▼▼▼▼▼

HEAVEN'S PRISONERS

Dir. Phil Joanou. Dist. Rank. Cert. 15. Dur. 132 Min.
Released: 17/05/96 US Box-office: $4.75 million

HAVE YOU NOTICED how many stars think that looking good in front of a camera qualifies them to be a producer behind it? In cases like Clint Eastwood and Mel Gibson they have handled their own careers with great insight, some others have turned good, strong material into a vehicle for vanity. This not the case with Alec Baldwin who, in his first production job, gives probably the best all-round performance of his career.

Lifted intact from the pages of James Lee Burke, he is Dave Robicheaux, ex-New Orleans cop, ex-drunkard and a character who lovers of hard-boiled fiction will be more than familiar with. He has retired from the stresses of the streets and taken up a shanty existence in the idyllic backwashes of Louisiana. But his past and his reputation are still there to bedevil him when, literally out of the blue, he and his wife Annie (Kelly Lynch) go into the adoption business.

The child they rescue from a crashed plane is an illegal immigrant, with bad connections on the mainland. Although totally innocent of the situation she is in, a storm of incident and accident whips up around her, sucking in Dave and his long-time nemesis Bubba Rocque (played ripplingly by Julia's elder brother Eric) and most of the local heavyweights. The film's secret weapon is Teri Hatcher who succeeds in shaking off her goody-goody Lois Lane image by playing pickled vamp Claudette, but she lacks the ragged edge the character needs to make you really want to slap her.

If Baldwin the family man is very quiet and subdued, Baldwin the ex-cop is all *noir*; scowling, beating and shooting first, asking questions later. Unfortunately, no one is intimidated by him and the whole situation gets rapidly out of hand.

Heaven's Prisoners is one of those movies we keep saying they don't make 'em like any more. The characters are more important than the action, the violence is dealt with in a workmanlike fashion and then moved on from. Yes we get the chase, yes we get the punch-up, yes we get the knife-wielding bad guy, but the point is that we also get a lengthy and detailed character study of a brave if foolish man gazing back into the abyss. That the abyss gazes also is an inevitable but still-effective characteristic of the genre.

If you're sick of two-hour pop videos with ever-bigger explosions and ever-smaller IQ's, if you pine for the days when Bogart and Mitchum slouched around in dangerous dark alleyways, you will find *Heaven's Prisoners* refreshingly old-fashioned.

JA ▼▼▼▼

THE HITCHER

Dir Robert Harmon. Dist. Beyond Terror Video Cert. 18. Dur 97 Min. Released: 1986. US Box-office: $5.75 million

THERE'S A KILLER on the road, his brain is squirming like a toad. And C. Thomas Howell stops to give him a lift. With the killer's knife at his throat, Howell begs *"What do you want?"* The chilling answer, in whispered tones: *"I want you to stop me."* That's the set-up right there. One of the most compulsively simple synopses in modern cinema, leading to a gripping road-movie with no pretensions to the grandeur it achieves.

The film's ace-in-the-hole is, of course, Rutger Hauer, still glowing from the success of *Blade Runner* some four years earlier, not yet a straight-to-video stalwart. He plays the enigmatic psycho, one of the last of his kind since the term 'Serial Killer' had not yet reached the ubiquity it now enjoys. He has no back story, no obvious motivation. He is an enigma. When asked where he's from, he answers slyly: *"Disneyland."*

Indeed, he could well be a figment of imagination, a nightmare of pursuit made convincingly real. Yet, when Howell believes (erroneously) that he has his nemesis in his grasp, a caring, sympathetic smile creeps across Hauer's face. It is almost as if he is sorry for what he has done to the boy, for taking away his innocence,

He dogs Howell, attacking him, then mysteriously leaving him alone. He sets him up, then frees him, only to set him up again. He pushes him, goads him. *I want you to stop me*. Eventually, inevitably, Howell turns and fights back, and then it is too late. This isn't a revenge drama, it isn't *The Terminator* where, when faced with an invincible enemy, tenacity and fate can still win the day; it is a tale about the complexity of psychology, about addiction to adversity. It's about father and son! It is a tale that stops, but doesn't end.

This battle of primal forces is played out against the bleak wasted splendour of the Mid-Western deserts, visible now in all their intimidating widescreen glory. The real America, it says, lies beneath a thin crust of civilisation. Drive away from the cities, away from their protection and you are completely on your own. You don't know what's out there.

Thankfully, this film didn't spawn a slew of sequels, so stands magnificently alone. Like its titular character it is inexplicable and unrepeatable. A beautiful, awful, terrifying, compulsive glimpse of the dark side. Hauer's best performance, bar none, and one of the half-dozen stand-out movies of the eighties now, finally, available in the only format a film should be seen in - 1:2.35 ratio widescreen!

JA ▼▼▼▼▼

JADE

Dir. William Friedkin Dist. Paramount (UIP). Cert. 18. Dur. 95 Min. Released: 13/10/95. US Box-office: $9.75 million

ALFRED HITCHCOCK has made a real comeback since he died. Hollywood is persistently disinterring his techniques in an attempt to make thrillers 'thrilling' again. Or should that be 'Hitchcockian'?

Jade, for prime example, unfurls with a big, meaty, 'Herrmannesque' score (actually by James Horner) over a moody 'Bassian' title sequence. This leads to a delightfully 'Kubrickal' opening scene as the camera prowls around a palatial and empty house. We faintly hear someone being brutally murdered off-screen.

This is a film scripted by Joe Eszterhas, so it tells the same basic story as *Jagged Edge*, *Basic Instinct* and *Sliver*. In common with these earlier drafts, it doesn't really have goodies and baddies, just shades of baddie. In other words: 'Eszterhesque'.

Here the Eszterhabitants include various chilly high-societites such as a promiscuous psychologist (Linda Fiorentino), an arrogant lawyer (Chazz Palminteri) and an ambitious Assistant DA (David Caruso), all interlinked by their penchant for uttering trademark 'Eszterhasbeen' psycho babble.

Fortunately, he doesn't have it all his own way. Director Friedkin is a master at using lighting, camera angles and editing to evoke a mature and moody urban jungle. *Un*fortunately, this subtle and serious technique clashes noisily with Eszterhas' penile dementia. The bonking scenes are so explicit and so numerous that eroticism becomes tedium. It seems that writer and director were attempting to make different movies, the result is disappointingly unfocused.

Undaunted, Friedkin falls back onto *his* trademark: a spectacular and frighteningly plausible car-chase. I'm sure I heard someone yell 'You Friedkin maniac!' at one point.

Great performances. Great music. Great to look at. Shame it's the same old story.

One final word of warning: don't pay too much attention during the first ten minutes, otherwise you might notice the big red neon arrow pointing at The Culprit, and that would certainly spoil your enjoyment.

***JA* ▼▼**

JOHNNY MNEMONIC

Dir. Robert Longo. Cert. 15, Dur. 105 Min. Dist. FoxGuild Video. Released: 26/05/95. US Box-office: $19 million.

SO, HOW DOES William Gibson's Hollywood debut fare in a market already cluttered with cyber-thrillers from *The Net* to *Hackers*? As you might expect, he digs further into the ramifications of future-tech than any of his competitors - even *Strange Days*. He explores how an entire society - and a global society at that - can be affected by technological development. He shows how scientific progress can become evolution. More than any other writer in Hollywood, he is accustomed to working in the future, it isn't a foreign country to him.

As the story begins Johnny is about to upload 320 gigabytes of information into his wetwire. This is a shockingly visceral experience, like taking a stationary roller-coaster and pulling twenty virtual gees. Unfortunately 320 gig is way too much for him and he begins to suffer the first shaky symptoms of NAS.

Earlier, a slow crawl of text had patiently explained that the world of multi-national power corps is falling apart because of the cerebral disease Nerve Attenuation Syndrome. The Holy Grail of the Man/Machine Interface is now a global reality, replacing hardware and software with wetware. The NAS disease is the organism's rejection of the artificial implants.

It is a world of new flesh, where no one has to be how nature made them, where rôles are constantly being re-negotiated. This is the future, and it doesn't work. Welcome to 2021, some eighteen months after the setting of *Blade Runner*, the original science-fiction noirmare and spiritual father of Cyberpunk culture. This slow-crawl of information is deliberately designed to evoke *Blade Runner*, the swooping flight over a virtual landscape that follows consciously reminds you of the apocalyptic LA skyline of 2019.

There are several reasons for Gibson and director Robert Longo to evoke *Blade Runner*, partially, I suspect, because Gibson has never hidden the fact that his seminal creations of The Sprawl and Cyberspace came out of his perceptions of the early eighties, a time when popular culture was swamped with *Blade Runner* references.

This film is crammed almost to choking with allusory and literal quotes, either from his own earlier works, or from the omnipresent *Blade Runner*. As Johnny is about to beat one of his assailants over the head he quips: *"Time to die!"* Ralphi Face, Johnny's agent, holds court in a bar that is half Tech Noir, half Taffy's. But, on a more fundamental level, the very story of one man with a finite amount of time to download his data before it pollutes his nervous system and kills him, is taken as much from the computer game *Burn Cycle* as it is from Rudolph Maté's 1950 *noir* film *D.O.A.* It may well be that Gibson isn't afraid to quote his peers, but there comes a point when doing so leaves room for little else.

Where *Johnny Mnemonic* falls down, it does so because of the self-confessed lack of experience Gibson and Longo have in movies. Gibson's script, although messy, is simply in need of tightening up, but that needs a good strong director, which, unfortunately, Robert Longo is not.

This film pulsates with great ideas and convincing futurology, but the flaccid pace and frankly bizarre casting betray the potential shown. *Johnny Mnemonic* is a disappointment, not just because I, along with many Gibson fans, have been waiting a long time for him to put his vision on screen, but because the lost potential bleeds out of nearly every scene. They came so frustratingly close, yet missed by light years.

JA ▼▼▼

JUDGE DREDD

Dir. Danny Cannon Dist. FoxGuild. Cert. 15. Dur. 96 Min. Released: 30/01/ 95. US Box-office: $34.5 million.

THE MOVIE ADAPTATION of the *2000AD* character Dredd was always going to a problematic proposition - especially with the persistent involvement of super-egos Schwarzenegger and Stallone. Well, we all know who won-out and got to (briefly) don the helmet. But the question remained, was this Oscar winner (yes really, although it was twenty years ago!) capable of acting like a single-minded, one-dimensional clone with a vicious streak a mile wide and a sarcastic sense of humour? Sounds like Stallone's entire filmography, actually.

Then there was the question of young Danny Cannon. Nothing in his only other movie, *The Young Americans*, gave any indication that he was capable of taking a $70 million budget in his stride whilst juggling the heftiest special-effects shopping list ever assembling in Britain. Would he be able to keep Stallone's vanity in check? Would he want to stick close to the source material, or do a *Batman* to it? Would it be any good?

Surprisingly, I am glad to report that the answer to most of those questions is *yes*! Anyone who grew up reading the early adventures of Dredd as he trundled across *The Cursed Earth* and battled *Chief Judge Caligula*, will be overwhelmed by a nostalgic familiarity. Writers William Wisher (*Terminator* 2) and Steven E. De Souza (*Die Hard*) have immersed themselves in these early adventures, and reproduced the feel and the black humour of those late-seventies British fantasies. The cynicism and nihilism which originally formed the judge's 'personality' (only to be leeched out as he became more popular) are there, if toned down for the American market. The fear of the police state, the suspicion that any law enforcer who hides his identity and shoots first can't be considered entirely trust-worthy, and the commentary on the insanity of living like caged rats in big cities, are all present here.

The detail which has been lavished on the look of the film is awe-inspiring, and the opening fly-by through the towering blocks of Mega City One is jaw-droppingly impressive, even reduced to small-screen dimensions. It has taken 'em thirteen years to surpass *Blade Runner's* vision of the future city, but surpass it they have. The buildings have that hunched-up armadillo look which artist Mike McMahon introduced, and the loving attention to minutiae which would be missed by all but the saddest of Dredd anoraks, is a positive delight.

And now the but ...

But, all this sterling preparatory work and the startling designs, all the beautiful effects, marvellous sets and witty one-liners are for naught. Betrayed. Shafted. Left languishing by a script which pulls out all the stops to create as many clichés as it can. Armand Assante chews the furniture with misplaced passion as the evil Rico, Max Von Sydow is stately but obviously doomed as the Chief Judge, Joan Chen is only there so Diane Lane has got someone to kickbox with, and the promised invasion of homicidal clones ... just sort of ... fizzles out.

Ruined by an ending which has obviously been so brutally hacked in order to obtain a teen-friendly certificate that it is rendered nonsensical. At 96 minutes it feels very light for a big-budget buster of blocks - about half an hour light - I had hoped that they would see sense when it came to the video release and present the full movie, for which I consider this to be merely the promo. Unfortunately, 'twas not to be. Maybe they'll try and milk a 'special edition' out of it further down the pike. Until then, this is really only for sad fan-boys like meself.

JA first hour : ▼▼▼▼, second half-hour: ▼

THE JUROR

Dir Brian Gibson. Dist. Columbia Tri-Star. Cert. 18. Dur. 118 Min. Released: 02/02/96. US Box-office: $22.5 million

IT LOOKS LIKE a Grisham movie. It tastes like a Grisham movie. It feels like a Grisham movie. But it ain't (it's better than that).

Demi Moore plays artist Annie, who is that blight on the landscape of modern God-fearing America - a single mother. She is enrolled for jury duty on a big mafia murder trial and is confidently assured that her identity will be a closely guarded secret so she will be totally safe. Yeah.

Hardly have the titles done rolling than The Teacher (a mafia hitman, so-called because once you've met him you've learned your lesson!) is wiring her home for sound. As played by Alec Baldwin, he is the James Bond of gangsters, quietly spoken, genteel, sophisticated, and not fond of having his decisions countermanded. The Don may look upon him as the hired help, but he knows he's really in charge!

With a voyeuristic zeal that DePalma would be proud of, he studies Annie and son Oliver, watching and listening, learning which buttons to push in order to get her to do precisely what he and The Family wants. In essence this boils down to: *get the jury to vote not guilty, or I kill your son*. Cue those million-dollar tears she leaks so well.

The premise is as old as the hills and the show-down pure tosh, but the package is held together by the bond between Moore and Baldwin. Their relationship is much more than victimiser and victim, after all, once this unfortunate murder-trial business is over ... well, the young lad does need a father!

Young Joseph Gordon-Levitt is very watchable as Oliver, making him more than the typical gee-wizz kid we all hate and fear. Despite mom's attempts to shield him from what's going on, this kid ain't stupid.

But the most fascinating aspect of this film are Annie's sculptures - they are enclosed in boxes and the only way to inspect them is to stick your hand inside and feel. The message of this is, of course, don't be fooled by outward appearance. It may look like a Grisham movie. It may taste like a Grisham movie. It may feel like a Grisham movie. But it ain't (it's better than that).

JA ▼▼▼

KILLING ZOË

Dir. Roger Avary Dist. Polygram. Cert. 18. Dur. 111 Min. Released: 19/08/95. US Box-office: $400, 000

"EXECUTIVE PRODUCED BY *Quentin Tarantino*" barks the advertising on the video sleeve. As anyone who is familiar with *Killing Zoë*, or its director, Roger Avary, will tell you, this technical credit isn't the only connection between this film and the remarkable Mr T.

Back in the days when he worked at *Video Archives*, Quentin Tarantino counted amongst his friends and work-mates one Roger Avary. Besides watching loads of movies together, Roger and Quentin devised a sketch based upon the supposed homosexual subtext of *Top Gun*. The pair also collaborated on scripts. On graduating from their unique film school, the two friends set about making their own movies. Tarantino wrote and directed *Reservoir Dogs*, a crime movie about a botched bank robbery. Avary, meanwhile, wrote and directed *Killing Zoë*, a crime movie about ... a botched bank heist.

In addition to the theme, the films share a number of other similarities. Indeed, *Killing Zoë*, with its pop culture posturing, big guns, drugs and quick-fire dialogue, really does appear to be crying out to be called 'Tarantinoesque'. In truth, many of the things we have come to consider hallmarks of man behind *Pulp Fiction* actually have their origins in Avary's debut. The heroin sub-plot, the animated square Uma Thurman draws in the air, neither of these features were in the shooting script for Quentin's classic until after he had seen a preview of his friend's film. As he would hi-jack the *Top Gun* riff (which he himself performed as part of his cameo in Rory Kelly's *Sleep With Me*) and Avary's *Pandemonium Reigned* (which became the gold watch episode in *Pulp Fiction*), Tarantino also stole elements from Avary's first feature.

None of which is to suggest that Avary is a superior artist to his ex-colleague. He isn't. A story about a gang, led by the drug fuelled Jean-Hughes Anglade, who storm a Parisian bank, *Killing Zoë* really can't hold a light to *Reservoir Dogs* or *Pulp Fiction* (It's better than *Four Rooms*, but then, what isn't?). As a writer, Avary has none of his friend's passion or sincerity. As a director, he has none of Tarantino's verve.

What *Killing Zoë* does have is good actors. Besides the ever-watchable Anglade, there are a brace of good performances from Julie Delpy and Eric Stoltz as the boy and girlfriend who find themselves on either side of the fence during the aforementioned fracas.

Alas a couple of good performances do not a good film make. The simple truth is that *Killing Zoë* isn't a very good film. Avary clearly has ideas (the film's chock full of them), but he lacks vision. Not so much an awesome debut, more another successful conquest for the magpie that is Quentin Tarantino.

RL ▼▼

KISS OF DEATH

Dir. Barbet Schroeder Dist. Fox Video. Cert. 18. Dur. 100 Min. Released: Spring 1995. US Box-office: $14.75 million.

THIS IS SOMETHING of a change of pace for director Barbet Schroeder. After earning the acceptance of *The Academy* with *Reversal Of Fortune*, he went on to make the 'from hell' pot-boiler *Single White Female*. Now he has given us a remake of Henry Hathaway's 1947 curio *Kiss Of Death*, which featured Victor Mature as the sap caught between loyalty for *his* family and *the* Family, and Richard Widmark's debut as the snickering badguy.

Now we have David Caruso, fresh from jumping ship on *NYPD Blue* (what a great career move that turned out to be!) as Jimmy the sap with the heart of tarnished gold, and Nicholas Cage (prior to drinking his way to an *Oscar*) as the thoroughly-nasty Little Junior.

Jimmy has a few too many scruples for a man who lives in a world where most people kill their enemies and sell their friends for a buck. Jimmy believes people like that deserve and appreciate loyalty. He also believes that having a wife and daughter doesn't make him vulnerable. It does.

He soon finds himself caught between Cage's homicidal wide-eyed loon on one side, and the great Samuel L. Jackson of the DA's office, who will hand him over to the mob as soon as send him to an expensive prison, on the other. Not the safest position to be in.

Throughout the film, Jimmy is passively passed back and forth between the supposed forces of good and evil and it is testament to Caruso's charisma that, given this essentially formulaic material, he actually makes you care for the guy; even if his descent into hell is more than inevitable.

Cage is on rare form, all nervous ticks and worried expressions. One is left with the indelible impression that he deeply resents the name 'Little Junior' and is over-reacting accordingly. But the man of the match is Sam Jackson who hardly has a line of dialogue, yet steals every scene he walks into.

There have been nastier and more cynical films like this - *Serpico* was one, the more-recent *Romeo Is Bleeding* another - films which stare long and hard at the madness of our urban society (and don't tell me that American society isn't our society), and give us slightly less than no reason to feel safe in it.

Kiss Of Death is a dirty tale, but someone had to tell it.

JA ▼▼▼

LAST DANCE

Dir. Bruce Beresford. Dist. Touchstone (Buena Vista). Dur. 105 Min. Cert. 18 Released: 03/05/96. US Box-office: $5.75 million

IT'S NOT THEIR FAULT. They couldn't possibly have predicted that Tim Robbins was making one too, and that it would be so damn good. It's just bad timing. Unfortunately, as you watch *Last Dance*, your mind is constantly drawn back to the similar-but-much-better scenes in *Dead Man Walking*.

Sharon Stone is continuing to strive for critical acceptance in a rôle where, try as she might, she doesn't come close to persuading you that she's a stupid, bitter con of twelve years standing. She is Cindy Liggett, a resident of a small, almost convivial death row in the quietest, cleanest prison I have ever seen on screen.

We are introduced to her via Rick Hayes, played by Rob Morrow (late of *Northern Exposure*) who is the preppy brother to the Chief of Staff to the State Governor. Despite having no experience of anything (except women and drink) he is handed a well-paid job on a plate, in The Clemency Office, and his first case is to decide if there is any reason not to kill Ms. Liggett.

His boss is the fractious and bored Randy Quaid, proving that, despite the evidence of *Kingpin* and *id4*, he is capable of giving a good performance once in a while. He informs Morrow that more women will be executed from now on: *"Because of the women's lobby! They all want equal treatment in the eyes of the law."* He knows that his job is pointless, the Governor never grants clemency, but he keeps plugging away, playing the game, not creating ripples, in the hope that one day ...

As Morrow swallows his first ever taste of responsibility and Stone begins to rely more and more on him, a man who has confessed that golf is the nearest thing in his life to religion, you can't help but feel sorry for Stone's character. Then, as she progressively falls in love with this limp, spiritless sop, you can't help but feel sorry for Stone's career.

When the film tries to be sensitive, it underscores with plaintive violins, which nudge the proceedings straight into sentimentality. When Stone leaves her home of twelve years to be taken to isolation, in preparation for her last day on Earth, the tears in her guard's eyes and the mute tribute as her fellow prisoners clatter their mugs against their bars, is more parodic than powerful. This is the scene that Richard E. Grant pitched to Tim Robbins in *The Player*, and the scene he so skilfully avoided adding to *Dead Man Walking*.

Bruce Beresford's early Australian movies, his 1991 Canadian historical drama *Black Robe*, even the sickly-sweet *Driving Miss Daisy*, all show him to be a talented director capable of meatier and for more self-assured work than this. *Last Dance* is slight work from all concerned, neither cruel nor unusual.

JA ▼▼

LAST MAN STANDING

Dir. Walter Hill Dist. Entertainment. Cert. 18. Dur. 100 Min. Released: 20/09/96 US Box-office: $13.75 million (after two weeks)

"NO MATTER HOW LOW YOU GO, *there's always right and wrong!"* This is the opening line of *Last Man Standing*, and could well be the line Walter Hill wants carved on his headstone one day. All Hill movies are essentially the same: set against a Western landscape (whether carved out of the urban waste-lands of modern-day cities or, as here, in the sand-blasted deserts of the Tex-Mex border during Prohibition) and concerning a man (or men) whose fierce individuality must be fought for and hard-won.

Although credited with being a remake of Akira Kurasawa's *Yojimbo* (as opposed to Leone's spaghetti-western version *A Fistful of Dollars*), Hill's script actually goes back to the work which inspired both films: Dashiell Hammett's *Red Harvest*. Unwilling to give up entirely on the desire to make yet another western, he also draws on the Eastwood character, not, surprisingly, so much from *Fistful* ... but more from *High Plains Drifter*.

Bruce Willis is The Man With No Hair, driving out of the desert into a town called Jericho (population 57 and dropping like a stone), like an exterminating angel. *"One thing's for sure, you wouldn't find Jericho anywhere on the map!"* So, we are into the landscape of the imagination, rather than any tangible place.

The town is a self-perpetuating anomaly. It is owned by two gangs, who compete over importing its liquor. There is no sigh of export, so the alcohol is for the exclusive use of the town, yet, with about half-a-dozen exceptions, the only people left in town are the gang members. They are therefore fighting a bitter and brutal war, over nothing.

Key among those exceptions are the barman/sidekick, the Irish gang-leader Doyle's Mexican girlfriend/hostage, and Bruce Dern's anything-for-a-quiet-life sheriff. *"Do yourself a favour,"* he advises Willis, all neighbourly, *"You're on your own here, get yourself a firearm!"* Well, he needn't worry on that score, as Willis proves momentarily, with one of those hand-cannons that sends victims flying thirty feet backwards (in slow-motion).

As Willis begins to play the two gangs off each other, making as much money as he can, he keeps hearing, in hushed tones, about the towns real monster - Hickey. Then, one night, a car rumbles into town and Christopher Walken, a brutal scar dividing his face, steps into Hickey's shoes.

As the inevitable show-down with Hickey draws ever-closer, Willis becomes more interested in Doyle's captive; *"My fear is my curse"* she tells him at one point. *"What's yours?" "I was born without a conscience"* he answers, without irony. Of course, you know that he is going to rescue her and bring both gangs down on his head. He may not have a conscience, but there's still that niggling right and wrong thing!

We are not exploring new territory here in Jericho, but few directors use these motifs as well as Hill, and he hasn't used them so expertly himself, since *48 Hrs* back in 1982. The gauntlet Willis must run to achieve some temporary redemption is a bloody and operatically violent one - I don't think I've seen so many bullets fired since John Woo's *Hard Boiled.* The sepia photography is stark and suitably bleak, Ry Cooder's seismic bass-lines (apparently played on a steel guitar bolted to the floor!) deafen and chill by turns.

Granted, the film's title kind of gives away the ending, but then the outcome is never in doubt, as Hickey says, standing in the burnt-out bones of a road-side diner, the wind spiralling sand around his feet: *"It's always gonna come down to something like this"* - a stand-up shoot-out between two battered warriors. No, the pleasure comes from the assurance of the handling, the mastery of the medium displayed by Hill and, believe it or not, the lightness of his touch.

"Somewhere along the line, it all got personal," confesses Willis, clambering back into his trusty Ford, *"Can't say it went according to plan; but I was right about one thing - they were all better off dead!"*

***JA* ▼▼▼▼**

THE LAST SUPPER

Dir. Stacy Title Dist. Electric Pictures. Cert. 15. Dur. 94 Min. Released: 05/04/96. US Box-office: $329, 000.

THE LAST SUPPER is a delicious black comedy from film journalist-turned-director Stacy Title which shows once again just how vibrant America's independent film scene is these days. 95% of this film takes place in one room and its adjoining garden, yet the subjects it addresses involved the entire Western world.

Lets imagine that the pre-eminence of far right-wing politics in our society is having as detrimental an effect on disadvantaged minorities as far-left wing politics have traditionally had in the East, it's preposterous I know, but bear with me. If that were the case, privileged intellectual Americans would be enraged by the fact, and sit around talking vehemently about what they would do - hypothetically - to make the world a better place if - for the sake of argument - they had the chance.

This film looks at what could happen if a group of students, as idealistic and insular as any of their breed, got it into their heads to actually try and save the world from those deluded maniacs on the right wing. This determination comes partially from an intellectual challenge they set themselves (*"If you were a time traveller and met Adolph Hitler before he grew up, would you kill him?"*) but mostly from their chance meeting with a truck driver called Zack.

Played stridently by Bill Paxton (*One False Move, Trespass* and, most recently, *Apollo 13* and *Twister*), Zack is an ex-Marine, proud as hell of his country who, when they start to dig at him (for being a working class hick mostly) makes the extraordinary statement *"Hitler had the right idea."* This, of course, is a red flag to their bullishness and they start laying into him with their sharpest comments and pithiest one-liners. He, in return, pulls a hunting knife and threatens to gut them. In the ensuing scuffle, they manage to re-deploy his knife, and so bring his miserable red-neck life to a no-doubt long over-due end.

As they set to and bury him under the tomato plants in the garden, they theorise about killing political extremists as an after-dinner pursuit. It's easy, it's fun and it makes the world a safer place for Liberals to live in. Gradually, as the conversation continues, their perspective evolves from 'what if' to 'when'. Deciding that stabbing is too messy and too ... well, physical, they opt for a far more civilised form of execution - poisoned wine.

So begins a ... one hesitates to call it delightful, but it is ... parade of self-righteous, deluded and egotistical guest-stars led by Charles Durning (last seen in *The Music of Chance* and the Coens' *The Hudsucker Proxy*) as the Reverend who believes that homosexuality is a disease and AIDS the cure, and Mark Harmon (who I last saw as Maddy's suitor in the TV show *Moonlighting*!) as the smooth predator who insists that rape victims are just vindictive dissatisfied lovers. Needless to say these two gentlemen are swiftly served their poisoned chalice.

Inevitably the coterie begin to bicker, their violent tendencies surfacing unpredictably because they had set themselves an intellectual challenge and forgotten to work possible emotional reactions into their equation, presumably because, being students they don't actually know what genuine emotions are yet.

Throughout, proceedings are punctuated by the enigmatic Ron Perlman (last seen speaking French in *City of Lost Children*, but probably best known as Vincent in the TV series *Beauty and the Beast*) who plays a pundit with wealth and taste, a sort-of thinking-man's Howard Stern. When he inevitably enters their cloistered world, he gets invited around for dinner and they prepare an extra-special decanter for him. So the show-down is set, the saviours of the Liberal world matched in mortal confab with The Right Wing incarnate, a set up which allows director Title and scribe Dan Rosen to ... ahem ... have their wine and drink it.

The Last Supper comes dangerously close to being too clever for it's own good on occasion, but the cracking dialogue and determinedly straight-faced performances save it from over indulgence. It will of course mean nothing to those myopic bigots it so skilfully targets (and no, I don't mean the homophobes and sexists) who will doubtless see the film at their local arts centre then discuss it over dinner.

Courtney B. Vance steals the show as Pete, the instigator of their hobby. As the only black man in the group he could, I suppose, be considered to be the only one with first-hand experience of the intolerance he hates, but this isn't dwelt upon in the film. He's convinced that they are objectively doing the right thing, the noble thing and, what's more, he's enjoying himself.

So, no car chases, no big explosions and no slack given to either political extreme in this biting satire which manages to avoid looking like a talking-head movie, despite the fact that its budget kept it closeted pretty much in that one room. With what little money she had, Title managed to persuade a few name stars to donate a day or two of their time, thereby giving the film the only kind of clout Hollywood truly understands. As with *Curdled, The Last Supper* is a film to look out for, then, in a few years time, when everyone is talking about Stacy Title's latest blockbuster, you'll know where it all began.

JA ▼▼▼▼

LEON

Dir. Luc Besson Dist. Touchstone Home Video. Cert. 18, Dur. 106 Min. Released: (France) 28/09/94, (US) 08/11/94. US Box-office: $32.25 million. A 'Version Integrale' Director's Cut was released in France 26/06/96 with some 25 minutes of additional footage.

MONSIEUR BESSON'S last film, *Nikita*, was the perfect Hollywood action movie: brash, post-modern and ultra-violent, filled with bright colours, vivid images, a pounding soundtrack and some of the most chilling action/violence sequences yet set to celluloid. Problem was, it wasn't made in America, it featured no big stars and - worst of all - the dialogue was in bloody foreign. Consequently, it wasn't until the limp English-language remake (*The Assassin* a.k.a. *Point Of No Return*) that anyone paid attention.

Curiously, the power of *Nikita*'s scenario is such that, even those who only saw John Badham's soulless re-hash, were excited and inspired by it.

Inevitably, Hollywood came a-calling, and Besson, who has always enjoyed dallying with different working-environments, took up the invite. With *Leon*, his first all-English language and (supposedly) all-American movie, he has effectively made his response to the Anglicised *Nikita*, but has also taken the chance to re-assess.

Your friendly neighbourhood Cleaner is back, slightly transformed, but once again in the form of Jean Reno. The *femme* extremely-*fatale* Anne Parillaud has been boiled down to twelve-year-old Natalie Portman, and the emphasis has shifted to make her a guest in his world, rather than the other way round. Meanwhile, Danny Aiello takes on the Tcheky Karyo rôle as Tony, Leon's scarily calm employer, a man with a heart of pure cold.

Unlike *Nikita*, there is a single easily-identifiable nemesis, the madman-of-the-people Gary Oldman, whose performance swerves dangerously close to too-much, but stays just the right side of the line as he chews up the furniture and enthusiastically murders recalcitrant informers to the strident accompaniment of Beethoven (he likes to hum an inspirational tune when gunning down women and children).

After an opening sequence comparable in its self-contained perfection to that of *Raiders of the Lost Ark*, *Leon* expands into a witty and (I hesitate to write this) heart-warming tale of two like-minds - one an infantile adult, the other a precocious child.

As with all Besson's work, this film is too stylised, and the characterisations too far beyond the pale, for you to mistake this film for standard American naturalism. It is an urban fantasy, hyper-real, but in ways that very few post-modern, self-referential American movies begin to approach. The internal dialogue and obviously complex back-stories are hinted at to add colour, never over-played to create drama or pathos. You don't mistake these creations for real people, but, at the same time, you never doubt their credibility within their own crazy, mixed-up world; very much like ours ... only more so.

Leon doesn't take prisoners. By turns chilling and charming, brutal and barmy, Besson has arrived on the Hollywood scene rather like his titular character: silently and unexpectedly. He then blows away all the empty, formulaic movies that surround him, before melting away into France once more.

JA ▼▼▼▼▼

LONE STAR

Dir. John Sayles Dist. Rank Cert. 15. Dur. 135 Min.

DAVID CRONENBERG'S next film will apparently be called *Crimes of the Future*. John Sayles' latest could easily have been called 'Crimes of the Past'.

Sam Deeds is the Sheriff of Frontera Town in Texas. His quiet, workaday world is thrown into turmoil when he is called to the site of a recently disinterred skeleton, found at the back of an army firing range. The only hints to the skeleton's identity are a Masonic ring, and a rusted black Sheriff's badge.

Sam's immediate thought is that the has found Sheriff Charlie Wade, who disappeared in 1957 after an argument with Buddy Deeds, Sam's father, who was then just a deputy but, in Wade's absense, became the town's most respected Sheriff. Sam's problem, in the week when the new town courthouse is about to be dedicated in his dad's name, is to investigate a murder, several decades cold, whose prime suspect is a man only he seems not to have loved.

Making full use of glorious Cinemascope frames, Sayles has woven another magical tale of complex characters in a powerful landscape. As with the recent time-pieces *The Confessional* and *Dolores Claiborne*, a simple shift of lighting or pan across a room serves to transport us back to a time when Kris Kristofferson (reborn as the insidious Wade) faced-off against a young, sassy deputy (Matthew MacConaughey).

Yet, rather than being this film's sole stock in trade, the murder mystery is merely the hanger on which many garments are hung. Sayles' primary concern is the racial mix of America, to reflect this, he has chosen a Texan border town, crammed to bursting with Mexicans, Blacks, Whites and mixtures of all three.

The fighting between these different groups is demonstrated in two consecutive scenes, one featuring a racially-motivated shooting, the other showing a PTA meeting where the white parents are strenuously resisting having Texas' history told from the Mexican perspective. The race war is fought on many fronts. However, this being Sayles' most careful, and caring script to date, these scenes also reflect Sam's resistance of his own past.

Sam is surrounded by a culture-clash (beautifully symbolised by a little old lady who stares myopically at a *Gameboy*, unable to put it down), which, again, has its roots in history. Wise old barman Otis Payne keeps a shrine to the Seminole Indians who, he explains to his grandson, were African slaves who ran with a tribe of native Indians and eventually found a home in Mexico. They were as racially-mixed as the enemies of white-folk could be.

Subplots are layered in leisurely depth in *Lone Star*, there is the 1957 hunt for illegal immigrant Elario Cruz - and the fate of his family in the modern day. There is Sam's re-awakened feelings for his childhood sweetheart Pilar. Then there is army colonel Joe Morton's return to his home town, and halting attempts to make peace with Otis, his father. If the film has a fault, it is that this plot is one too many, it only underscores Sam's relationship to Buddy, it doesn't add anything to an already rich mixture.

Meanwhile, Sam finds that pursuing his dead father is like investigating Godot. Buddy is omni-absent, yet ubiquitous. The flashbacks to Wade's reign of terror are the most kinetic scenes in the film, dripping with venom and blood; whilst the present is a much more diplomatic period. Corruption no longer needs a gun, it needs a deciding vote.

The message of this film, if it has one, is simply that all is not necessarily how it seems, knowledge is not necessarily a blessing and nobody is perfect. A mature, liberal and open-minded philosophy if ever there was one, as purveyed in a mature and liberal movie. Sayles' best since the similarly multi-layered *City of Hope*, and, given another viewing or two, possibly his best film to date.

JA **▼▼▼▼** ½

MAXIMUM RISK

Dir. Ringo Lam Dist. Columbia Tri-Star Cert. TBA Dur. 95 Min. Released: 13/09/96 US Box-office: $14.25 million to date

FOR ALL HIS FAULTS, Jean-Claude Van Damme can certainly pick directors. Having 'revived' the career of Peter Hyams and introduced John Woo to the States, he now headlines Ringo Lam's first foray into La-La Land. Jean-Claude really is the work-horse of the Hollywood action scene, churning one out every six-months, regular as clock-work; each one timed carefully to avoid competition and earn him at least one week atop the box-office chart. I suppose it's a formula that works, so why change it?!

As a piece of formulated film-making, *Maximum Risk* is neither as diverting nor as different as *Hard Target* was. It doesn't really stand-out from the action-movie mainstream, which is a shame given that Lam is the spiritual father of *Reservoir Dogs*, and therefore partially responsible for the renaissance in Hollywood shoot-'em-ups.

The very-promising opening sequence, in the streets of Southern France, features J-CVD dying a nasty death. Cut to local cop, also played by ol' J-C, who discovers that the corpse is actually that of the brother he never knew he had. Determined to find out how and why his brother wound-up cold on the mortician's slab, J-C assumes his identity and takes his return flight to New York.

Precedent would indicate that a new eye on the New York skyline can make it look alien and new. Not so with Ringo; failing completely to exploit the similarities between New York and Hong Kong, and therefore leaving his documentary, fleet-of-foot style back home, he fails to distinguish himself. Curiously, he is much more at home in the low-rise vistas of Nice.

The film's middle-act is therefore a leaden bore, plodding from one lumpen chase to the next. However, there are moments to hint, teasingly, at what might have been. The lengthy and convoluted fight in the sauna, played-out to the accompaniment of an accordion, develops into the highlight of the New York story. The film doesn't come alive again until the production has moved back to France for a show-down which is masterfully handled and sparkling with all the energy and imagination of a great Hong Konger.

Unfortunately, these great set-pieces are too few and far between, being separated by a tedious array of moments like the one when J-C and new girlfriend (inherited compassionately from his ex-brother), whilst being held hostage, manage to distract their captor's attention long enough for a quickie against the bathroom door. Yeah, right.

JA ▼▼

MISSION:IMPOSSIBLE

Dir. Brian De Palma Dist. Universal (UIP). Cert. 12. Dur. 125 Min. Released: 22/05/96. US Box-office: $200.5 million to date

A DE PALMA MOVIE is an event. A De Palma version of a favourite crime series from the sixties is an eagerly awaited event. How closely will he stick to the original's structure? How elaborate will the impossible mission be? Which Hitchcock film will he rip-off this time? All important questions which I have been waiting nearly two years to answer.

Mission:Impossible The Movie begins with the *original* version of *that* theme (not the modern re-mix) set to a montage of images from the upcoming film (just as the original series did with each and every episode). This is a bravura moment and an exhilarating way into the adventure. However, the pace set by Lalo Schifrin's legendary track and the slashing edits that accompany it, slacks off as the first mission patiently unfolds.

The off-duty IMF (Impossible Mission Force) are chattier and sassier than their TV counterparts, but on duty they are higher-tech and slicker, if somewhat lacking their predecessor's panache. Tom Cruise is like a kid with a new toy, as team leader he gets to wear some completely unconvincing rubber faces and be generally bossy. And what a leader he is, within fifteen minutes of that title sequence, he's managed to cut the cast list substantially down to size and is on the run from his superiors who believe that he arranged for the assassination of his own team.

So they have taken a hallowed and highly successful trademarked concept, and ripped it apart. The film turns into a manhunt as Cruise attempts to piece together what happened and find out who sold him out (he should have just asked any member of the audience, 'cos they all know). This contrivance also serves to take a celebrated ensemble-cast format and turn it into a one-man-against-the-world story.

De Palma has assembled a world-class cast for this film, and yet Cruise still conspires to get most of the screen-time all to himself. The only problem with this is, he did it all before as Mitch McDeere in *The Firm*, and wasn't greatly charismatic then. Cruise needs actors to bounce off, he built his career on working with the best both infront of and behind the camera, and learning from them, stretching himself to not be outshone by them. He doesn't have the gravitas to carry a film on his own, but works best in company. The scenes of him agonising alone ring hollow but, when he decides to assemble a new team and so has Ving Rhames (Marcellus Wallace from *Pulp Fiction*) and Jean Reno (Leon from *Leon*) to respond to, he and the film come back to life.

In order to prove his innocence, the new unofficial IMF must break into (and out of) the CIA headquarters at Langley. Cue the sequence we've all been waiting for: silent and efficient, worked almost entirely without dialogue, but set throughout to that metronomic music - the team work their way into the most closely guarded room in America (with a convenient crawl-space and air-conditioning duct built into its ceiling). This sequence is deliciously silly - but reminds you what the whole endeavour was supposed to be about. Forget the conspiracy and the manhunt, stick with the caper.

While you laugh at the stupidity of Cruise's chosen mode of entry (hanging from wires, counterbalanced by a sweating Frenchman) you are still drawn to the edge of your seat by the tension of waiting as you experience the first quintessentially De Palman moment in the film - watching a droplet of sweat work its way across Cruise's glasses, threatening to drop onto a pressure-sensitive floor and give the game away. And then, just when you think they've gotten away with it ... but no, I won't spoil it. This scene, with the time and care and trouble that went into its execution is every bit as rivetting as the great poolroom scene at the beginning of *Carlito's Way*. De Palma pulls out all the stops: penetrating close-ups, agonising slow motion, and an unerring ability to put the camera right where you want it to be. Masterful.

The only other scene where thirty years of directing experience comes to the fore concerns Cruise's realisation of exactly what has been going on around him. We see alternative versions of flashbacks as the voice-over cautiously tells us a completely different and contradictory story - a moment of pure unadulterated cinema.

Other than this, De Palma's main contribution has been to stop this film careering into the kind of ecstatic emptiness of young contenders like Michael Bay. It is not a study in form over content, and as such sits ill in the roster of summer releases. Its pace is slower, its contrivances are less well rehearsed, its aspirations are slightly higher and therefore its failings are more disappointing.

Certainly, *Mission:Impossible* is not the film I had hoped it would be, nor is it the film it could have been had more control resided with the writer and director and less with the star and producer. Never the less, it has moments to treasure, music to adore, and prospective sequels by the score. The advance rumour was that this film would out-Bond *Goldeneye*. It doesn't, but it leaves the prospect of an interesting battle in the years to come as 007 and IMF tussle to create the most spectacular espionage movies ever made.

JA ▼▼▼▼

MULHOLLAND FALLS

Dir. Lee Tamahori. Dist. Entertainment. Cert. 18. Dur. 106 Min. Released: 26/04/96. US Box-office: $11.5 million

NEW ZEALAND DIRECTOR Lee Tamahori was responsible for 1994's box office smash *Once Were Warriors*. In *Mulholland Falls* he again explores the bone-crunching dynamics of the all-male group. But now the setting is the early-50s and the group is a crack squad of Los Angeles cops investigating a routine murder case which goes out of control. Tamahori's male clique places *Mulholland Falls* in a direct line of descent from the films of Howard Hawks, a director who regularly celebrated the tensions and camaraderie which exist between men of action in westerns and war movies.

When Ellery Coolidge (Chazz Palminteri) encourages leader of the 'Hat Squad' Max Hoover (Nick Nolte) to open up more, Hoover replies that this is not the way of the real man: *"You must carry your own water."* Such a line would not have seemed out of place coming from John Wayne's trail boss in Hawks' 1948 western *Red River*. What lends poignancy to *Mulholland Falls* is that the personal rapport among Hoover's team and their *mano-a-mano* methods of dealing with law breakers are starting to make less and less sense in a world in which impersonal bureaucracy and mass nuclear annihilation have become the new Zeitgeist.

Other Hawksian echoes crop up throughout the film. Its Los Angeles recalls the mean streets of LA in *The Big Sleep*. Significantly, in the opening scene Max and his men take a hoodlum out to Mulholland Drive overlooking the city and throw him over the edge. The idea of LA as a mythical sewer complex of lawless apartments and tacky offices connected by the swish of busy expressways lurks in the back-stories of both films.

Festering amidst its decay in the Hawks film sits Colonel Sternwood, wheelchair-bound and dying of a rare blood disease. Representing a more honourable age, he is the precursor of a military-industrial regime headed by John Malkovich's cancer-ridden General Timms which has become corrupted by the winning of the war and the splitting of the atom. The post-war post-Hawks world is a complicated one in which the army is out of line and even Max Hoover's ethical carte blanche has been compromised by his infidelity with the dead Allison Pond (Jennifer Connelly).

Now too crime-infested to afford a fundamentally decent man breathing space, LA, as in such classic depictions as Polanski's *Chinatown*, is more metaphor than metropolis, and so the final conflict must take place beyond the city limits over the salt flats of Utah. Setting this displacement from the city to a sparse, almost allegorical setting, seems obliquely reminiscent of Tarantino's *Reservoir Dogs*. Here the 'dogs', united by their distinctive 'uniforms', like the members of the 'Hat Squad' in their custom-made suits, move through a universe consisting not of distinctive locations but of homogenous urban space, rather like the anonymous desert brush punctuated by the rocky outcrops which provide cover in the classic western. The LA of *Reservoir Dogs* is not the holiday destination of guidebook literature, but, like *Mulholland Falls*' Utah, the stage for the resolution of all-male conflicts surrounding private and public notions of law and order. Hardly surprising, therefore, is the fact that Tarantino and Tamahori's films contain two of the most impressive line-ups of male stars working in Hollywood today.

The nuclear threat scenario of Tamahori's film also invites comparison with Robert Aldrich's film noir, *Kiss Me Deadly*. Indeed, as that film dates from 1955, it often feels as though, in some mythical movie realm, Ralph Meeker's hot-headed Mike Hammer and Nick Nolte's short fuse Max Hoover are brothers under the skin and are both on the trail of the same 'MacGuffin.'

Interestingly, *Mulholland Falls*' mood and themes seem to pick up where *The Big Sleep* left off, anticipating the hysteria of the Aldrich universe in which the government cannot be trusted and private dicks have to make up the rules for themselves. It is as though, the squad disbanded, his wife gone, and left with a faulty past, Max must now face up to an apocalyptic future as an atom without influence. One of the pitfalls of mainstream American cinema is that movies often conceived as hybrid narratives combining a range of successful formulas at the development stage all too often look that way at the viewing stage. The overwhelming impression left by Tamahori's first American film is of a script which touches many another movie on its circuitous way to resolution. But this is no bad thing since *Mulholland Falls* adds up to more than a routine 'clothes 'n' cars' nostalgia opera, being a tribute to a bunch of Hollywood characters who once were warriors.

***RA* ▼▼▼▼**

MURDER IN THE FIRST

Dir. Marc Rocco Dist. Warner Bros. Cert. 15. Dur. 110 Min. Released: Spring 1996. US Box-office: 17.5 million

IN 1949, 15-year-old Henri Young was arrested for stealing five dollars from a food store. Sentenced to serve out his time on Alcatraz, he spent virtually the whole of his sentence in solitary confinement. On being released back into the prison community, Henri promptly killed the man he believed to be responsible for his being mistreated. Sentenced to death, all that stood between Young and the hang-man's noose was naïve attorney, James Camphill.

Sadly, *Murder in the First* fails to recreate the real-life drama in its telling of the case of Henry Young. Part of the problem lies with first time director Marc Rocco and his inability to keep his camera still for more than a couple of seconds. By far the greater portion of the blame can be attributed to leading actors Bacon, Slater and Oldman.

For a film widely praised for its acting, it is amazing just how inept the performances actually are. Kevin Bacon, usually a likeable, laid-back actor, takes this rare leading man opportunity with both hands and then tramples all over it, playing Young's limp, thick-lip and even thicker Bayou accent right up to, and over, the edge. As the warden, Gary Oldman gives the sort of wretched performance we have come to expect from him. Surrounded by so much ham, Christian Slater seems even more bland than usual. His inability to conjure up the charisma his crucial part demands is very apparent in the scenes he shares with his on-screen brother Brad Dourif. As desperately as Dourif tries to underplay his small rôle, he is still a damn sight more interesting than Slater's foppish, law school graduate. A cracking cameo from R. Lee Ermey as the avuncular judge further underlines the shortcomings of the leading men.

Perhaps aware that the performances aren't quite up to scratch, Rocco wields his camera in all manner of different directions. While all this hand-held stuff might work well in action movies, it doesn't play to good in a conversation piece like this.

Overwrought when it ought to be understated, laughable when it should be affecting, *Murder in the First* never looks like reaching the lofty heights it sets itself. It can't even aspire to the well-meaning of a Stanley Kramer movie. At a time when film is taking a kicking for the way it deals with history, Rocco's film commits the cardinal sin of treating a crime against humanity like TV movie-of-the-week material.

***GH* ▼▼**

MUTE WITNESS

Dir. Anthony Waller Dist. Columbia Tristar. Cert. 18, Dur. 90 Min. Released: 15/09/95. US Box-office: $1 million

***MUTE WITNESS* BEGINS** with an homage to *Halloween*, then descends into the silliest and most protracted death-scene since Ernie Wise last took to the stage. From the word 'go', we are not sure if we are expected to be frightened or amused; and the movie continues to confound expectation.

The setting is a movie studio on Moscow, where an American film-crew is making a tacky horror movie. Our heroine is Billy the make-up girl, who is mute. In classic stalk'n'slash movie style, she gets locked into the studio over night. Yet, unlike any s'n's since *Halloween*, this film actually manages to be genuinely scary.

Over the years there have been many films like this, but few have come so completely out of the blue. The horror movie is a dead art-form, having been surpassed by the splatter movie. The spy saga became history with the end of the Cold War; and thrillers all seem to drop from the same mould (the director's casting decisions telling you whodunit before you even know what they dun). Yet *Mute Witness* contains ingredients from all these recipes and still comes over as a refreshing breath of stale air.

It would be priggish of me to reveal who has playfully been cast as the obligatory Mr. Big - especially as he is simply credited in the titles as 'Mystery Guest' - but suffice it to say that you will be pleasantly surprised.

If this film has a fault, it is that Waller has felt the need to Tarantinize it with too-many references to the great works of his predecessors. I noticed moments lifted from Hitchcock, Kubrick, even Russ Meyer, but these just add to the garden of delights he has planted. Funny. Exciting. Chilling. Devious. This is one of the most impressive debuts of recent years. Seek it out and see for yourself. That is an order!

JA ▼▼▼▼▼

THE NET

Dir. Irwin Winkler Dist; Columbia Tri-Star Cert. 15. Dur. 108 Min. Released: 28/07/95. US Box-office: $50.75 million

SPEAKING FOR MYSELF, I don't need much excuse to think about Sandra Bullock, but when I do, gazing myopically at a computer screen isn't really how I see her. Never the less, here she plays Angela Bennett, a computer nerd. She shops, chats, plays and works from home, via the modem, so she rarely if ever meets people. She is part of Hollywood's new techno-toys club (see also *Disclosure*, *Copycat* and *Assassins* for a look at how the Internet isn't, or *Hackers* to see how it should be).

The main reason she uses these handy-dandy tinker-toys to help her avoid the world outside, is her mother - she has Alzheimer's and doesn't recognise her daughter from one day to the next. It's almost as if Angela wants to compensate for her mother's lack of memory by storing her own on hard disc.

This is not only sad, it makes her vulnerable. Given the right access codes, anyone can break into any computer, reading secrets and changing facts into fiction.

Angela suddenly becomes an unperson - her driving licence, credit cards, house deeds, her whole world has gone. Deleted. Now no one recognises her, it's not just her mother. Her neighbours never see her, so can't vouch for her identity; she's part of a virtual community, not an actual one, consequently her identity comes down to a simple matter of access codes - if you know 'em, you can take over her world.

What the makers have done is very cunningly apply new technology to an old-fashioned thriller. Hitchcock always told us that innocence was no excuse, and that no one was safe anywhere - even in the shower. Through hallucination and psychology, he suggested that identity and reality where often negotiable values. Well now, through the wonder of the silicone chip, identity and reality are simply ones and zeroes in a data stream, and they are eminently vulnerable to attack.

Would you know how to cope if your bank account suddenly disappeared, or your house suddenly belonged to someone else? Scary, isn't it. And it's not science fiction any more. Nowadays villains can cause more chaos with a laptop and a mobile phone, than their ancestors ever could with guns.

The Net is a tense and effective thriller. It suggests that, despite what the propagandists would have us believe, the danger presented by computers doesn't stem from over-active, mischievous teenagers, but, as ever, from the powers that be. Computers are potentially the greatest force yet devised for social control. How many of us genuinely understand them? How many of us can use one to its fullest extent?

The Net suggests that we are progressively being left further and further behind by the march of technology, possibly to the extent that we are almost akin to the peasantry of the Middle Ages, powerless to resist, yet entirely dependent upon the minority who do know what's going on, and have some say.

The Net has some important things to say, and it is to their credit that the film-makers chose to wrap their message in a seat-edge thriller. After you've watched it and you return to your home, office, shop, or bank, you won't look at the computer screen you will inevitably find there in quite the same way again.

JA ▼▼▼▼

NICK OF TIME

Dir. John Badham Dist. Paramount (CIC) Cert. 15. Dur. 90 Min. Released: 24/11/95. US Box-office: $8 million.

THERE'S A FUNDAMENTAL PROBLEM with *Nick of Time*. It has a great central premise, then proceeds to betray itself every chance it gets.

For example: Christopher Walken hatches an elaborate plot to blackmail some poor schmuck into assassinating a State Governor. Why? *Well, because he himself can't be seen to be at the convention the Bonaventure Hotel* (the one last used in the depressingly similar, but incalculably better, *In The Line Of Fire*) *when the Governor is killed.*

Okay, I can swallow that. But why, if that's the case, does he enrol Johnny Depp as said schmuck, then follow him around like a suspicious puppy, threatening him, cajoling him and yelling at him in a style that even a blind, deaf and stupid secret-serviceman would notice. *Ah, well that's because he knows he's safe, because the secret service are in on the deal.*

What, all of 'em? Okay, fair enough. But if that's the case, I'm forced again to wonder why he doesn't just waltz in there and do it himself? *That's because he needs surveillance camera footage of Depp doing the deed.*

Ah, I see, to avert suspicion, like. Hmm. Well then, why, at the end, when all else fails, does he go after her himself, anyway? And where are the police when all these shots are being fired? *Ehm ...*

And then there's the gimmick on which the whole confection rests - its use of 'real time', yet there are slow-mo sequences, hallucinations and cut-aways! *That's a homage to John Woo and his way of playing with time!*

But, there's a sudden jump of almost ten minutes. He spends so much time looking at clocks its positively transparent that, by the time he's 64 minutes into the plot, you're only 54 minutes into the film. Where does the time go? *Ahh ... well ...*

No, I'm sorry, Badham's direction is strident and effortless, but he does seem so bored with this sort of film nowadays. Nevertheless, he brings the best out his performers, and wrings-out what tension there is in the script. Unfortunately, it's not enough, consequently a promising first half is scuppered by typically lacklustre committee-written ending. They would, I can't help but think, all have benefited from taking a little more time!

***JA* ▼▼**

ONCE A THIEF (ZONGHENG SIHAI)

Dir. John Woo Dist. Made In Hong Kong. Cert. 15. Dur. 100 Min. Released: (Hong Kong) 1990.

THIS IS THE SLIGHTEST of the John Woo films yet released in this country; even so, it stands head and shoulders above the rest of the straight-to-video market this year. Although it stars Woo's lucky-charm, Chow Yun Fat, it wears quite a different guise from any of the other films they have made together - it's an unashamed comedy.

I'm afraid I've always had a problem with Chinese comedies - it has something to do with the minor detail that they're just not funny in translation. Consequently, the shenanigans of Jackie Chan *et al* remain something of a closed book to me, I tend to fast forward through to the stunt scenes.

It hardly need be said that Woo is a better director than Chan, consequently even the so-called funny scenes here are worth watching for the extra information they contain. Also, in typical Hong Kong fashion, scenes change tone and direction as if Aristotelian Unities were going out of fashion (what do you mean 'They are'?) and therefore even a party-pooper like me isn't bored for long.

The story concerns a *menage à trois* of art thieves, Joel, Cherie and Jim, so it is only appropriate that it begin with a hilariously unlikely raid on a moving truck in Southern France. Taking inspiration from the fount of all heist movies Jules Dassin's *Du Rififi Chez Les Hommes* (a.k.a. *Rififi*, 1955) and *Topkapi* (1964) with maybe just a hint of Hitchcock's *To Catch a Thief* (1955), this is a breezy and brash high-speed ride.

In flash-back we are introduced to the children's abusive guardian - the mastermind of their early crimes, and, by contrast, the benevolent policeman/uncle who rescues them from the gutter. Later, their dilemma becomes a struggle between these two forces as their ex-guardian wants them dead whilst their ex-uncle is the inspector in charge of bringing them to justice. So, even though the presentation may be totally different, the regular Woo concerns of group-loyalty over minor concerns such as legality, are here for all to see.

The set-pieces are crafted with the usual Chinese precision, the stunts being no less demanding of the actors and stunt-performers than in the more serious movies. Where this film scores is in the shoot-outs, which are text-book demonstrations on how to empty a clip without actually hitting anyone. The body-count is low, the violence skilfully skirted round and, consequently, this is a great way for the young and uninitiated to get into Hong Kong action cinema.

An interesting aside for you, Allied Productions have just turned *Once A Thief* into an American TV series (which, if I may say, it is perfectly suited for) and the pilot movie was directed by Woo himself. He obviously wanted to make sure they got it right, so hired the best man for the job ... himself.

JA ▼▼▼ (by Woo's standards) ▼▼▼▼ (by everyone else's)

PRIMAL FEAR

Dir. Gregory Hoblit Dist. Paramount (CIC) Cert. 18. Dur. 125 Min. Released: 04/04/96. US Box-office: $56 million

AS USUAL, Richard Gere plays a depressingly rich, deplorably successful professional (this time he's a lawyer, but he's pulled the same schtick as an architect, a psychiatrist and a corporate raider before now) whose self-confidence is overshadowed only by his vanity. His opening monologue concerns his belief that there is no such thing as truth, only the relative truth he, the defence lawyer, relates to the jury.This is the key to the movie - truth and justice are not based on evidence or on provable fact - they are based solely on belief and perception.

So what else is new?

This film is shot through with chilly autumnal colours, reminding this viewer of Lumet's bleak take on the legal profession *The Verdict*.Although Gere doesn't literally chase ambulances like Paul Newman did, he is morbidly attracted to the big cases because they further his own career (and earn him 40%). In the pursuit of the raw materials out of which he will manufacture his truth, Gere (whose character is, one need hardly add, named Vail) finds himself clambering over cardboard condominiums beneath the sheltering arches of downtown bridges. He doesn't notice the suffering around him.

So what else is new?

Well, they've found a mildly witty way of having their prime suspect be both guilty and innocent, thereby throwing up another smokescreen between the jury and objective truth, which Vail proceeds to use to the advantage of his bank-balance.

Maybe it is simply that court-room dramas have lost their bite since we all got so heartily sick of seeing what the reality (objective or otherwise) was like with the O.J. case. Maybe it is that this particular tale is too reminiscent of too many of its predecessors (Gere's own *Final Analysis* comes most readily to mind), but whatever the cause, *Primal Fear* fails to chill with is coldness, fails to alarm with its corruption and fails to entice with its dilemmas. It also fails to give its audience even the remotest hint as to why the hell it is called *Primal Fear*! And that's the truth.

JA ▼▼

PUBLIC ACCESS

Dir. Bryan J. Singer Dist. Imagine. Cert. 18. Dur. 90 Min. Released: (US) 1993

FULL MARKS to anyone who fingered *Public Access* as evidence of two major new talents. It scooped the *Grand Jury Prize* at *Sundance* in 1993, if not a proper UK release, which seems unfortunate now that writer Christopher McQuarrie and director Bryan J. Singer have hit so big with their follow-up, the sensational *The Usual Suspects*.

Not, to be fair, that *Public Access* offers us many clues of the grandeur to come. The smart ensemble playing of *Suspects* is absent here, instead, the film is carried almost entirely by the unsettlingly thick-lipped and charismatic Ron Marquette. He is Whiley Pritcher, the mysterious buttoned-down stranger who one day walks into the little middle-American town of Brewster and the little middle-American lives of its buttoned-down residents.

Almost Whiley's first act is to pay up-front for four Sunday 'family hour' slots on the local public access cable-TV channel, announcing that he will host a call-in show called *Our Town*. *"What,"* he asks, *"is wrong with Brewster?"*

The answers are slow in coming, but eventually the seething underbelly of the town is exposed in all its petty squabbles and bigotry, and the question becomes not 'what' but 'who' is wrong with Brewster.

Public Access is a terribly measured affair. The film is in no apparent hurry, and proves it in a series of very effective long, languorous zooms and tracks across the studio as Whiley broadcasts, telling us one thing and showing another. The film looks and sounds superb.

Marquette is perfect for the piece, whether he's in his sensible Republican suit or naked, scrubbing out the bathtub. What he is, we discover, is a sociopath, and that, in turn, is where the film eventually fails. Once the killing starts, it cannot sustain the stifling atmosphere of before, and ends up shooting for one too many targets - the serial killing, the media manipulation, the politics - losing impetus somewhere along the way. The end should be scary but is merely necessary.

Public Access has too much of an agenda to generate as flesh crawling, disorienting an ambience as that masterpiece of small-town paranoia *Blue Velvet*, but the debt owed to David Lynch is huge in its shades of both Lumbertown and *Twin Peaks*. It's an ambitious and impressive debut, and it's ultimate disappointment, one senses, has more to do with a failure of technique than nerve.

***GH* ▼▼▼**

THE ROCK

Dir. Michael Bay. Dist. Buena Vista. Cert. 18. Dur. 130 Min. Released: 07/06/96. US Box-office: $133.25 million to date

LIKE MICHAEL BAY'S previous movie *Bad Boys*, this white-knuckle-techno-thriller begins with a night-time raid on an unsuspecting building. General Ed Harris leads his adoring band of ruthless marines against a U.S. army weapons dump in order to liberate a flight of chemical weapons. He intends to take said weapons to Alcatraz Island, where he will launch them against San Francisco and kill several million people, unless the Government admits to its black ops policy and honours the soldiers who have died in illegal operations.

Not the most ignoble of motives, but not quite as democratic as convention would like, so a plot is hatched to defuse the situation. Nick Cage is a chemical weapons specialist who, along with grizzled ex-Alcatraz prisoner Sean Connery and good-guy marine Michael Biehn, is to lead the attack to re-take the island and make the missiles safe.

Die Hard cut away all the detours in action films, it took away the need for romantic interludes and boiled down comedy side-kicks to the bare minimum. *Speed* tore away much of what was left by simply filling the screen with so much incident and pacing the whole endeavour so that there was no time for detours.

The Rock weaves a very complicated multi-strand story together by adopting *Speed's* pace but, in order to pack more characters and locations in, cuts out unnecessary conventions like establishing shots and breathing space. One incident follows straight on from the next to such an extent that, by the end of the first reel, you've been drawn so far in that to sit for more than three minutes without a car chase, explosion or stunt of some description, has the most patient of backsides jiffling with boredom.

The plot is stitched together out of threads we have seen a thousand times before; this film doesn't pretend to be showing us anything new, so why waste time re-introducing it. The characters are from entirely familiar stock, their rôles and relationships instantly defined: Nicholas Cage is effectively Luke Skywalker, taking advice from Obi-Wan Connery whilst being led into the jaws of the enemy (*that's no island, it's a battle station!*) by Han Biehn. Meanwhile, Hans Zimmer is John Williams, pounding out his *Crimson Tide* score again, endlessly, hypnotically, throughout the action.

As with 1995's *Die Hard With A Vengeance*, the action sequences are shot in close up with a hand-held camera and with editing that cuts almost down to the individual frame. Don't try to focus, don't try to concentrate, just allow the sound and fury to wash over you.

So the audience is passive, pupils wide, brain in neutral, the perfect state in which to enjoy a rollercoaster ride. But rollercoasting isn't a spectator sport, it can only really be enjoyed by participants. Unfortunately, for all the reasons outlined above, I simply couldn't engage with this film. I didn't care whether the characters (and by extension San Francisco) lived or died, because experience of these movies had taught me to know exactly who would die, when and by whose hand. With no light and shade, no charismatic characters (no one to compare to Travolta's barn-storming performance in *Broken Arrow*, for example) and no hope of an original idea, there was nothing for me to hold on to.

It seems that more can indeed be less, more names above the title, more stunts and more explosions adds up to less cumulative effect. Don't get me wrong, I can be as much an airhead as anyone when it comes to action movies - but I need an engaging lead performance, I need some attempt at emotional conflict, I need stunt sequences that don't come straight out of the mould ready formed. If there's going to be an astronomical body count, you have to want the badguys to die and, by the same token, want the goodguys to live. John Woo and Robert Rodriguez continue to show us that mindless violence doesn't have to be entirely mindless to still be fun.

The Rock isn't an abject failure, thanks to director Bay's MTV background it is certainly beautiful to look at, and Connery is given some nice lines to throw away when Cage asks him about his past as a British secret agent (geddit!?). As usual Harris acts everyone else off the screen, but, after a promising pro-active start, his character just seems to peter out. Unfortunately the three credited script writers haven't really exploited the wonderfully rich potential of the scenario they were handed.

And I was so looking forward to watching Haight-Ashbury bite the big one.

***JA* ▼▼**

SHALLOW GRAVE

Dir. Danny Boyle Dist. Polygram. Cert. 18. Dur. 92 Min. Released: (UK) 06/01/95. (US) 10/02/95 US Box-office: $2.75 million UK Box-office was $7.5 million, and the worldwide total eventually came to: $20.5 million.

WE WATCH DANNY BOYLE'S debut because we are told it's fresh, it's smart and scary and funny. And, for the most part, it is. It only lasts 92 minutes, and from the off comes on like an express train. We like it precisely because it is NOT a period adaptation nor one of Ken Loach's patronising middle-class diatribes. And, best of all, it looks *American*.

Then we watch *Shallow Grave* again and it begins to dawn that there is something seriously wrong with this adrenalised post-Thatcher yuppies-in-jeopardy flick.

The plot we know: three twentysomething professionals look to rent out a room in their Edinburgh flat. After humiliating a string of aspirants, they alight upon the enigmatic Hugo (Keith Allen), who promptly keels over and dies on them. But, before they can do the right thing, the threesome unearth a suitcase of cash under the dead man's bed and cross an invisible line: dispose of Hugo and they can keep the dosh themselves.

There is still a lot to be admired in here. Boyle, along with writer John Hodge and producer Andrew McDonald, know this is their calling card. Thus, from the beginning, we get the *Sunset Boulevard*-esque posthumous voiceover, and the fast-cutting montage of (very funny) interviews that establish the three as very much anti-heroes. The set design is striking, especially the disorienting, cathedralic flat with its shopping centre-size entrance hall. It tells us that we should take the following with a shovelful of salt.

Hugo has sprawled naked on a deep-red sheet for days, like something out of a Peter Greenaway wet-dream, before they get round to burying him. The scenes at the shallow grave itself are oblique; grisly details are conjured by the sound of saws rasping through bone. Visually and aurally the film remains striking, as does its willingness to dispense with pedantic detail.

The problems are more structural. From the start we anticipate David (Christopher Eccleston) to be our anchor. Hodge clearly thinks the same, thus throws us mid-way by having him the one to snap first. The problem being, as amusing as we might initially find Alex (Ewan McGregor) and Juliet (Kerry Fox), they soon begin to grate. When the put-upon Cameron punches Alex out at the ball, we cannot but cheer. And by the time the thugs fetch up, the treatment metered out seems wholly justified. The playing is fine - but they are hamstrung by the script.

And, incidentally, has anyone ever stopped to consider that turning the corpse over to the authorities doesn't actually preclude keeping the cash? In point of fact, the heavies might have been forced to reason that their ill-gotten gains had gone the same way. But then, we wouldn't have much of a movie of common-sense prevailed, would we?

Eccleston is a fine actor (witness TV's *Our Friends In The North*), but he can do nothing with the robotic David. When he starts living in the attic, drilling spy holes, the abrupt shift rings hollow. Likewise Juliet's gravitation towards David at the payoff, to shift our sympathies on to the irritating Alex. The bald fact is, by the time of the climatic showdown we wouldn't mind seeing them all dead.

The final 'twist' is a one-shot. On repeated viewing it becomes farcical: would David not have checked the case before leaving? And given all that's happened, why does Juliet wait until she's in the car? Alex is clearly going nowhere. It makes for a nice shot but precious little sense, and (with Andy Williams' ironic croon on the soundtrack) points up the huge debt this film owes the Coen brothers. Didn't we see this done first and better in *Blood Simple*?

All of which is not to deny the film its sense of fun. It's a black comedy that manages to be frequently black and occasionally very comic. It proves that Hodge can write (the incidentals are excellent), and that Boyle is prepared to shrug-off the television straight-jacket so afflicting British cinema. And, as if to prove it, in the meantime they've hooked-up with the awful Irvine and become the country's most successful drug peddlers. For all its flaws, at least *Shallow Grave* is not yet more bum-numbing frown and gown heritage cinema, and to that we raise a (qualified) glass.

GH **▼▼▼**

SMALL FACES

Dir. Billie and Gillies McKinnon Cert. 18 Dur. 90 Min.
Released: (UK) 12/04/96, (US) 14/07/96.

Glasgow, 1968, three brothers are surrounded by a world on the verge of revolution, yet their reality is not controlled by the new world order, but by something very old - tribes. Bobby, the eldest, belongs to The Glen, one of the many gangs in the city. Alan is the middle brother who aspires to Art College, whilst the youngster, Lex, is barely in his teens. He is played by newcomer Iain Robertson, one of those unnerving child-adults, a pudding face and glistening, lively eyes that blaze with delight or anger.

Malky, leader of the rival Tongs gang and for whom *"mental is a state o' mind"* has been shot by Lex with an air-rifle, has lost his girlfriend to Alan and is the bitter enemy of Bobby: *"You have tae admit,"* he muses philosophically *"tha's quate a fam'ly!"*

Small Faces is about families, both of brothers and gang-members, and the pressures that environment can place on such kinships. It's also a film about earning respect, which is sometimes achieved through the blood of rival street-gangs (as demonstrated literally in the horrific ice-rink attack) or, as the emigreé, Uncle Andrew proves, through getting away to better yourself.

Overshadowed by the colossal *Trainspotting*, this film actually owes more fealty to Coppola's *Rumblefish* than to anything home-grown, concentrating on the loyalties that can draw you away from your dreams. The advertising blurb inevitably tells us that *Small Faces* ranks alongside *Trainspotting*, but, in time, it will be seen as having more in common with Scorsese's *Mean Streets*.

SC ▼▼▼

STRANGE DAYS

Dir. Kathryn Bigelow Dist. Universal (CIC) Cert. 15. Dur. 145 Min. Released: 06/10/95 US Box-office: $7.75 million

SET ON NEW YEAR'S EVE 1999, this cyber-noir epic occurs a little too close to home for comfort. It depicts city streets choked with riot police and armoured cars, a world where the just are afraid to walk the streets, and the unjust have discovered a new drug: Squid Clips. The first ever Virtual Narcotic.

If you want to experience the full tapestry of life, rob a bank, fall off a building, have sex with ALL the beautiful people, all without leaving the sweaty confines of your easy-chair, then you need Squid Clips. And the man to get them from is Lenny Nero - played by Ralph (call me Rafe) Fiennes. A bottom-feeder, he clings to some delusion of morality by refusing to peddle snuff chips. Excitement, fine. Criminal, no problem. Pornographic, why not? Deadly, no way!

The Maguffin which comes his way is, inevitably, a Squid Chip which could bring down what vestige of social control LA has left. It is an eye-witness account of a cop cold-bloodedly murdering a too-conspicuous-for-the-establishment's-own-good rap-singer. Obviously this plot was meant to evoke the Rodney King incident, but this reference has now been supplanted by the Tupac Shakur murder, which shook the American music-biz more recently.

The various plots and subplots in this hyper-charged dystopian action-movie weave around each other, with only the creaky serial-killer-in-the-fold story letting the side down. Although the brutal and shocking sequence where he rapes and murders his first victim whilst recording it for posterity using the Squid technology, is a real punch in the gut. All the more painful when you remember that this film was directed by a woman! Bigelow wisely only runs this before your disbelieving eyes once - after that you get to squirm as Lenny shows other people what you've just seen. Their facial expressions bring the violence home more powerfully than a desensitising re-run would.

Ralph Fiennes continues to be a significant presence, drawn to dangerous rôles like a moth to a flame. Angela Bassett is characteristically powerful as Lenny's only friend Mace - when this woman pulls a gun on you, you don't mess around, you run! Juliette Lewis is once-again vacuous as the used-up rock star, Faith, whilst Tom Sizemore in a very bad wig, chews the furniture as Lenny's ex-partner Max.

Although *Strange Days* is far from perfect, it milks dry good ideas by the bucketful. This is the film *Johnny Mnemonic* should have been. See it on the big screen if you can, but do see it

***JA* ▼▼▼▼**

STRIPTEASE

Dir. Andrew Bergman. Dist. Rank Cert. 18 Dur. 110 Min.
Released: 28/06/96. US Box-office: $32.5 million to date

SOMEONE SHOULD HAVE TOLD Demi Moore that this is a comedy. Granted, her rôle as a separated mother who has to work as a stripper to finance her custody battle, doesn't leave much space for slapstick - but she doesn't have to appear so po-faced about it. Anyone would think she found taking her clothes off for money Demi-ning.

Now Burt Reynolds, he's not above letting it all hang out. Thankfully though, he manages here to keep most of it in. He plays Senator Dilbeck, a drunk and disorderly denizen of Capitol Hill, with a penchant for bad white wigs and bad white girls. His opening line sums him up as pithily and eruditely as ever I could: *"Poontang!"*

He makes his way unsteadily into The Eager Beaver (yes, really) and, as soon as he lays eyes on dancing Demi, decides he wants to lay everything else on her too. Like fractures in glass, or, probably more appropriately, swirls in a walnut whip, the movie's several plot lines all radiate from this one moment.

Several people of Demi's acquaintance, for several reasons, decide to blackmail Dilbeck over his visit to the strip club, after all, this *is* an election year. He hardly has time to notice, not that he would allow it to distract him from his one true purpose in life - being a pervert - before said blackmailers are sleeping with the fishes. Enter detective Armande Assante with the line of the film: *"Of all the lakes, in all the countries, in all the world, you had to float up in mine."* Now why does that sound vaguely familiar?

Director Andrew Bergman has long specialised in mixing straight crime motifs with comedy, beginning back in the seventies with his two excellent novels about the wise-ass private dick Jack DeVine: *The Big Kiss-Off of 1944* (1974) and *Hollywood and DeVine* (1975). His first movie of any note was *The Freshman* (1990), where he persuaded Marlon Brando to come out of hiding long enough to re-evoke Don Vito Corleone.

Pausing only to continue his love of disinterring seventies icons by weaving James Caan into *Honeymoon In Vegas* (1992) and Issac Hayes into *It Could Happen To You* (1994), both of which were led by Francis Coppola's nephew, young Nicholas Cage; Bergman returns to crime-comedy with *Striptease*.

The dark, dubious edge of Carl Hiaasen's novel has been supplanted by Bergman's clear, bright camera work. There is little sensation of threat here - except from Robert Patrick's grungy turn as Demi's ex-husband, a man who now uses his daughter as diversion while he steals wheel-chairs from hospitals. As he says when he meets Reynolds: *"So you're a congressman. We've got a lot in common!"*

Demi's talents are amply supported by Ving Rhames (the bouncer with heart of gold and a brain of jelly) and Assante, who gets second billing despite having nothing much to do. Of course, Reynolds is wonderful as a tribute to the political profession: *"Why are you so shiny?"* asks his aide with trepidation, *"You've never covered yourself with Vaseline, then?"* the Congressman replies, resplendent in Stetson, boxers and wellingtons.

But Demi is determined to play a serious rôle in a silly film. Now that she is a star of sufficient clout (apparently earning $12 million for this film, the most ever paid to a woman in Hollywood) she can make editorial decisions about the films she appears in. Presumably, therefore, she must be intent on making a seemingly noble statement about the resilience of womanhood and the responsibility of motherhood (her character's daughter is, after all, played by her real daughter, Rumer Willis).

All of this, I would suggest, is in order to make *Striptease* a politically correct porno-movie, by having the male viewer know and understand her character so well that, even draped three-quarters-naked over a chair, he can't objectify and therefore lust after her. Instead, he must sympathise with her plight; all of which serves to make the film's show-piece erotic dance numbers peculiarly sexless.

Problem is, this is supposed to be a seedy movie about seedy people. Ultimately, common decency can only be *un*common if it grows out of a dark and immoral background. Yet no one here is truly malicious. The good-guys are too good to be true, the strippers are just one happy family (they even like their boss) and the bad guys are slimy rather than sadistic (Vaseline notwithstanding).

Therefore, her moral stand, her drive to protect her daughter, her scheme to rid herself of the concupiscent Congressman, are all drained of the truth and poignancy Ms Moore seemingly hoped for. If you don't have characters to care about, and you don't have comedy to crease you up, you don't have much of a movie.

Get Shorty and *Birdcage* have both presented the cheap, camp personality of Miami far more convincingly than *Striptease*, which is a shame since their makers obviously learned a lot about the nature of the sun-drenched beast, from reading the works of Carl Hiaasen. I'm sure one of his books will make a good film. One day.

***JA* ▼▼**

THINGS TO DO IN DENVER WHEN YOU'RE DEAD

Dir. Gary Fleder Dist. Miramax (BVI). Cert. 18. Dur. 124 Min. Released: 01/12/96. US Box-office: $500, 000

GIVE IT A NOUN: *dogs, pulp, suspects*. Gary Fleder's arresting debut is of a piece with the hipsville smart-mouths, and yet maintains an odd distance. Certainly more son-of-Singer, less junior Tarantino. It is four-star gourmet fare, to a paunchy *Pulp Fiction* Big Kahuna Burger.

Denver belongs to Christopher Walken's wheelchair-bound Man With The Plan. He wants former gangster Jimmy The Saint (Andy Garcia) to pull an action - scaring the boyfriend of his feeble-minded son's ex-girlfriend. The hesitant Jimmy concedes (we all need money) and picks up his old gang: the damned Easy Wind (Bill Nunn); the married Franchise (William Forsythe); Pieces (Christopher Lloyd), a decaying porn-projectionist; and the lunatic mortuary assistant Critical Bill (Treat Williams). When it all goes south, The Man calls on nerdy out-of-town hit man Mr Shhh (Steve Buscemi) to excise Jimmy's 'buckwheats'.

What a service Mr Buscemi has been to the American independent movie scene, lending credibility by virtue of his immense talent to all manner of deserving causes. Be it as a scumball *or* a scuzzball, Buscemi has been excellent in all of his endeavours. As with *The Usual Suspects*, a strong script attracts skilful playing. Certainly, Garcia has never been better, carrying a little too much weight, tailoring just smart enough, he's charming more than cool. All the principles are very good, but the real wonder is ferocious and childlike Treat Williams, getting all the best lines (*I've been Godzilla, you've been Tokyo!*) in this, his first major film for six years.

The script for ...*Denver* was a hot property in Hollywood for almost a decade before the film was made. When you see the film, you can understand why Scott Rosenberg's screenplay attracted the attention of such big-name players as Jack Nicholson, James Woods and Sean Penn. The post-*Pulp Fiction* frenzy to find literate crime-stories brought it out of moth-balls, and you wonder why they ever doubted it. Only Garcia's romance with balloon-lipped Gabrielle Anwar doesn't work. She's there solely to keep him around town and does little with a thankless part. (At least she's better than the fearful Uma Thurman, who was originally mooted for the picture.) Fairuza Balk as a druggy prostitute is much better.

That remarkable title - from the closing Warren Zevon song - is perfect. Jimmy's gang are dead from the off: the things they do in Denver are already for the dead.

What elevates Scott Rosenberg's screenplay above the norm is that, for all its humour, it takes death seriously. People are not clipped for laughs, and they don't die easy. Daringly, the film employs two running commentaries: from old-timer Joe Heff (Jack Warden) in a malt bar booth; and the touching, slightly sugary pre-mortem videos Jimmy records for his failing Afterlife Advice business. Rosenberg's brilliant, authentic-sounding schtick - 'boat drinks', 'buckwheats' - is really super-stylised prison/biker/gang speak. Glasses should also be raised to Director of Photography Elliott Davis for his impressive *noir* compositions (keep your eye on those backgrounds, there's an Edward Hopper painting in there somewhere).

In the end then, with its occasionally over-size sets, cracking repartee and real emotional undertow, ... *Denver* resembles nothing so much as the classic Coen brothers post-mod gangster-ride *Miller's Crossing*. It talks the talk and it walks the walk, for sure, but in a sincere and beating heart has something the garish Querantino can't provide. Give it a name.

GH **▼▼▼▼▼**

A TIME TO KILL

Dir. Joel Schumacher. Dist. Warner Bros. Cert. 15 Dur. 130 Min. Released: 24/07/96. US Box-office: $106. 75 million to date

A TIME TO KILL opens with two card-carrying, good ole Southern red-necks (complete with Confederate flag in their truck) raping and brutalising a ten year-old black girl called Tonya. Because they can. This deeply disturbing sequence is shown in cruel close-ups of ropes being tightened, blood being spilled, childhood being stolen. It is to director Schumacher's credit that he has succeeded in making this scene sickening, whilst the full extent of the violation is played-out in the viewer's mind, not on the screen.

Needless to say, I've been scanning the trade mags, looking for the news report of author John Grisham serving a subpoena on himself so that he can answer for the emotional shock this scene may engender in its hapless audience. No luck, but I'll keep checking.

I digress.

The monolithic Samuel L. Jackson plays Tonya's father, Carl Lee, and his rage is as tangible as his daughter's pain. Feeling as, I suspect, any loving father would, he can't see beyond his need to make the rednecks suffer. He wants revenge - he may call it justice, but he knows it's revenge. So, he breaks into the court-house and, in front of half the town's judiciary, machine-guns the red-necks into mince-meat.

It is a particularly satisfying moment.

So begins the court-case; as Carl Lee stands trial for his life on two counts of murder. Suddenly we're right back in familiar Grisham territory. His protagonist is the usual down at heel lawyer (the really rather excellent Matthew McConaughey) ... assisted by ever-reliable spunky law student (the wasted Sandra

Bullock) and our old-favourite, the grizzled mentor (drunken, that is) Donald Sutherland. Over on the other bench we have the ubiquitous ambitious DA (a hammy Kevin Spacey) the regulation-issue sheriff with a heart of gold but a duty to perform (stalwart Charles Dutton) and, in case this all began to seem a little polite, the essential trouble-making brother to the deceased (Kiefer Sutherland, doing his trade-mark hard-eyed psycho routine again).

Amazingly, Grisham managed to pack everything on which he has built his 'reputation' into this one tale. He might as well have never put finger to keyboard again, it's all here. But enough wish-fulfilment, let's stick to the facts.

The huge crowd Schumacker has drawn together all acquit themselves as admirably as the *Janet and John* script will allow, but then they should be able to breeze through rôles they've all played, or seen played, dozens of times before. Particularly resplendent are Patrick MacGoohan as Judge Noose (yes, subtle innit) and Kurtwood Smith as the leader of the local KKK, the fearsomely named Stump Sisson. Ashley Judd tries her best with the usual thankless task of being the wife, mother and Achilles' Heel to the hero, but she hasn't got much to work with.

The main problem, from the thesps' perspective, is that they're practically elbowing each other out of the way to get their moment centre-screen; put simply, they're just too thick on the ground. Case in point: all the publicity material leads you to believe that this is a Sandra Bullock starring vehicle, and if you go to see it on that understanding, the first 75 minutes will prove a significant disappointment, as will the last 30, because she's hardly in it, there's no room.

A Time To Kill is a contrived, almost flippant depiction of a deeply serious subject, especially in these days when the perceived proliferation of violence in society is all the news can seem to find to report. The collateral damage that explodes around the case reaches riotous proportions, with bungled assassination attempts, bombings and kidnappings following in quick succession. Moral ambiguities are hinted-at, played-with, but never really addressed.

Indoors, the court-room drama manages to hold a little more water, providing powerful and emotional viewing, and really allowing the pedigree of the gathered multitudes to shine through the mongrel material. MacGoohan insists early on that there won't be any grand-standing in his court, when, in fact, he allows little else

At heart, *A Time To Kill* is a simple, old-fashioned tale about rich white folks and their poor black neighbours. It has pretensions of profundity as it attempts to investigate the turbulent grey area where white and black meet. Unfortunately, the film gets confused by its own ambition and then seriously wounds itself as it plunges headlong into melodrama for its finale. Any legal council who blubbers while he's summing up his defence would, I suspect, not be long in looking for another career.

The curdled motives behind this piece, the hollowness of the original source, the choice of spectacle over speculation and the jostling of far too many good character actors, does no justice to either the significance of the issues under discussion, nor the surprising quality of the key performances on display.

JA ▼▼▼

TO DIE FOR

Dir. Gus Van Sant Dist. Rank Films. Cert. 15. Dur. 107 Min. Released: 22/09/95. US Box-office: $21 million

THE NUMBER OF FILMS where radical Canuck director David Cronenberg appears in front of the cameras is a select one. The number that are actually any good is good deal shorter. His rôle in this latest from the maverick Gus Van Sant is small, but significantly more than just a head-up-and-grin cameo.

On this evidence, what Cronenberg and Van Sant have in common, is an instinctive understanding of the fundamental unreality that the mass media in general - and television in particular - is transforming into The Everyday. From the former's *Videodrome*: *"Television is reality, and reality is less than television."*

Suzanne Stone (Nicole Kidman) would not understand the distinction, that there even was a distinction. She exists for television. *"On TV is where we learn who we really are,"* she says. She may only be the weather girl on the local cable channel in Little Hope, New Hampshire, but it *is* television, and *all* television is good. She has also just had her husband Larry murdered.

Buck Henry's fine script portions Suzanne's tale into media-friendly chunks. She addresses us straight to camera to explain, maybe even excuse herself; there are interviews with those that knew her; voice-overs; talk shows. *To Die For* is a media overload from which we learn that Larry, at the prompting of his family, was eager to start a family and, her career threatened, Suzanne determined to defend herself by the only means at her disposal: she lured a trio of local high-schoolers into shooting him. *"It was the most exciting time of my life,"* one of them later says.

If we needed confirmation, Van Sant's film proves once and for all that Mrs. Tom Cruise is a formidable screen actress. Suzanne is, if you will, a highly selective bimbo. If it doesn't further her career, she can exclude it from her orbit like it simply no longer exists. She is relentlessly dim to everything that isn't either in front of a camera, or about getting in front of a camera. She needs a husband, she gets one. She needs him disposed of, she will do whatever is necessary. Her manipulation of the America's youth is cruel and glacial, and provides some of the best moments in the film.

Joaquin Phoenix, brother of the late River, is excellent as Jimmy, the boy Suzanne literally seduces into murder, and Alison Folland even better as the overweight, monumentally insecure Lydia. Matt Dillon, star of Van Sant's terrific *Drugstore Cowboy*, is unusually sympathetic as Larry.

Coming off the back of the calamitous *Even Cowgirls Get The Blues*, Van Sant badly needed a hit and found one in this knowing, black comedy. His tone is a little uneasy for the first third or so, leaving the film feeling slightly bitty, sliced into a few too-many sound-bites. In fact. it's not until Suzanne kick-starts her game plan that her director seems entirely comfortable, going on to serve up a second half that is particularly delicious.

The more she is convinced that TV is enriching her as a person - that the studio lights are revealing an inner star - the more facile and meaningless Suzanne becomes - in complete contrast to this funny, bitter, bitingly intelligent little film.

GH ▼▼▼▼

TRAINSPOTTING

Dir. Danny Boyle Dist. Polygram. Cert. 18. Dur. 90 Min.
Released: (UK) 26/02/96, (US) 19/07/96. US Box-office: $12 million to date

AT THE TIME OF WRITING, *Trainspotting*'s world-wide box-office take is $60 million (about £45 million) and still rising, making it the second most successful British film ever, after *Four Weddings and a Funeral*. Why? The accents are indecipherable south of Hadrian's Wall, let alone west of the Pecos, so how has the film grabbed the attention of so many people?

Because of its humanity. Stylistically the film is like *Casino* with humour, essentially plotless, with a crowd of delinquent protagonists, driven by Renton's painfully honest voice-over. The music is the heart-beat and ironic undercurrent of the piece, accompanying daring swoops into and out-of reality, scaffolding for the crackling pace of the editing.

The film's style is what has made it a Mecca for students, and this year's poster of choice, but the style coruscates across a script which is wittier, more daring and better-considered than any this year. The energy and imagination here are a quantum leap from the conceit of *Shallow Grave*, yet the principles behind it are the same. That film deliberately made its central characters soulless, here Renton and Co are tragic fools. *"The streets are awash with drugs you can have for unhappiness and pain, and we took them all. Fuck it, we would've injected Vitamin C if only they'd make it illegal."*

When he is with his parents, Renton's world is flecked with dull rusty browns and proceeds in agonising slow-motion, but his drug-den is bright and vibrant, with strong, warm lighting and vivid red walls. *"Choose life"* are the opening words. But Renton *"...chose not to choose life. I chose heroin; and the reason? Who needs reasons when you've got heroin."* The appeal is easy to see. British cities seem so dull as movie locations, look at *The Young Poisoner's Handbook*, or *Jude* to see squalor and architectural misery as only we Brits know it. Yet, here, when seen through drug-fogged eyes, Edinburgh is vibrant, colourful, brash, dangerous and ferociously alive.

Although never presented as exactly desirable, the film approaches drug abuse with an understanding and amused eye - and then, one morning, that all changes. The image of the baby in the cot, still and blue, stays with you. That single, pivotal image re-directs the movie. When looking impotently down on the body, all they can think to do is 'cook up', to shoot more shit into their veins and forget about it all for a few hours. This is when you see drug addiction for what it really is: pathetic, desperate, selfish and dehumanising.

In the scarifying 'cold turkey' scene, with a clockwork baby looming down on him and Dale Winton twisting the knife into his parents, Renton tries himself and finds himself guilty. After this, he doesn't take drugs 'recreationally' again. But then 'uncle' Begbie - quite simply the most ferocious character committed to screen since Pesci's turn in *Goodfellas*, brings the cold, creeping certainty of disaster back into Renton's life.

It is during this final act of the film that a vestige of plot does take form, involving a drug sale and the resulting bag of money, which brings about the same dilemma as *Shallow Grave*. How much is friendship worth?

Renton decides, wisely and with a clear head, that his 'friends' are also his main problem. Taking the money and leaving them will solve all of his problems in one go, so he makes the selfish and immoral, yet perfectly correct decision: *"I'm cleaning up and moving on. I'm choosing life. I'm gonna be like you!"*

As the December/January nomination-frenzy is still ahead of me, I have no idea which films will be in the forefront of the Academy's mind when it comes to awarding statues in March 1997, but, as of October 1996, the only film that is in serious contention for any of the big Oscars, is *Trainspotting*.

***JA* ▼▼▼▼▼**

2 DAYS IN THE VALLEY

Dir. John Herzfeld Dist. Entertainment. Cert. 18. Dur. 104 Min. Released: 27/09/96 US Box-office: $10. 5 million

THIS IS THE FEATURE-FILM debut of director John Herzfeld and, it being a Tarantinesque ensemble heist-movie, you'd think he was as young buck, hot out of film school. Not so, he got his breaks as an actor way-back in *Kojak* and *Starsky and Hutch* and, as a TV director, he discovered Michelle Pfeiffer. I point this track-record out, because it explains the sophistication and confidence of *2 Days...*, a film which he also wrote.

Although there is a certain amount of band-wagon jumping here, given that crime is very hip in Hollywood; you can't resist feeling that Herzfeld wasn't so-much inspired by Tarantino to produce this script, but rather, in the way of *Things To Do In Denver...*, simply used it as a springboard to get an already-existing script up and running.

2 Days ... begins disparately, with four separate stories, all seemingly unconnected.

1: Teri Hatcher (Lois Lane, and *Heaven's Prisoners* veteran) wakes-up from a drug-induced sleep to find her boyfriend has had his head blown off next to her, while she slept. James Spader (*Music of Chance, Crash*) and Danny Aiello (*Leon*) speed away from the scene of the crime, having just executed said boyfriend. Then Spader sets up Aiello to take the rap.

2: Greg Crutwell (last seen in his kegs in Mike Leigh's *Naked*) is a particularly obnoxious art-dealer, who suffers a massive attack in the middle of Ventura Boulevard. Across the road someone is stealing a car, but they kindly take a detour from their joy-ride to deliver the screaming Englishman to a hospital.

3: Award-winning director Paul Mazursky (*Down and Out in Beverly Hills*) plays an award-winning director, who has fallen on hard-times and is on the verge of becoming homeless. The only thing keeping him from killing himself is his dog Bogey. So he sets about trying to find a home for Bogey.

4: Jeff Daniels (*Speed*) and Eric Stoltz (*Killing Zoë, Pulp Fiction*) play disgruntled Vice cops Alvin and Wes, the former on the verge of a nervous breakdown, the latter desperate to get promoted to Homicide. In between arguing over the merits of busting massage parlours, they almost drive into a hysterical Teri Hatcher who, half-dressed and dowsed in her boyfriend's blood, runs out into the street.

How these groups of characters are drawn together, how they interact, and the deeply buried secrets that exist between many of them, make for very enjoyable viewing. However, the text is too dense to weave together into a satisfying pattern, but there are enough delightful details for you to ignore the short-comings of the big picture:

Aiello holding a gun on his hostages whilst cooking pasta for them.

Spader shoving a fistful of ice down his trousers when his girlfriend Helga (statuesque newcomer Charlize Theron) turns him on.

Hatcher and Theron laying into each other in a fight that John Wayne and Victor MacLaglen would have been proud of.

Also, in common with many of the more interesting Hollywood movies these days, *2 Days* ... has its share of uncredited cameos - notably Louise Fletcher, Keith Carradine, and Lawrence Tierney who sits sullenly in bed, listening to Hatcher and Theron fighting next door, and assumes that that's how kids today have sex.

The over-all result is of a novel, possibly in need of some tightening-up, rather than of a film. Individual scenes are a delight, running motifs (such as the importance of timing) are deftly handled and the comedy plays well against the drama. Although all the characters are eventually drawn together, *2 Days* ... doesn't manufacture the neat and convenient dénouement most films strive for. It trades on the peculiarities of LA city-dwellers, and retells the pressures that make their lives so far from ordinary, as Joel Schumacher's *Falling Down*, or Robert Altman's *Short Cuts* did. And it is to the likes of Altman that this film owes its allegiance, rather than trendy new kids on the block like QT.

JA ▼▼▼ ½

THE USUAL SUSPECTS

Dir. Bryan J. Singer Dist. Polygram. Cert. 18. Dur. 101 Min. Released: 11/08/95. US Box-office: $23.25 million

THIS DEVILISHLY CUNNING crime thriller starts at the end, segues back to the beginning, makes its eventual way to an absorbing middle and finally turns everything upside down with a magnificent dénouement, a mere minute before the end-credits roll. But, even if you haven't seen the film, you've probably managed to pick that much up. What you want to know is, after all the hype, is it actually any good? Indubitably!

The poster/sleeve image of the police identity parade was the starting point of the idea for Chris McQuarrie, the writer, and is the starting place of the plot. Five cons are brought together in the same room, they don't know each other, but they know *of* each other. Gabriel Byrne is an old-time hood, trying to get out of the game. Stephen Baldwin is the trigger-happy new-boy in town. Benicio del Toro is the indecipherable small-timer. Kevin Pollack is the matter-of-fact car-jacker and Kevin Spacey (who, need one remind you, limped away with an Oscar for this performance) is the planner and narrator.

Locking such an array of criminal talent into one room can't be coincidence, they think, but never the less band together to pull an audacious and lucrative heist. Problem is, the money they take belongs to the mythical Keyser Soze. If *Charley Varrick* thought he had problems inadvertently stealing from the mob, that was nothing compared to what Soze can do to you. A Hungarian refugee, we see, in flashback, how he executed his own family to make the point that no one can intimidate him. His acts of vengeance have reached legendary status, making him the bogeyman of the criminal fraternity.

And so the gang meet Soze's representative Pete Postlethwaite, who explains that, to make amends to Mr Soze, they must now do a job for him. They are sent to raid a drug deal worth $91 million. All of this is told in flashback by Spacey to police investigator Chazz Palminteri, who becomes progressively more obsessed with the ghostly Soze.

With a structure which could only be fairly described as labyrinthine, McQuarrie's script (which also won an Oscar) keeps you guessing and scratching your head throughout. What is so damn admirable though is that unlike most every other whodunit, this requires repeated viewings because, even when you think you've figured out *who* did *what* to *whom* in the library with the candle-stick, you still aren't quite sure *how*.

Nothing has been left to chance in this film, the direction is detailed and subtle, the performances beautifully balanced. *The Usual Suspects* demands your full attention and therefore, is best appreciated in the full widescreen ratio (I found myself watching those almost-off-screen corners suspiciously, just in case something untoward was going on there).

Without a shadow of a doubt, *The Usual Suspects* is one of the half dozen stand-out films (criminal or otherwise) of the last twelve months, it deserves house-room in any self-respecting film-fan's video library. Hopefully director Singer and scribe McQuarrie are in cahoots for the foreseeable future, which would make this film ... wait for it ... the beginning of a beautiful friendship.

***JA* ▼▼▼▼▼**